AF251262

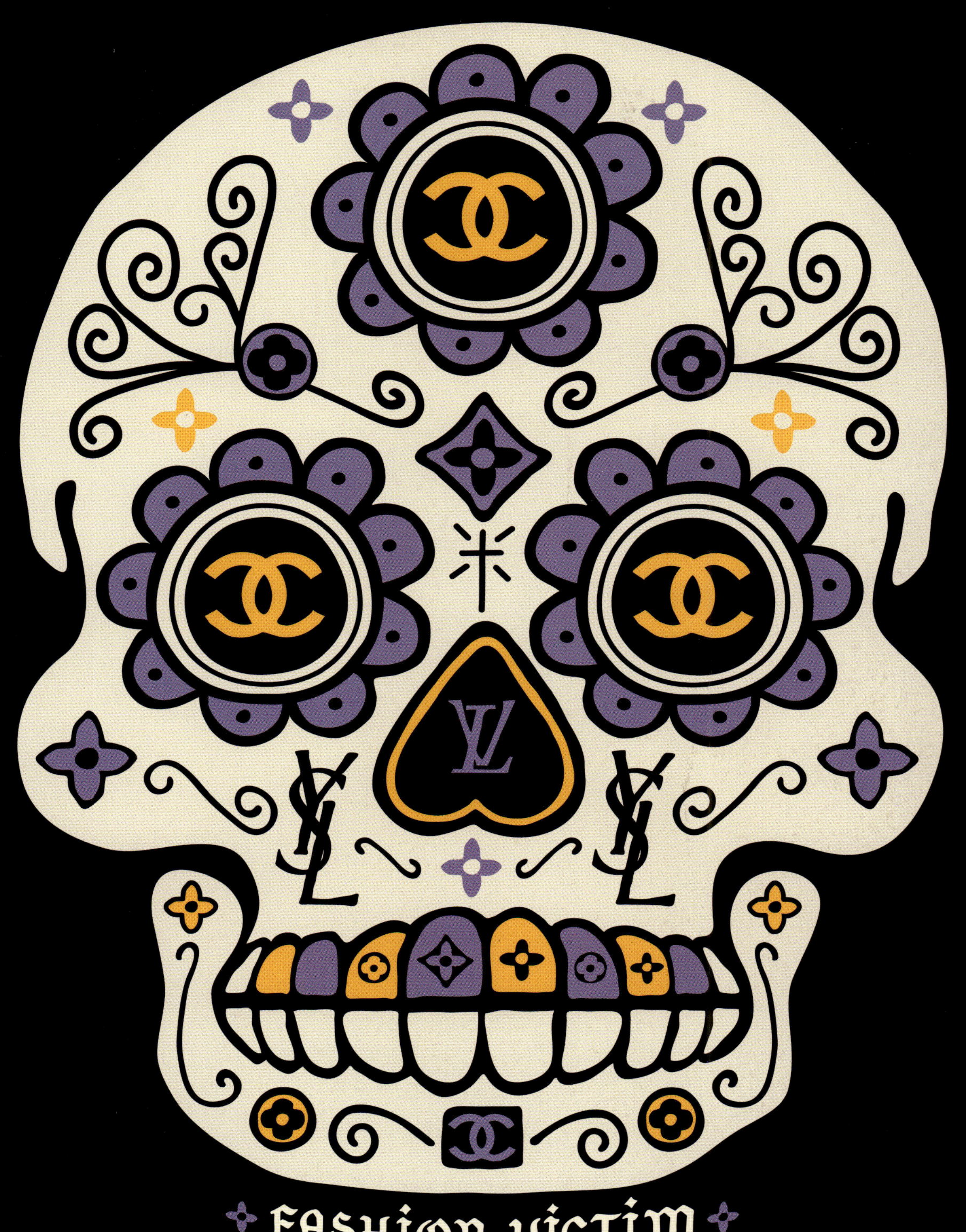
FASHION VICTIM

First Published in the United States of America in 2008

Gingko Press, Inc.
5768 Paradise Drive, Suite J
Corte Madera, CA 94925, USA
Phone (415) 924 9615 / Fax (415) 924 9608
email: books@gingkopress.com
www.gingkopress.com

ISBN: 978-158423-289-6

Printed in China

© 2008 JUXTAPOZ
www.juxtapoz.com

Produced by: R. Rock Enterprises
Design by: Kim Groebner
Project Manager: Z. Oxford
Special Thanks: Caleb Neelon, Shawna Kenney

Previous Page Image by Grotesk
Opposite Page Image by David Choe

Cover Image by Tomer Hanuka

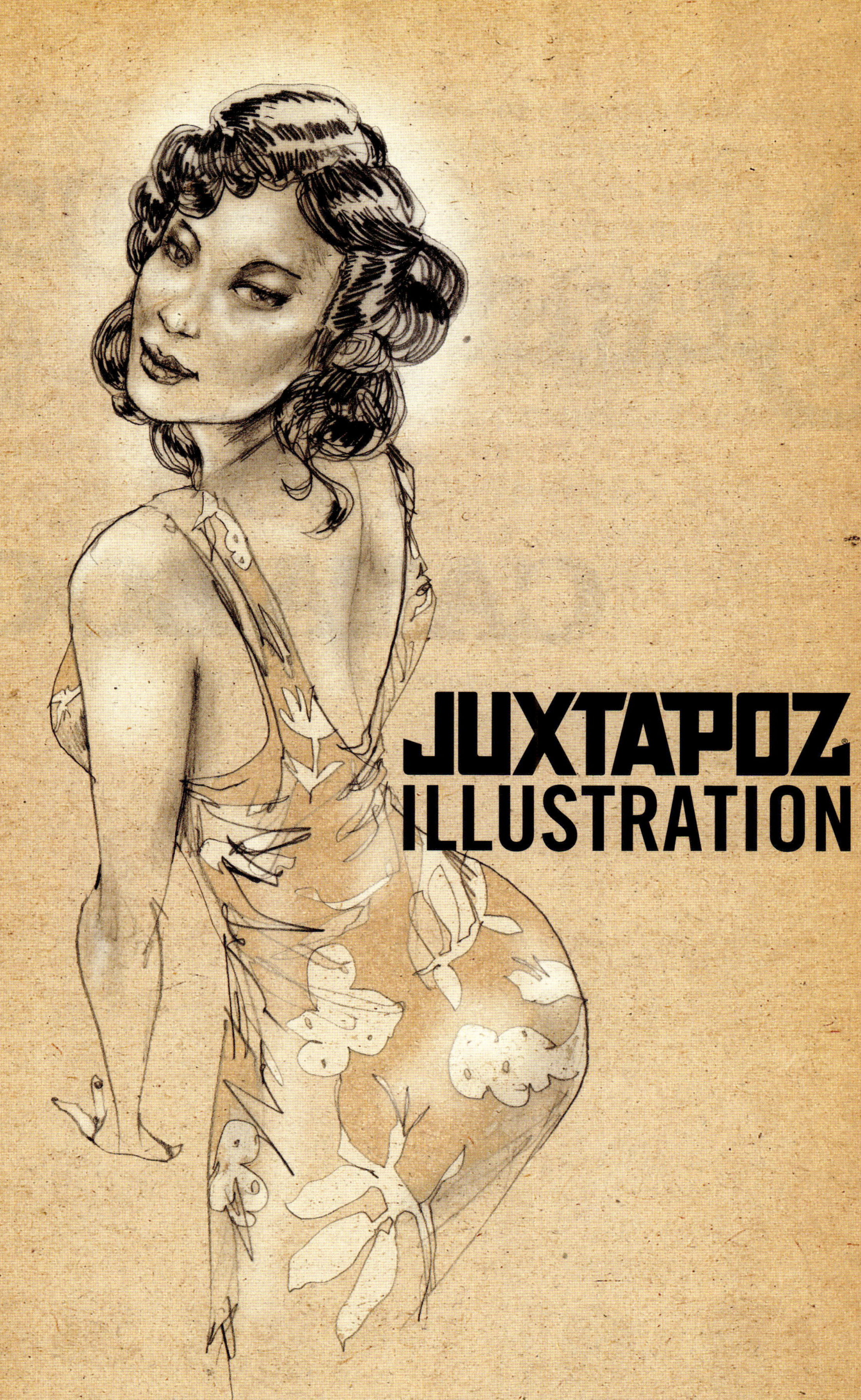
JUXTAPOZ
ILLUSTRATION

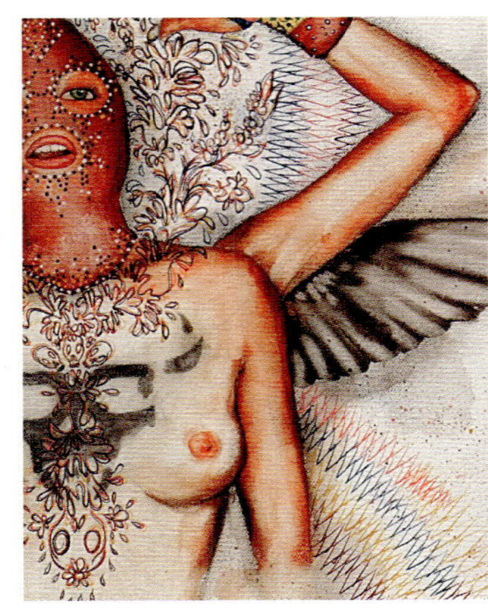
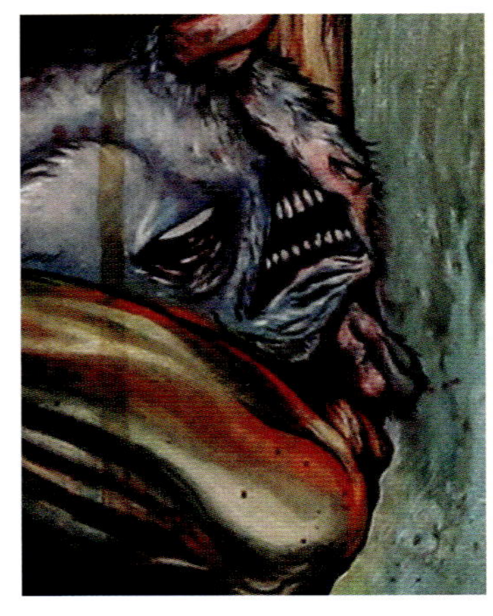
ADVENTURE
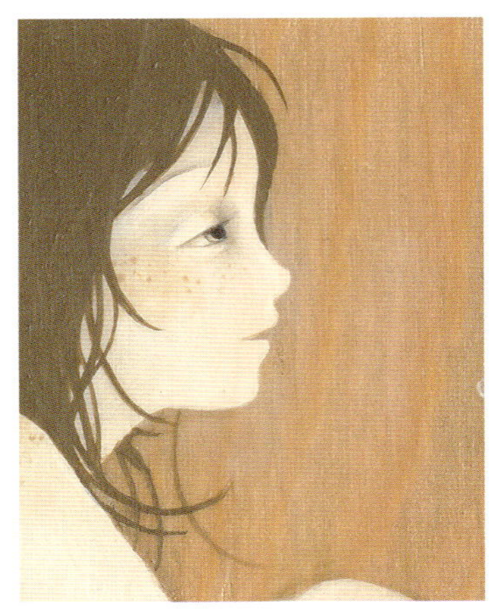
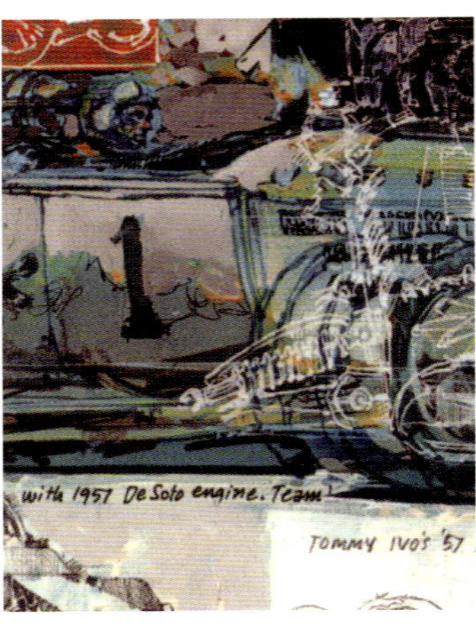
with 1957 DeSoto engine. Team
TOMMY IVO'S '57
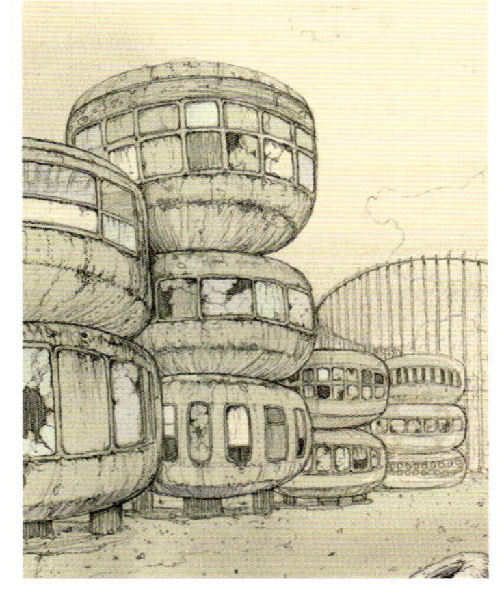
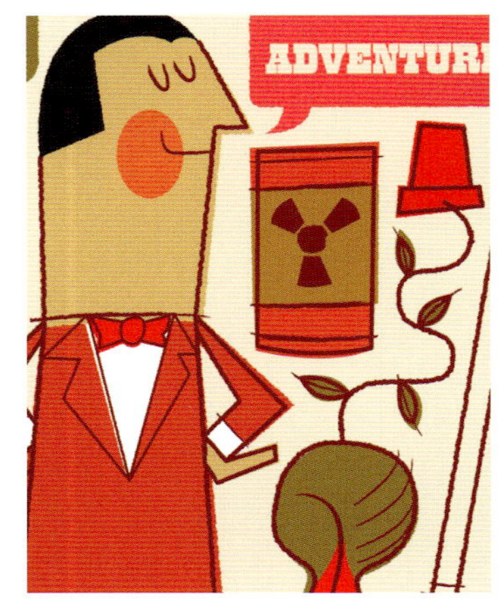
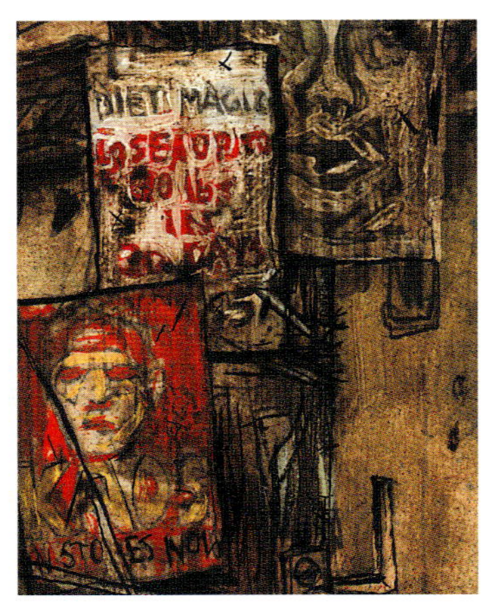
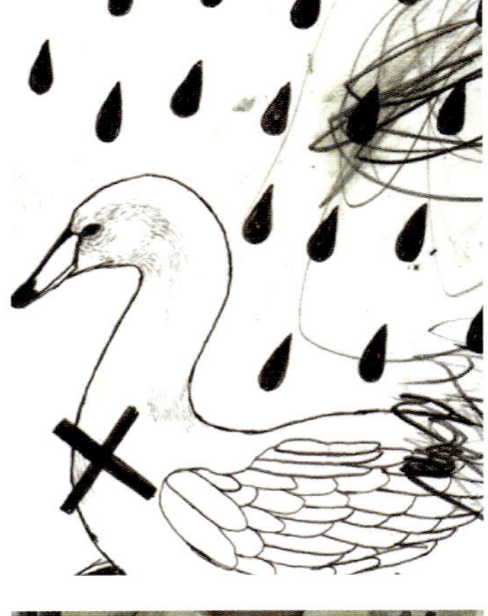
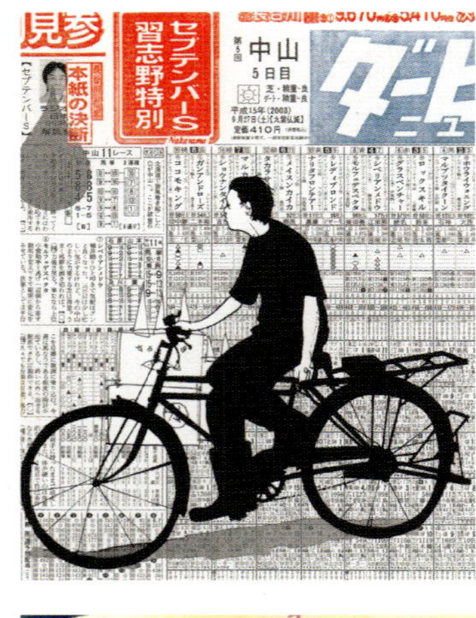
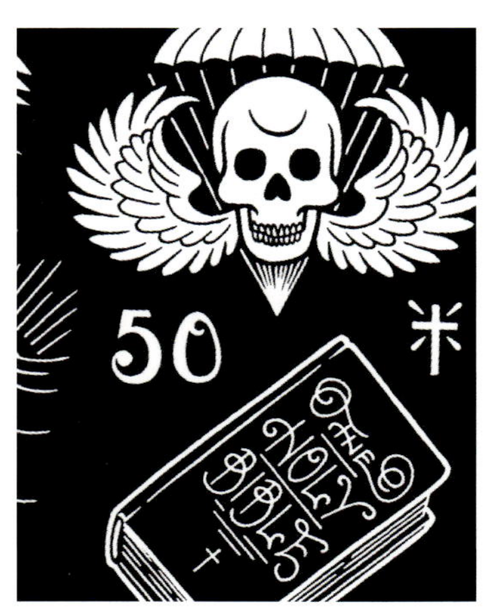
50
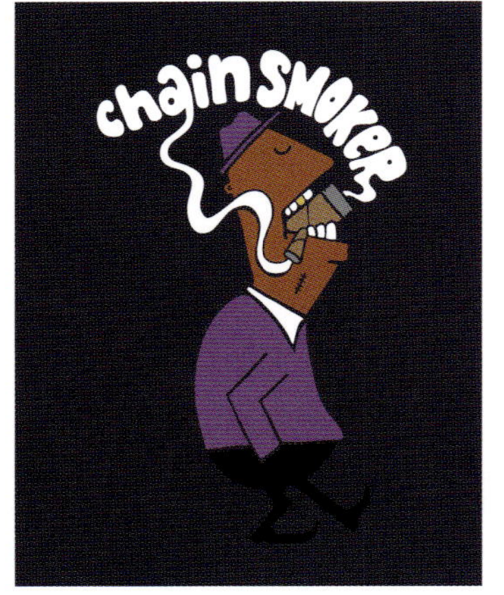
chainSMOKER
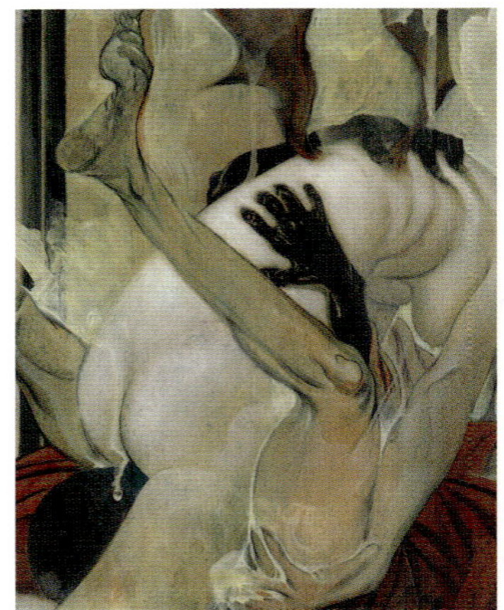
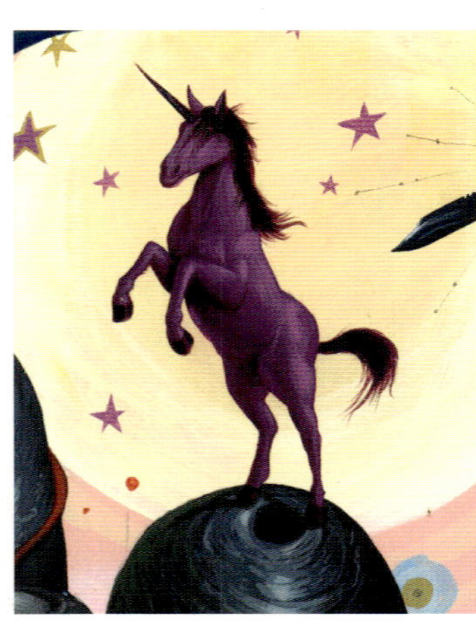
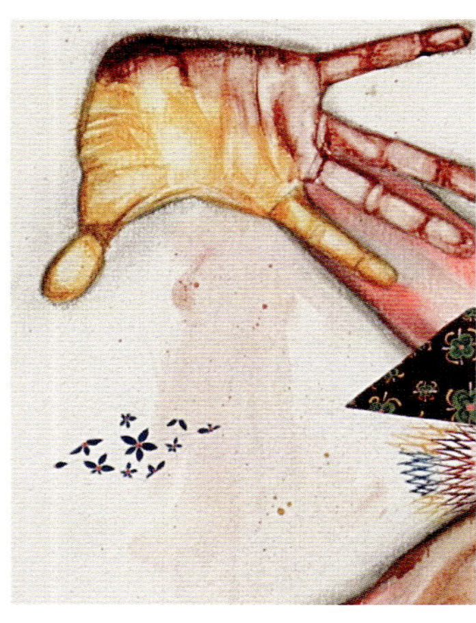
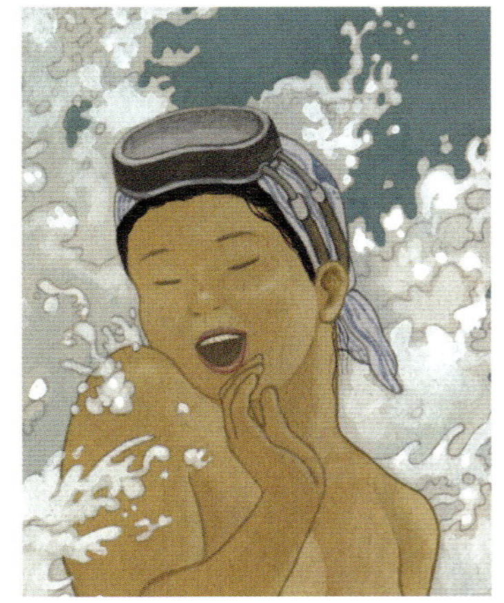
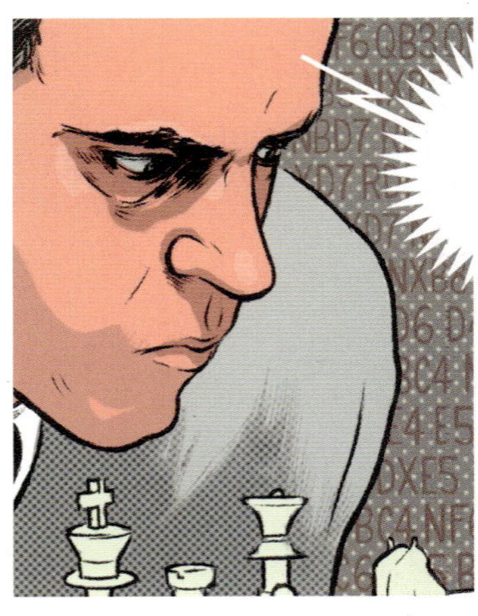

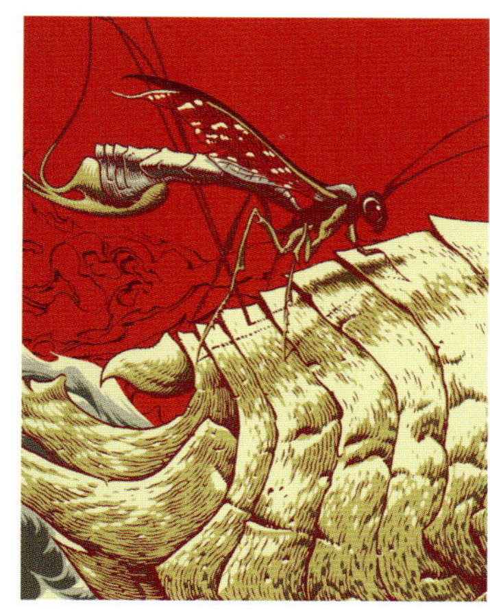
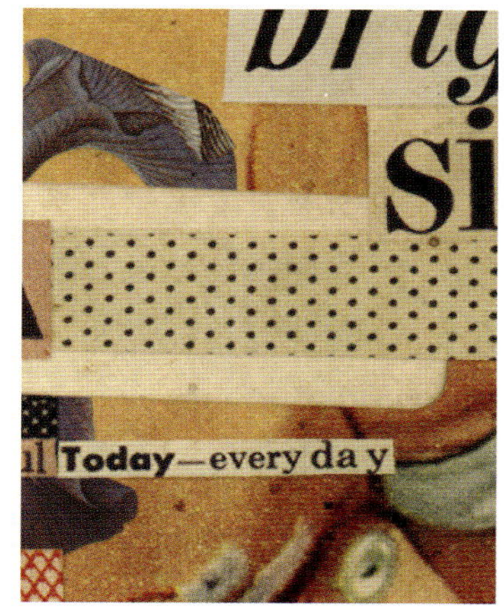
si
Today—every da y
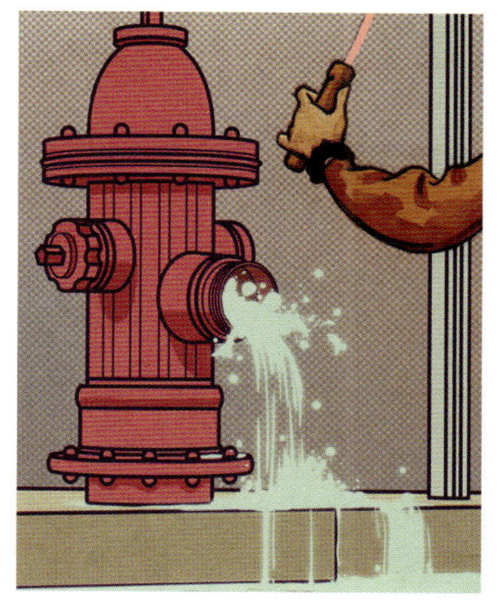
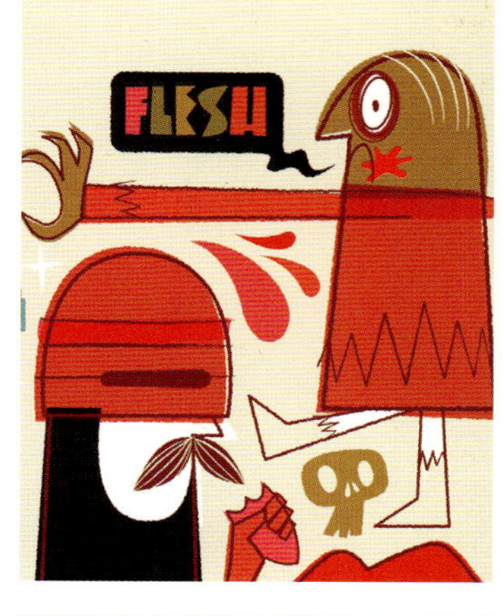
FLESH
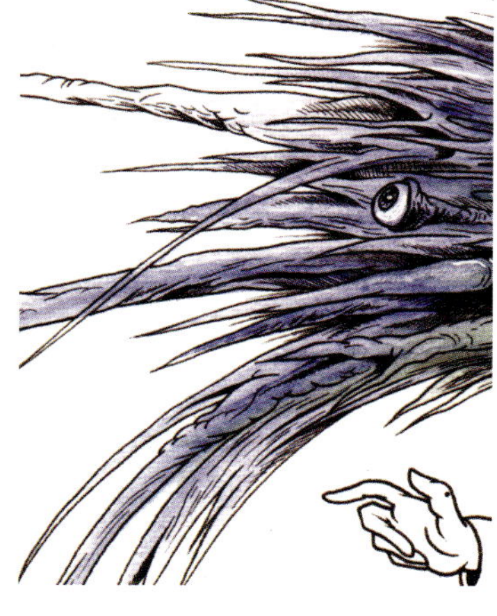
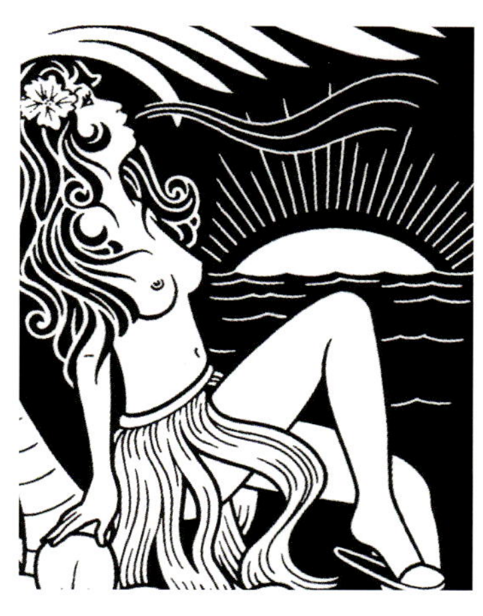
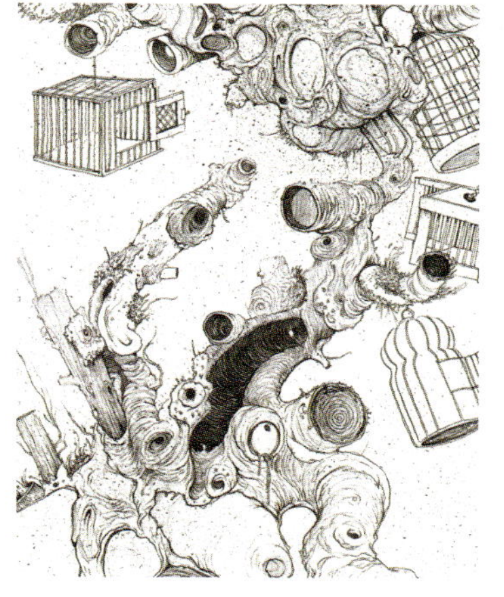
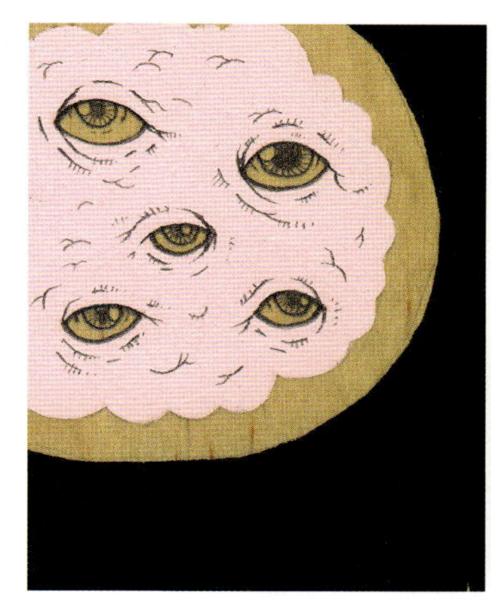
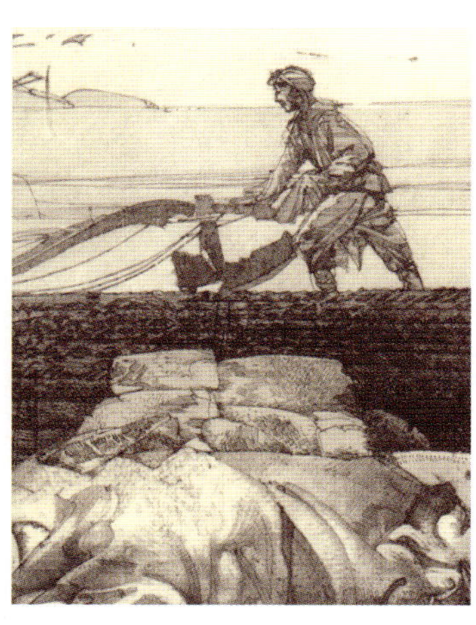
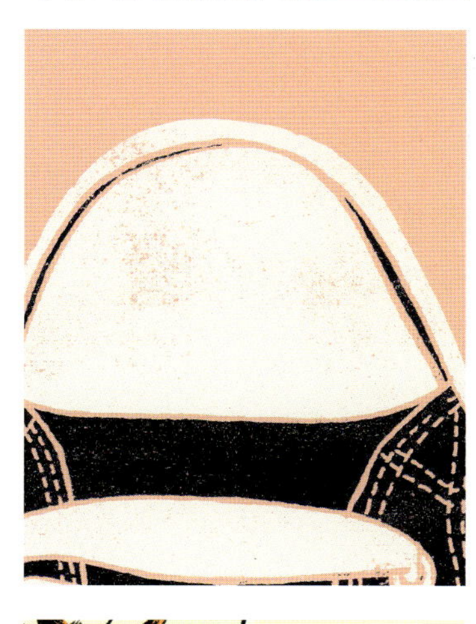
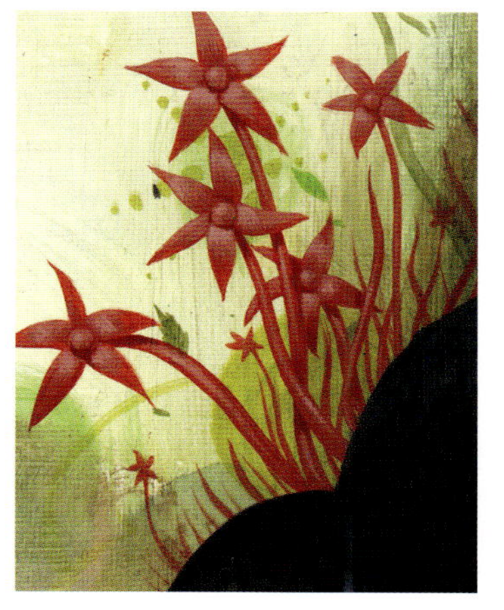
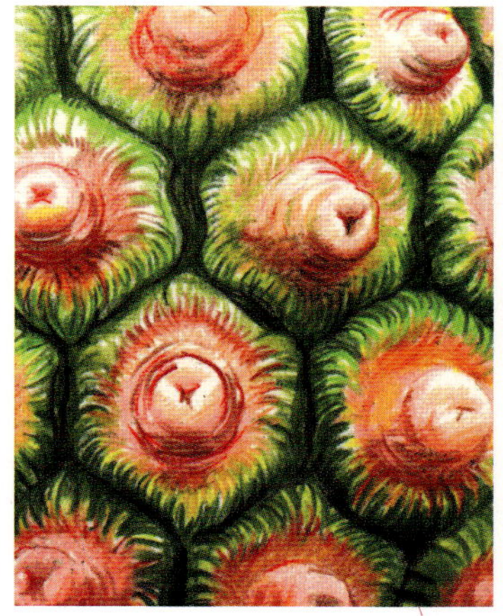
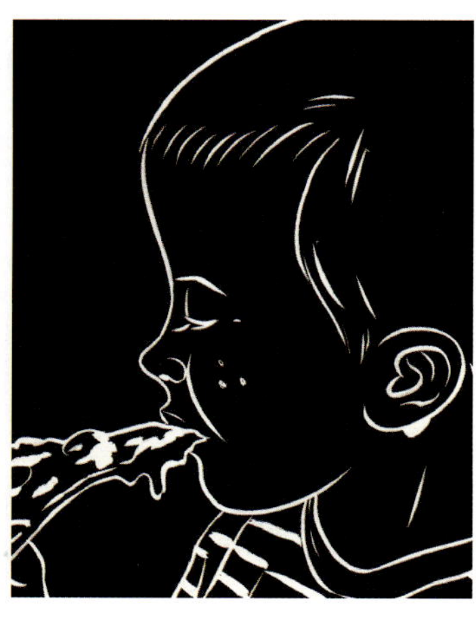
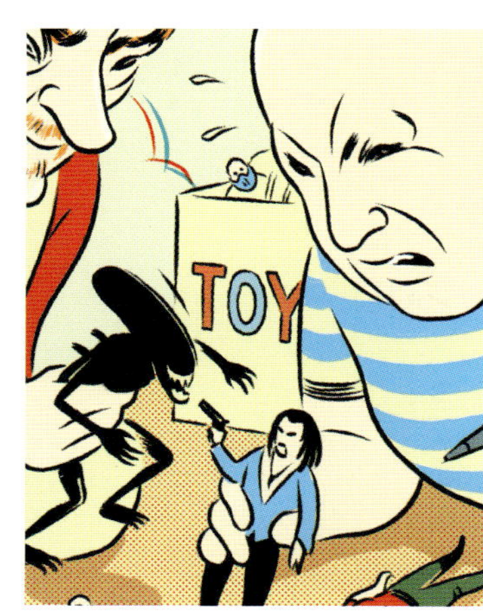
TOY
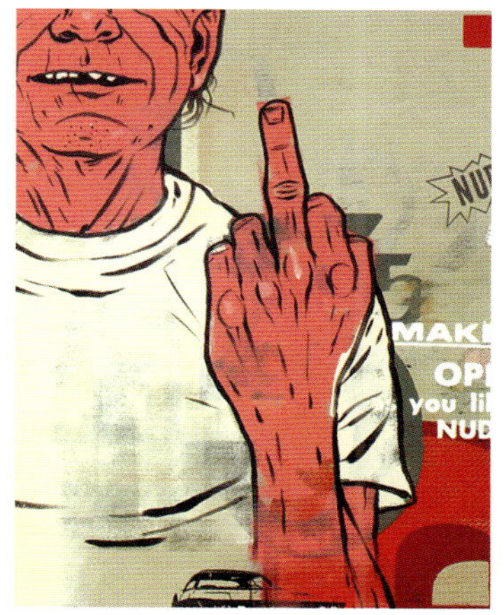
you li
NUD
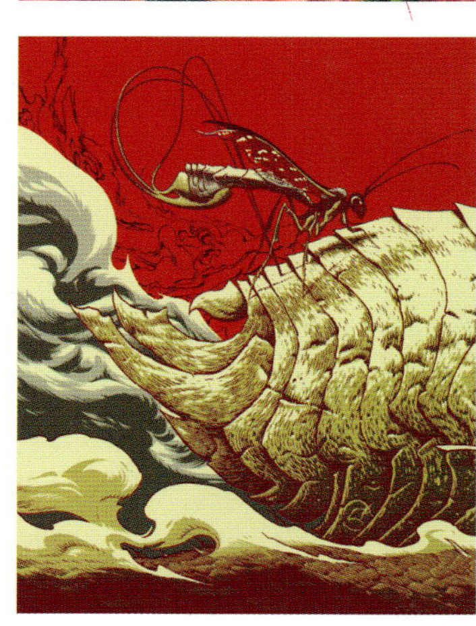

CONTENTS

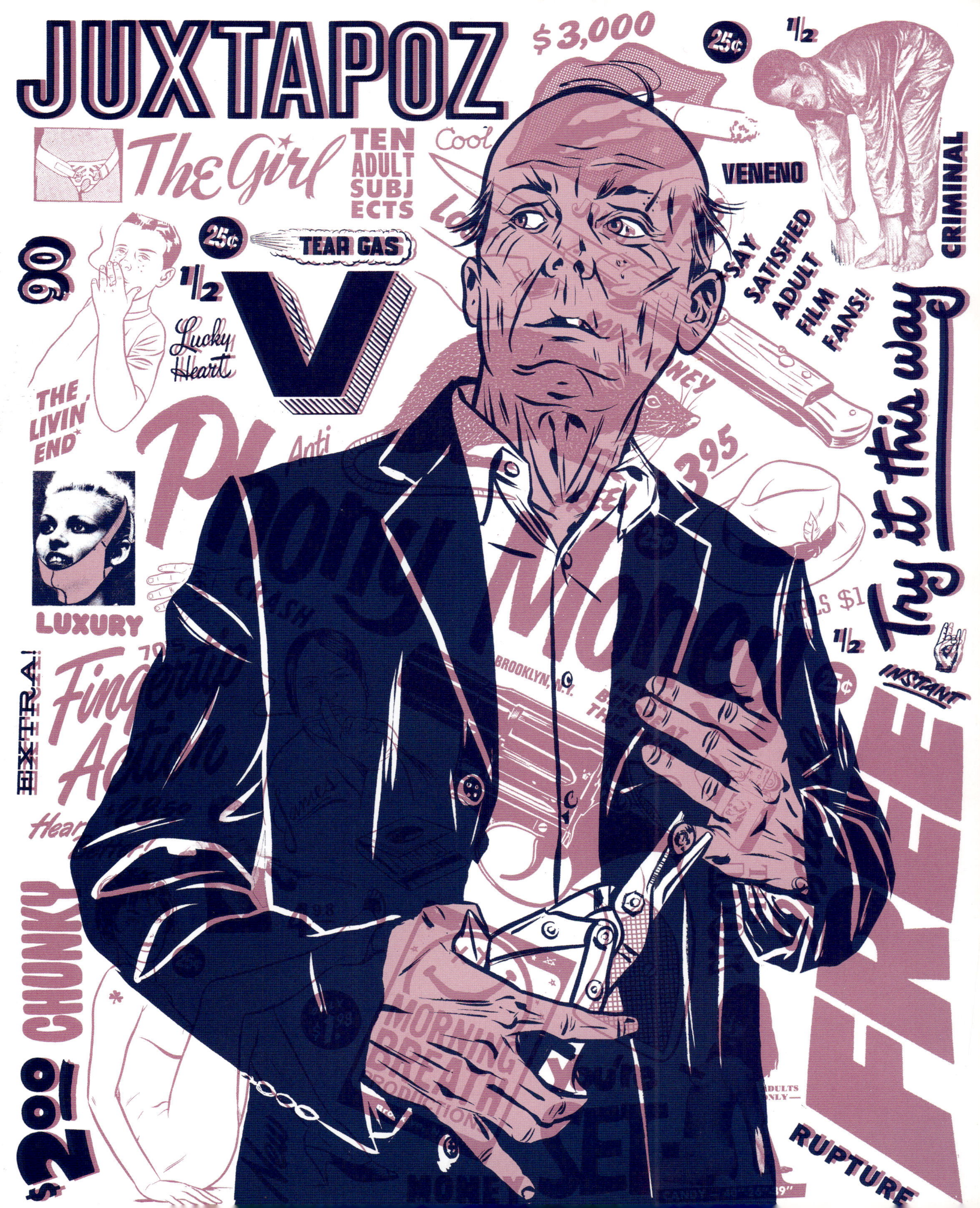

JUXTAPOZ
$3,000
25¢
½
The Girl
TEN ADULT SUBJECTS
Cool
VENENO
CRIMINAL
90
25¢
½
TEAR GAS
V
Lucky Heart
SAY SATISFIED ADULT FILM FANS!
Try it this way
THE LIVIN' END
Anti
3 95
LUXURY
BROOKLYN, N.Y.
½
INSTANT
EXTRA!
Fingertip Action
FREE
James
MORNING BREATH PRODUCTION
$2 00 CHUNKY
RUPTURE

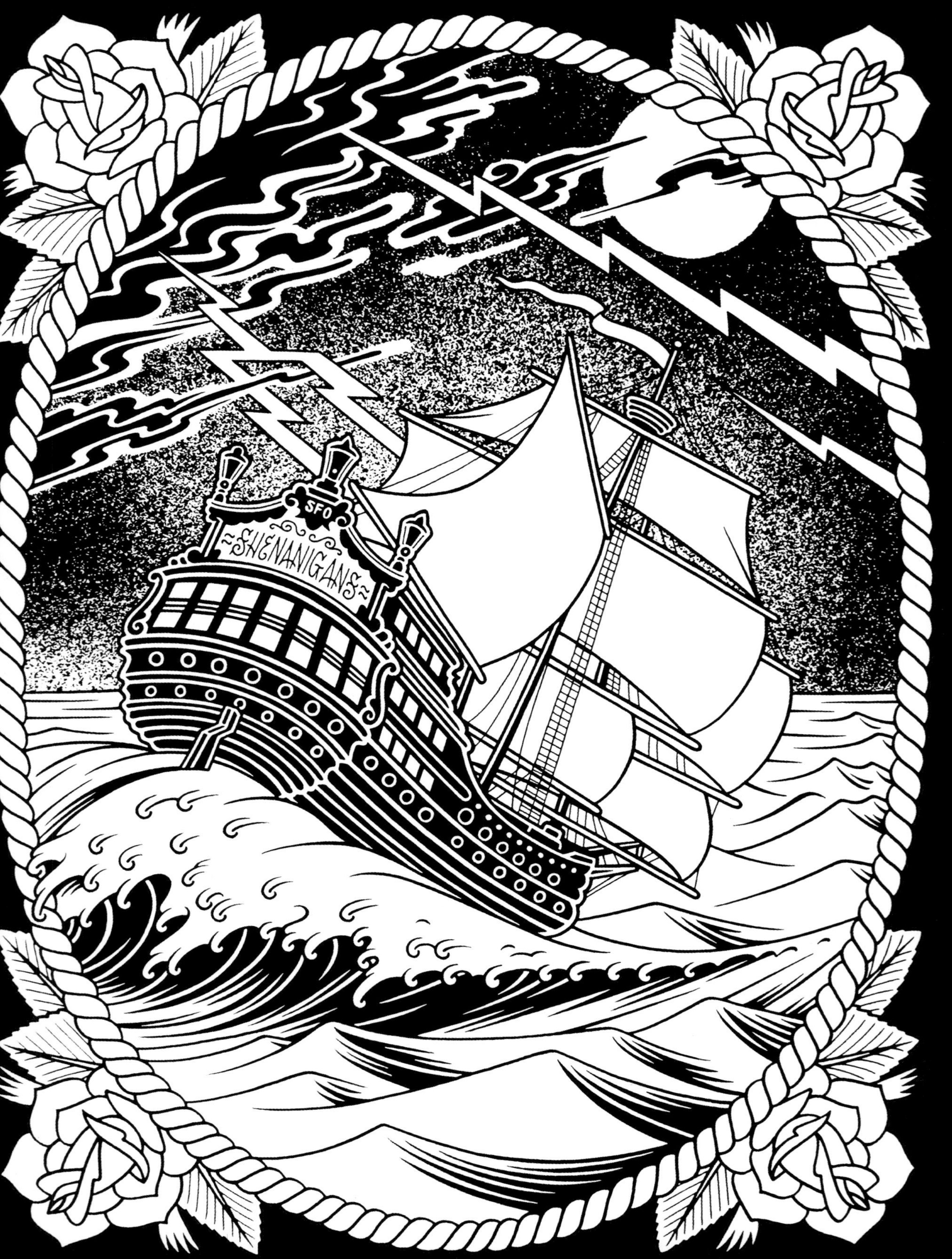

SFO
~SHENANIGANS~

INTRODUCTION

Robert Williams established *Juxtapoz Art & Culture Magazine* to document the exploding lowbrow art movement. When it was first published in 1994, the movement was still very much under the radar. For more than a decade, *Juxtapoz* has documented this movement in a way that had never been done before: validating the work in an intelligent format, from an insider's perspective. In the intervening years, *Juxtapoz* has re-branded and re-imagined itself to better represent a generation of artists intent on working outside the ossified art establishment. Now, *Juxtapoz* has re-invented itself by publishing a series of art books.

Juxtapoz Illustration is the first book in the series. This book showcases a kaleidoscopic array of illustrators. We purposely cultivated a wide range of artists who demonstrate the diversity—in style, aesthetic and philosophy—of the craft.

Juxtapoz Illustration features artists such as Aaron Horkey, Alex Pardee, Amy Sol, Barron Storey, David Choe, Evan Hecox, James Jean, Jeff Soto, Jeremy Fish, Kelsey Brookes, Michael Sieben, Mike Giant, Mode 2, Morning Breath, Nate Van Dyke, Sam Flores, Tomer Hanuka and more. The artists are briefly profiled, then allowed space to let their work do the talking. Some of the illustrators have appeared within the glossy pages of *Juxtapoz.* Others are new talents culled from all over the world. Whether you have read about them or not, each of these artists has experienced professional success and artistic accolades, while remaining accessible to commercial clients and collectors alike. They represent the phenomenal modern illustration movement perfectly. The world will witness more from these artists in all arrays of media—from toy and T-shirt designs to gallery shows to their own books and beyond. But remember, you saw them here first.

Image by Mike Giant

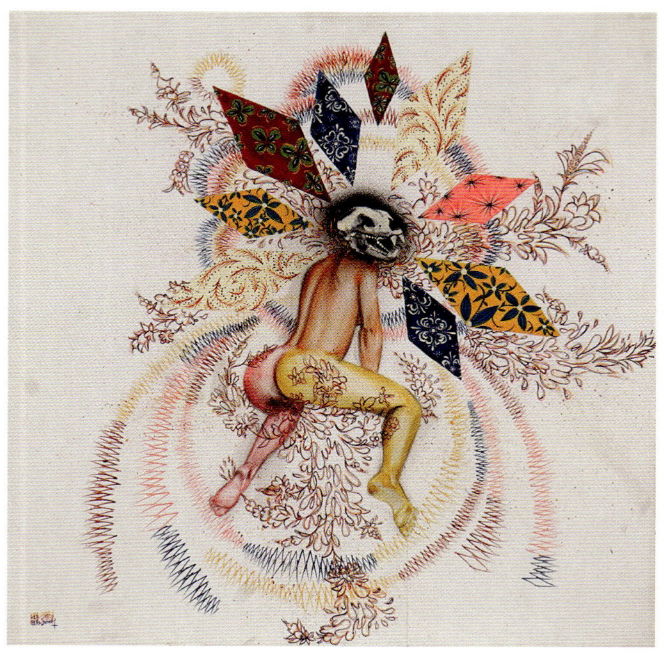

KELSEY BROOKES

Kelsey Brookes ditched his formal science training for an art career and moved from Denver to San Diego, for the surfing. He made a 'zine of his art at Kinkos, snuck into ASR, the monster surf and skate trade show, "and handed them out to anyone with a hand." Companies like OP and Insight expressed an interest, and he has since designed shirts for RVCA's Artist Network Program. Brookes has created prints for Pictures on Walls and sells his artwork through London's white-hot Lazarides Gallery. His work mixes beautifully rendered human body parts with psychedelic imagery, like pages from some anatomy book printed on blotter paper. "I use the human body a lot," he explains, "it's the root that my paintings grow from. I decorate and dress up the body with all sorts of things—animal parts, quilt patterns and plants." He feels that he's been living out his original fantasy. "All I wanted to do then, and mostly all I want to do now, is paint and surf," he says. "So my life now is like a dream come true, except in the dream I didn't have to eat Ramen noodles every night." It's also a dream open to anyone: "There is nothing exclusively unique to me that other people don't have or can't develop over time—this is very important to note. It is only necessary that you believe in your own abilities."

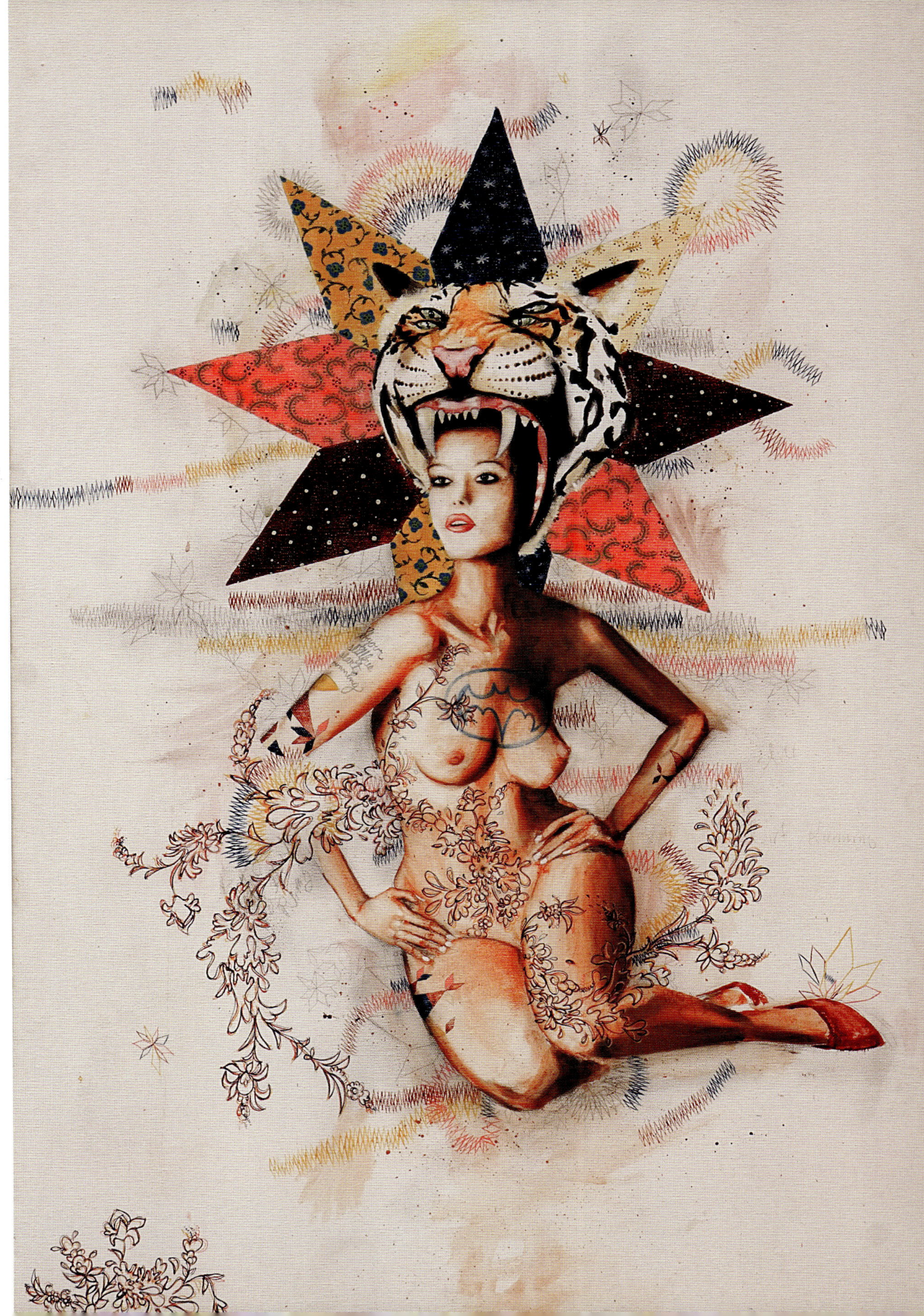

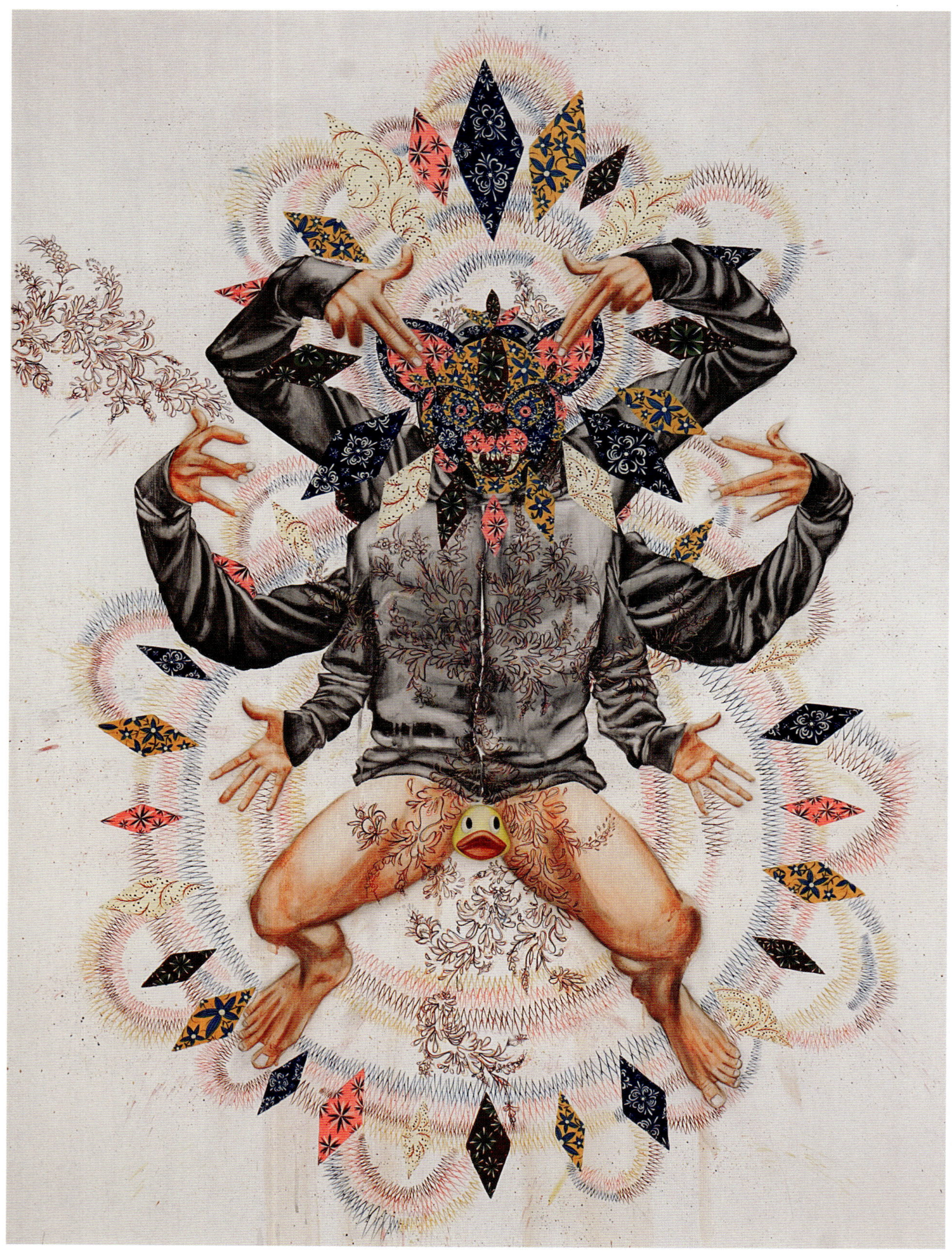

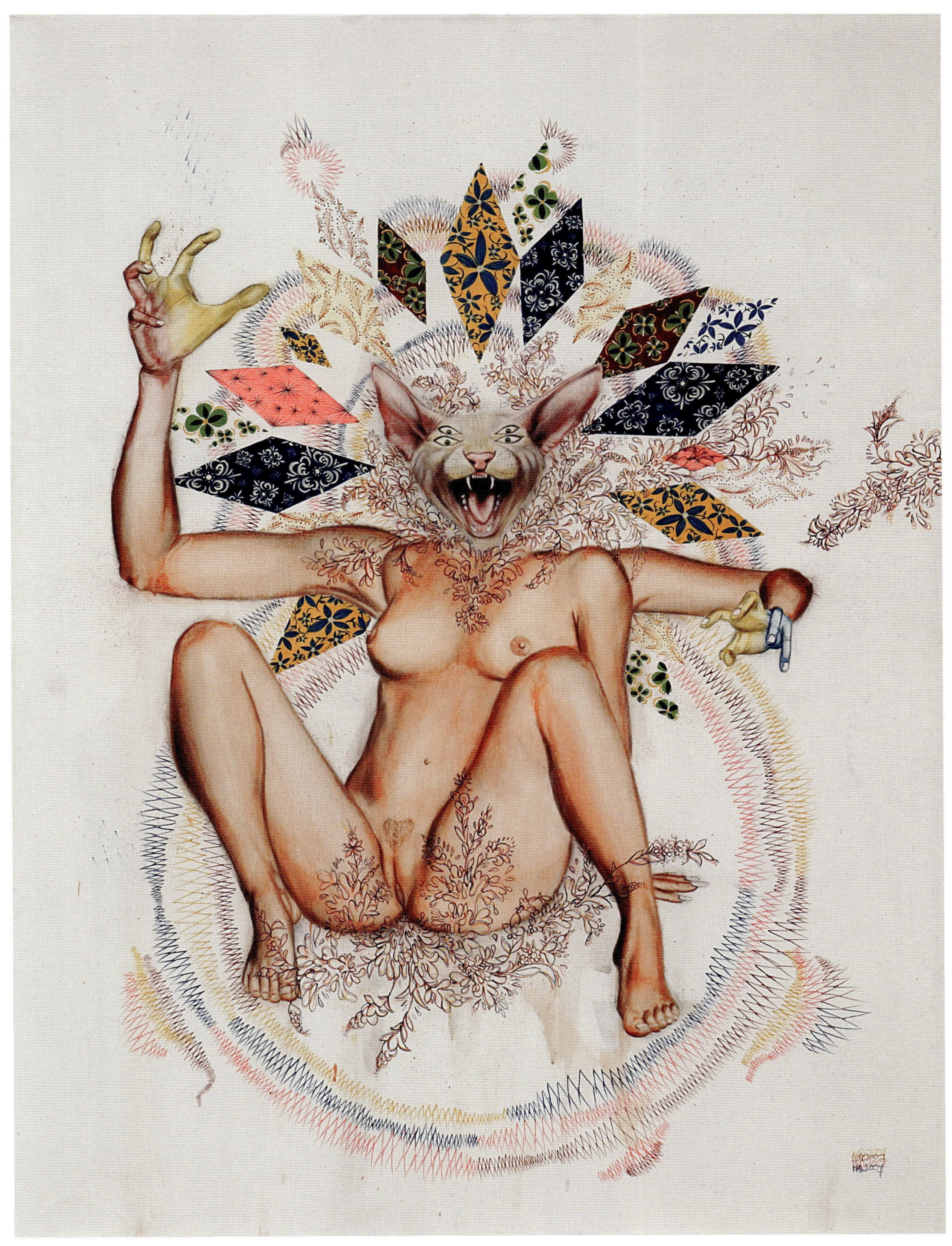

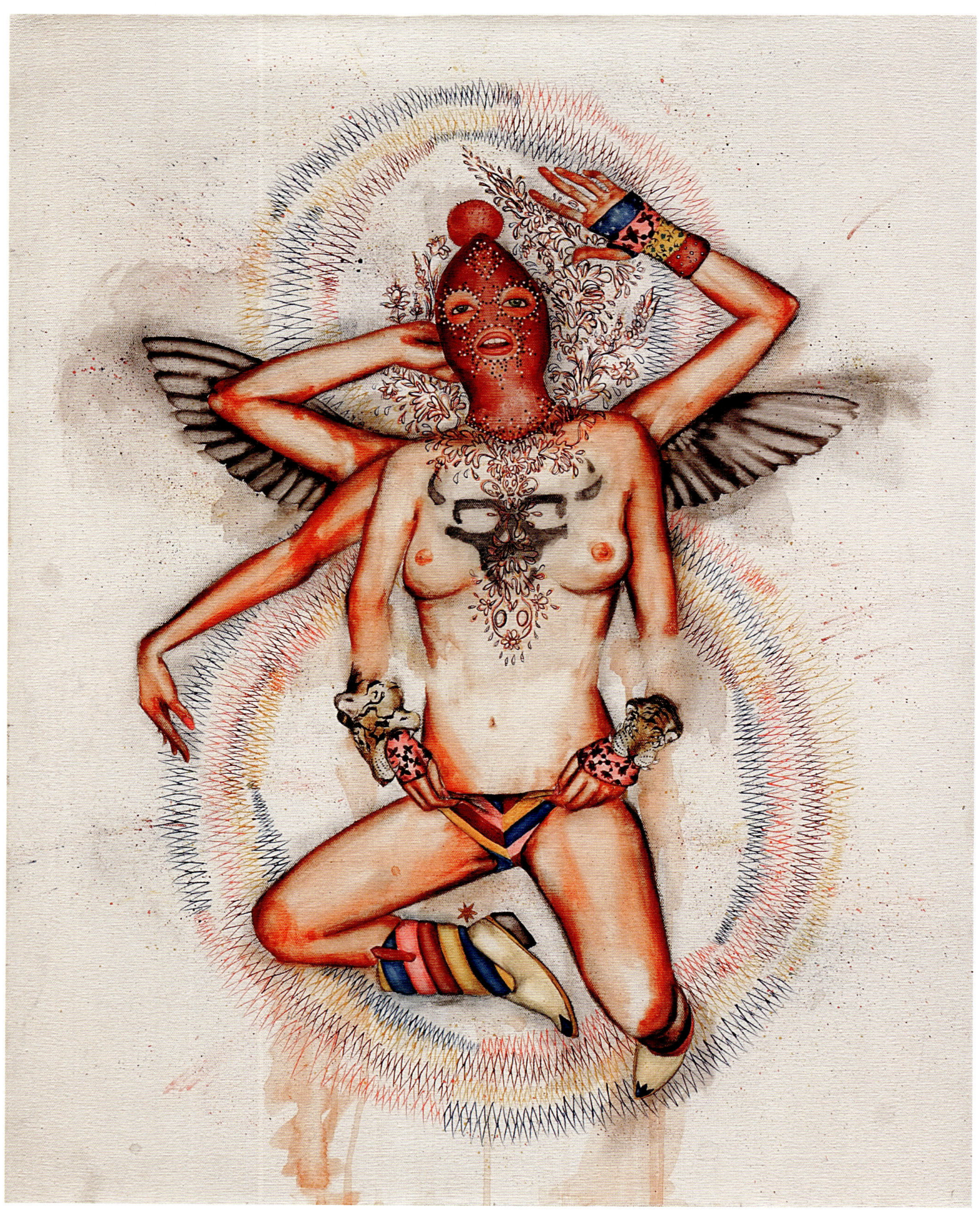

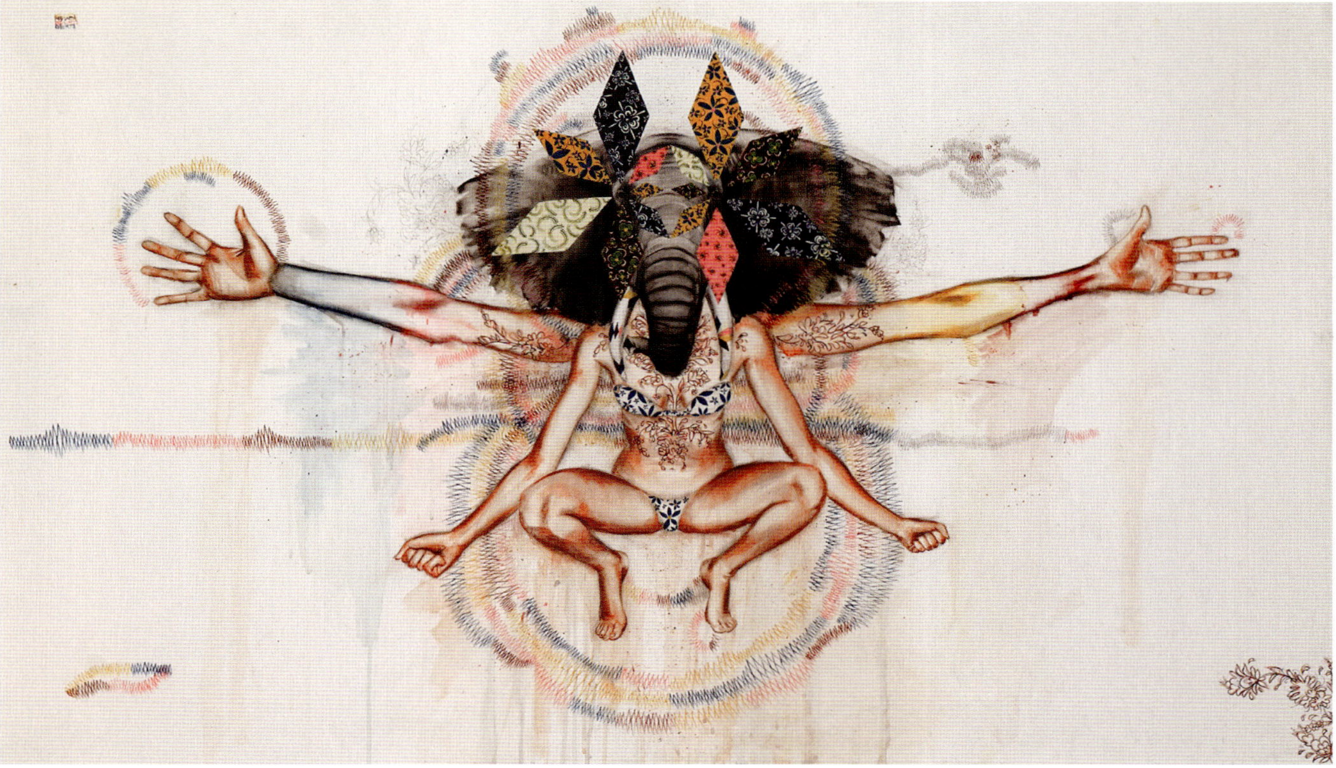

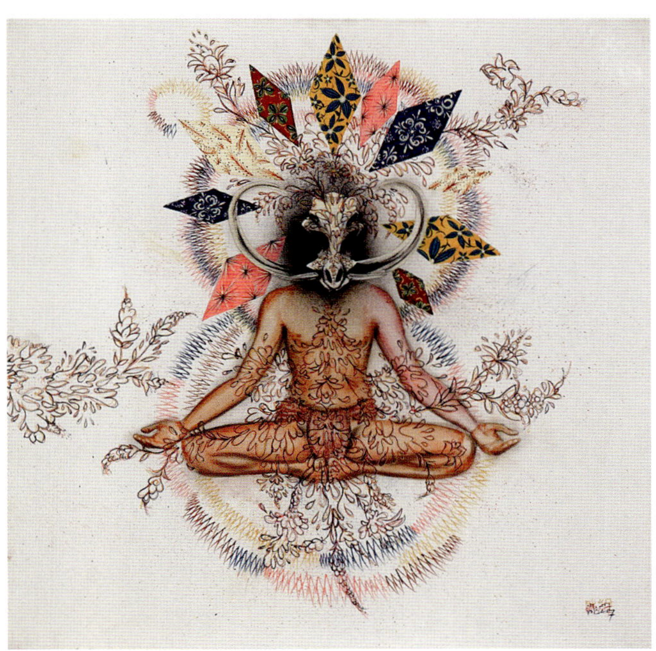

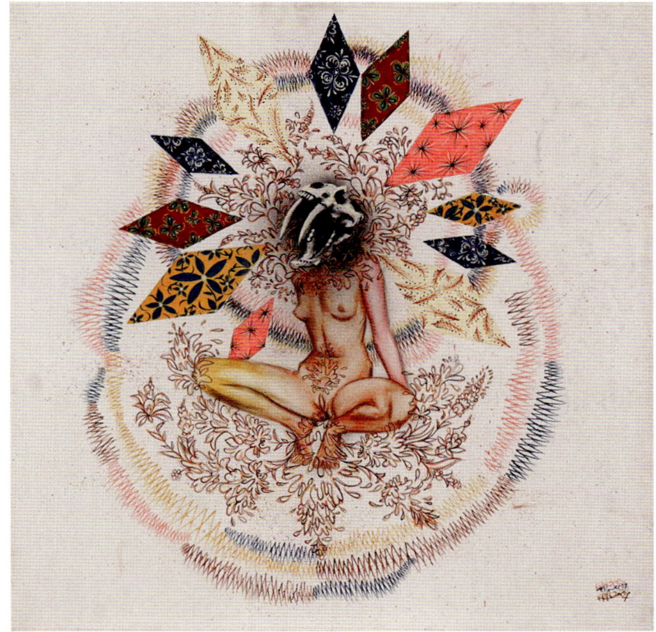

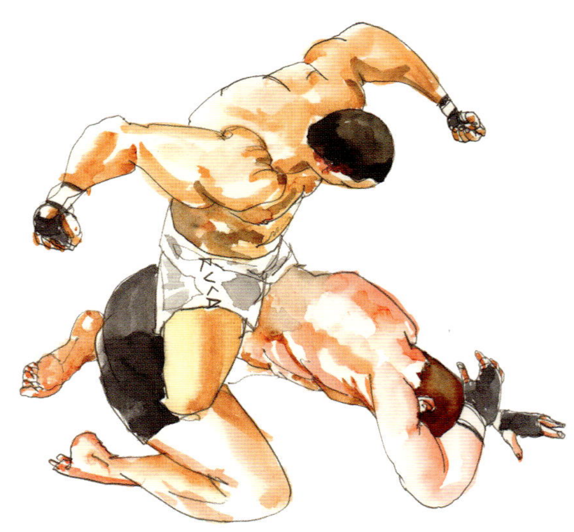

DAVID CHOE

David Choe's therapist says that he's dyslexic, clinically depressed, and has ADD and OCD. "All the prerequisites of being a decent artist," says Choe. As a child, Choe sketched the characters he watched on TV—G.I. Joe, He-Man, Robotech and Transformers—and used his drawings as makeshift toys. He continues to infuse this creativity into everything he does. While serving a 3-month sentence in a Japanese prison, he used soy sauce and his own urine as paint. His unabashed, dirty style has led to numerous jobs: album jackets for Linkin Park and Jay-Z, a DC Comics cover, freelance illustration for Hustler and car design for Scion, among many others. It was his first self-published book "Slow Jams" that launched his high-profile illustration career. "Everyone's an artist these days except illustrators," he laments. "Cooks are artists, haircutters are artists—everyone's a fucking artist. Ironically, the only real artists are illustrators. They create the look of society. Who is the real artist: Warhol? Or the dude that designed the Campbell's soup can? I never cared much for galleries and museums. All the art that was important to me was on the back of cereal boxes, candy packages, comic books… It's still a mystery to me how I ended up in the museums—I'm an illustrator."

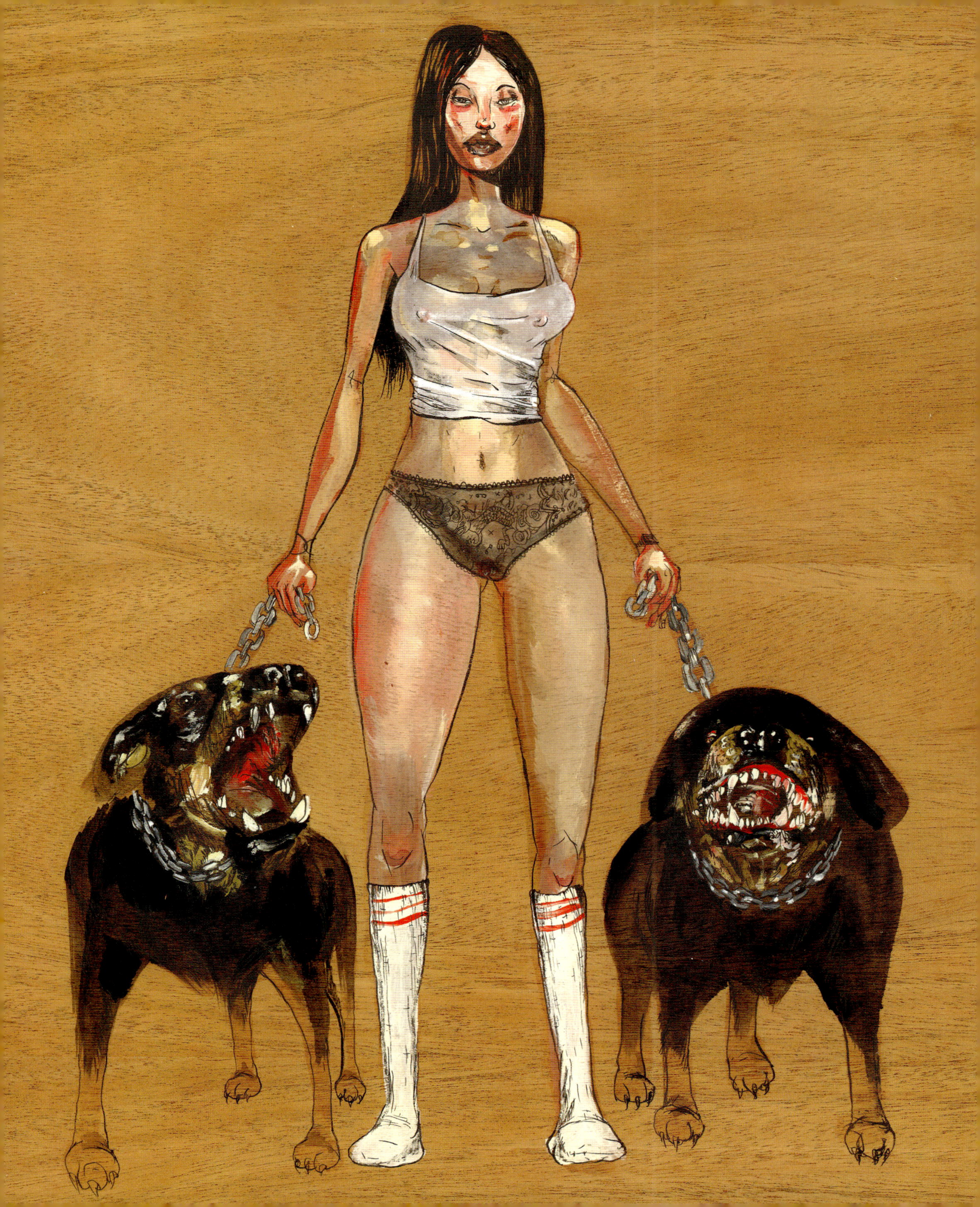

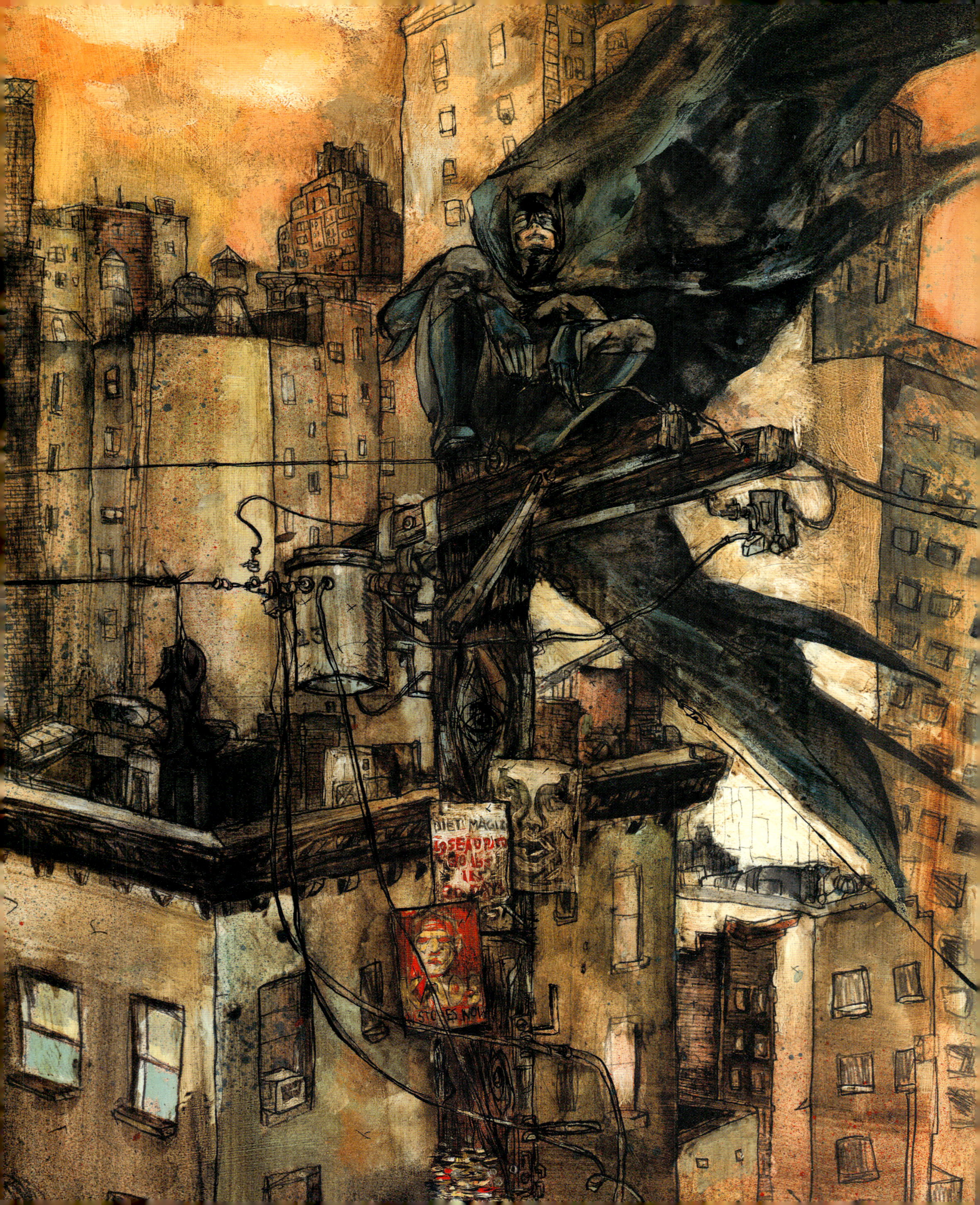
DIET MAGIE
L'OISEAU DIT
VOUS
LES
O DAYS
STO ES NOU

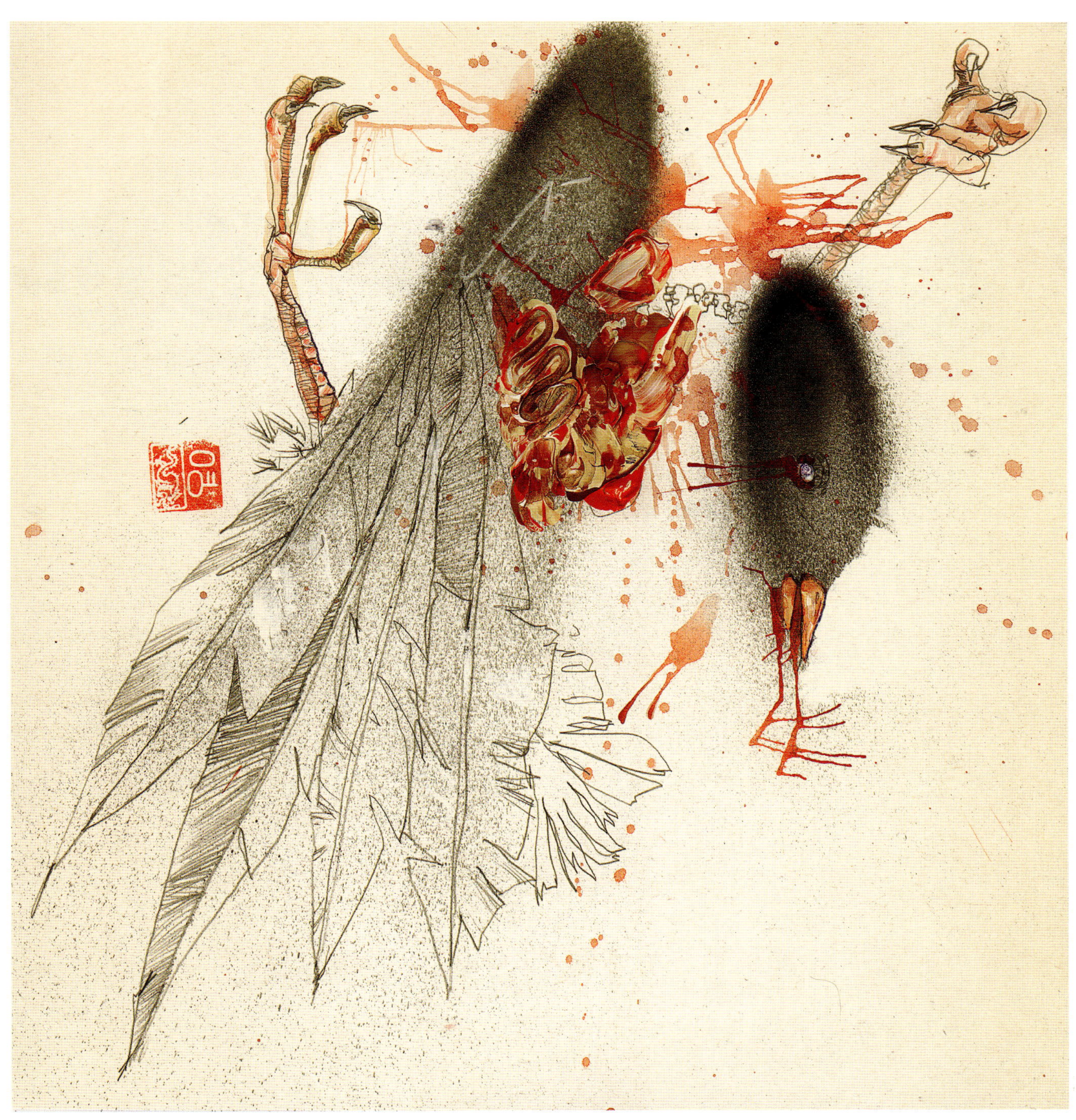

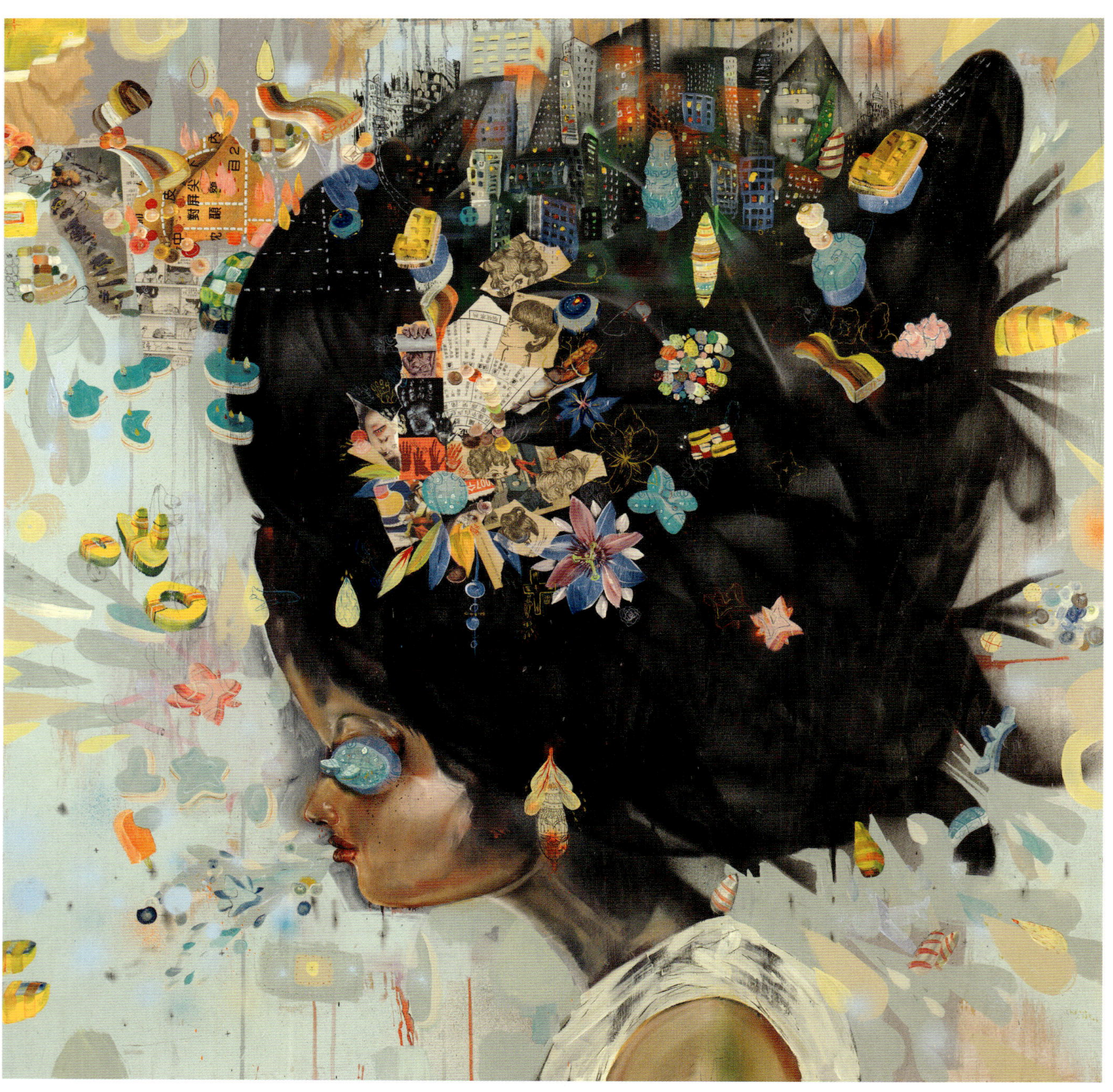

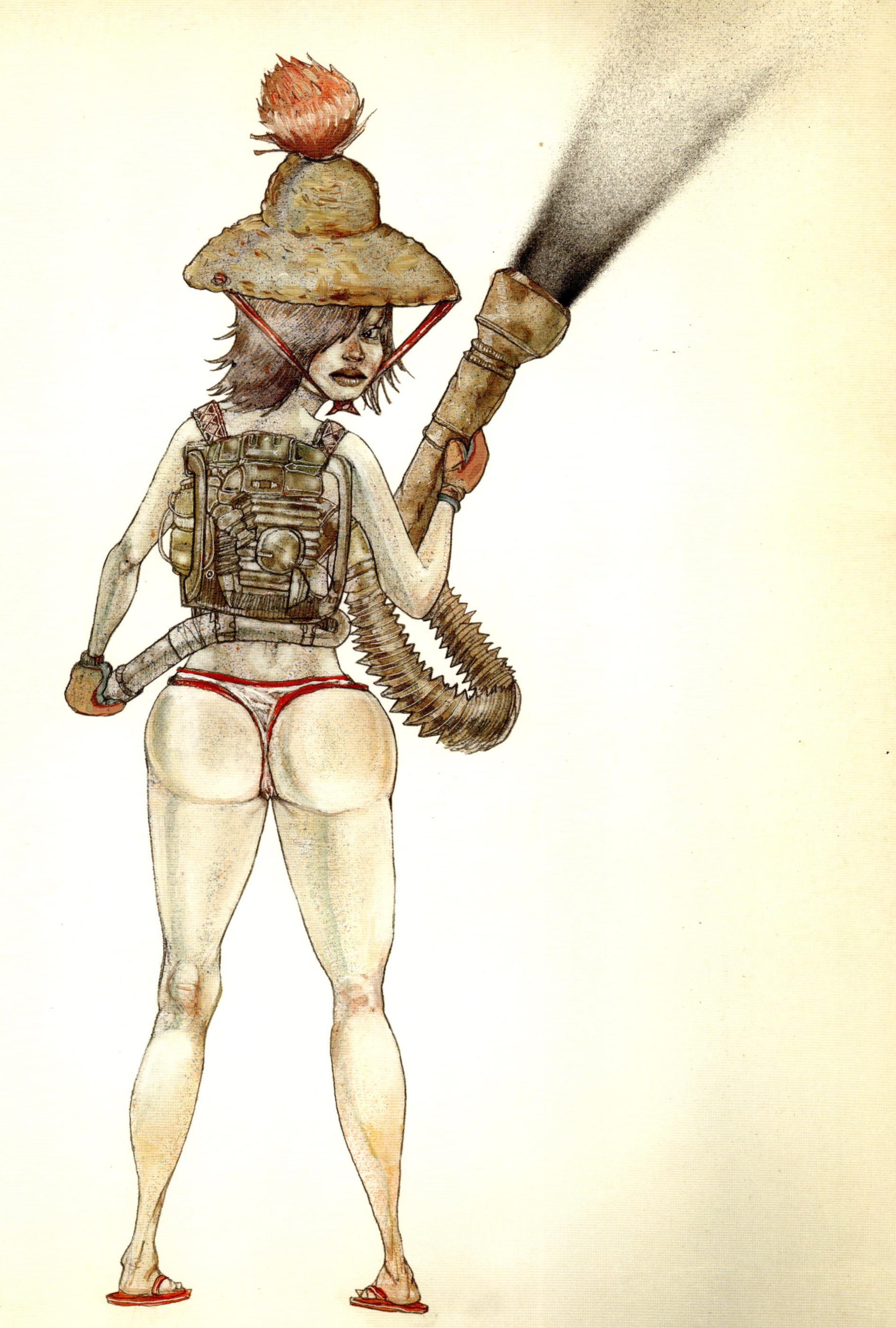

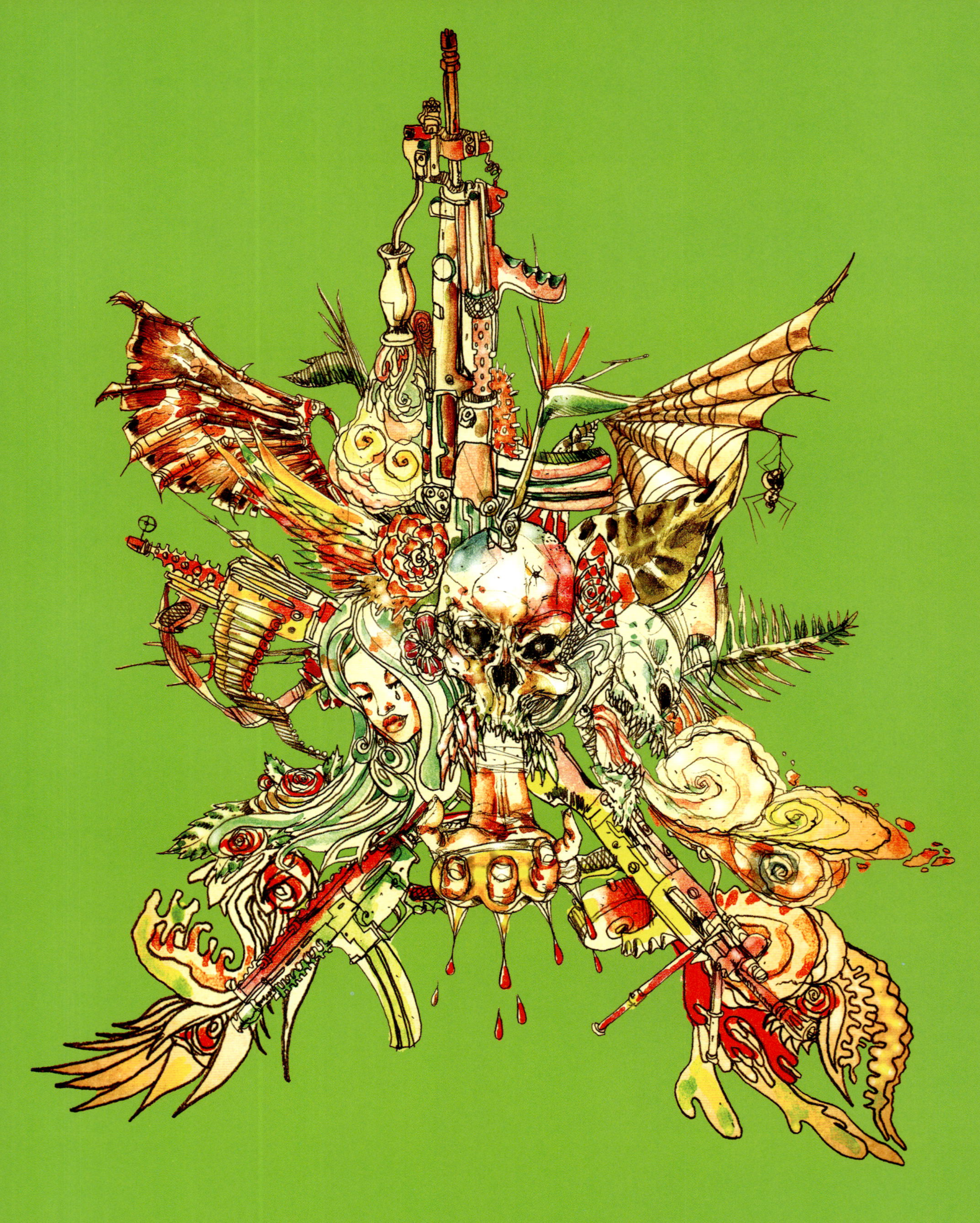

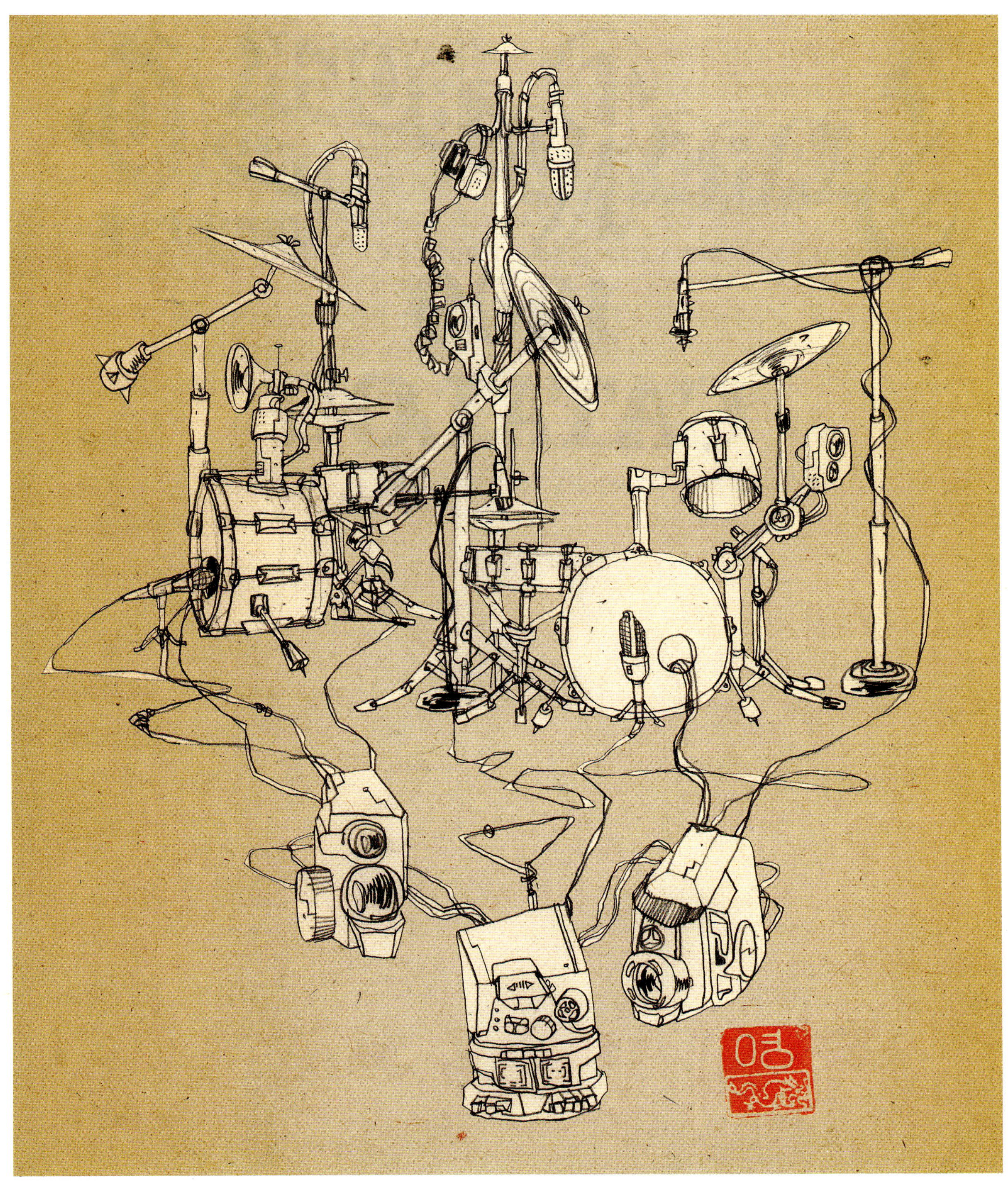

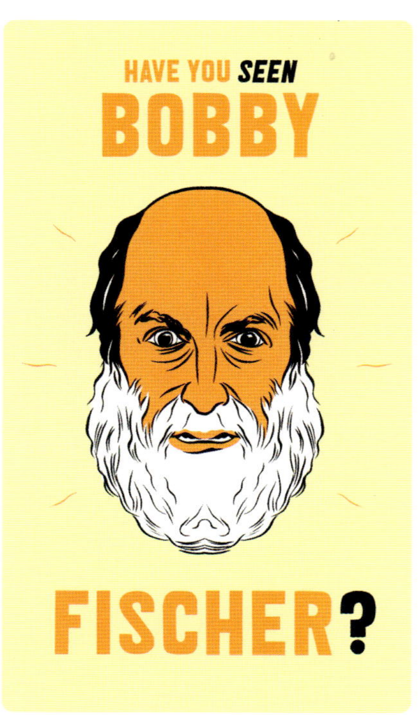

MICKEY DUZYJ

Born in a working-class immigrant neighborhood of Detroit, Mickey Duzyj's parents encouraged him to make art as a way to sustain and connect with his cultural identity. "Ukrainians," he explains, "have a great tradition of art, and I was exposed to all sorts of things—woodcuts,dyed and patterned eggs, and painting—from a very young age." As a high school student he visited a cousin in Albuquerque, who frequented the streets at night, and wrote graffiti in San Francisco with artists such as Mike Giant, Dalek, Felon and Amaze. The effect of his introduction into graffiti culture was trans-formative, and he carefully noted that the writers drew all the time: "It really made an impression on me." Duzyj returned to the suburbs to look for a similar community, and subsequently applied to the School of Visual Arts in New York City. He has lived in Brooklyn ever since. In 2005, he took the top prize at the collegiate Society of Illustrators competition. His client list has included Rolling Stone, The New Yorker, Esquire, Wired, and The Wall Street Journal; he has designed book-jackets, and skateboards for 5BoroNYC. Using limited color palettes has become a signature style for him. "I don't see why everything needs to be full CMYK all the time," he explains. "Especially when some of the most classic graphic images—flags, sports uniforms, the Coca-Cola logo—only have a few colors."

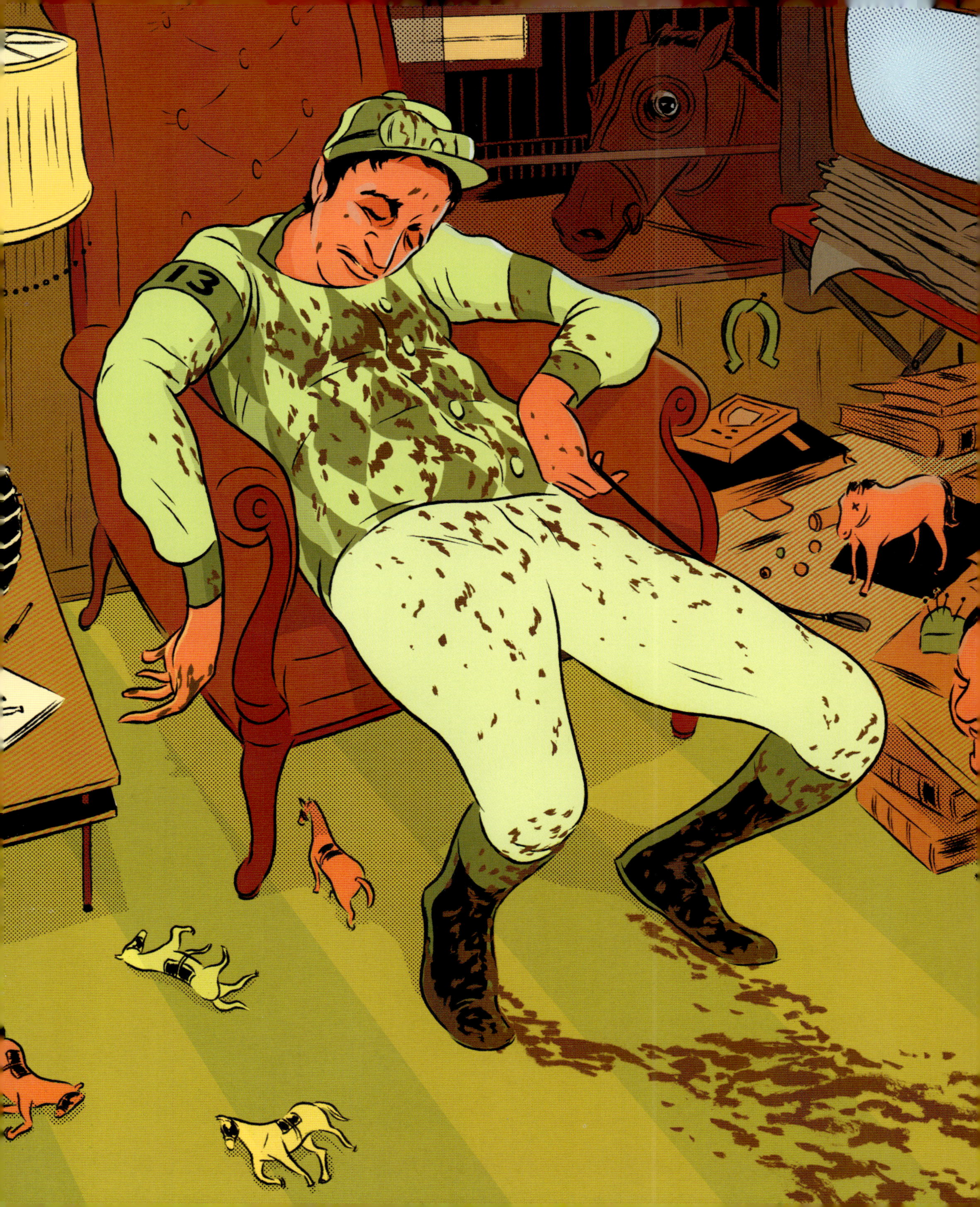

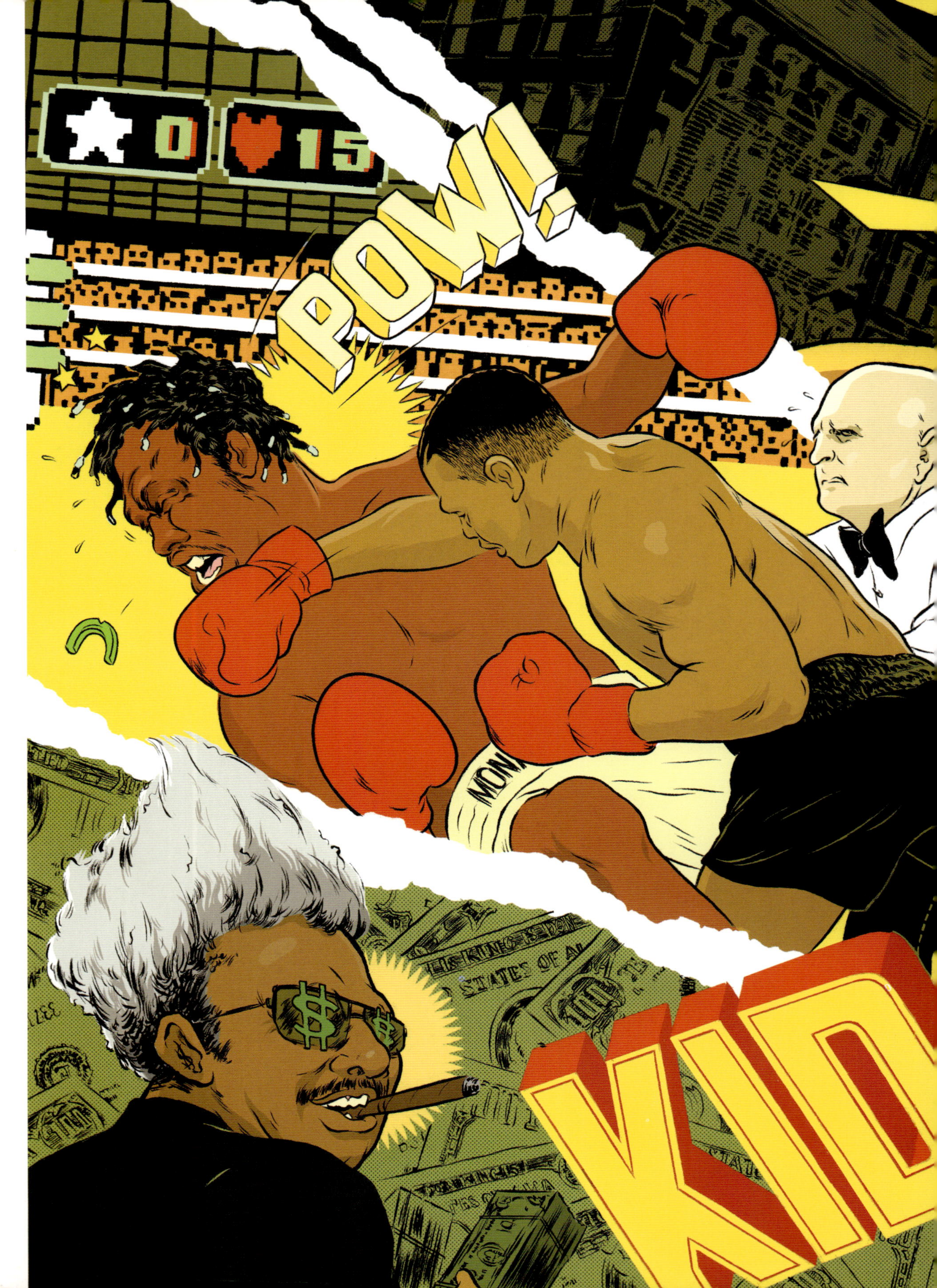

0
15
POW!
MON
KID

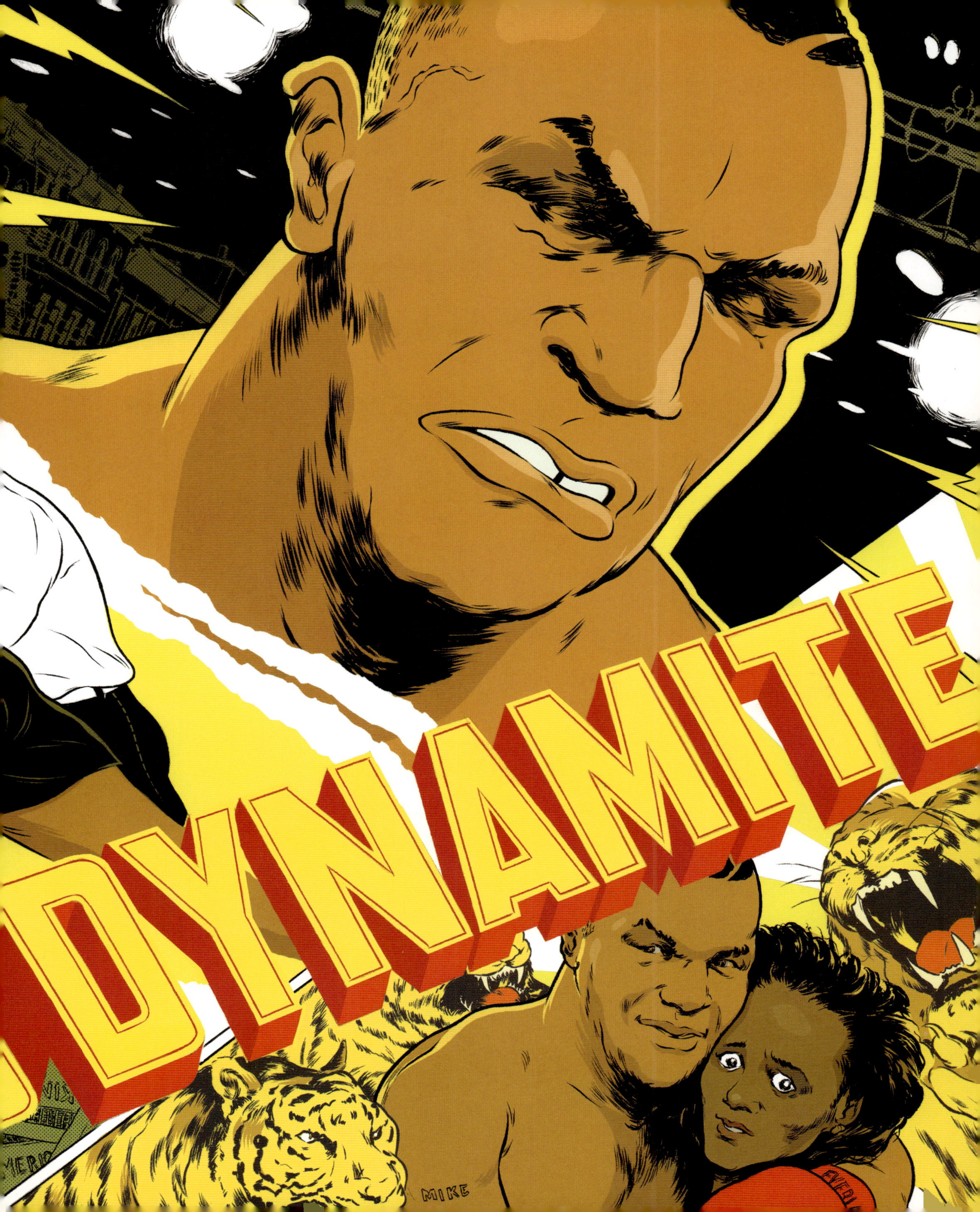

DYNAMITE
MIKE

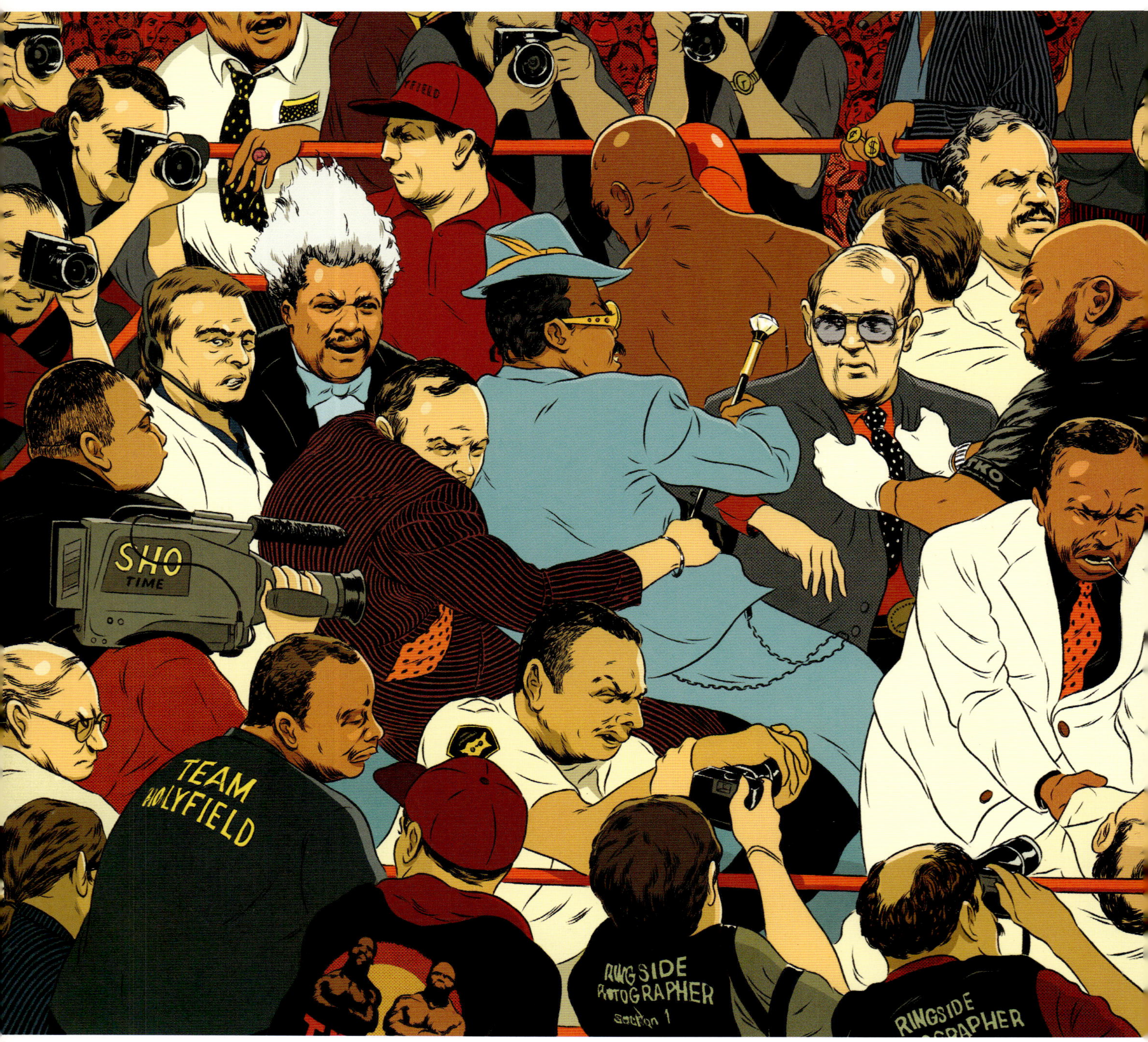
SHO TIME
TEAM HOLYFIELD
RINGSIDE PHOTOGRAPHER
section 1
RINGSIDE PHOTOGRAPHER

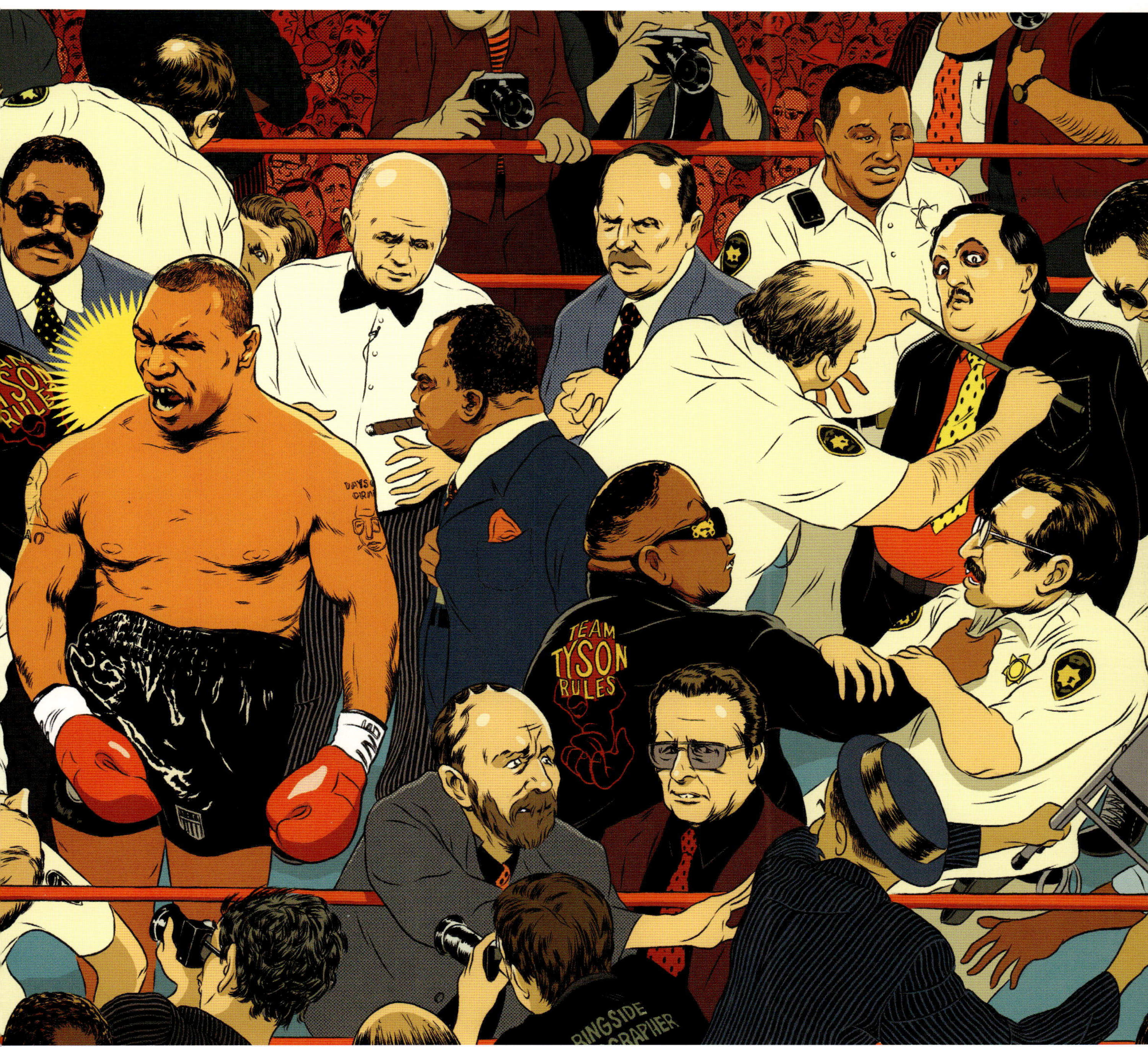
TYSON RULES
TEAM TYSON RULES
RINGSIDE PHOTOGRAPHER

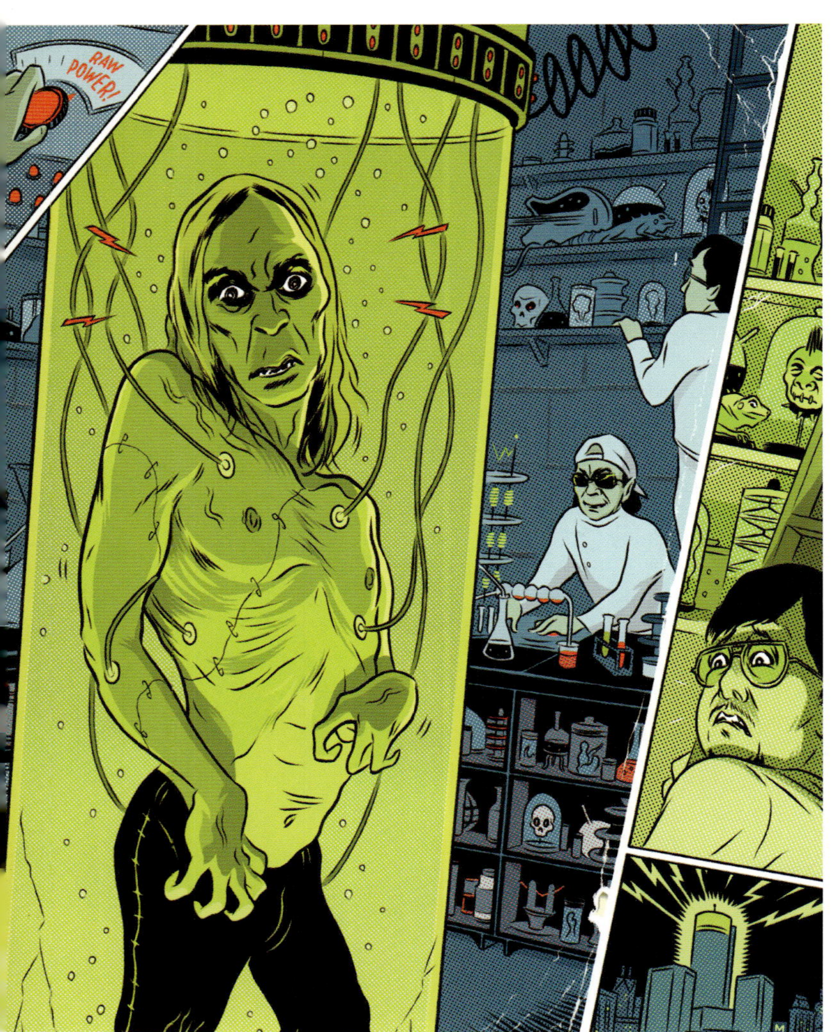

RAW POWER!

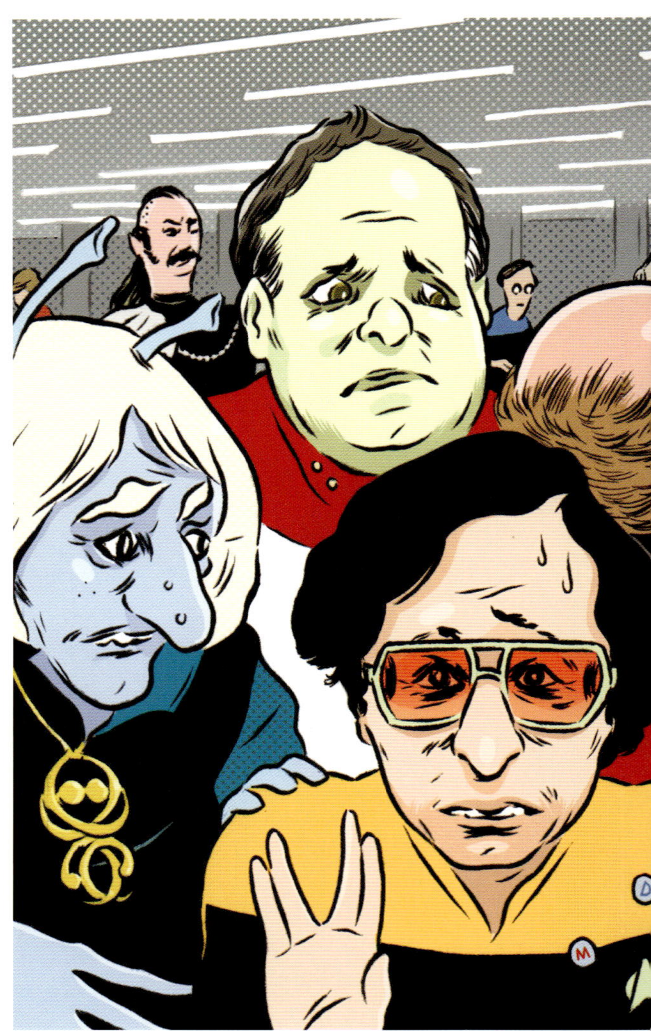

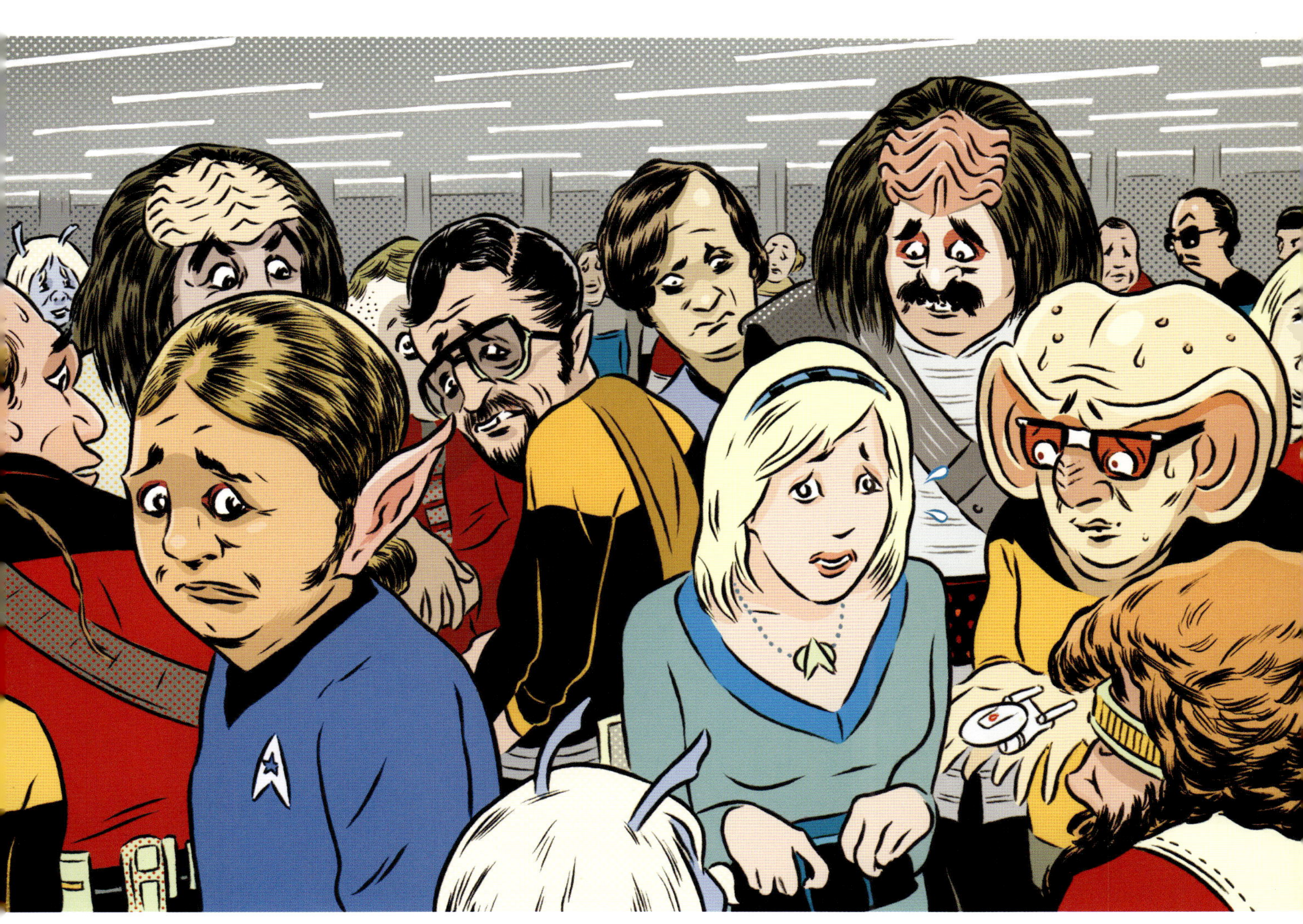

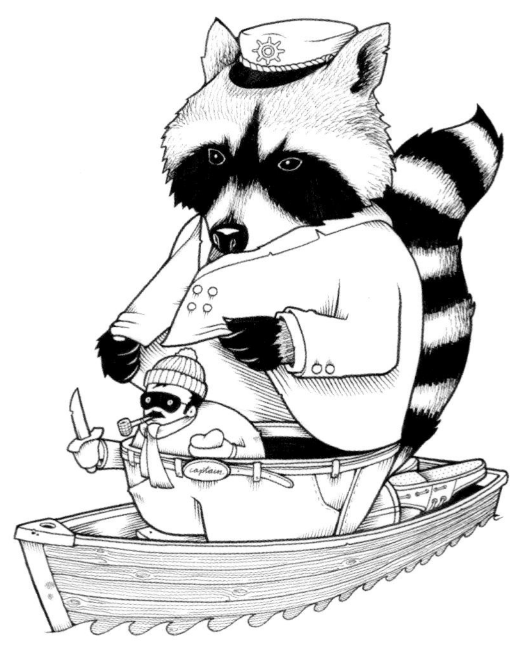

JEREMY FISH

Jeremy Fish tells a story, using what he refers to as his "library of characters and symbols," including silly pink bunnies who steer makeshift vessels across the sea and sky. But Jeremy's stories are told in a "Choose Your Own Adventure" fashion, because "You as the viewer get to decide the ending to the story, or decide that it sucks and walk away." Jeremy lives and works in the North Beach neighborhood of San Francisco — "you know, Jack Kerouac, Francis Ford Coppola, the old beatnik neighborhood, it's not really a business as much as it is a lifestyle." He also maintains a website, umbrellamarket.com, that sells T-shirts, prints and toys. He deems it "the coolest thing since canned beer." Last year, he collaborated with rapper Aesop Rock on a book titled "The Next Best Thing," a story about their mutual solution—or lack of one—for creative block. He has also designed vinyl toys such as the Turtlecamper and Bunnyskull based on his illustrations, as well as a shoe for Nike, with more projects to come. Despite his success, he says, "I am not that naturally talented. I have to work super hard to build a recognizable style to my stuff. I try to challenge myself constantly to improve technically and conceptually, while maintaining a similar storytelling aesthetic."

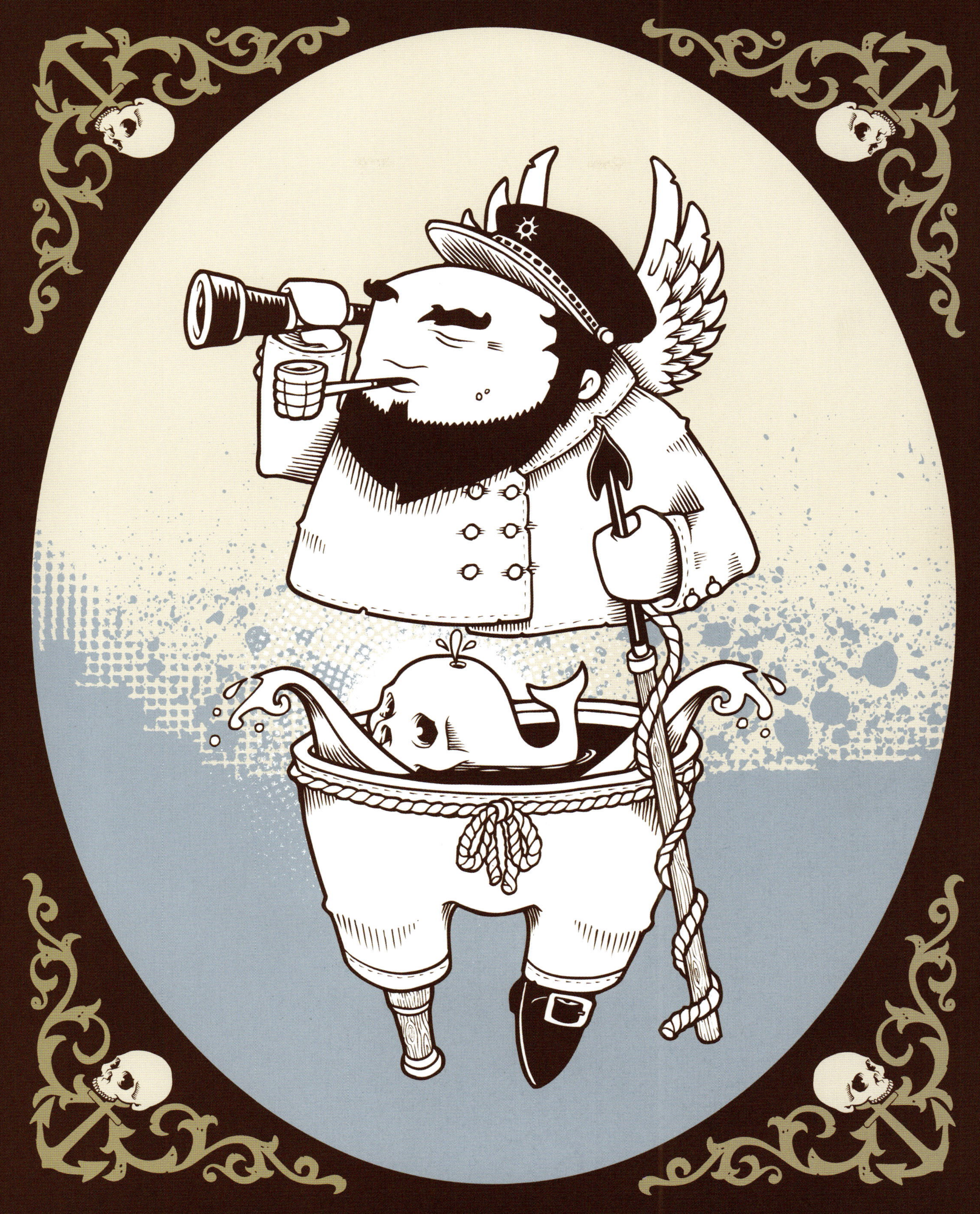

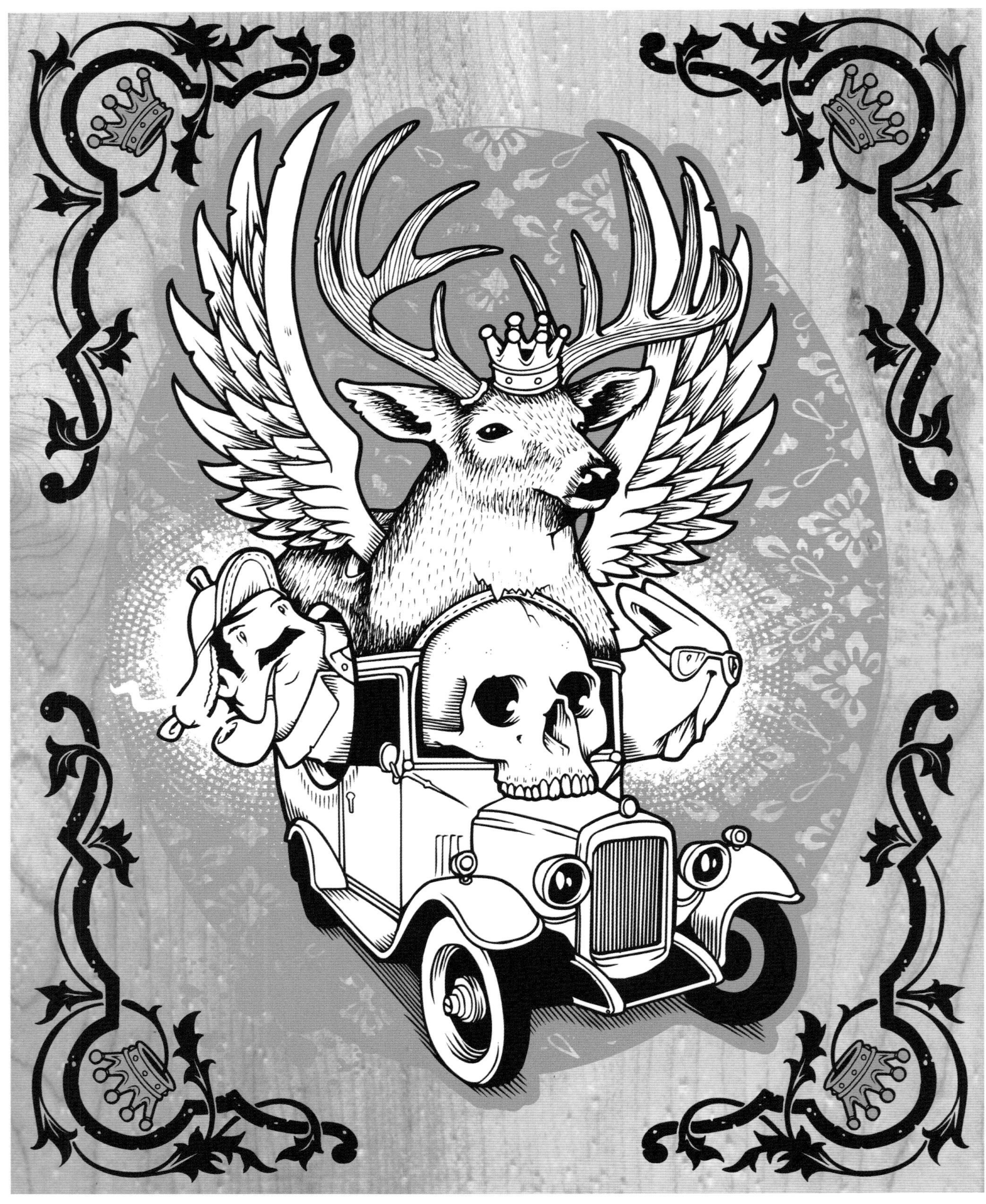

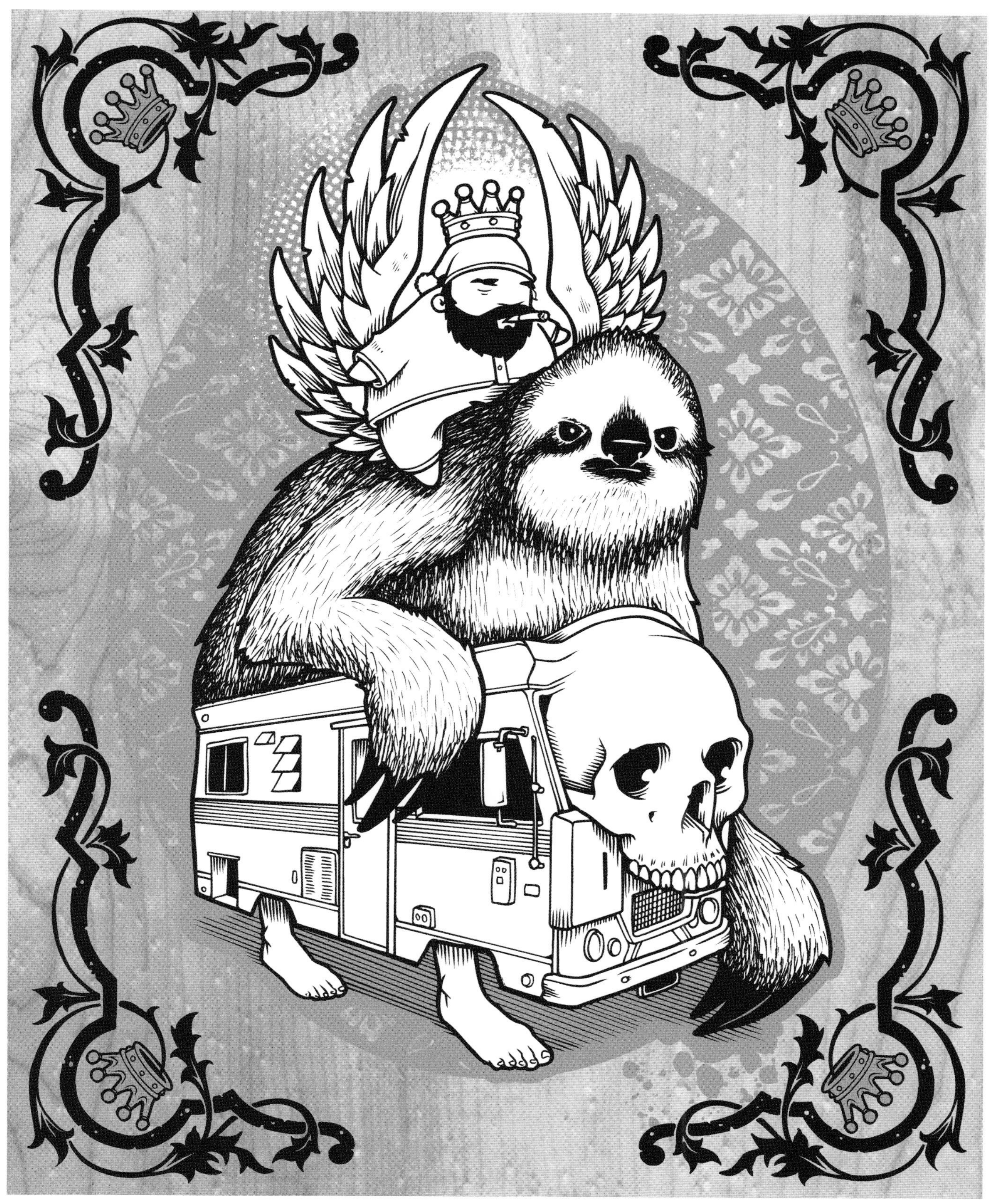

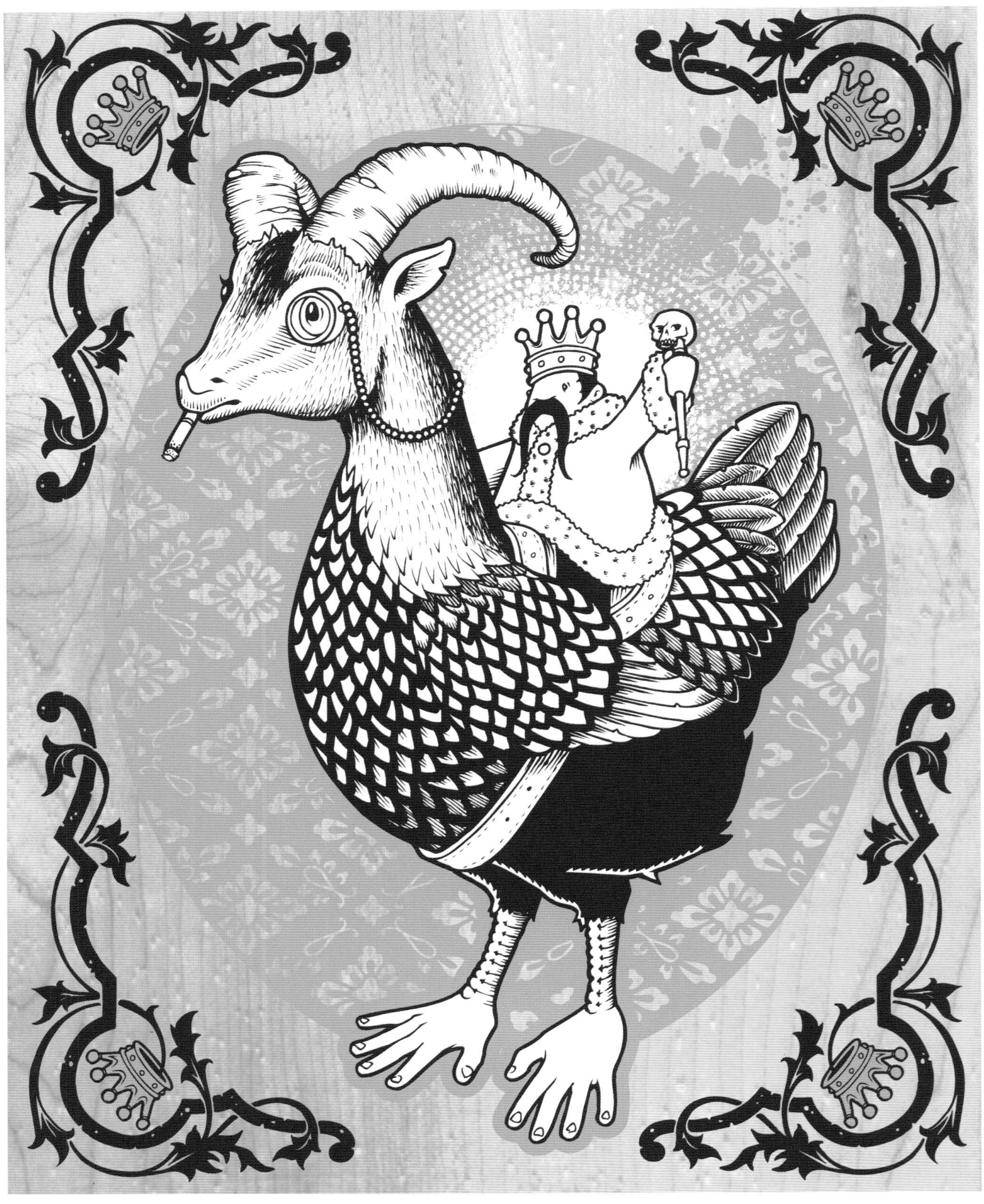

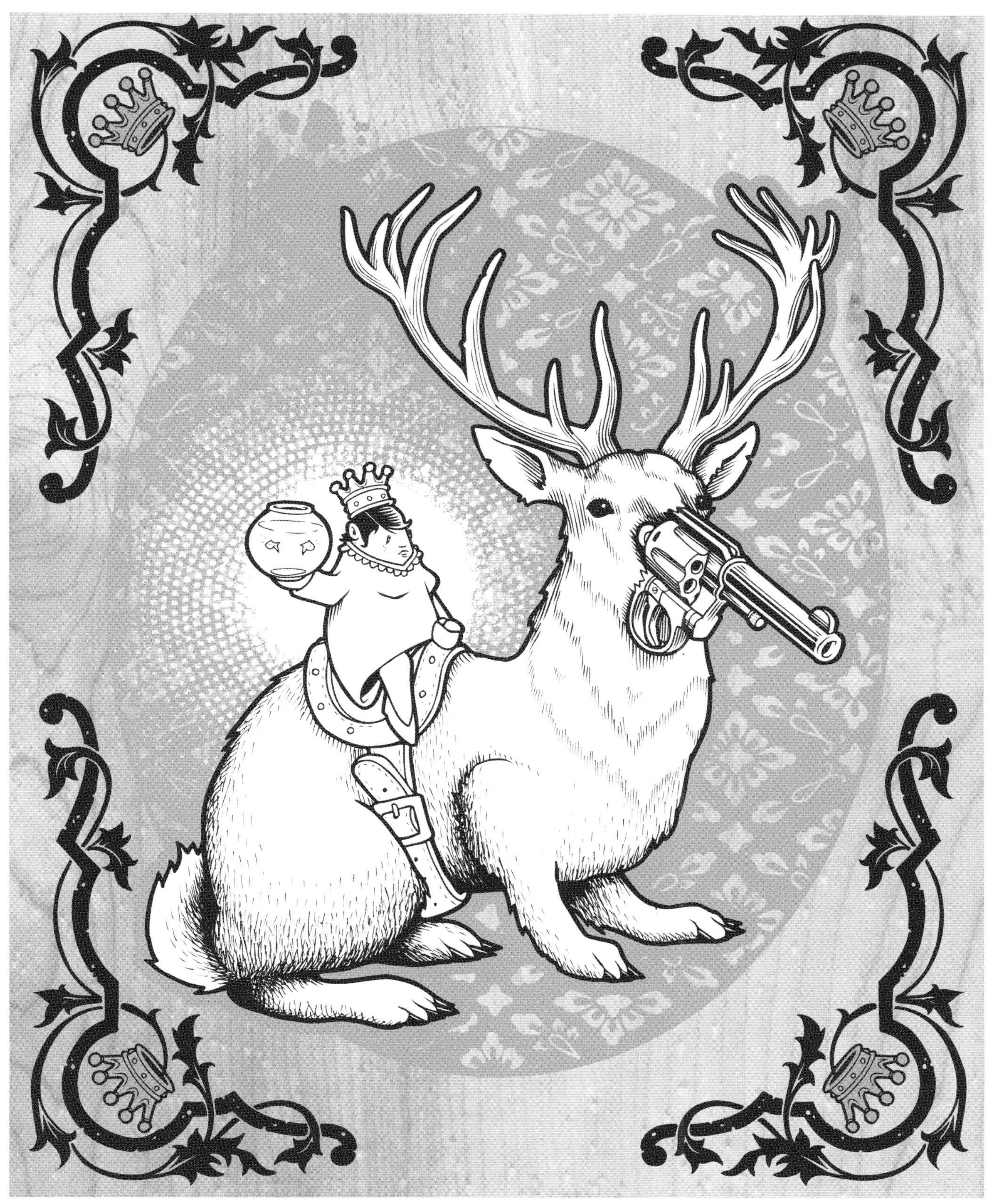

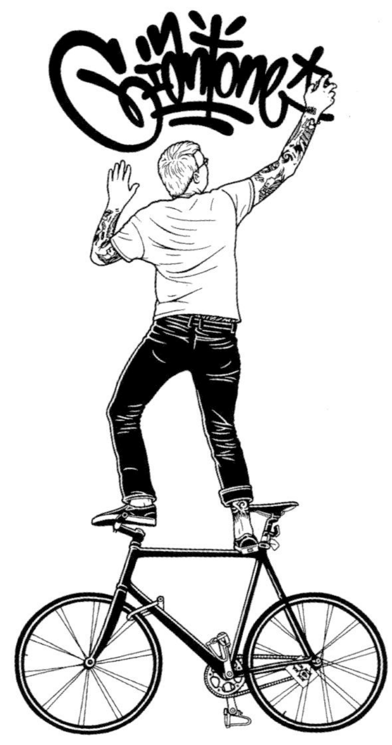

MIKE GIANT

Mike Giant has an instantly recognizable aesthetic—even if he doesn't think so. "I can't say what others see in my work," acknowledges the Albuquerque-based artist. "I can say what I hope viewers see: attention to detail, balance, grace, volume, depth, history and love." His thick black-and-white images are reminiscent of José Posada, albeit with a modern-day, graffiti-based twist. But Mike says it's simpler than that: "My aesthetic is the artistic manifestation of who I am. I stick with black and white because I'm colorblind. I draw skulls, roses, bicycles, girls and gods because that's what interests me." He is most inspired by books, grabbing a pile and pouring through each page in search of exciting imagery as rediscovered fodder for his sketches. His work has been shown all over the world — most recently in Paris. When asked how he got to where he is today, his simple response is, "One drawing at a time." In life and in art, it seems he likes to boil things down to their essence. It's fitting, then, that he enjoys illustrating because "it's the everyday-man's medium." He also tattoos and paints walls, and would like to produce music one day. "But for now," he allows, "I'm pretty happy spending 90% of my art time pushing Sharpies around on nice paper."

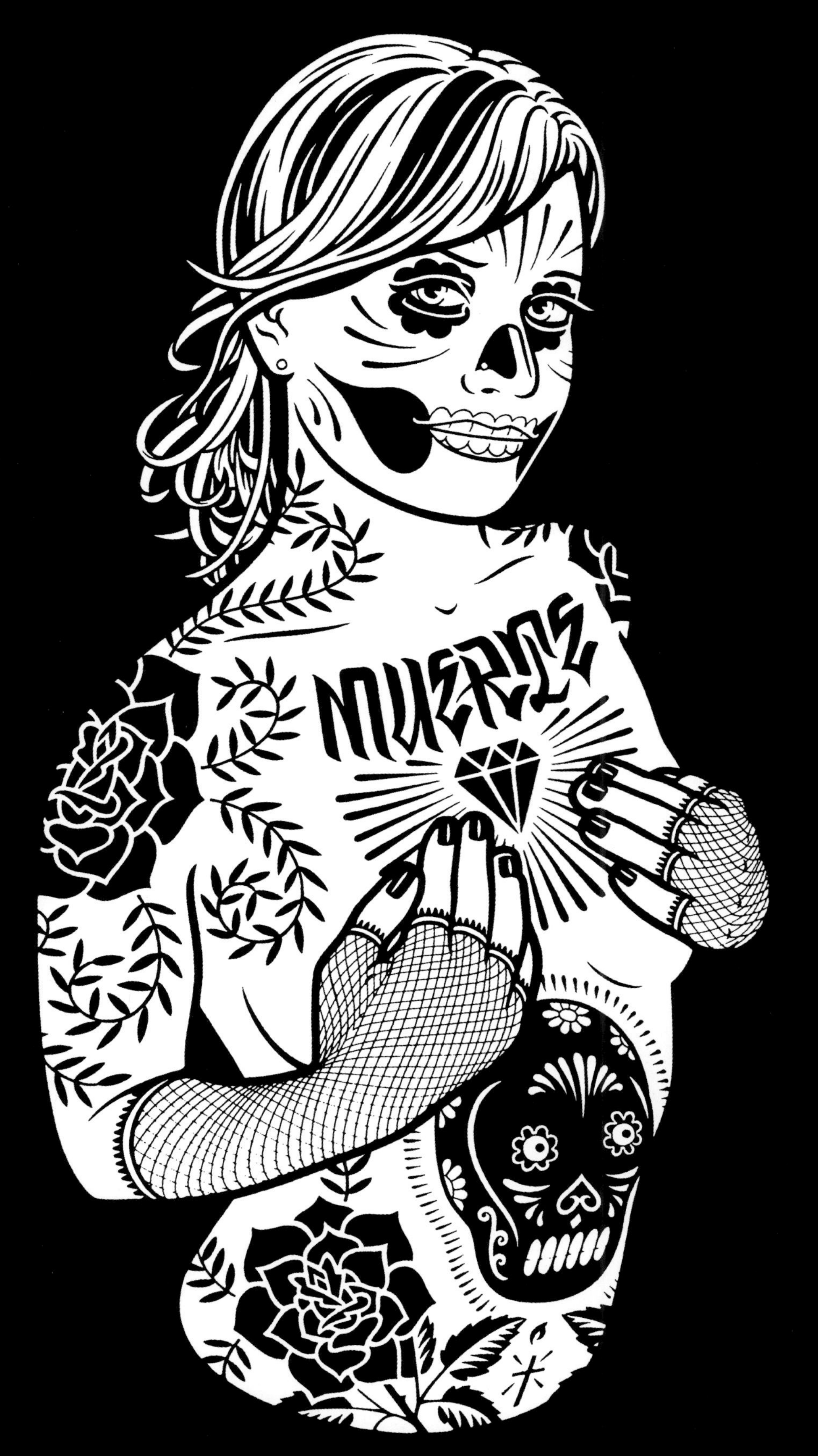
MUERTE

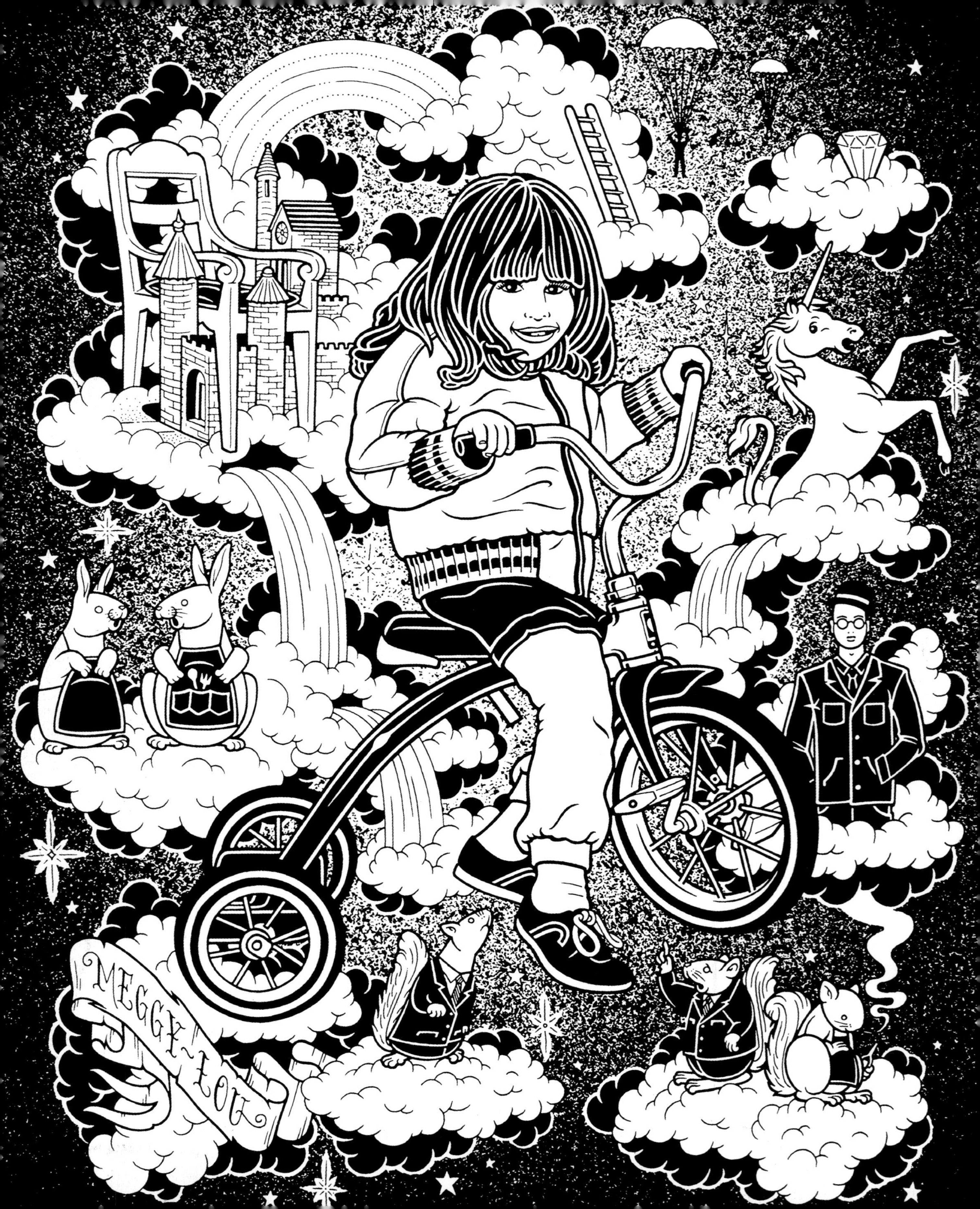

MEGGY-LOU

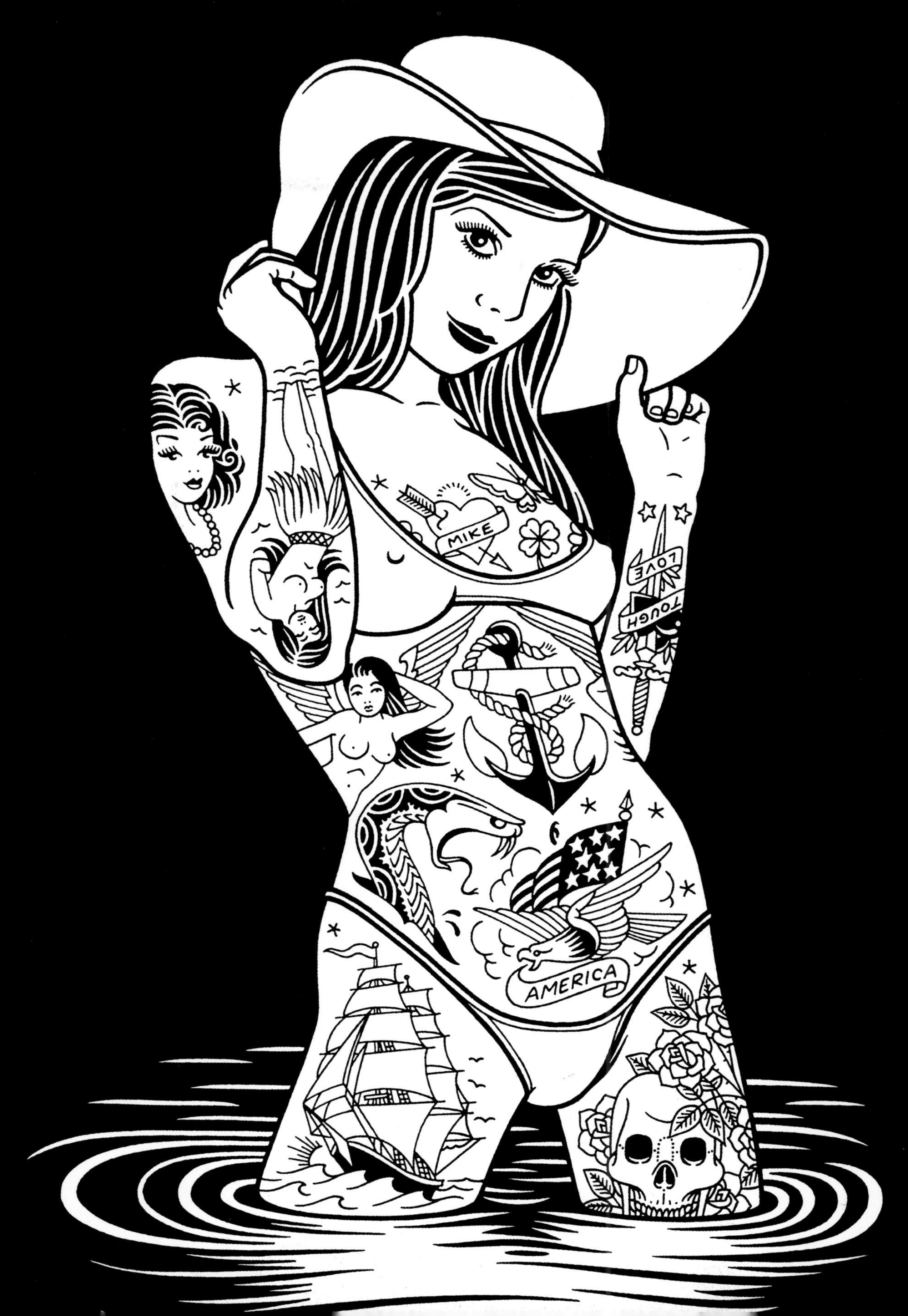

MIKE
LOVE
TOUGH
AMERICA

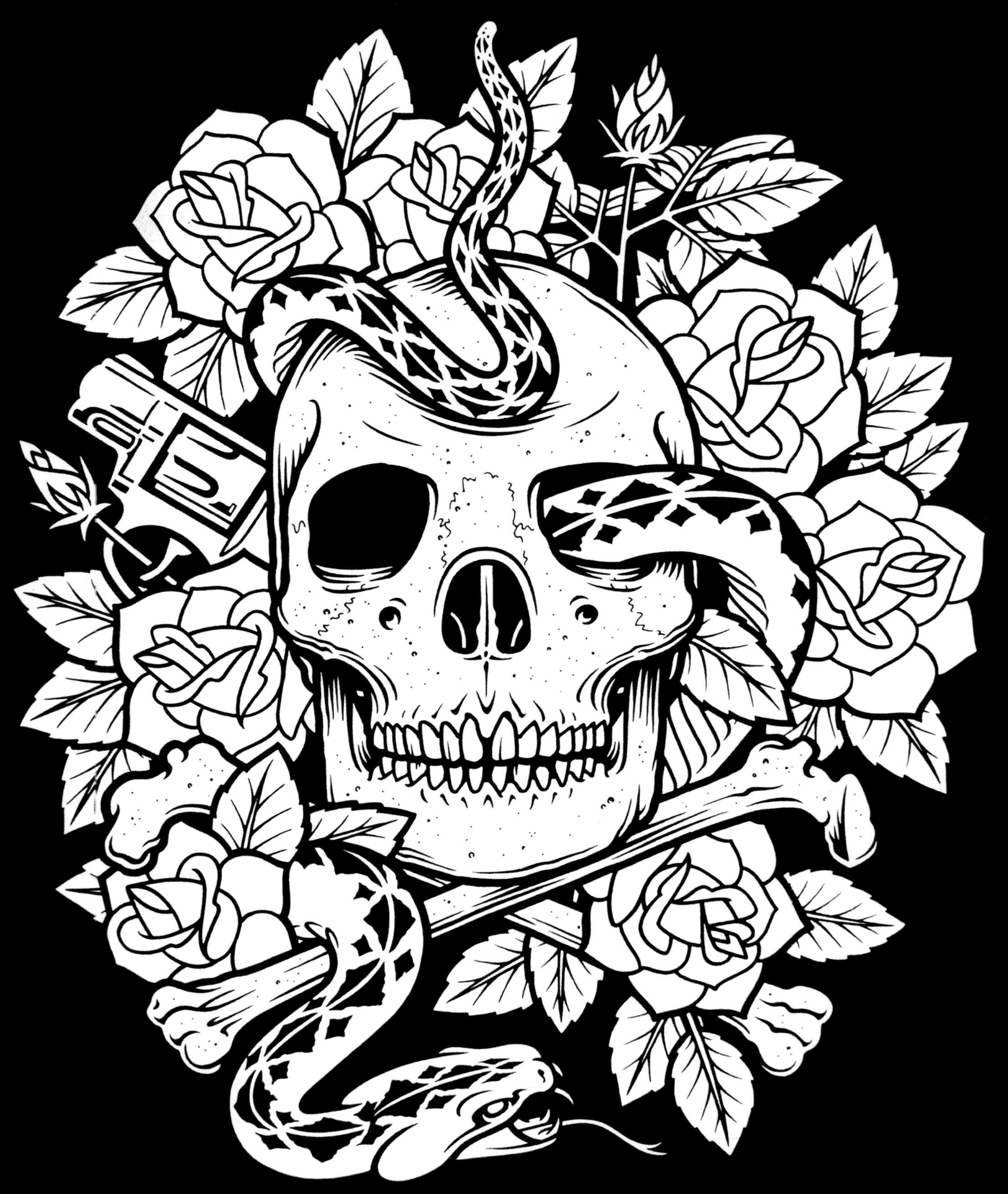

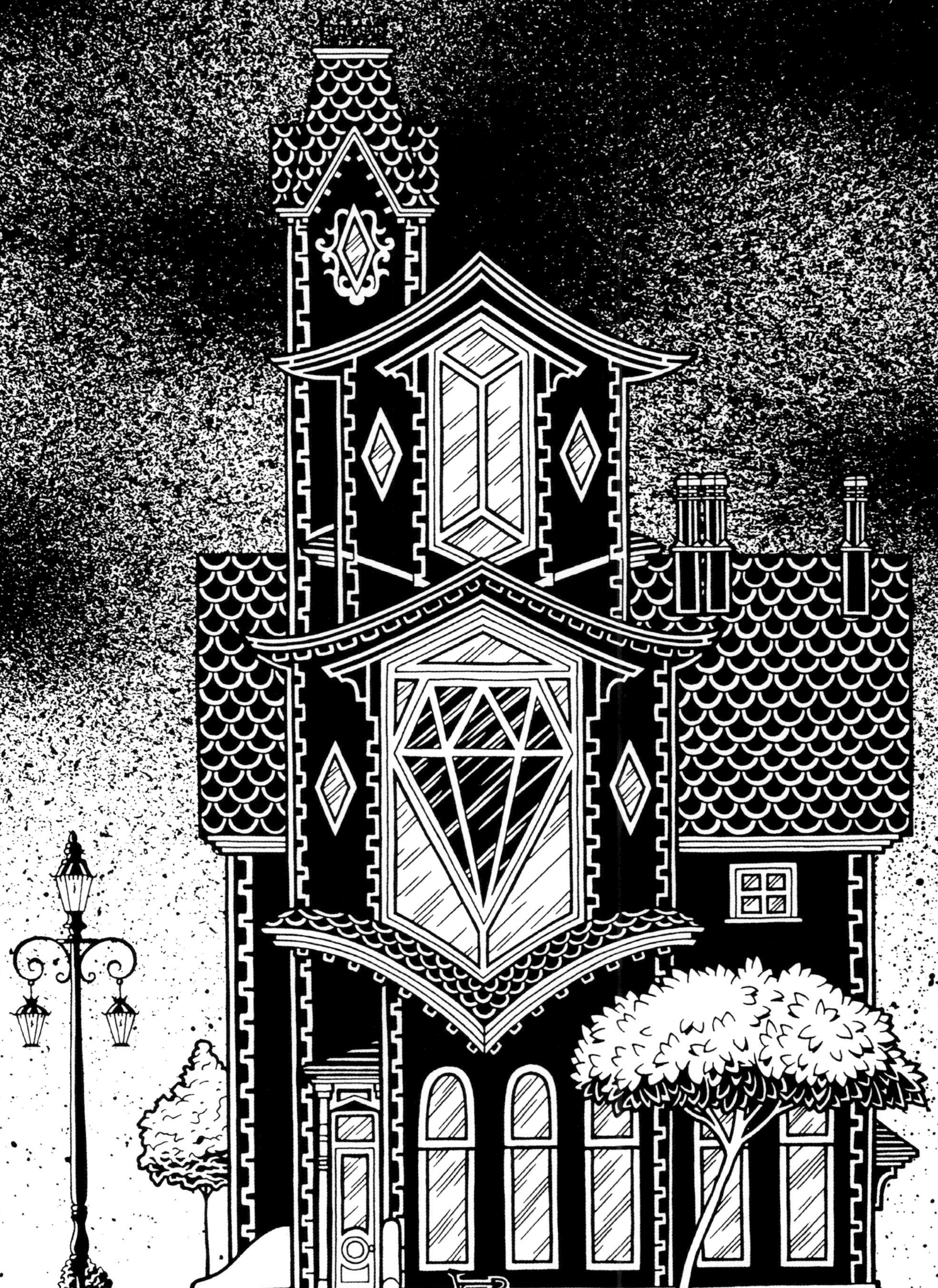

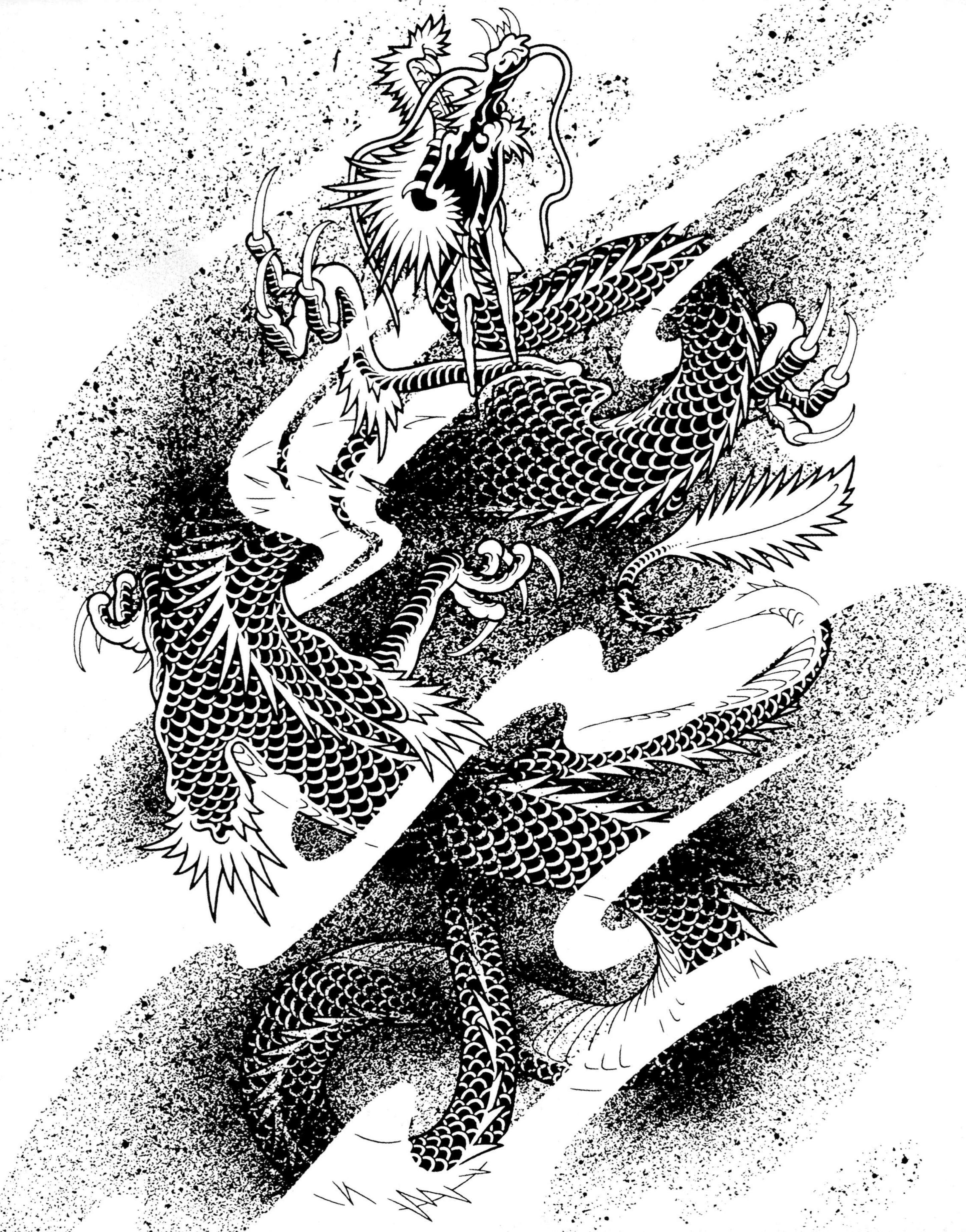

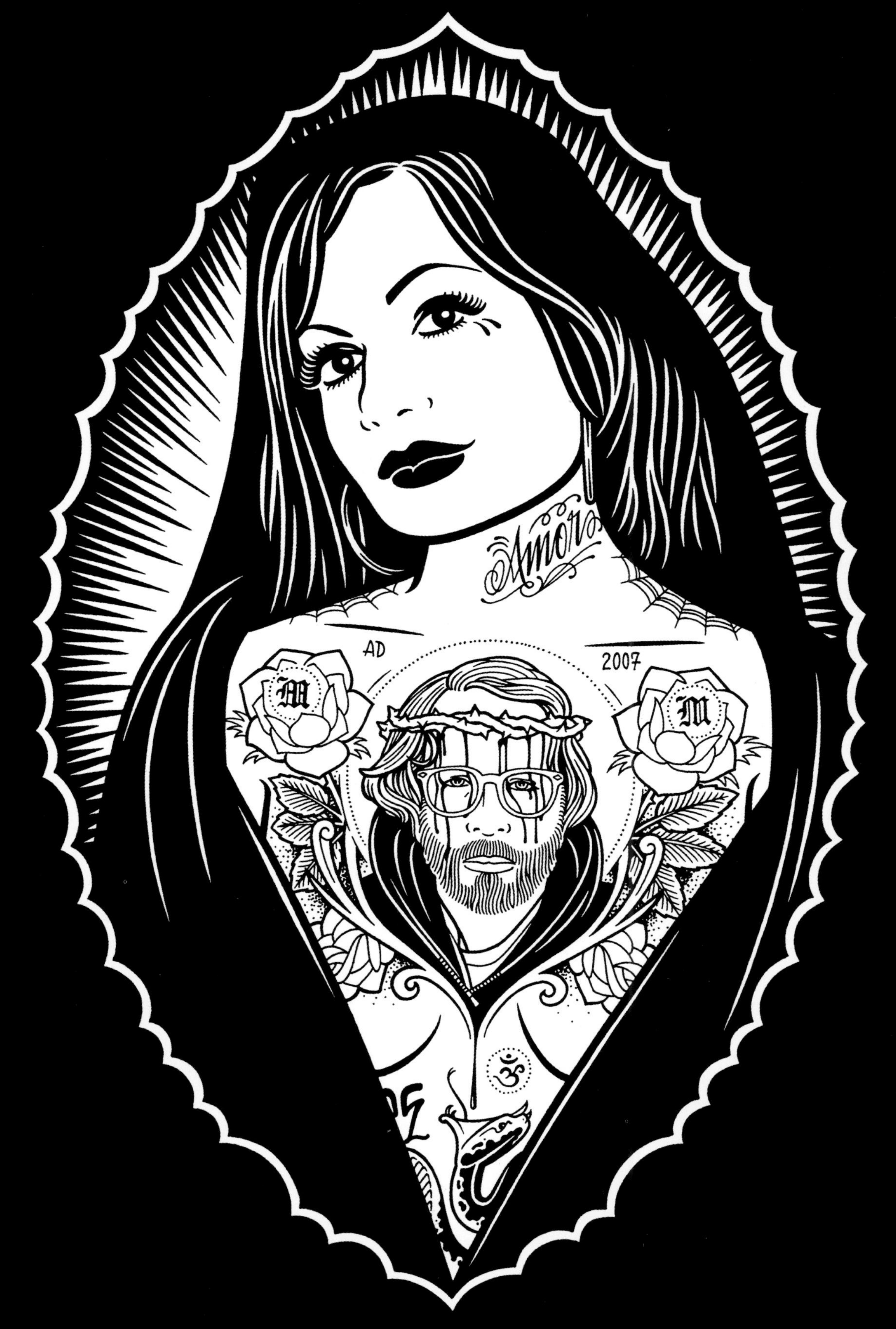

Amora
AD
2007
M
M

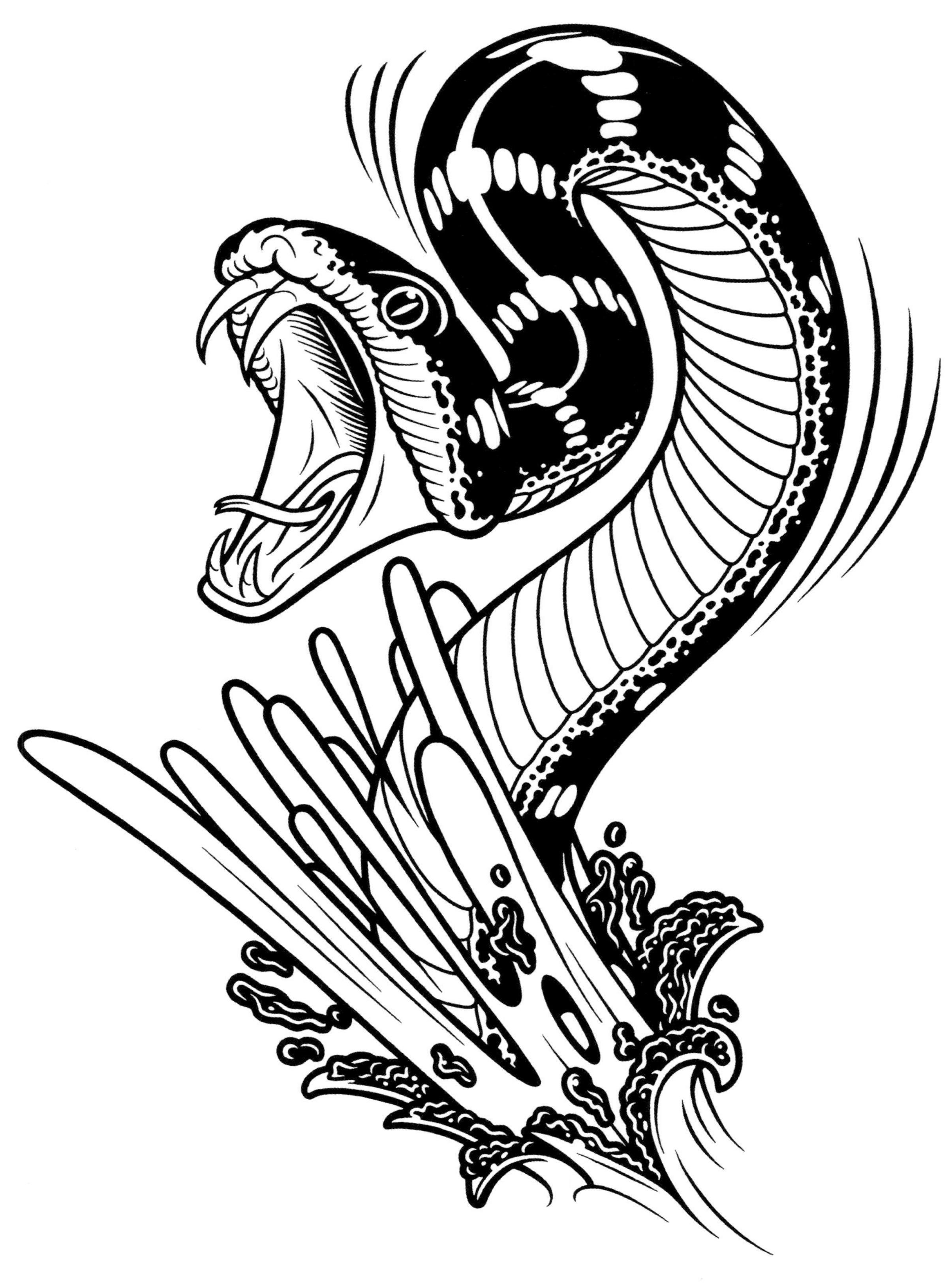

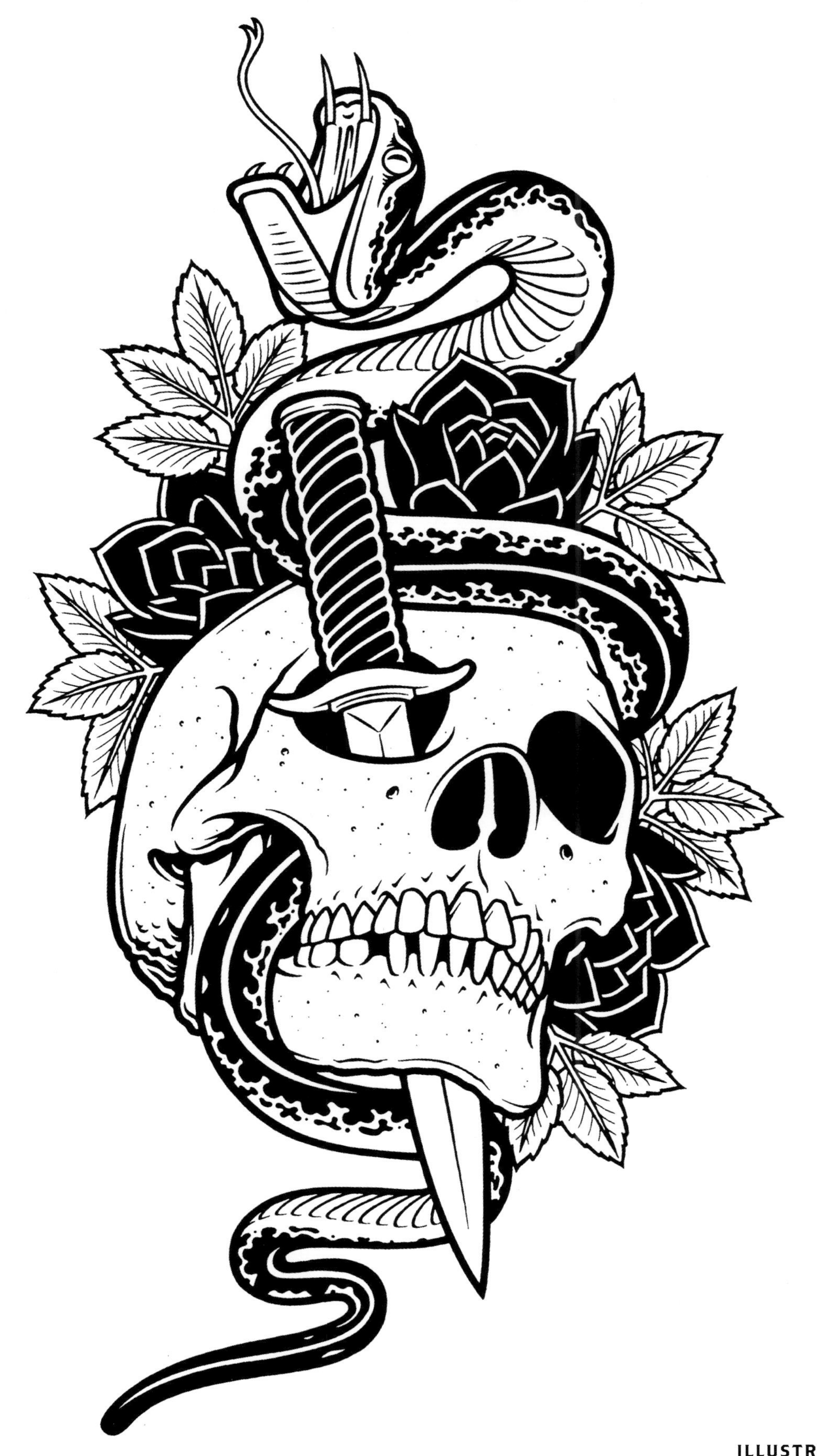

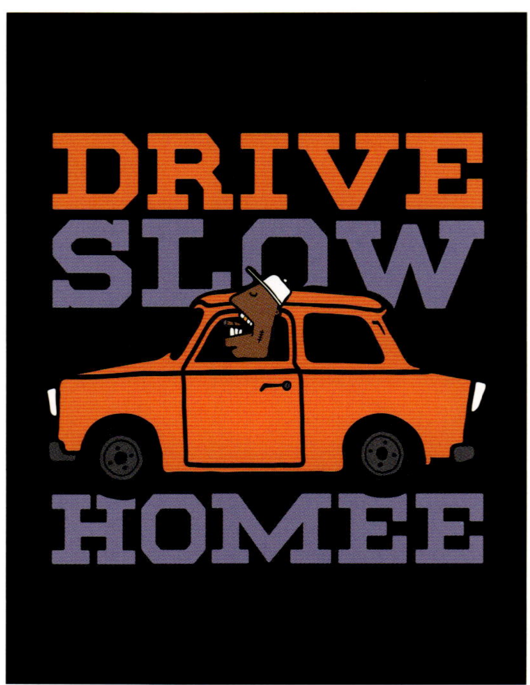

GROTESK

Originally from Switzerland, Kimou Meyer, aka Grotesk, now calls Brooklyn home. The borough has proven particularly inspiring for the transplanted artist whose work often features images of his surroundings —subway trains, graffiti, pigeons and elements of hip-hop. "When some clients meet me," he explains, "they wonder how come a Swiss guy like me is doing such 'Americana.'" Grotesk is also inspired by family, cooking, children's books, old cartoons, sign painters, vintage graphics and traveling. "I can basically be inspired by anything," he says. Until a few years ago, Kimou used busy computer graphics, but now he takes a minimalist approach. "I was overdosing on elements," he explains. "I tried to go back to the roots, simplify the style, the shapes, and add more hand-drawn elements, a more organic vibe. Now I try to find a more unique punch line: strong color, strong message and simple illustration." He finds illustration so appealing because it is easily absorbed by the masses. "It is the fact that regular people can enjoy it," he says, "not only the 'snobbish' art crowd." Kimou describes his work as "immature, strange, fanciful, unexpected and indefinable." In art school, he was told that his work looked too cartoonish; that he would never be a fine artist. "I took it as a compliment," he says, "and focused on it."

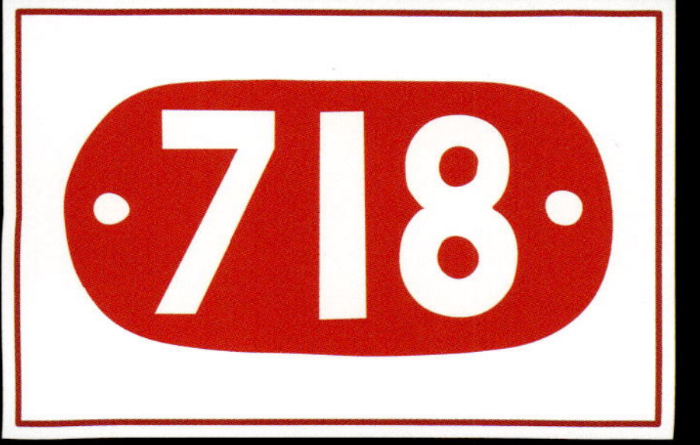

718

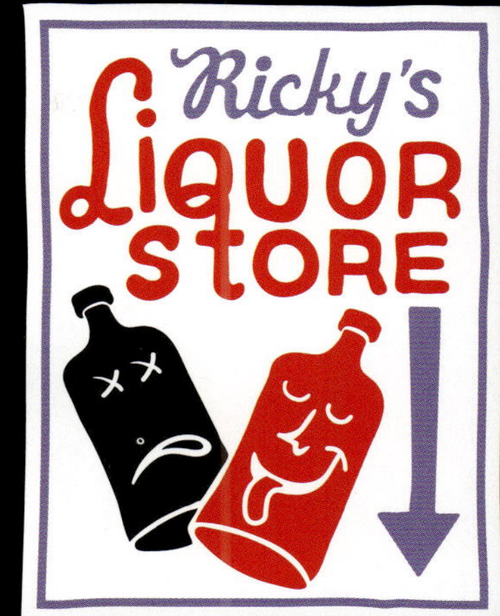

Ricky's
LIQUOR
STORE

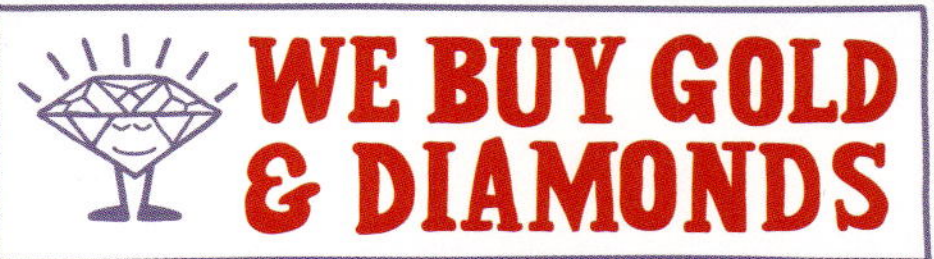

WE BUY GOLD
& DIAMONDS

EL GROTESKITO
TROPICAL PRODUCTS   DELICATESSEN AND GROCERY

Open
24/7!!!

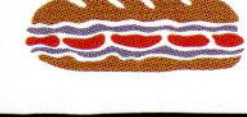
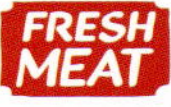

FRESH
MEAT

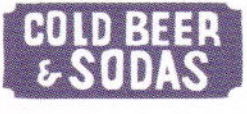

COLD BEER
& SODAS

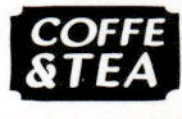

COFFE
& TEA

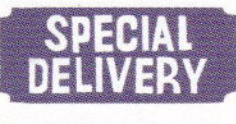

SPECIAL
DELIVERY

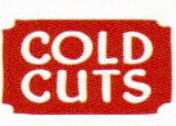

COLD
CUTS

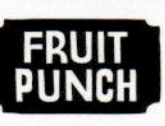

FRUIT
PUNCH

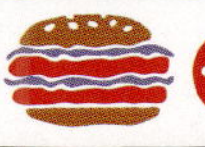
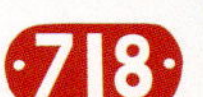

718

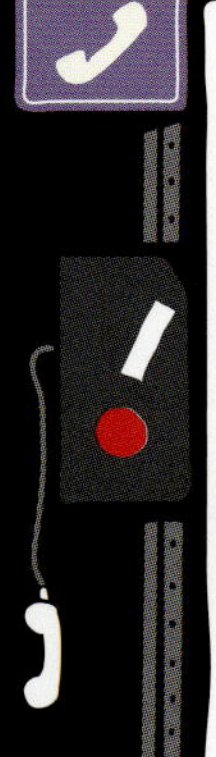

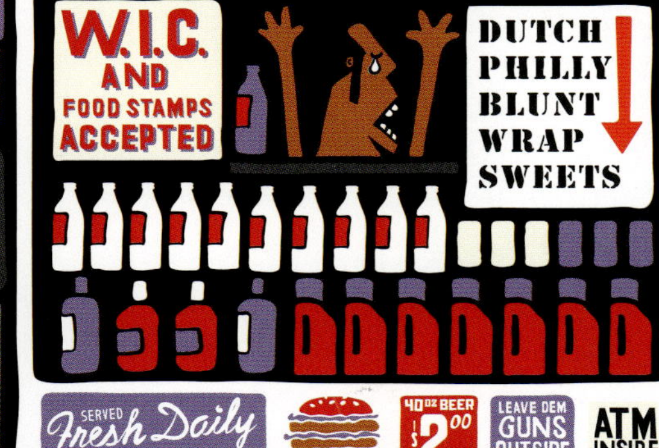

W.I.C.
AND
FOOD STAMPS
ACCEPTED
DUTCH
PHILLY
BLUNT
WRAP
SWEETS
SERVED
Fresh Daily
40 OZ BEER
$2 00
& UP
LEAVE DEM
GUNS
OUTSIDE
ATM
INSIDE

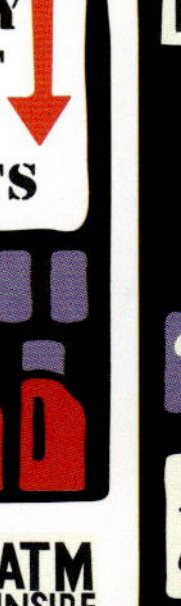

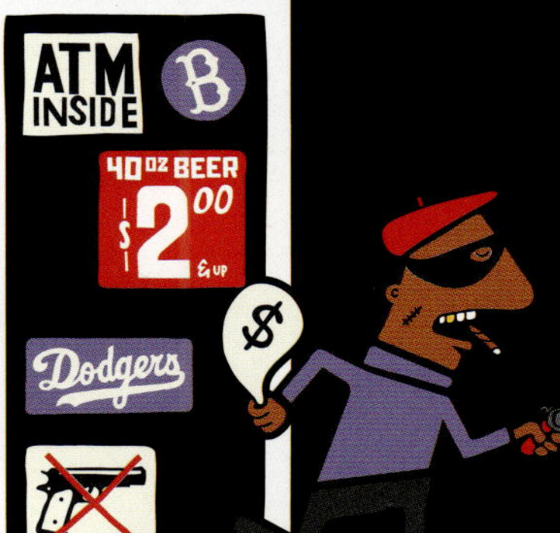

ATM
INSIDE
B
40 OZ BEER
$2 00
& UP
Dodgers
$

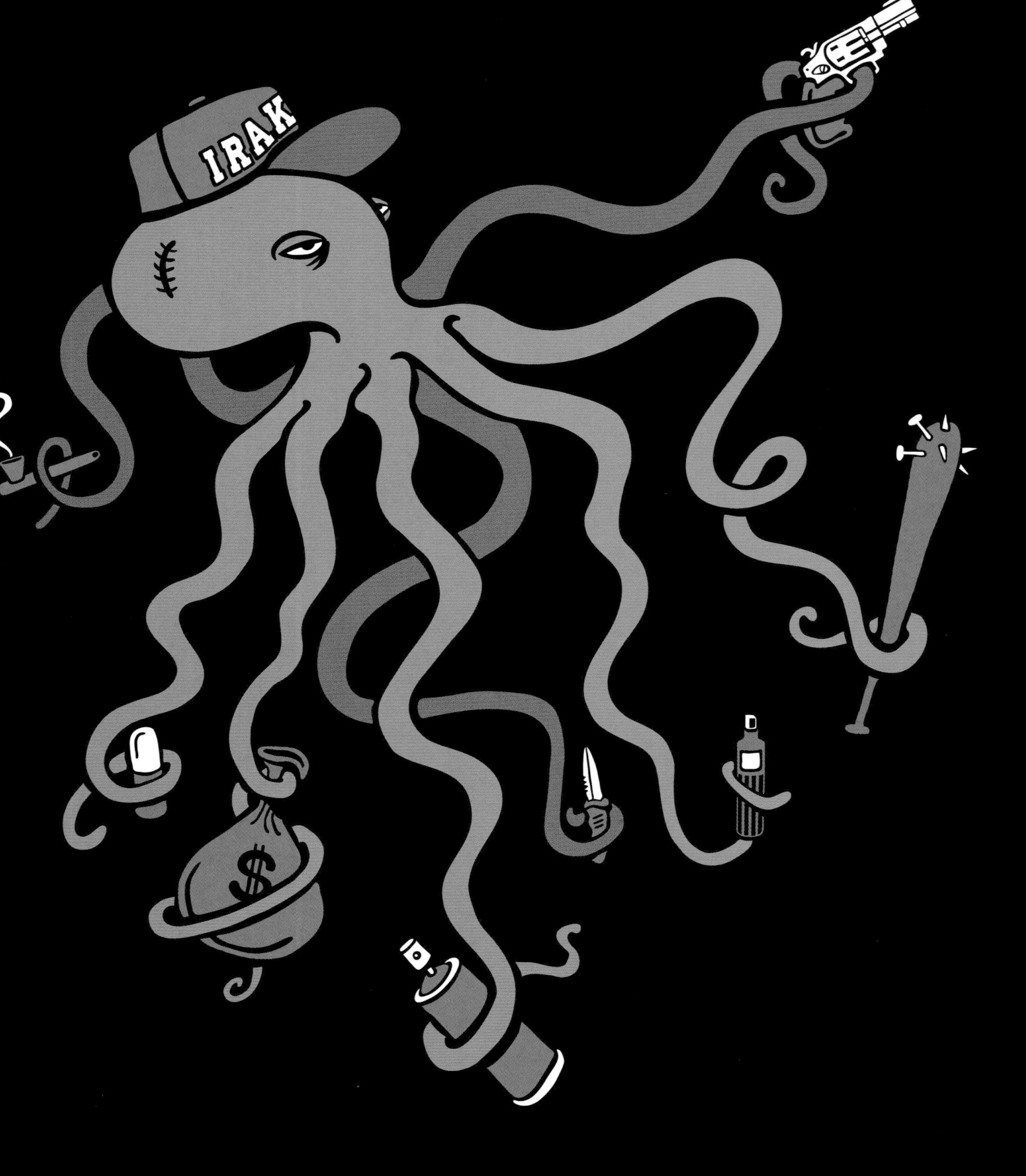
IRAK

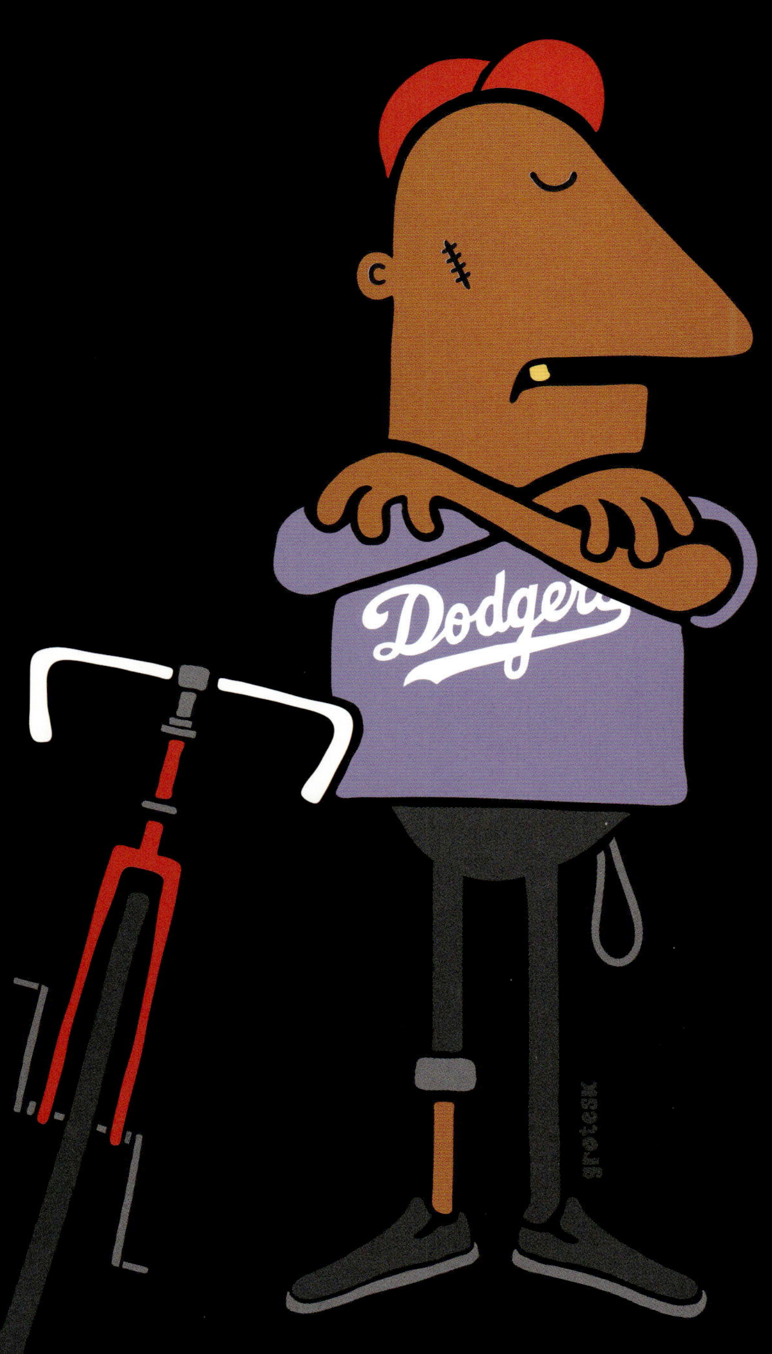

Dodgers
grotesk

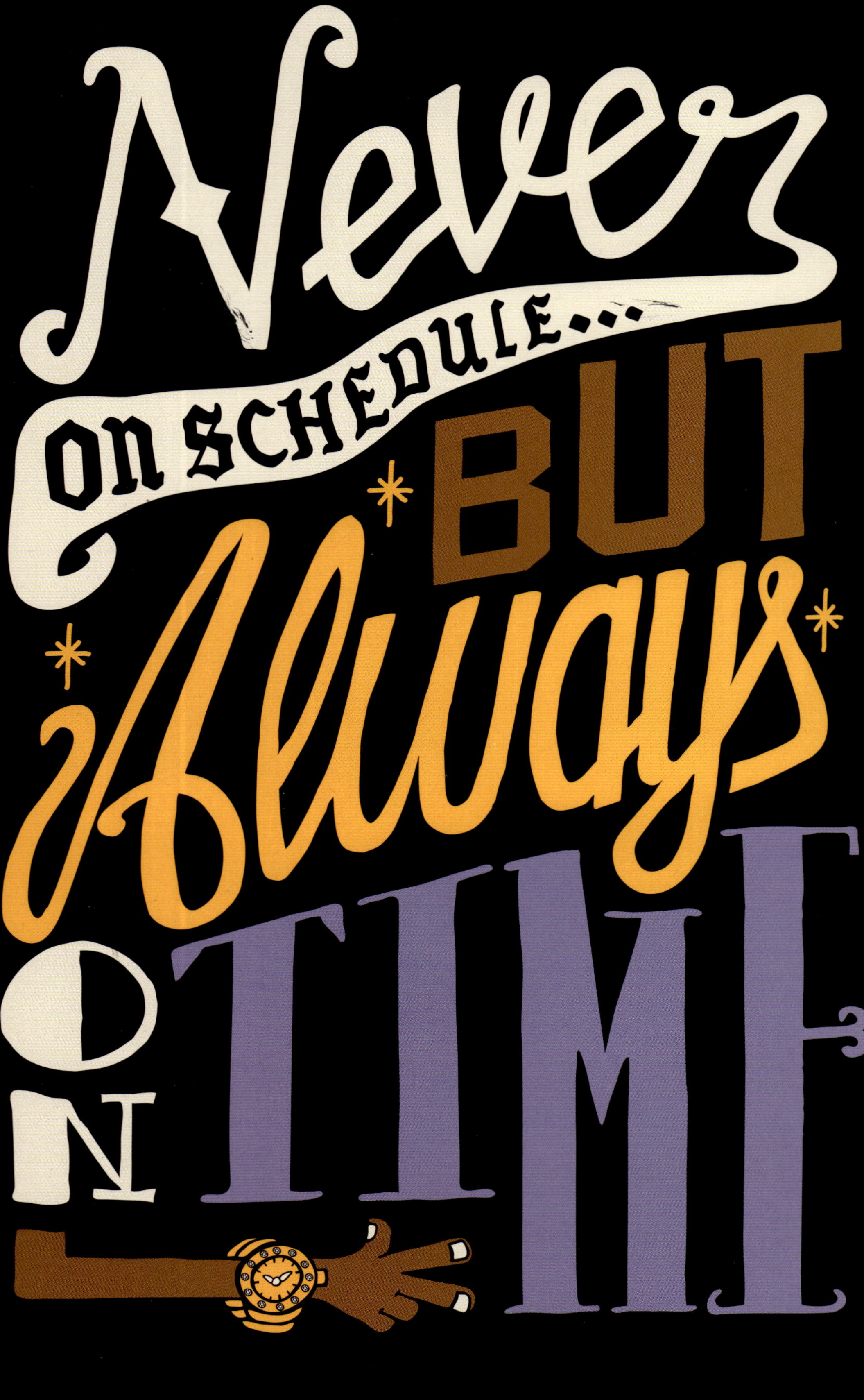

Never
on schedule...
BUT
Always
ON
TIME

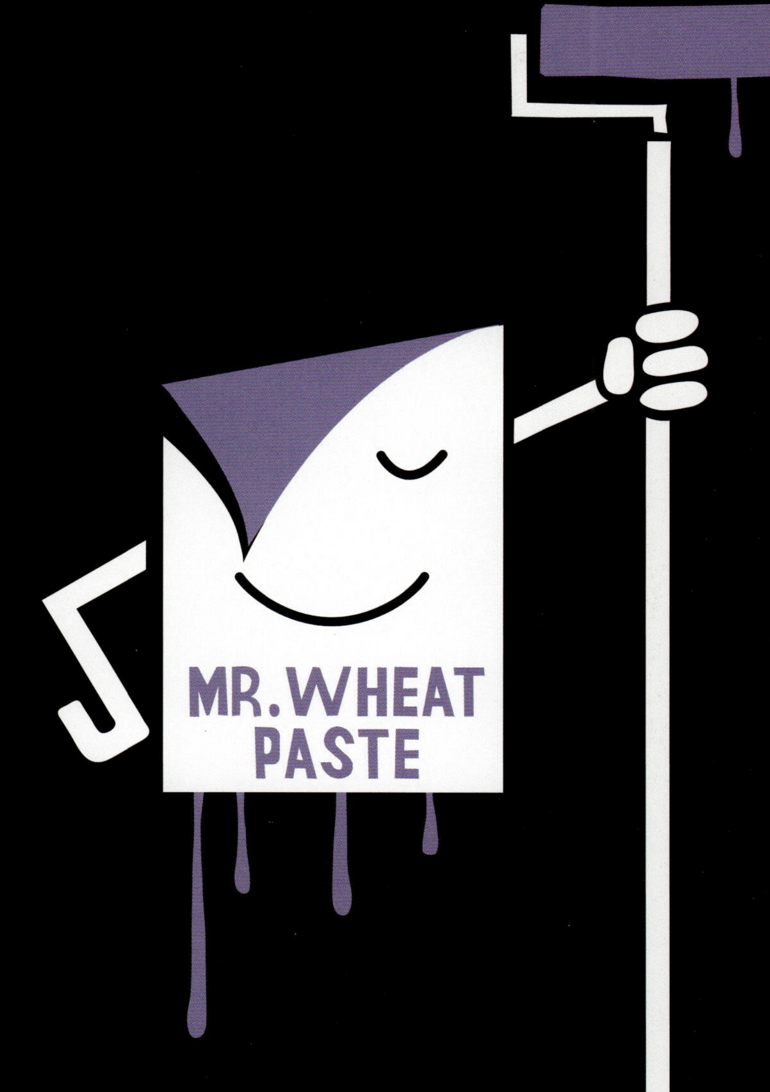

MR. WHEAT
PASTE

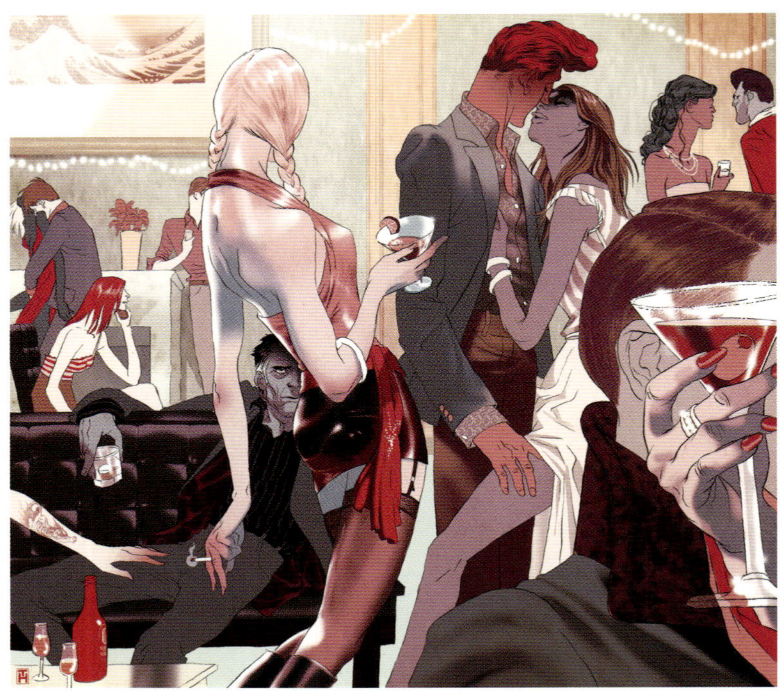

TOMER HANUKA

Tomer Hanuka was born in Israel, and moved to New York at 22. He was inspired by comics because they married words with images. "That lent a narrative approach to image making," he explains, "plus the insistent seduction of mass culture, so illustration seemed to fit right in that niche." He learned his craft by reading comic books, drawing from observation, avoiding exercise and not owning a computer. After graduating from the School of Visual Arts, Hanuka collaborated with a number of magazines, including doing two covers for the New York Times Sunday Magazine. He also illustrated the provocative book cover of "Marquis De Sade" for Penguin Classics. In just six years he has been awarded three gold medals from the Society of Illustrators. Hanuka's aesthetic is eclectic, with traditional scene-based storytelling at its core. His style is a mix of comics, Japanese woodcut prints and "Twilight Zone" reruns, conveying an atmosphere tense and dramatic, with the potential to spill into the horrific. The compositions are cinematic—just one of his images is as complex and entrancing as any full length science-fiction film. He is currently working on a graphic novel with his twin brother, Asaf.

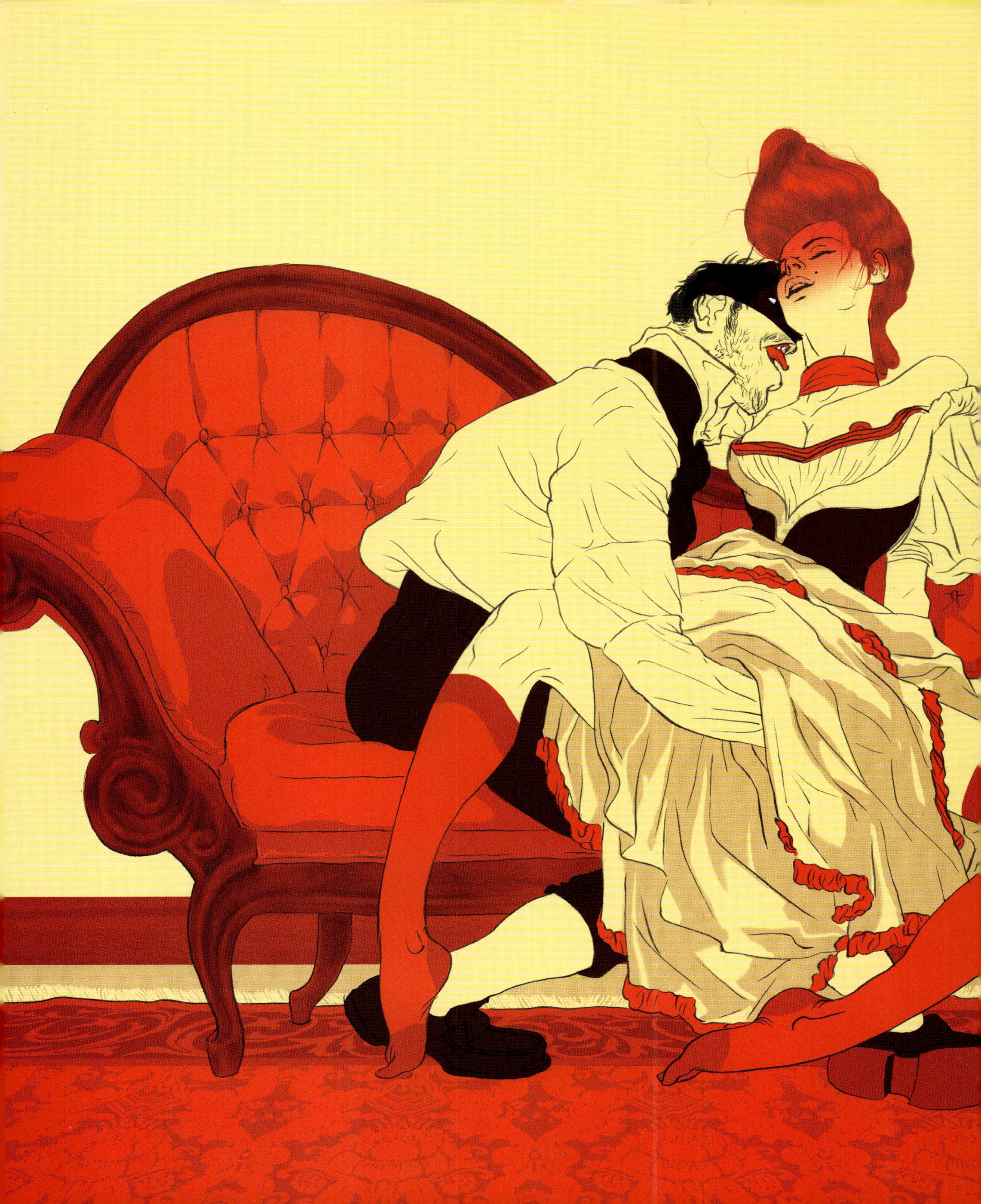

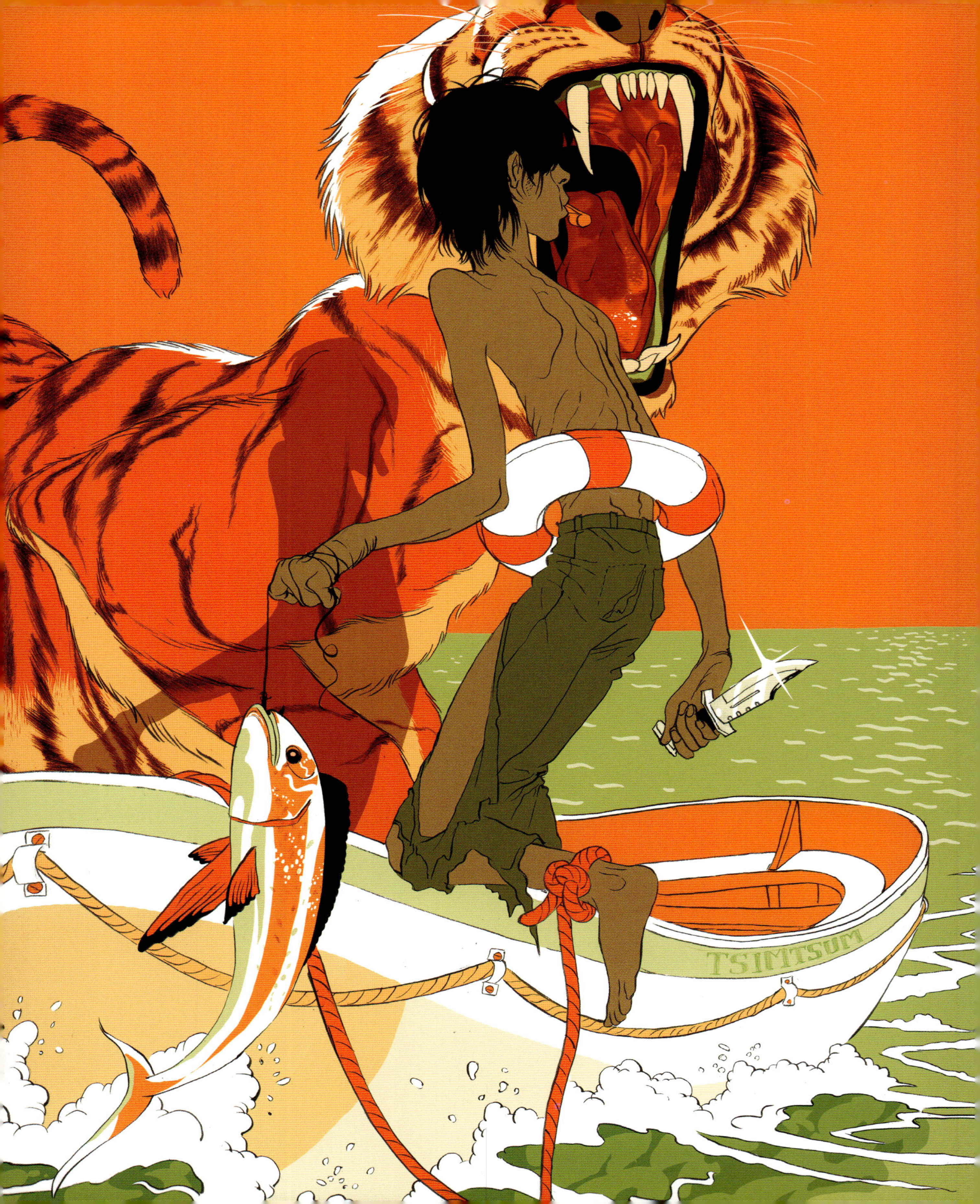

TSIMTSUM

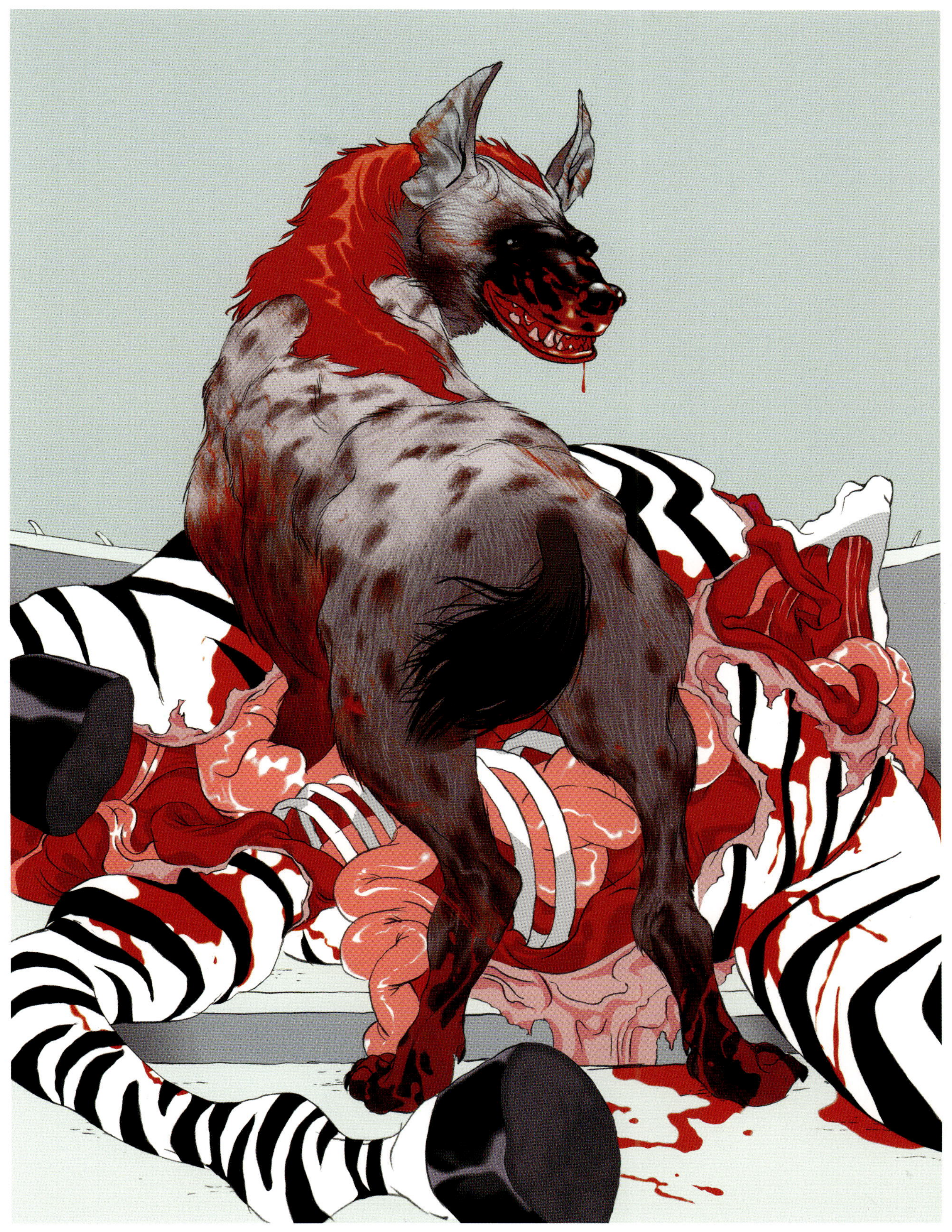

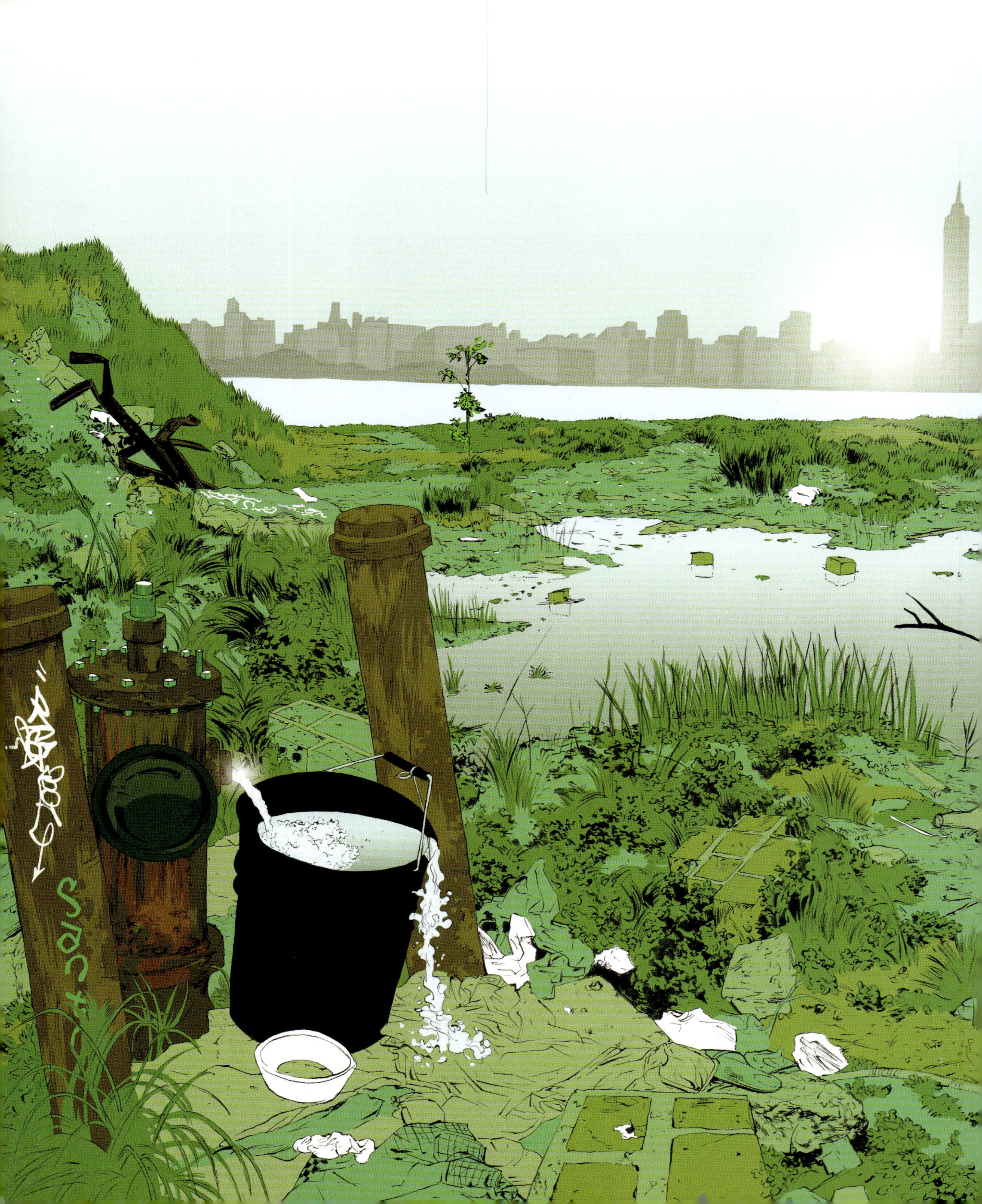

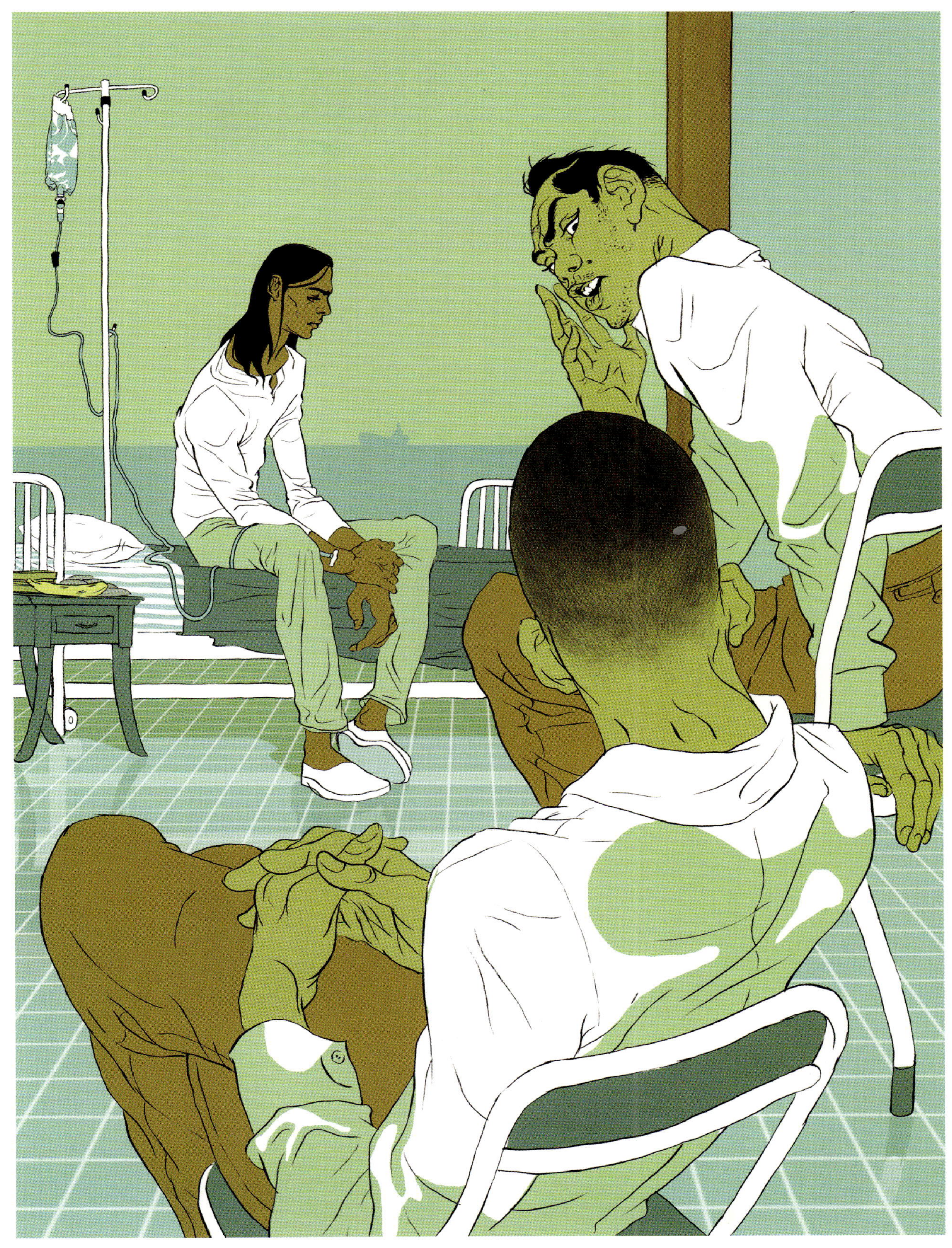

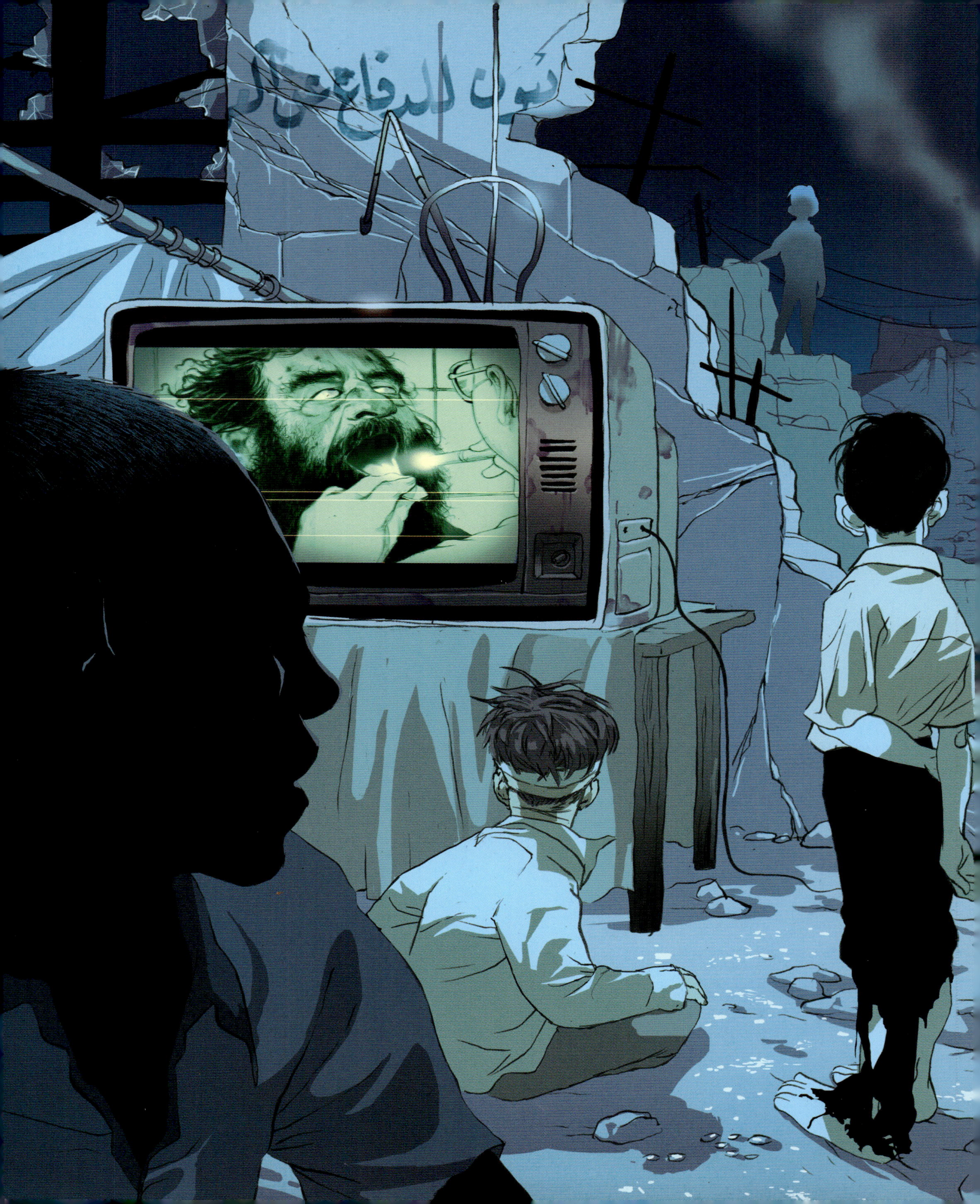

الدفاع

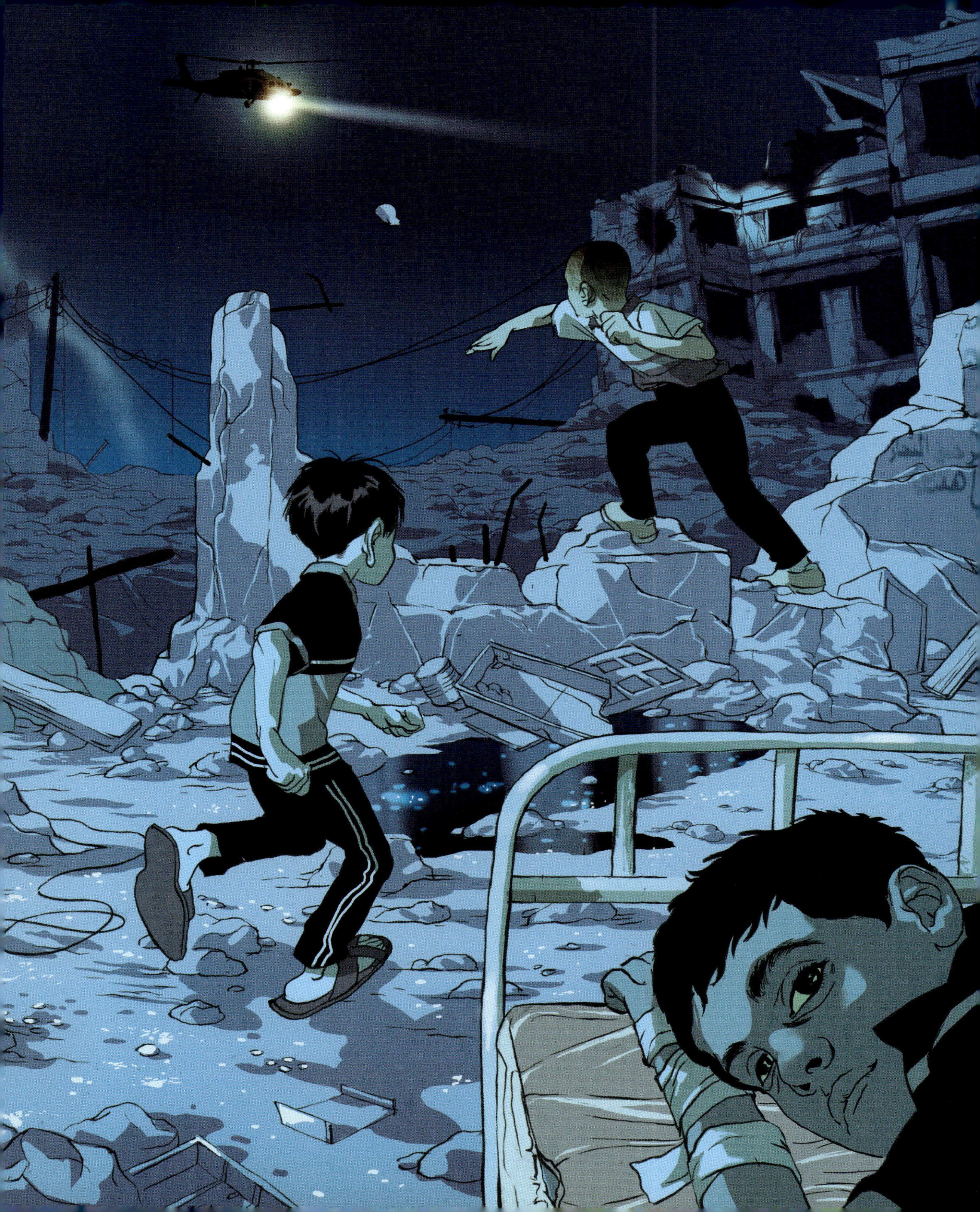

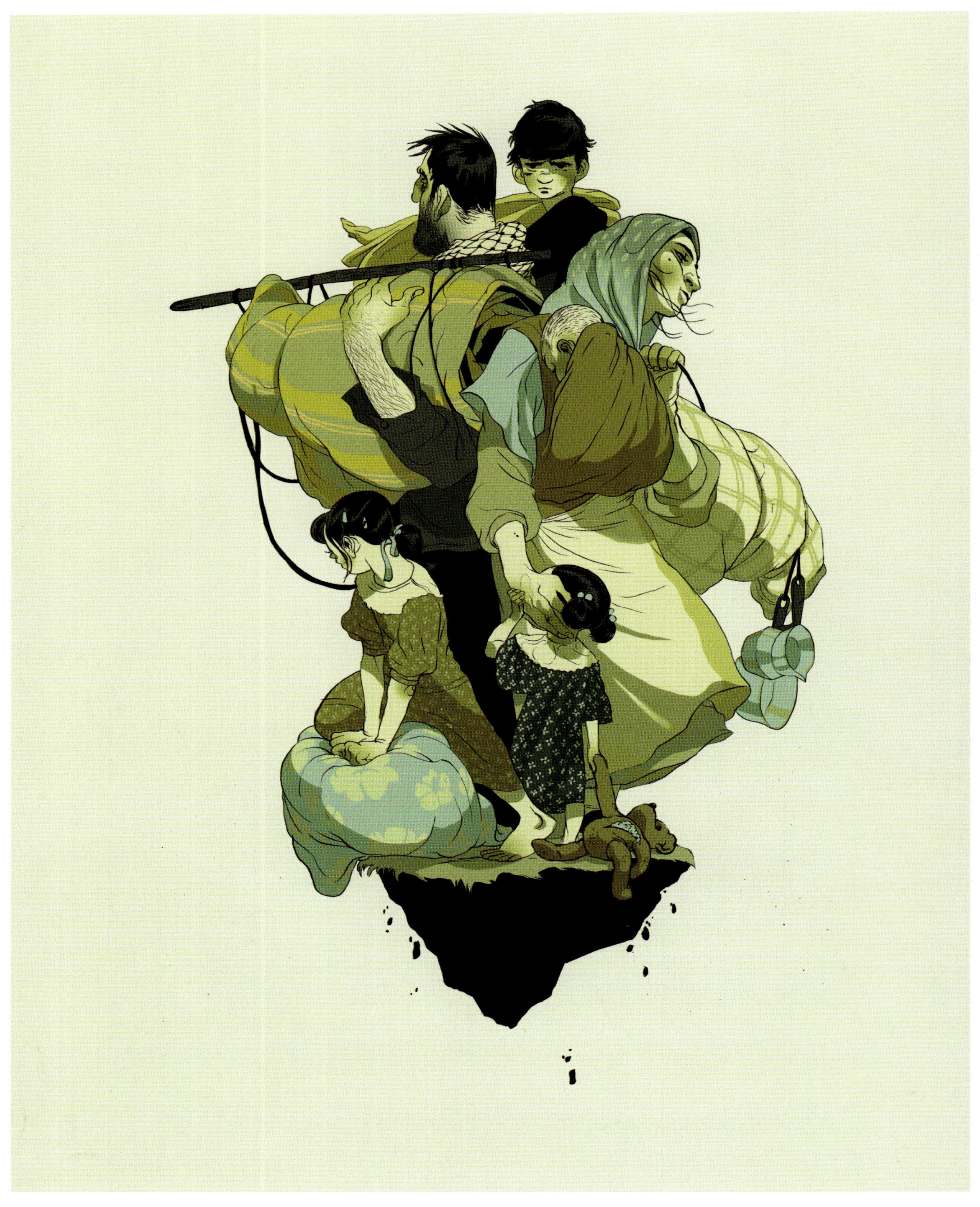

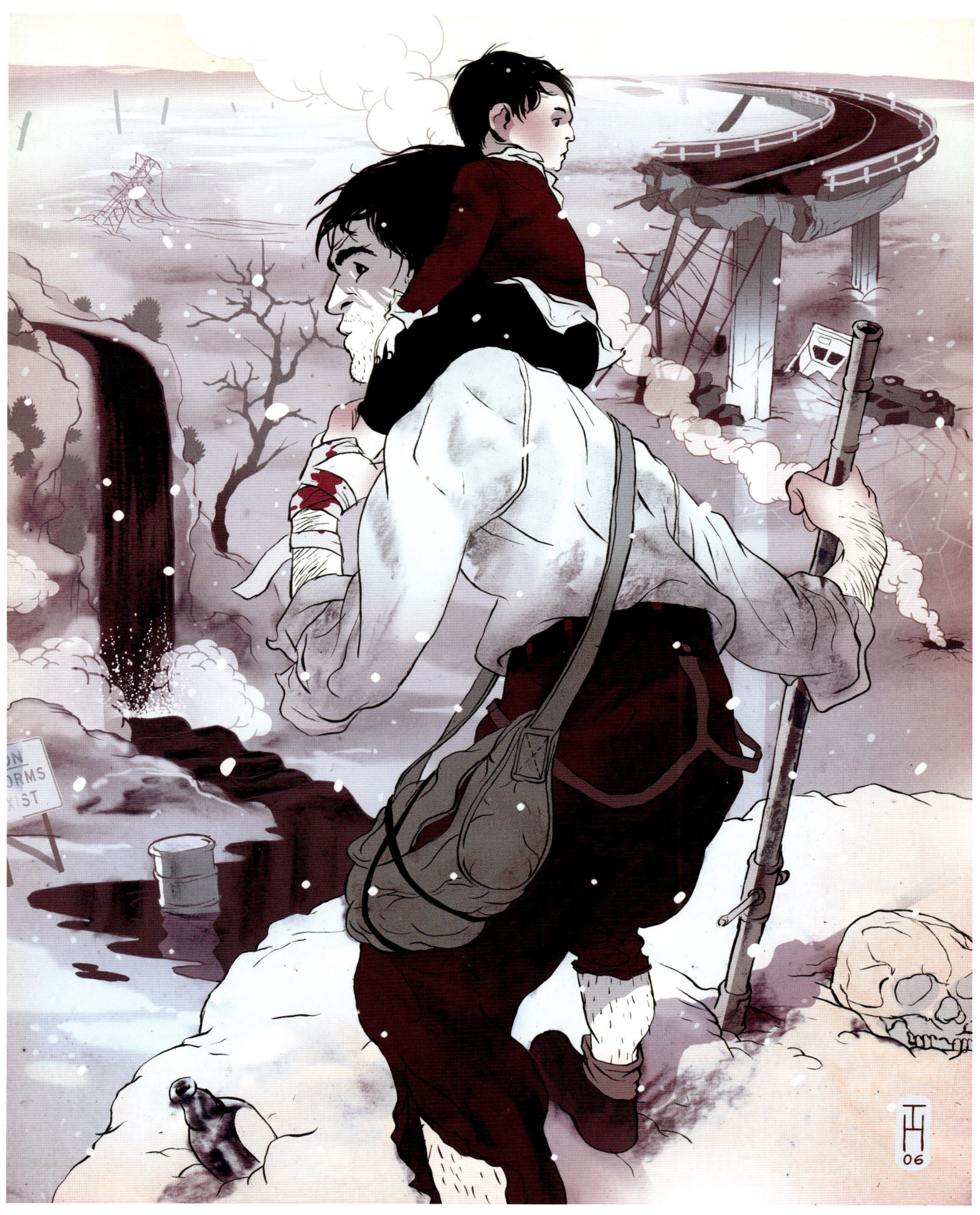
ON
ORMS
XIST

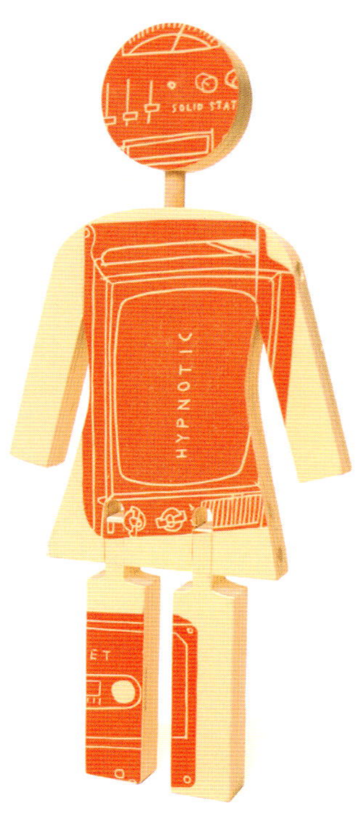

EVAN HECOX

Denver-based artist Evan Hecox is known for creating unusual skateboard graphics; he has produced several hundred over the past decade. But he is also a fine artist, who shows work all over the globe—Tokyo, Paris, Sydney—where he absorbs new cultures. "I think that's probably the most rewarding aspect of what I do," he says. Hecox is fascinated by the modern metropolis, he views them as giant living organisms. "I'm interested in the way cities are constantly being created and destroyed simultaneously, things are built and over time they decay, get re-painted 50 times, covered with graffiti, windows get boarded up, it all gets torn down and starts over again." His work displays a keen eye, that examines everyday occurrences in a novel way. "I see how a bunch of electric wires crisscrossing makes a beautiful arrangement, like tree branches," he says. "A scattering of cigarette butts dropped in a random pattern reminds me of a pile of leaves. Small things have meaning; I try to emphasize those sorts of things in my work." There is a darker side to Hecox's landscapes, but perhaps it is not apparent at first glance. "I try to make my work have a sort of instant visual appeal, but with an undercurrent that seems a little off," he explains. "Like a catchy pop song but when you listen closer the lyrics are actually kind of sad."

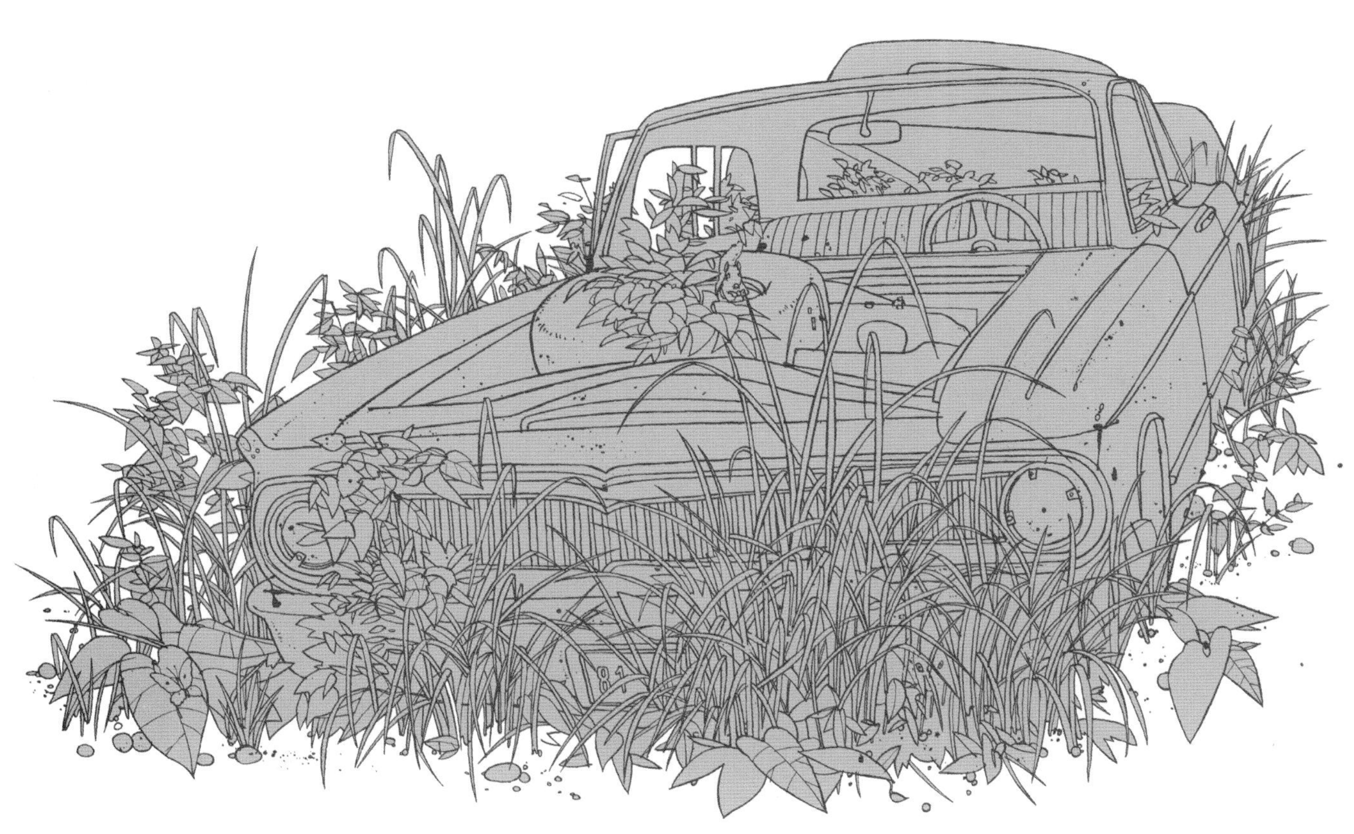

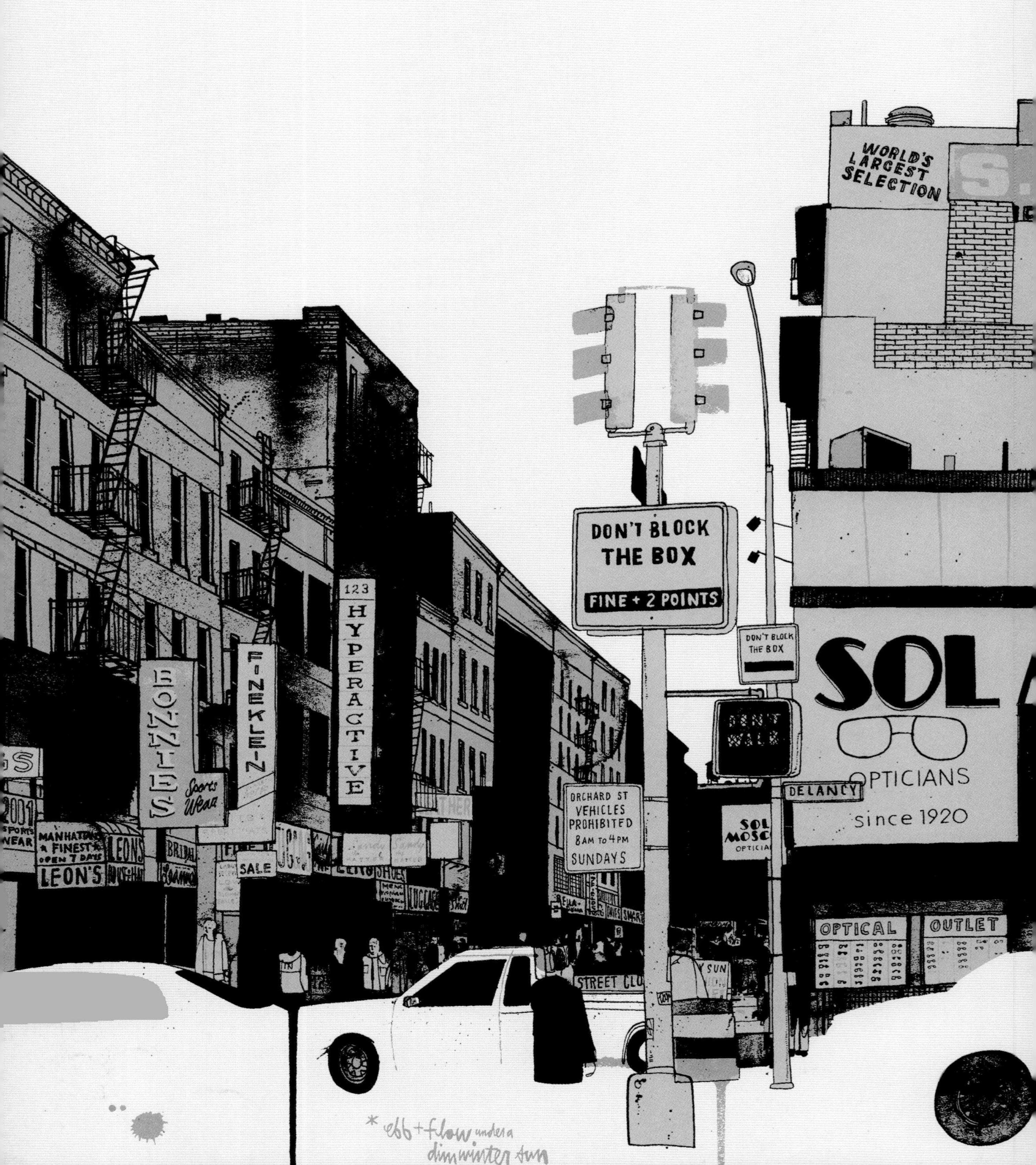

WORLD'S LARGEST SELECTION
S.
DON'T BLOCK THE BOX
FINE + 2 POINTS
DON'T BLOCK THE BOX
DON'T WALK
SOL
OPTICIANS
since 1920
SOL MOSC
OPTICIAN
DELANCY
ORCHARD ST
VEHICLES
PROHIBITED
8 AM to 4 PM
SUNDAYS
OPTICAL
OUTLET
123
HYPERACTIVE
BONNIES
Sports Wear
FINE KLEIN
MANHATTAN'S
FINEST
OPEN 7 DAYS
LEON'S
LEON'S
2001
SPORTS
WEAR
BRIDAL
SALE
LUGGAGE
STREET CLU
SUN
* ebb + flow under a
dim winter sun

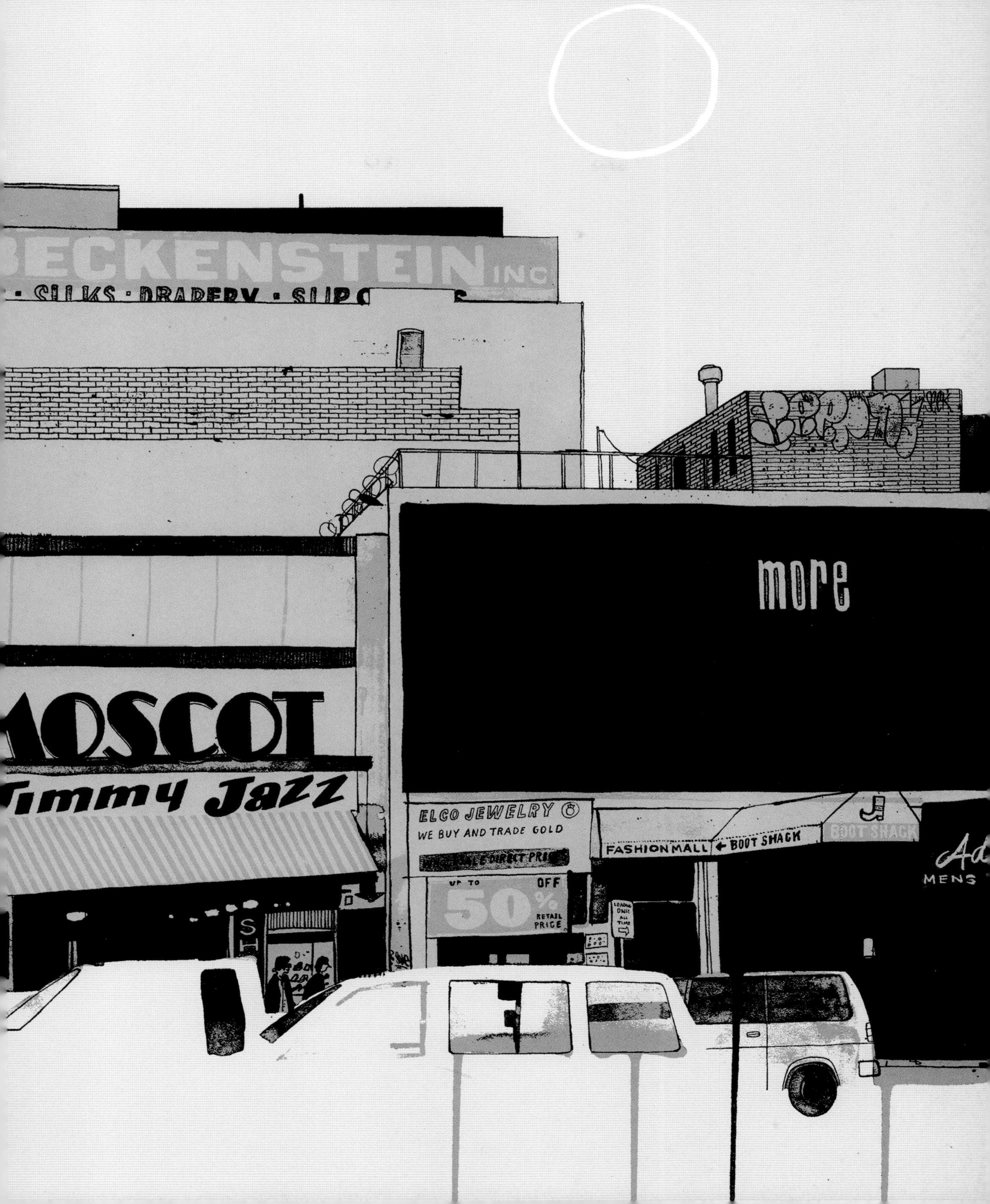

BECKENSTEIN INC
SILKS · DRAPERY · SUP
more
MOSCOT
Jimmy Jazz
ELCO JEWELRY
WE BUY AND TRADE GOLD
DIRECT PRICE
UP TO 50% OFF RETAIL PRICE
FASHION MALL ← BOOT SHACK
BOOT SHACK
MENS
LOADING ONLY ALL TIME

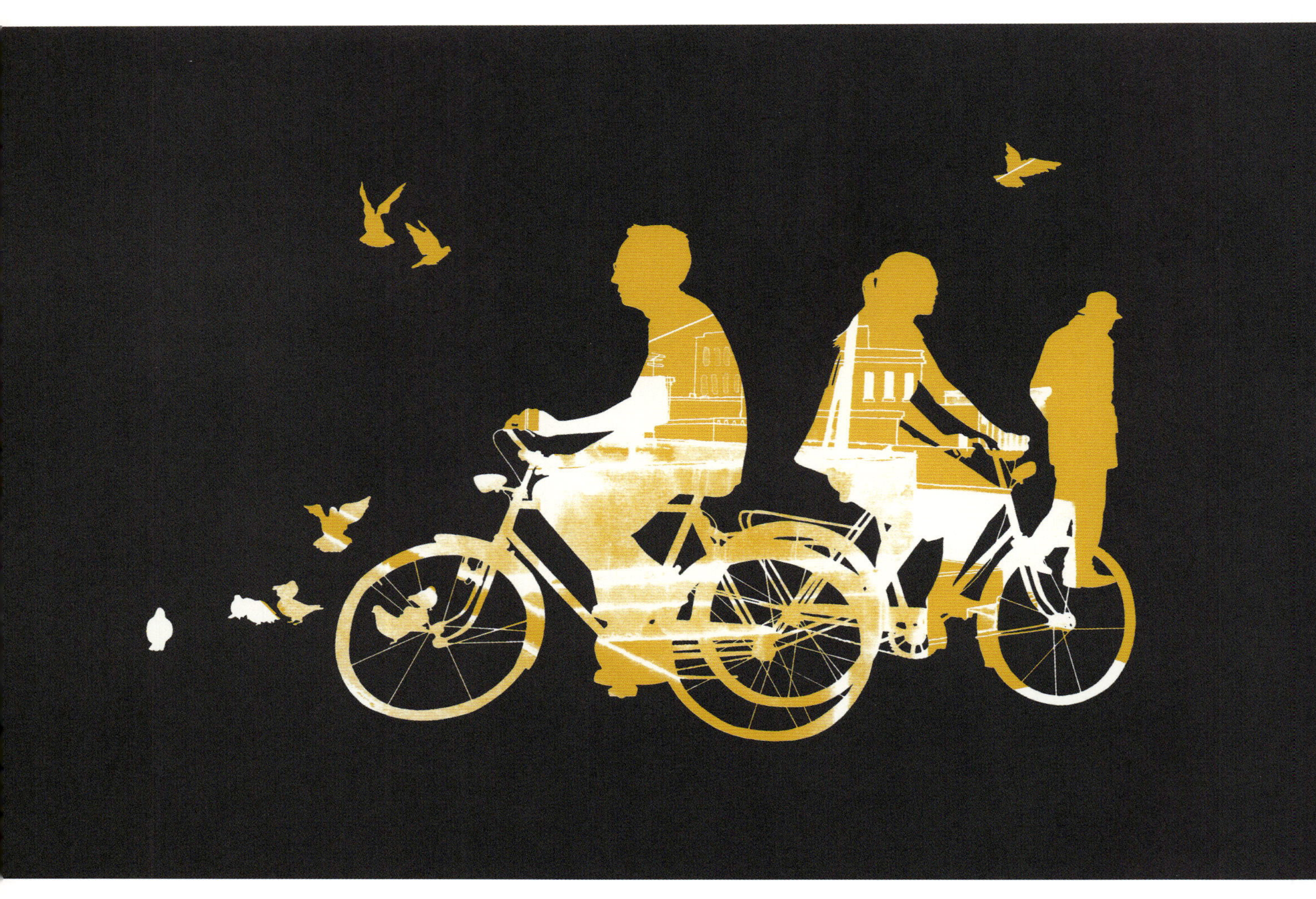

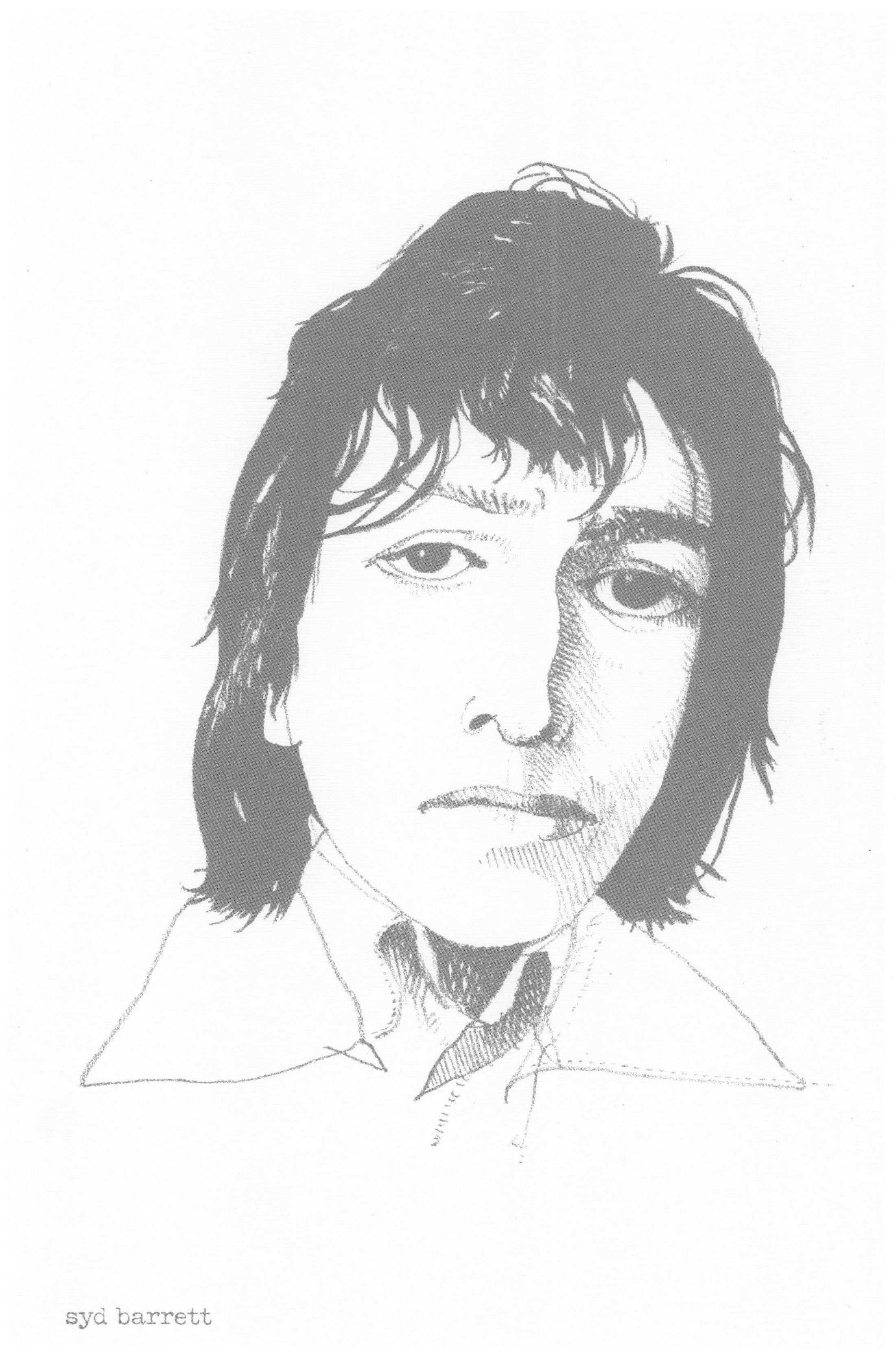

syd barrett

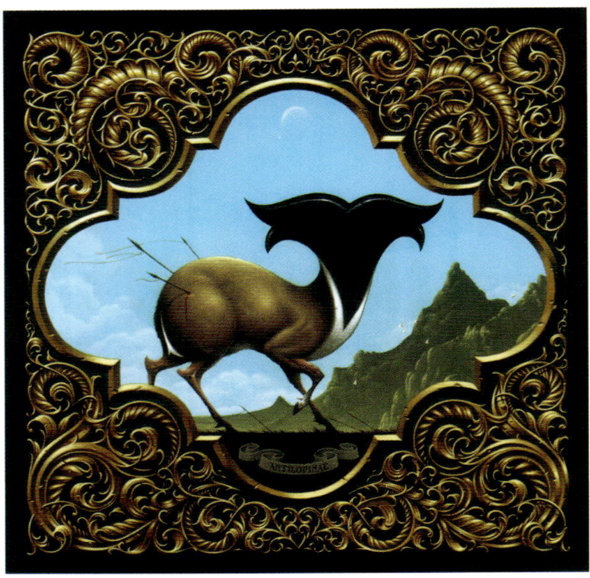

AARON HORKEY

Aaron Horkey was born and raised in the farming community of Windom, Minnesota, population 4,500. After spending his late teens and early twenties in Minneapolis, he returned home, and now lives in a town down the road from his parents in Mankato, which he calls "a bucolic whistle stop just west of the Mississippi." Aaron's father is a professional woodworker who handed down the obsessive attention to detail that defines the craft. His mother, a painter and illustrator, also influenced his work. Aaron was drawing constantly by age 3, and began his career as an illustrator at 10, when he sent in some designs to a temporary tattoo company unaware of his age. "I think they were a bit taken aback when I showed up with my folks," he says. While Aaron was in Minneapolis in the late '90s, he was a part of a fantastically creative scene, amid musicians such as The Doldrums, ANDP and Mangina, artists like the WND and HM graffiti crews, and the magazine Life Sucks Die, for which he contributed illustrations and beautifully updated art nouveau lettering. Returning home, he continued to design graphics for apparel, skateboards and album covers, as well as create his own artwork. "I could give a shit about client lists or the like," he explains. "The work I'm the most proud of is the really obscure stuff that I spend way too much time on; half a dozen people will ever see it and it makes me absolutely no money at all. Automatic drawing while I'm on the phone, envelopes, production notes, birthday cards—those are my major accomplishments."

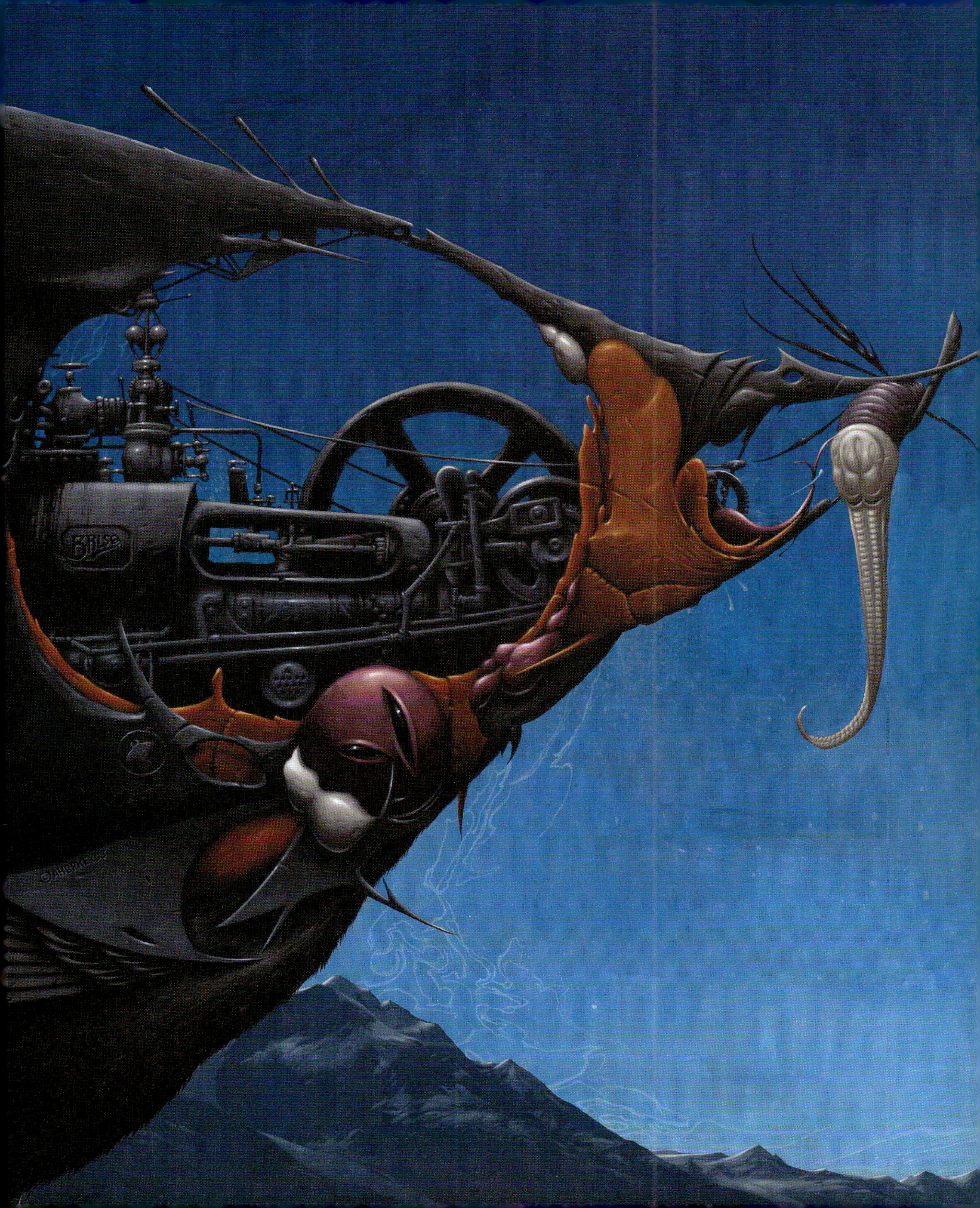

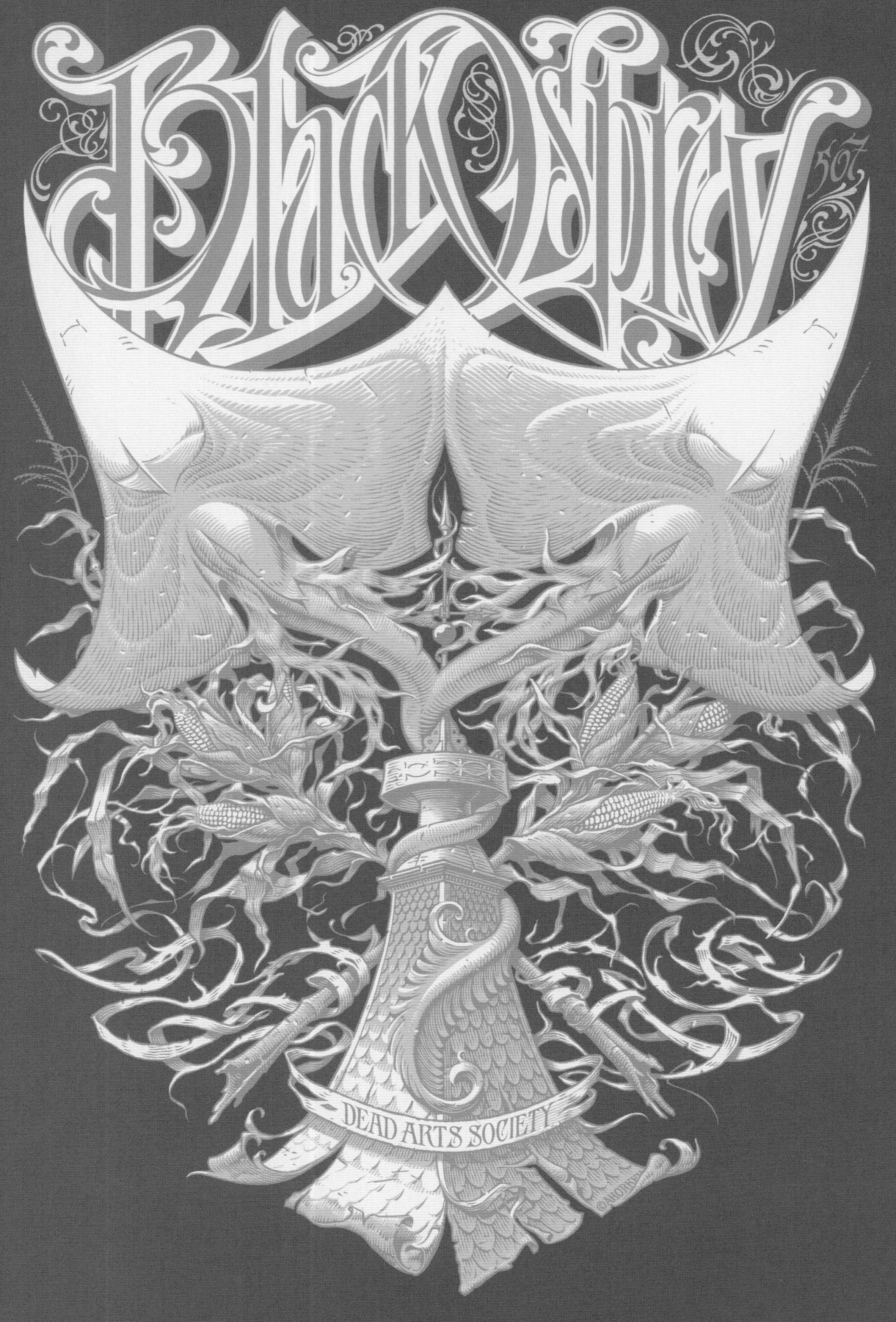

BlackBerry
DEAD ARTS SOCIETY

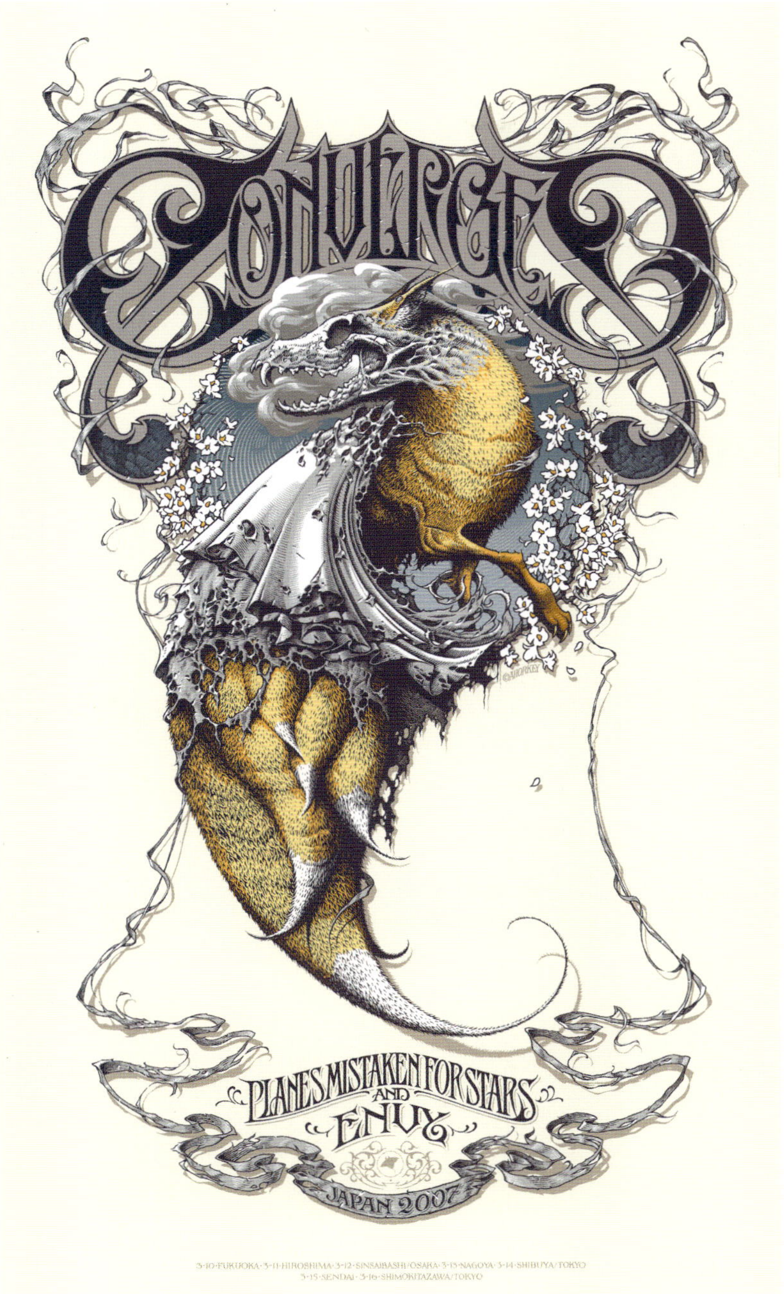

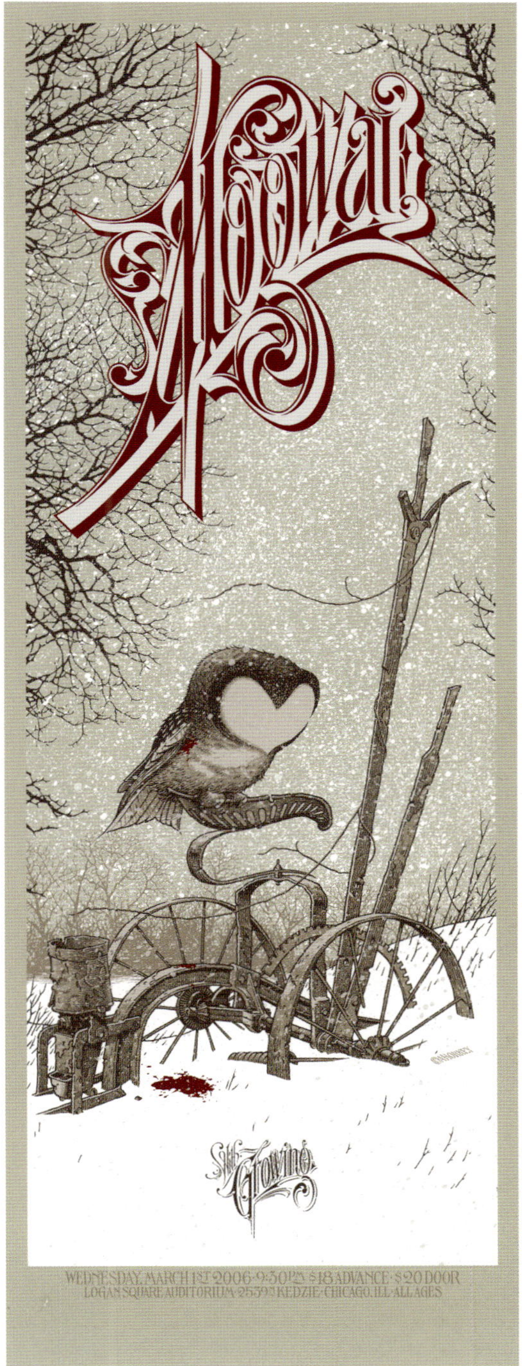
CONVERGE
PLANES MISTAKEN FOR STARS
AND
ENVY
JAPAN 2007
3·10·FUKUOKA · 3·11·HIROSHIMA · 3·12·SINSAIBASHI/OSAKA · 3·13·NAGOYA · 3·14·SHIBUYA/TOKYO
3·15·SENDAI · 3·16·SHIMOKITAZAWA/TOKYO
WEDNESDAY, MARCH 1ST 2006·9:30PM · $18 ADVANCE · $20 DOOR
LOGAN SQUARE AUDITORIUM · 2539½ KEDZIE · CHICAGO, ILL · ALL AGES

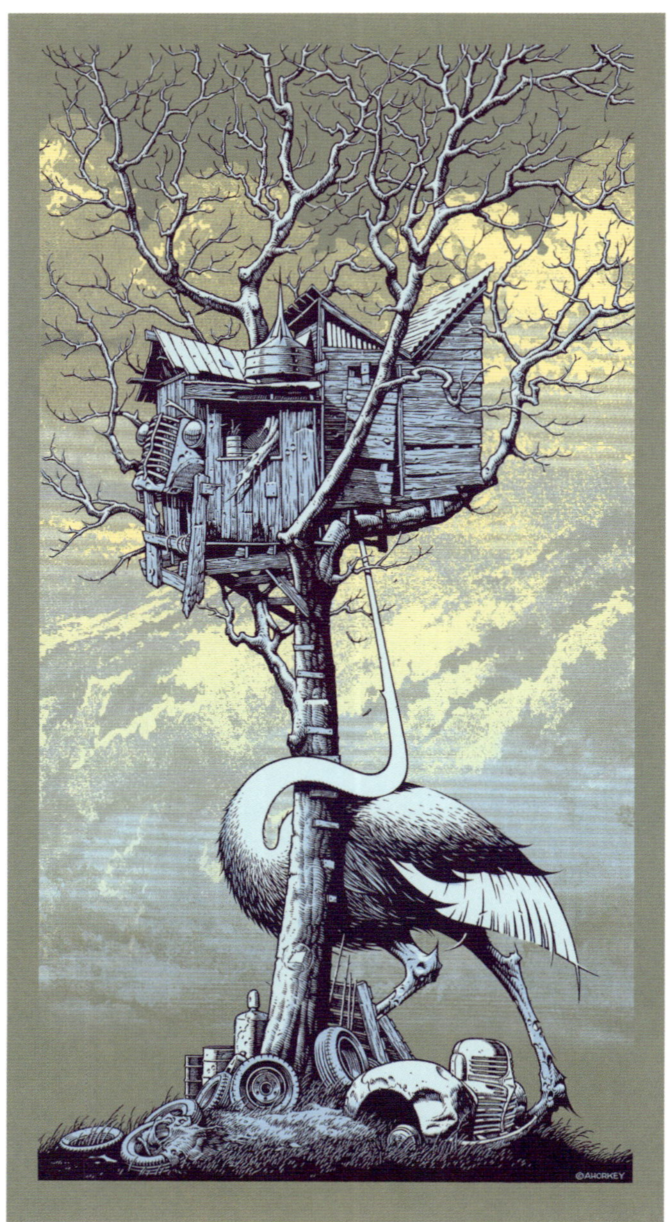 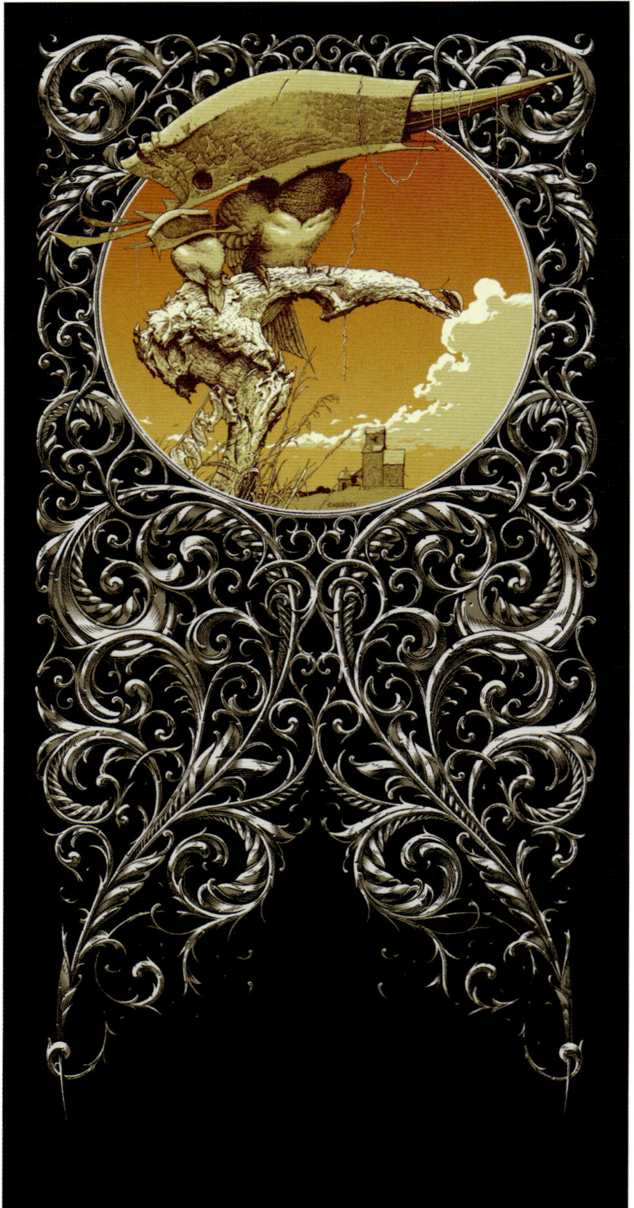

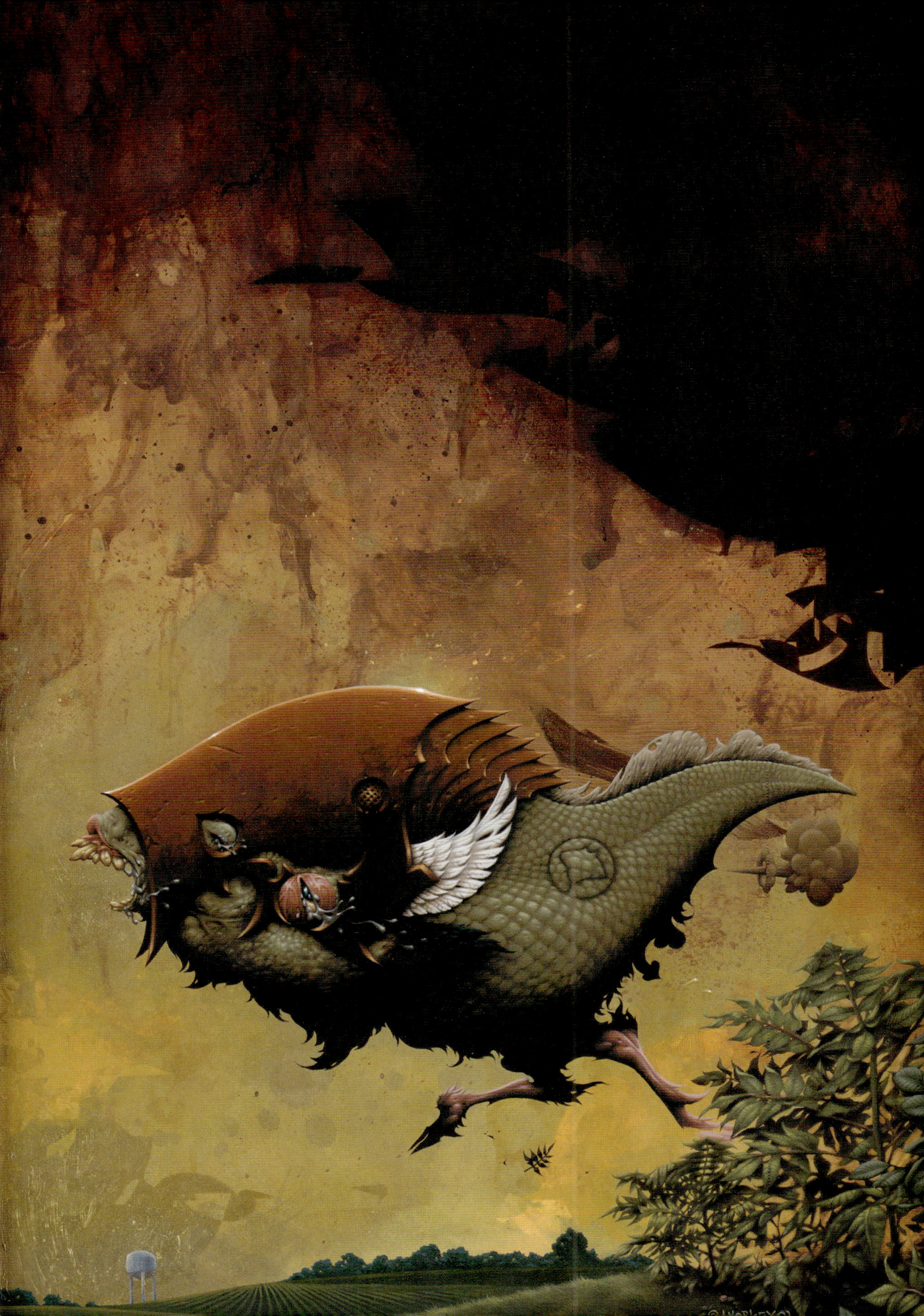

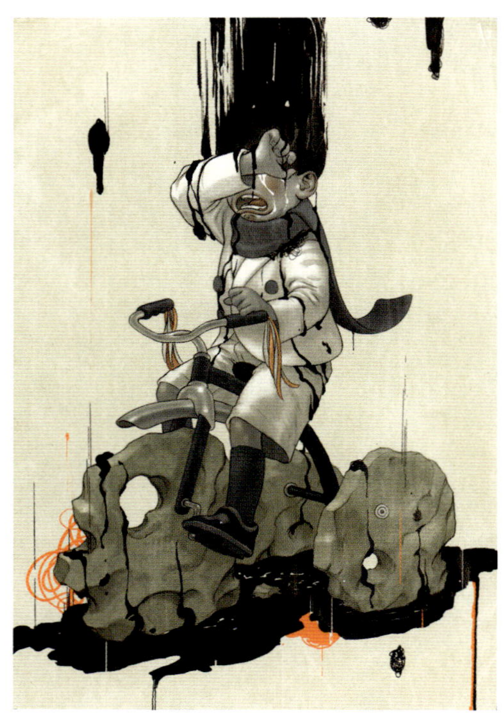

JAMES JEAN

Peer pressure drove James Jean into illustration. "I became addicted to the euphoria," he says. It's turned out to be a healthy habit as Jean's work has garnered a number of awards. As a cover artist for DC Comics, he earned three consecutive Eisner Awards and two Harvey Awards, among many others. Recently, he took home a handful of gold-and-silver medals at the Society of Illustrators of L.A. and the Society of Illustrators of N.Y. Jean has also worked with high-profile clients such as The New York Times, Atlantic Records, ESPN and Nike, to name a few. He got to this point by "a million years of evolution, intense pressure, a few pounds of fetid black goop" and a stint at the School of Visual Arts in New York. "I grew up reading comics," says the LA-based artist who was born in Taiwan. "But by the time I could tie my own shoelaces—in college—I developed serious ambitions to be a painter." After graduating, he returned to drawing comics. "My process is an ever-evolving search for ideas," he explains, "a play on drawing with a punch." Look for more of Jean's biting work in his second book, "Process Recess v.2."

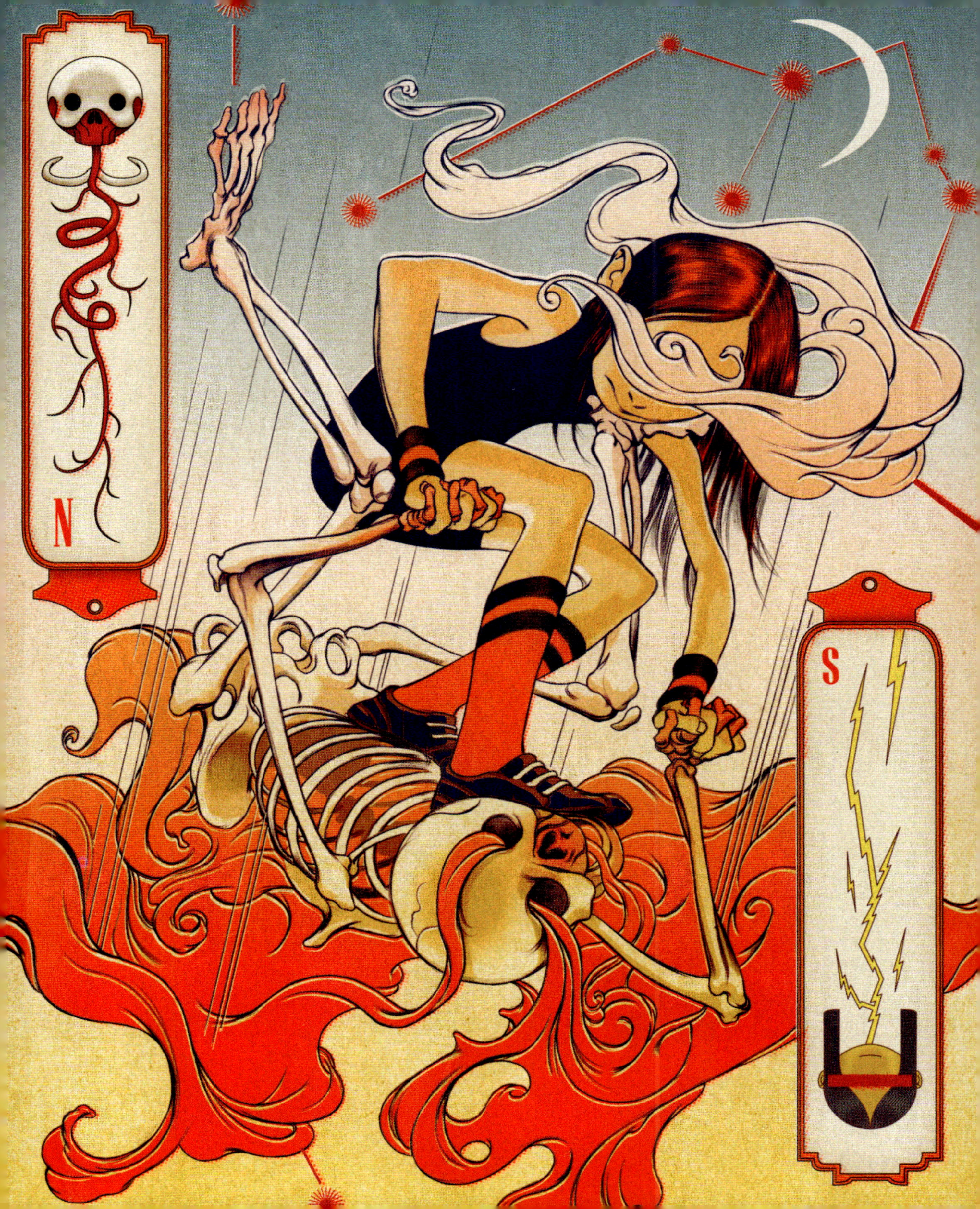

N
S

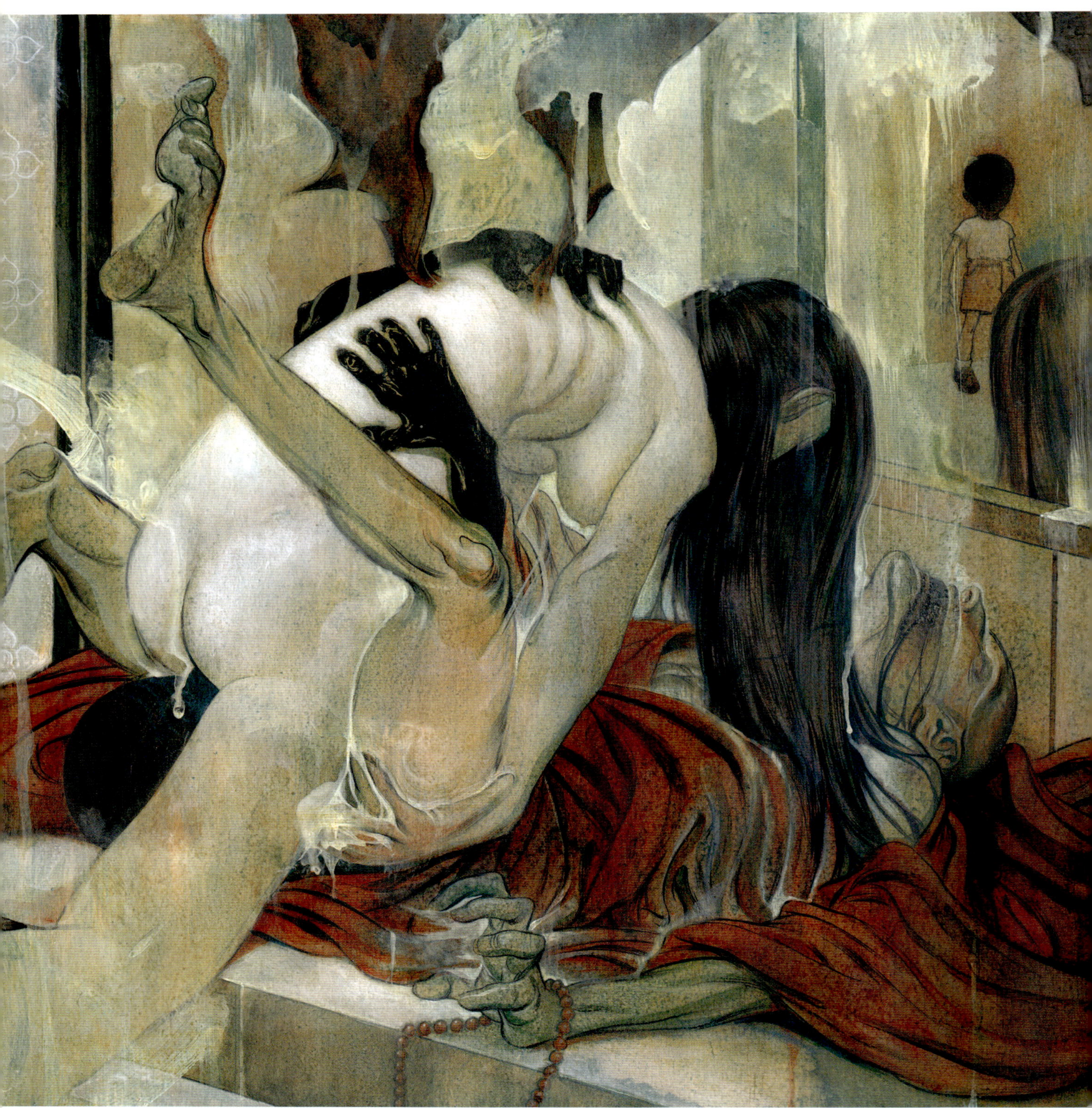

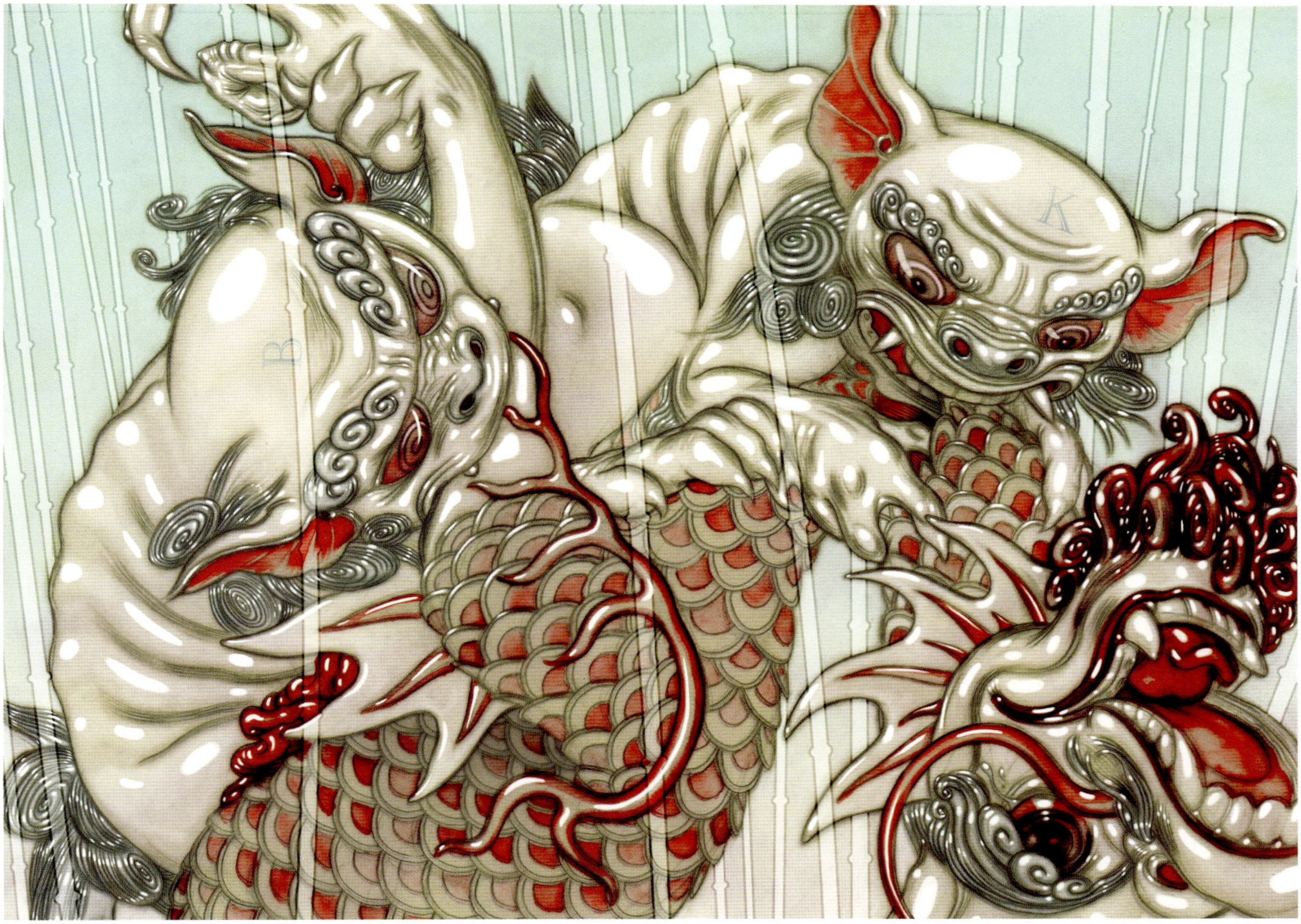

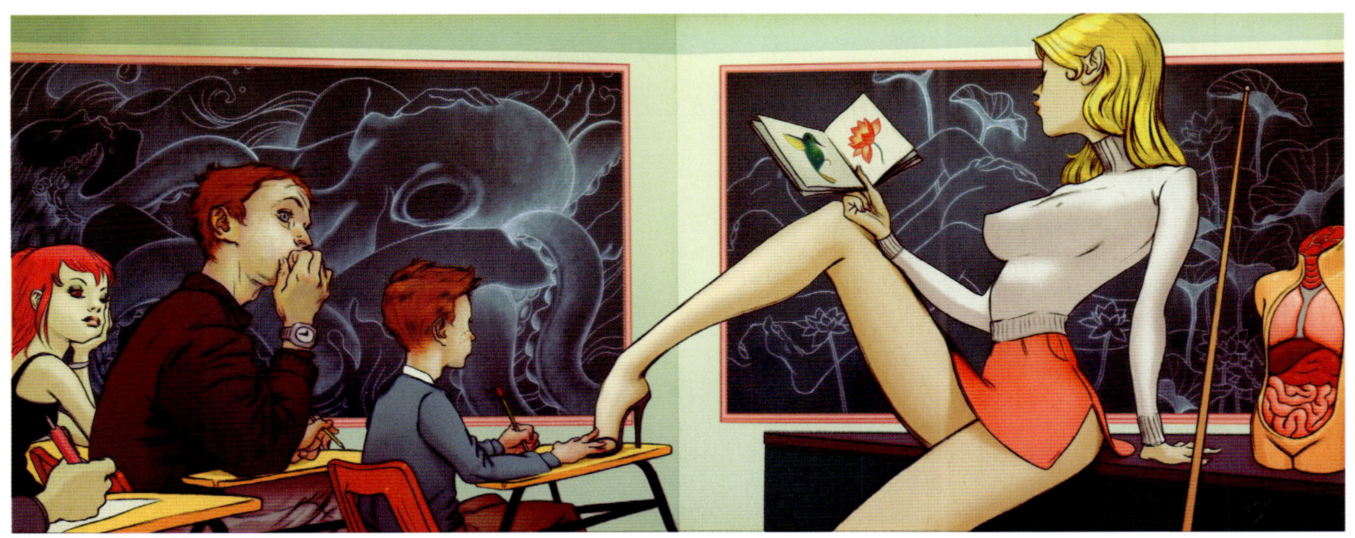

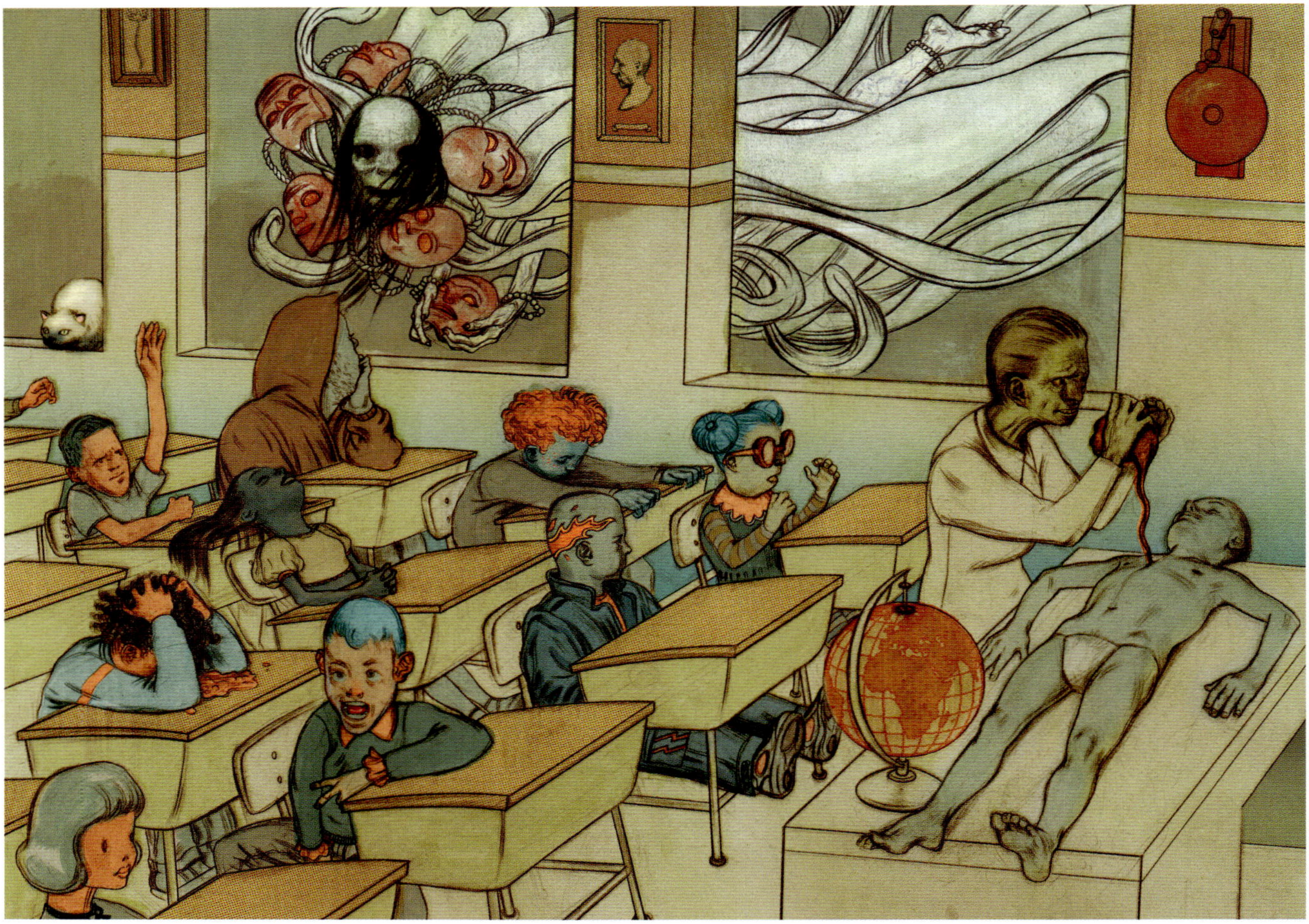

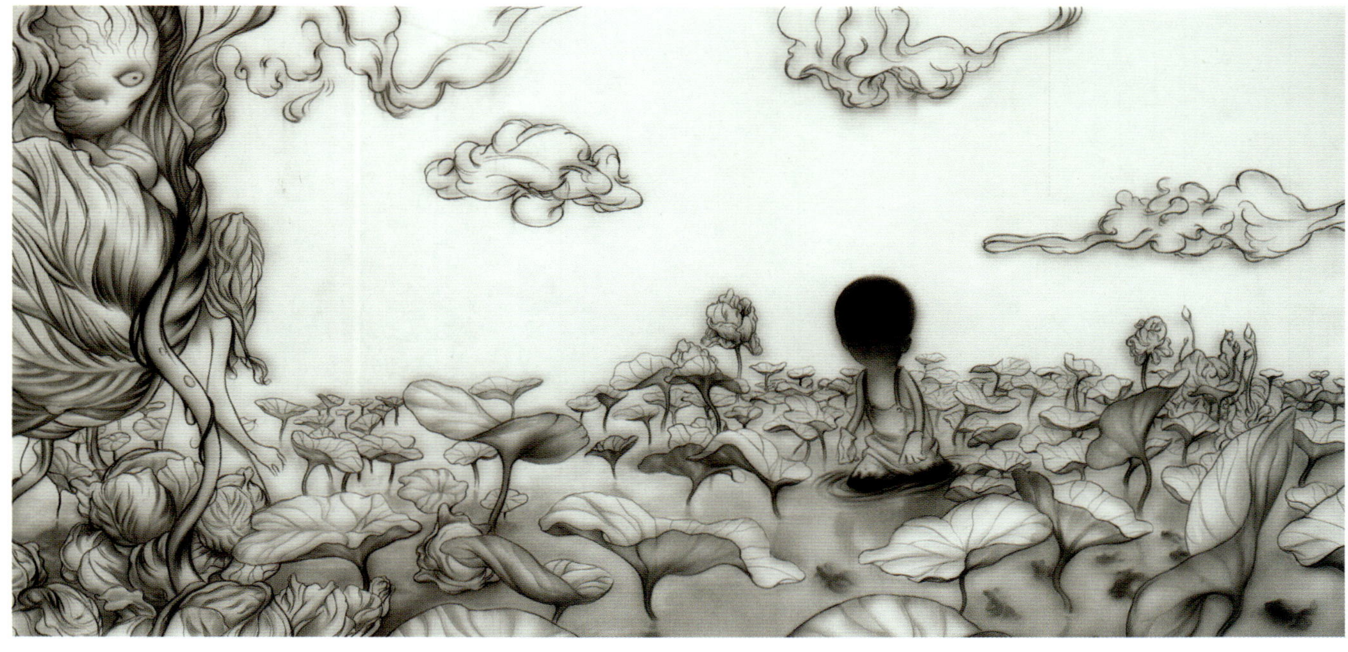

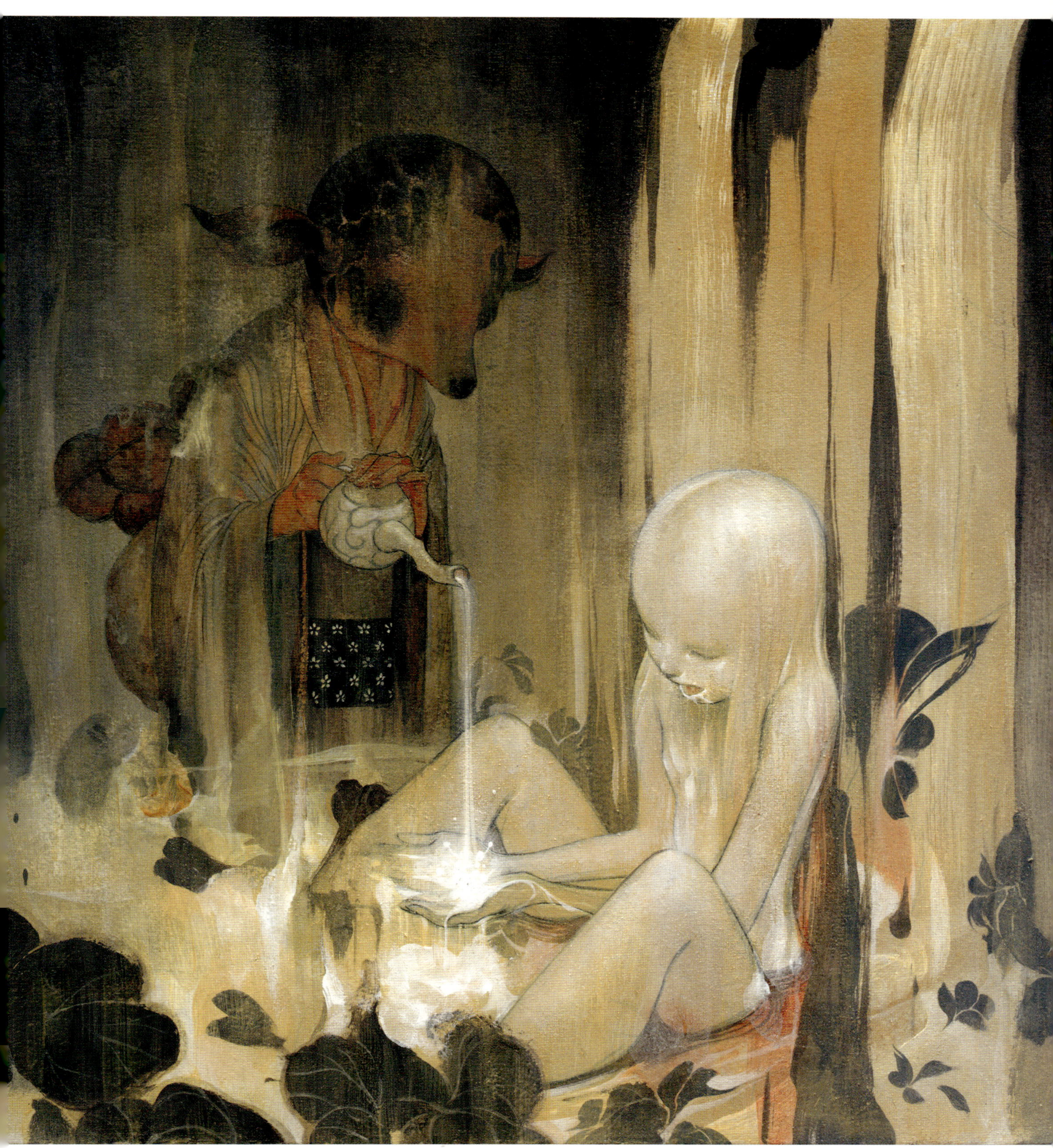

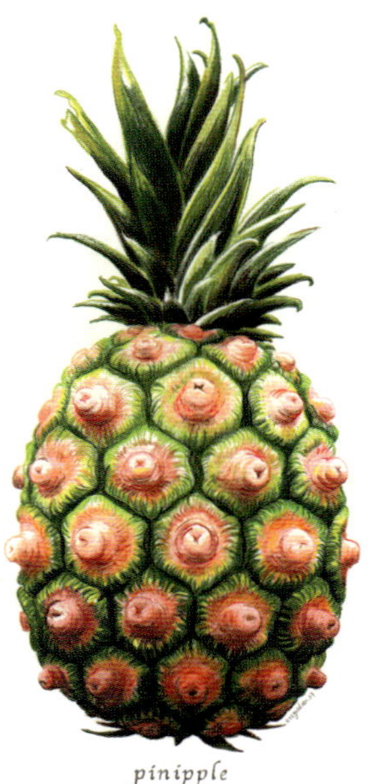

KOZY N DAN

Kozy and Dan met in college. "He used to harass me in class," Kozy says. "I did not," retorts Dan, followed by a "Well, maybe." Today the husband-and-wife illustrators work together as kozyndan. Their first gig was for Giant Robot, and shortly after they were asked to create album cover art for the band Weezer. Their panoramic work features complex urban landscapes with a twist; in one piece two giant sea slugs leave rainbow-colored slime all over the streets of SoHo. "We are really interested in the conflict between man and nature," Dan explains. Motion Theory, a small production studio, turned a handful of the couple's pictorials into a live action film for RESFEST. And last year, the Baltic Centre for Contemporary Art commissioned them. "I think that was a milestone for us," says Kozy. "We had never really thought our work would fit in that kind of environment. It really forced us to take stock and think about what this work is that we are making; what is under the surface of silliness." Still, the pair prefers drawing images of simple animals—or mutated yet endearing bunnyfish. As Dan observes, "Thematically and visually our work together was kind of born fully formed, which is to say it is as complex and silly and crude as it ever was."

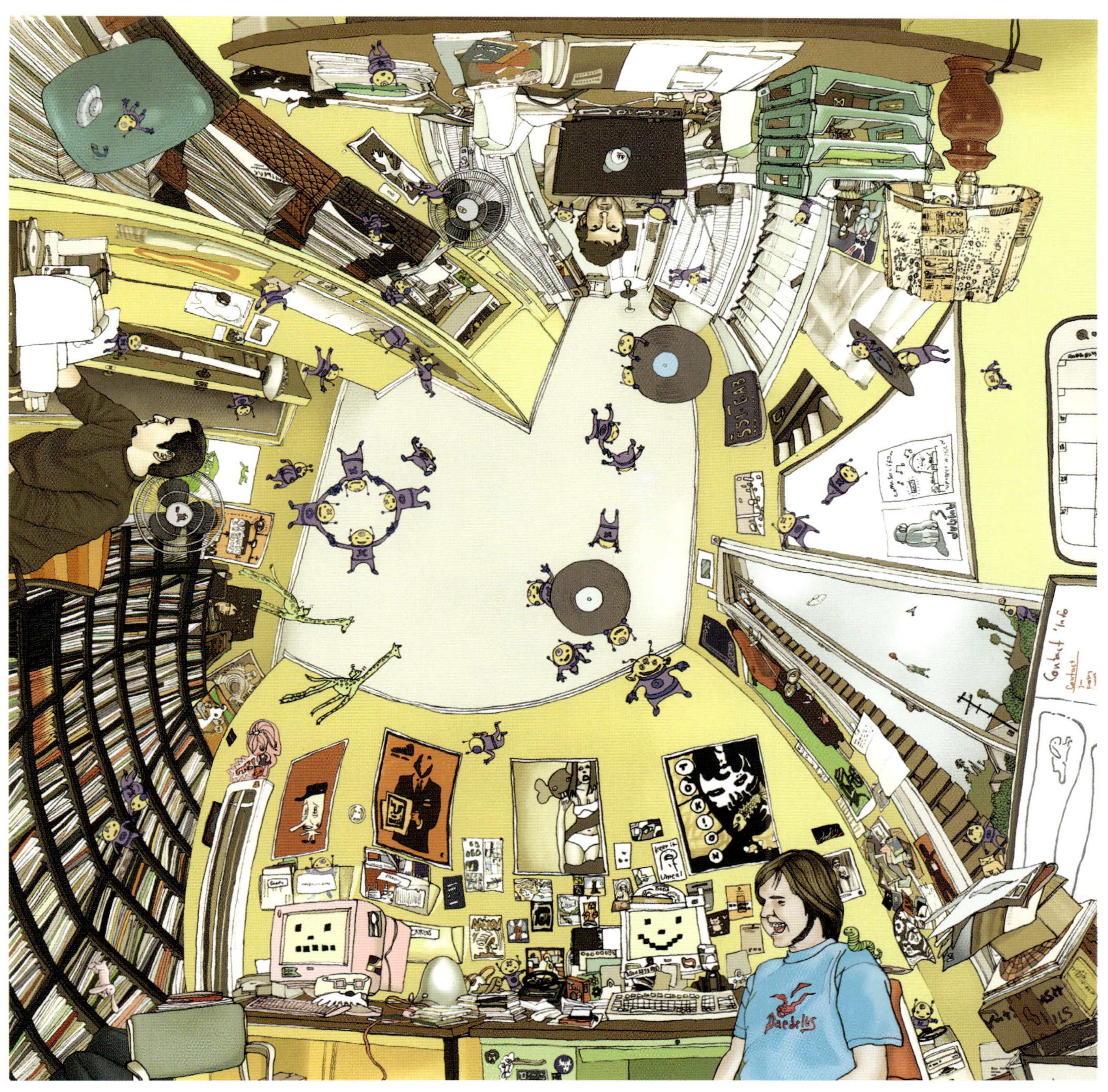

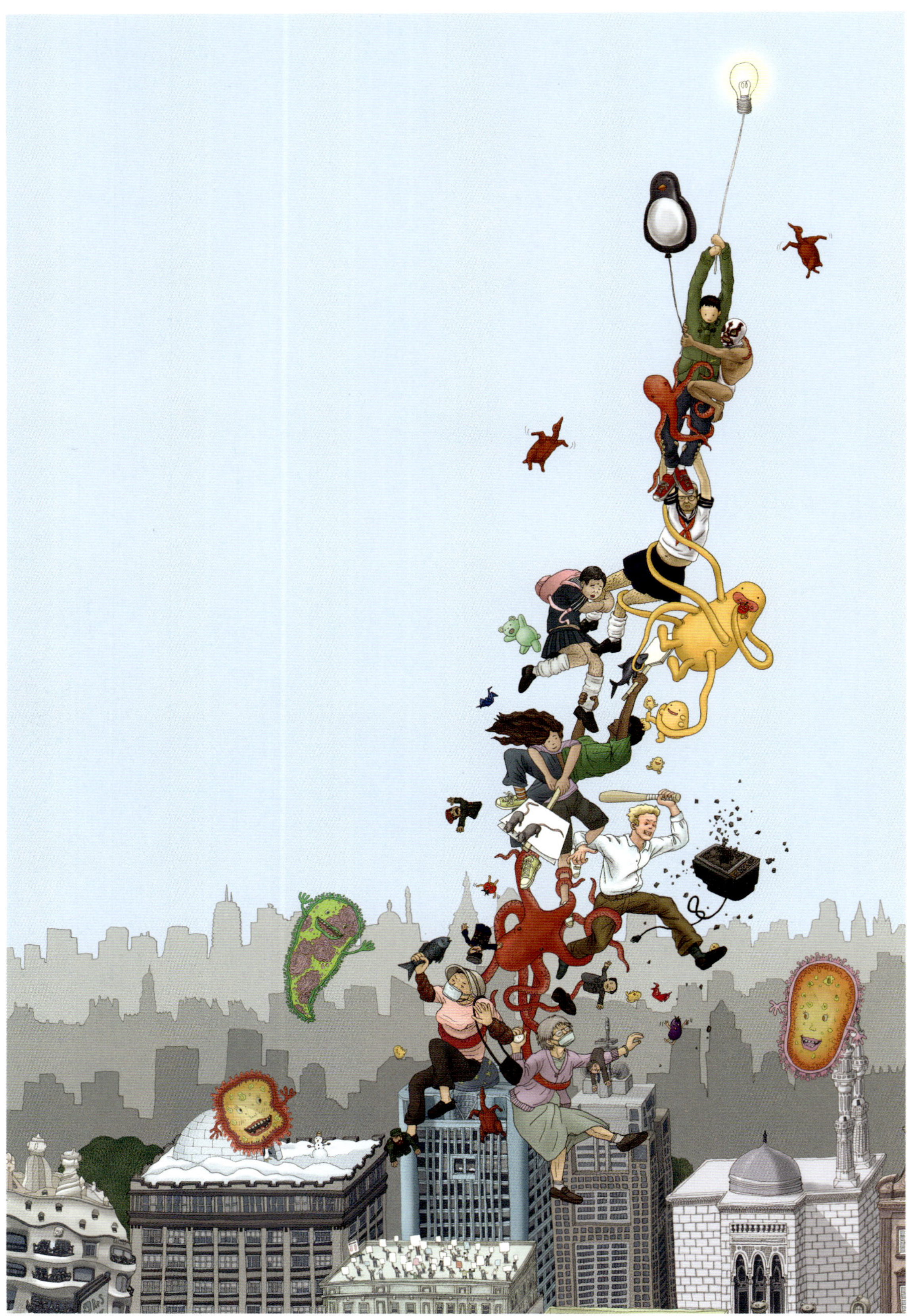

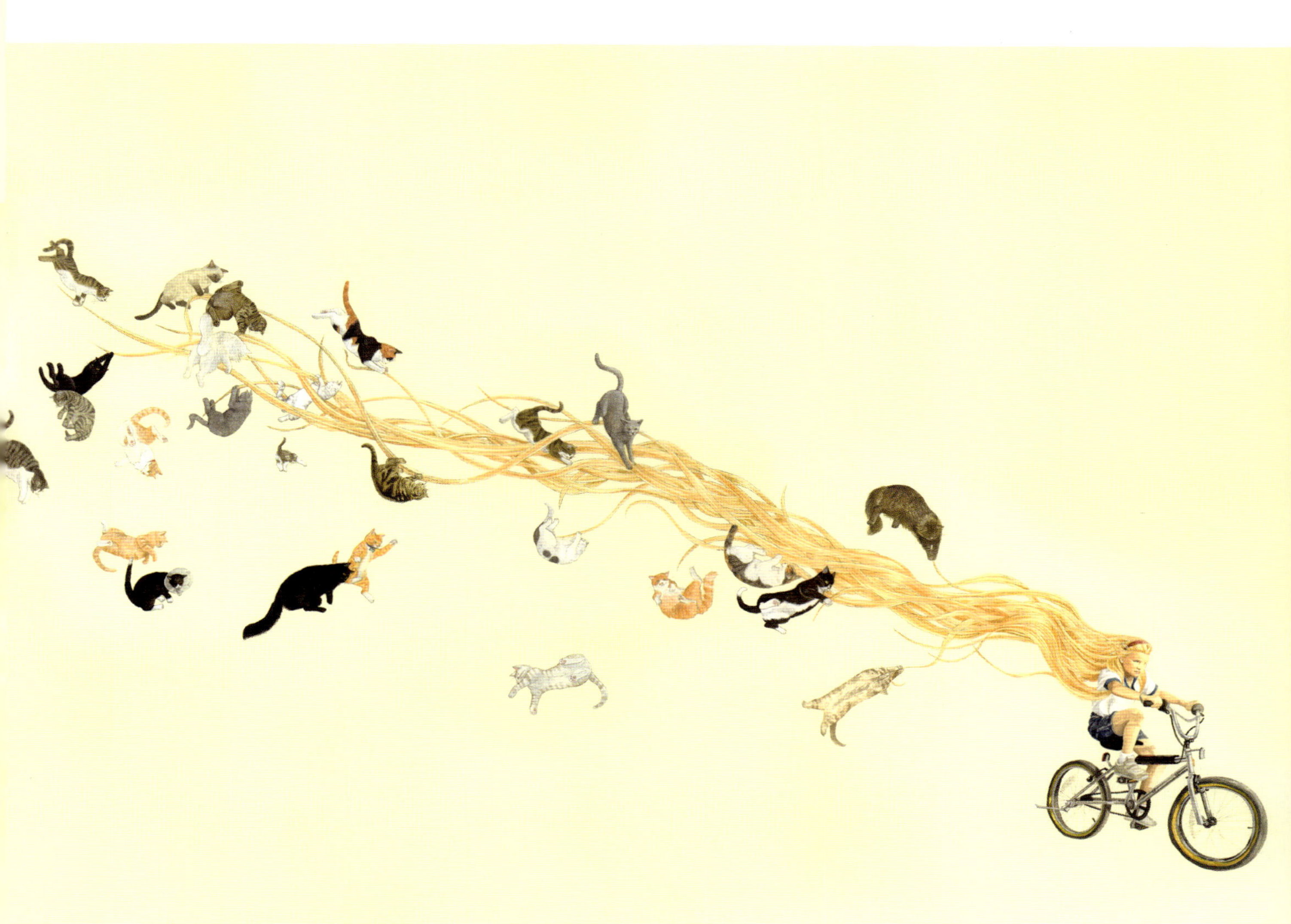

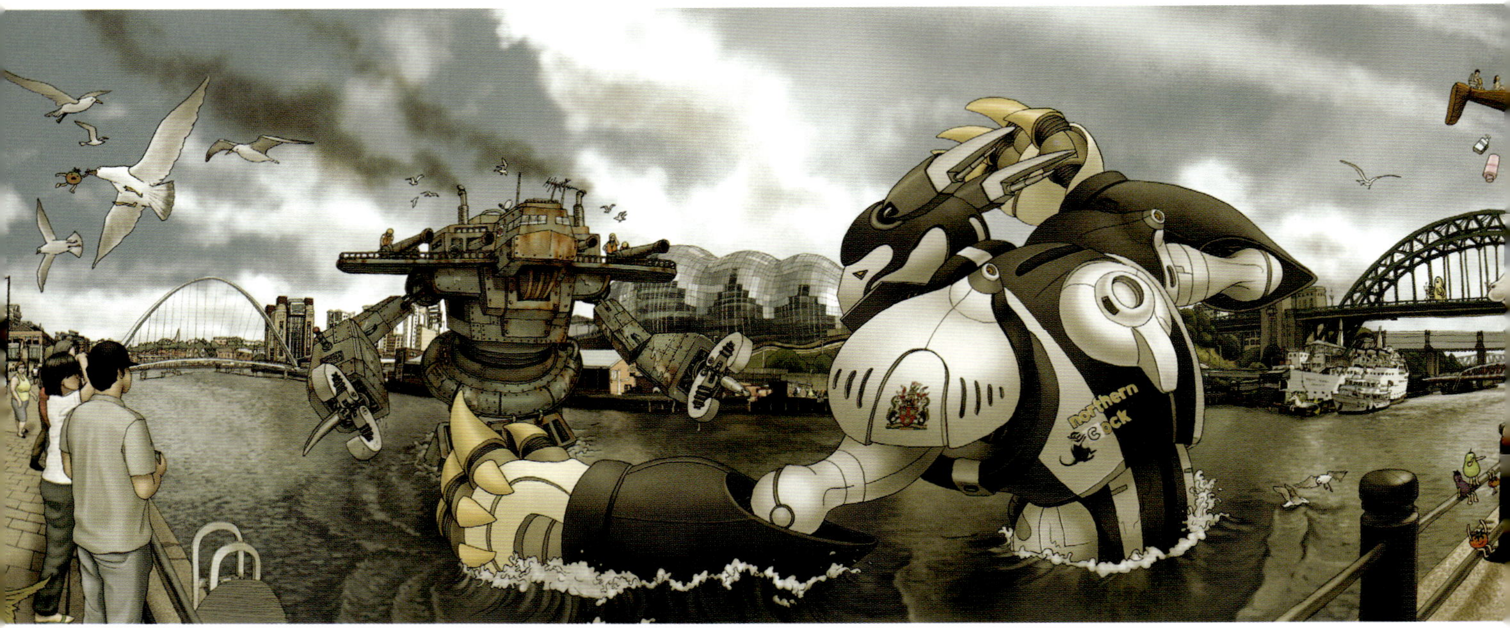

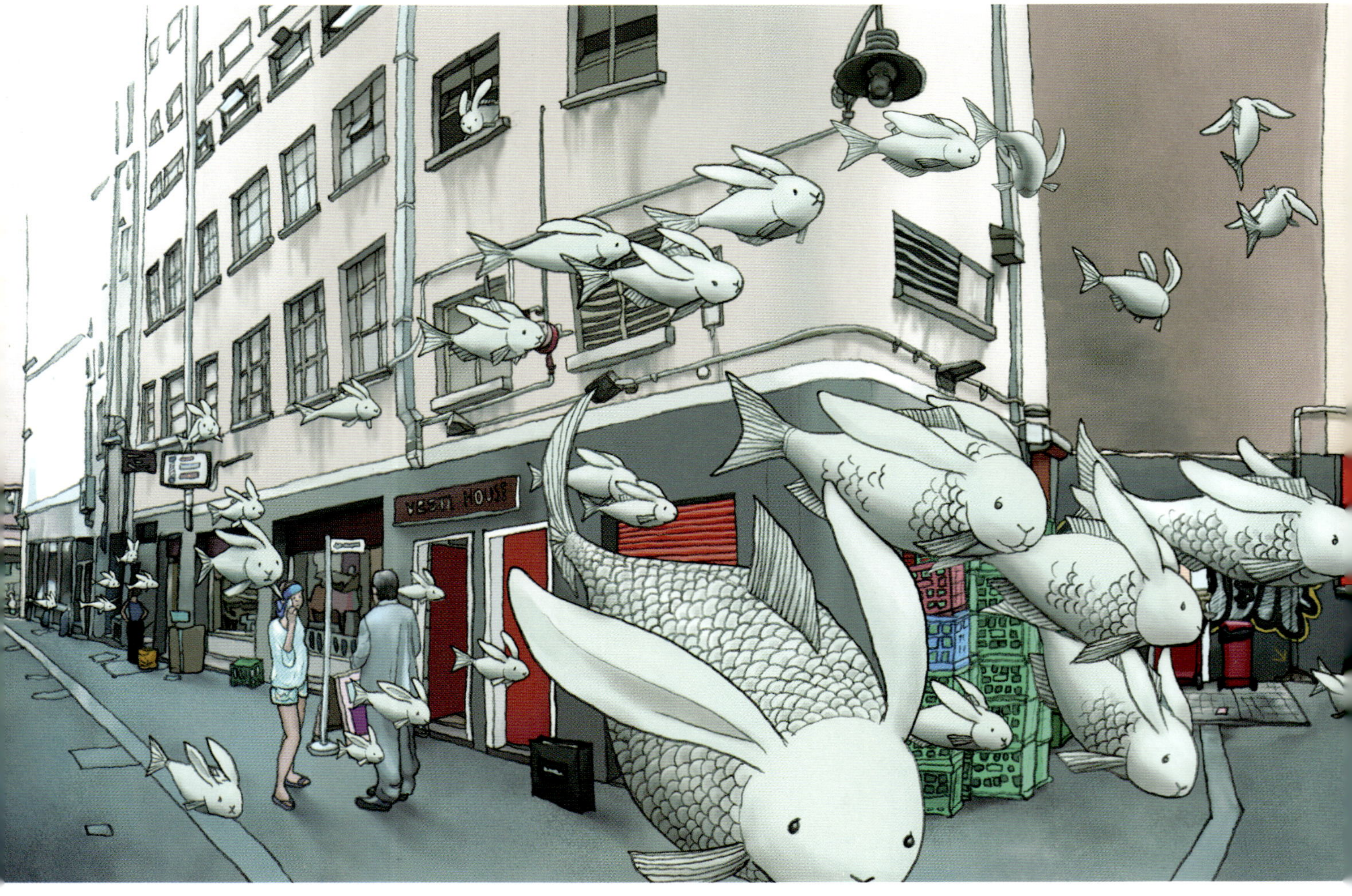

Northern
Rock

MESH HOUSE

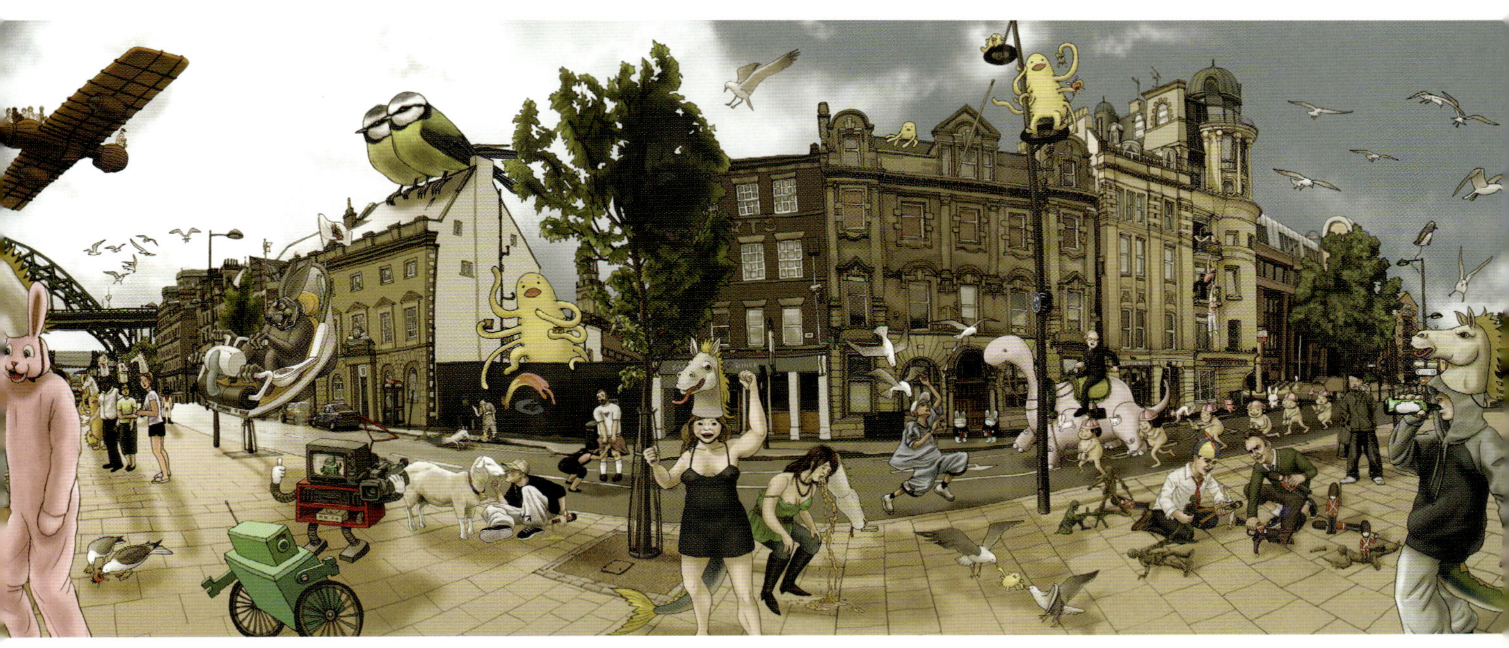

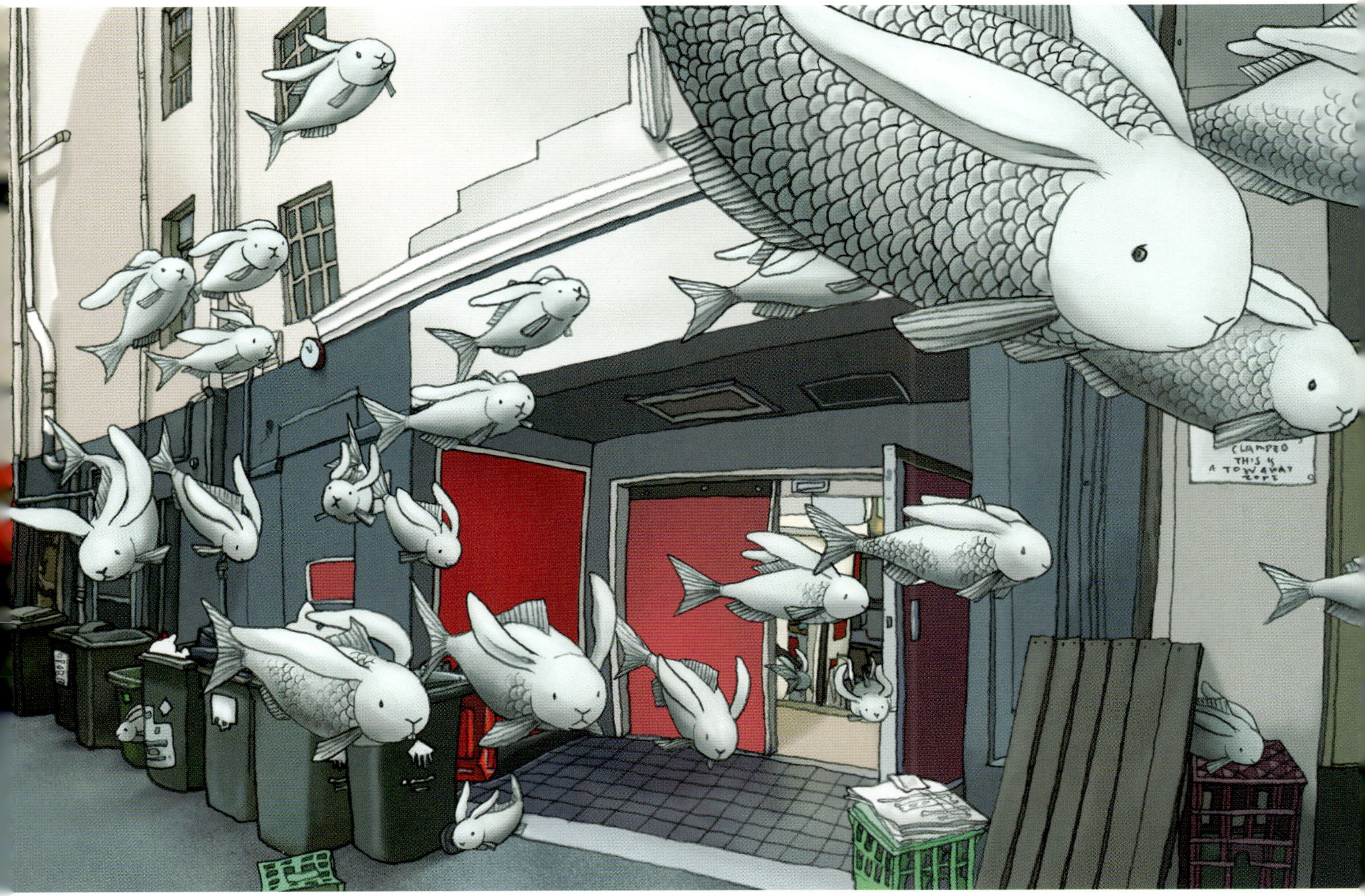

CLAMPED
THIS IS
A TOW AWAY
ZONE

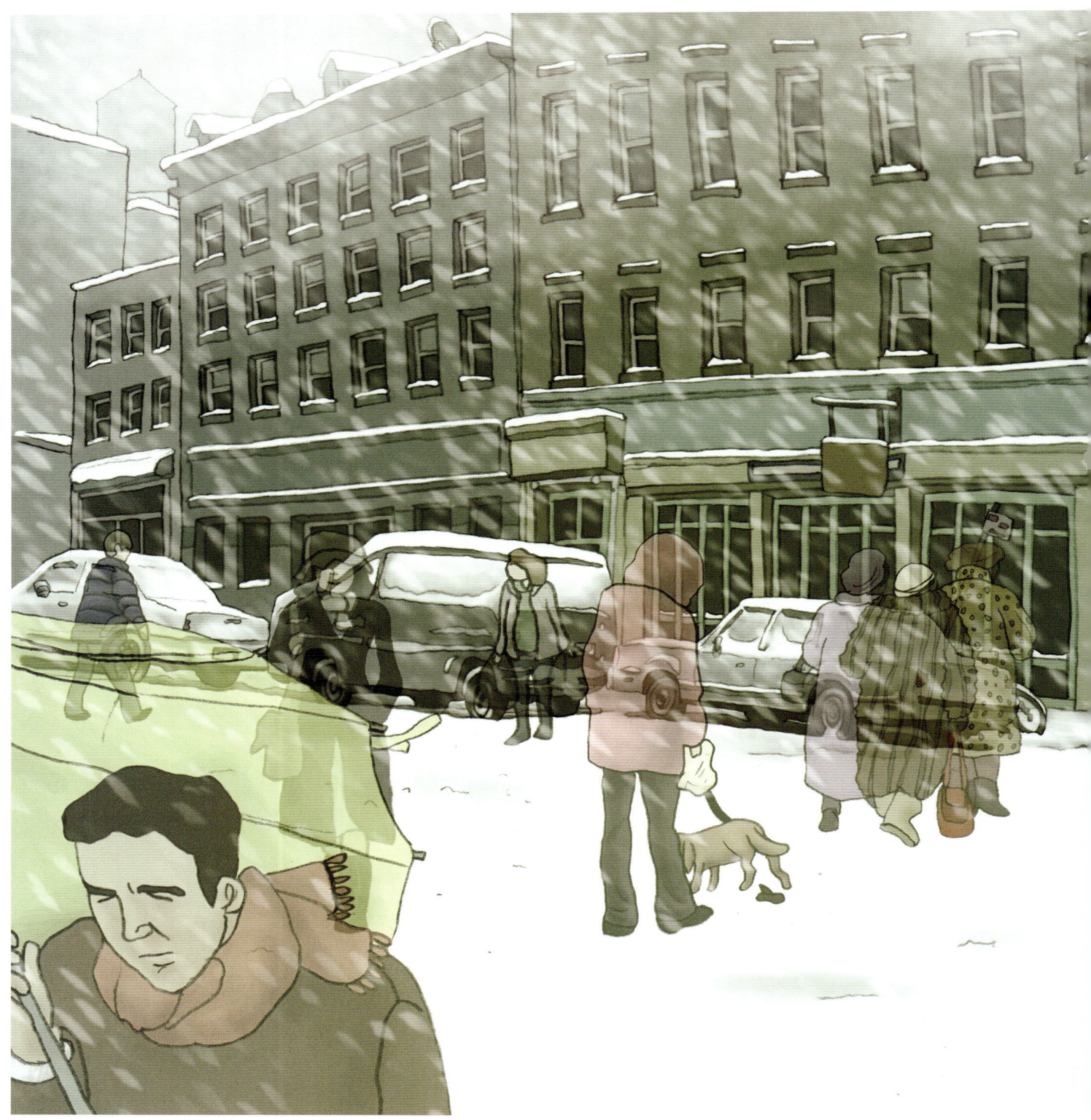

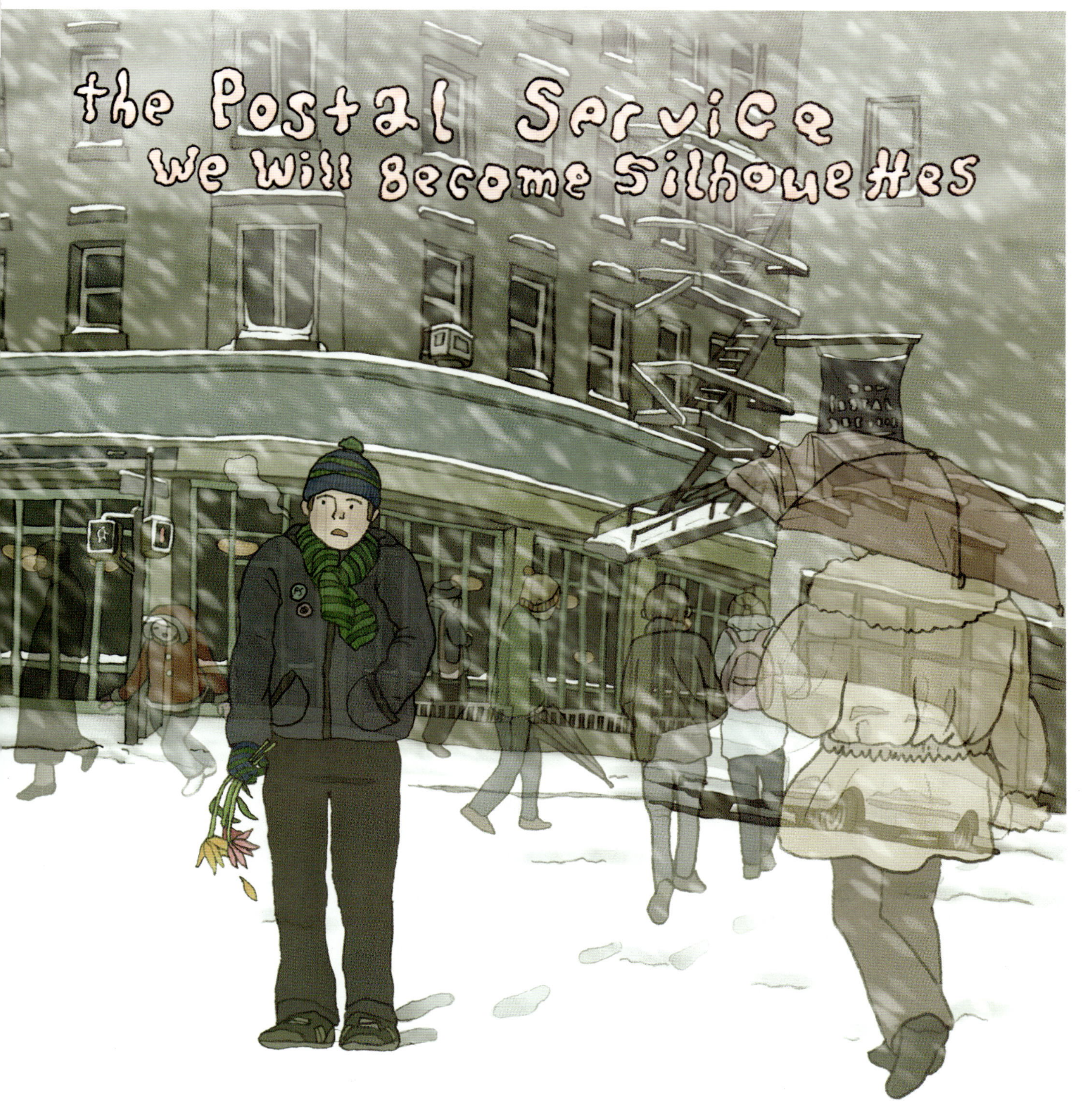

the Postal Service
We Will Become Silhouettes

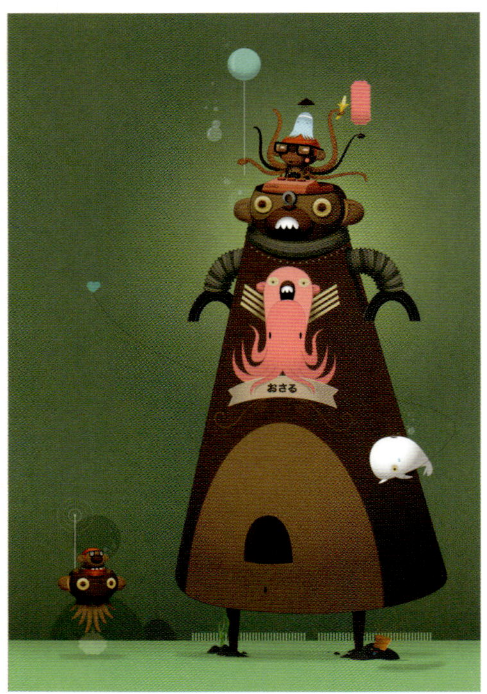

CHRISTOPHER LEE

Everyone has doodled cartoonish characters in the margins of their school notebooks during an interminable class. Sacramento-born Burbank resident Christopher Lee has proven it's no waste of time by bringing those little pictures into reality with his vinyl toy line, The Urbanites. Lee admires the clean and bold color that typifies the work of modern cartoon masters past and present, and cites Ray Patin, Mary Blair, Tim Biskup, Lou Romano and Pete Fowler as favorite examples. "Most effective characters," he explains, "aren't the ones that are drawn to technical perfection, but rather they're the ones that tell a story to the audience without saying a single word." He continues: "I try to bring a certain friendly charm to all my illustration work, which is usually expressed through the use of bold color, my choice of shapes and the small element of storytelling I try to incorporate into each piece." That approach has led to the opportunities to partner with clients such as Express Fashion, Computer Arts Projects and Honda, as well as exhibits in galleries. It was at a gallery show at Kidrobot in San Francisco that Lee connected with the marketing director for George Lucas' licensing company, who bought a piece and later offered him some work. Lee recalls, "The icing on the cake was probably the personal tour of the legendary Skywalker Ranch."

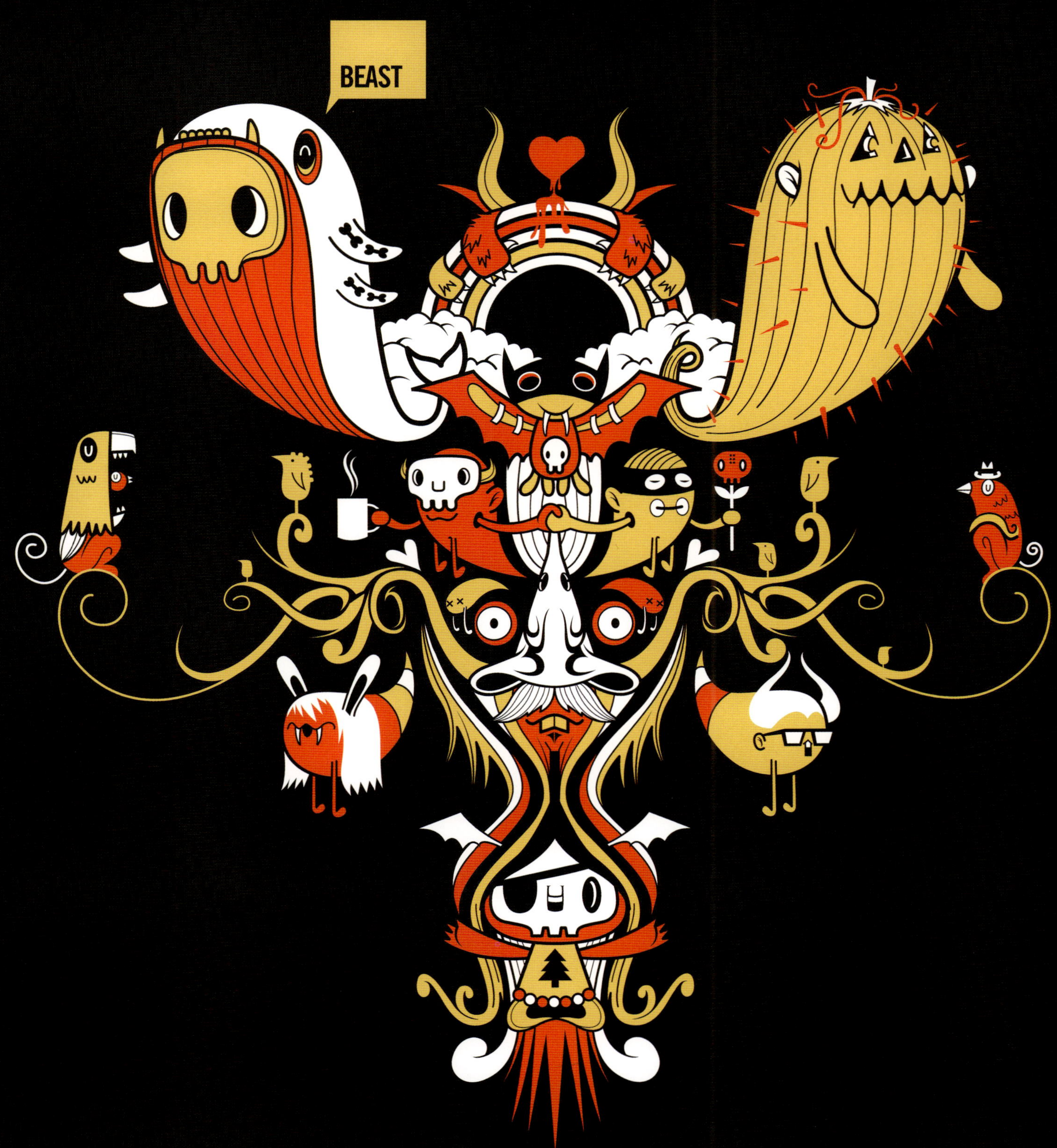
BEAST

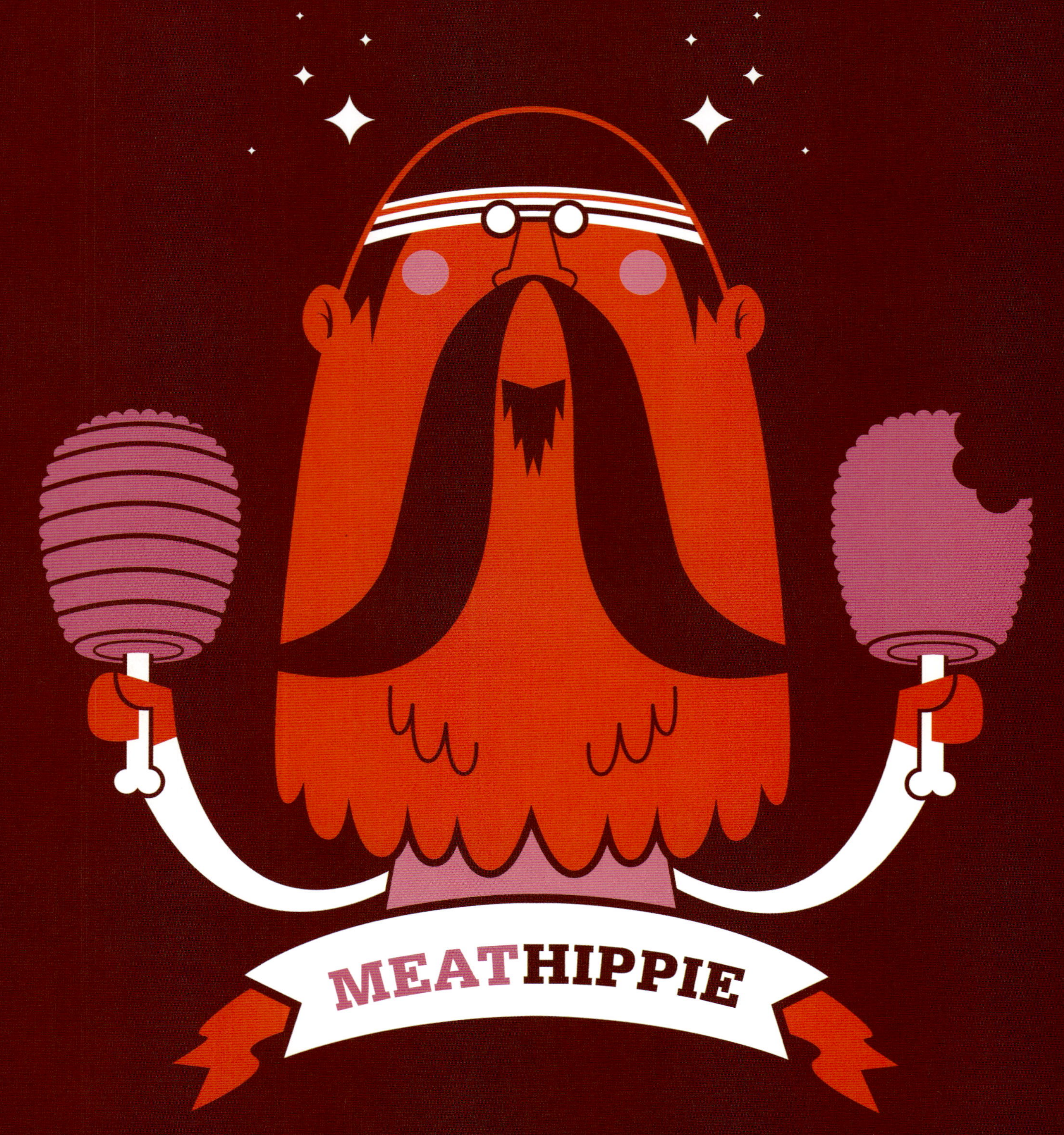
MEATHIPPIE

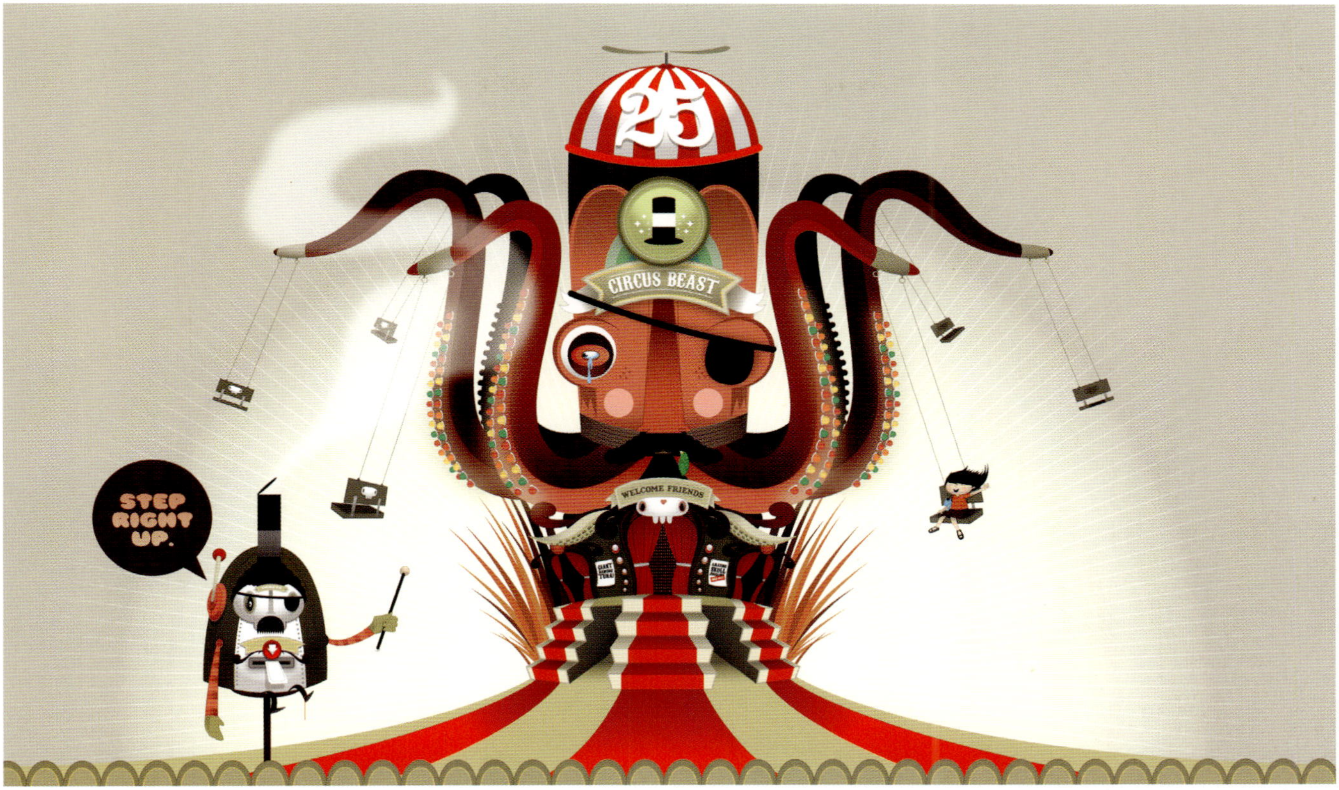

25
CIRCUS BEAST
WELCOME FRIENDS
STEP RIGHT UP.

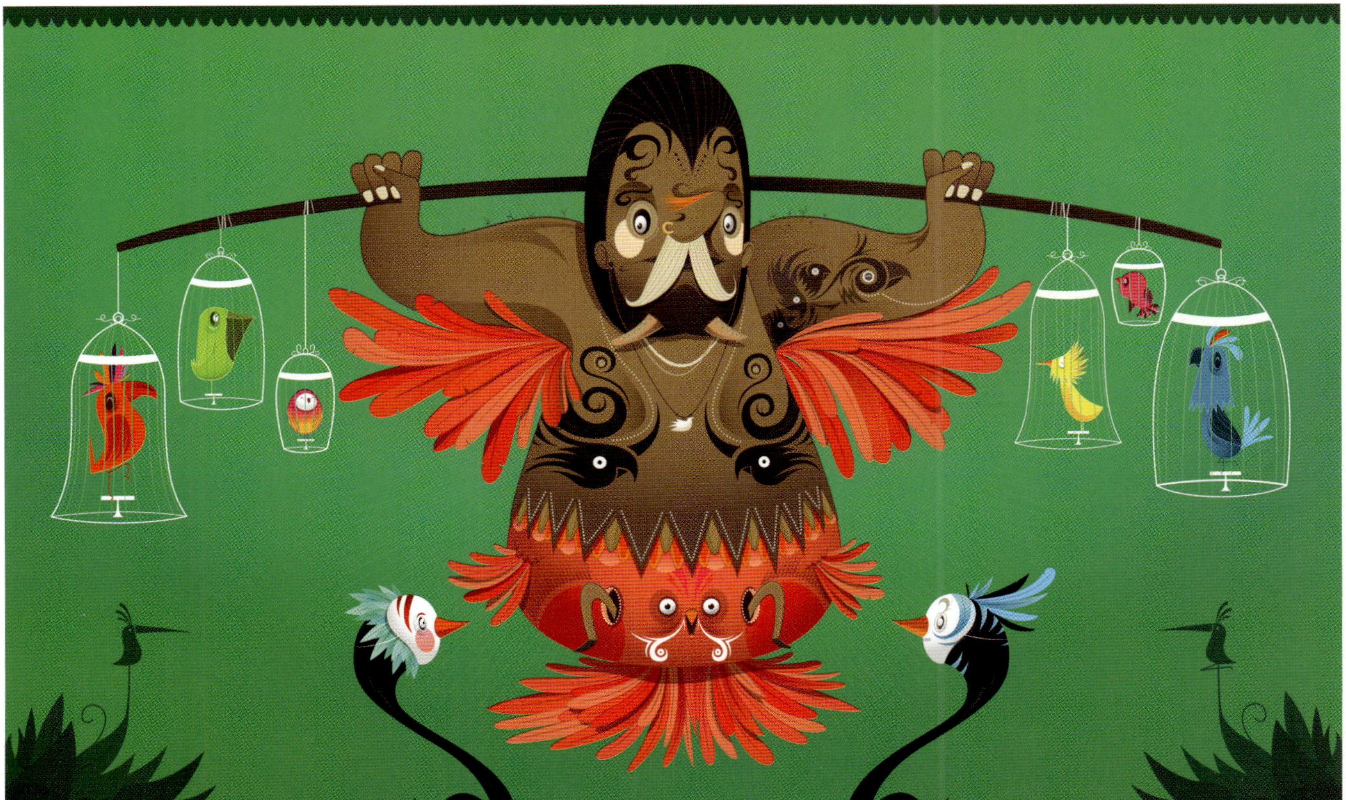

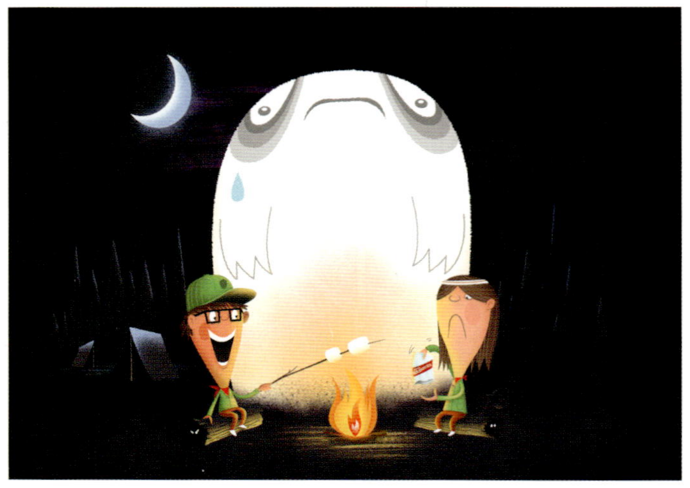

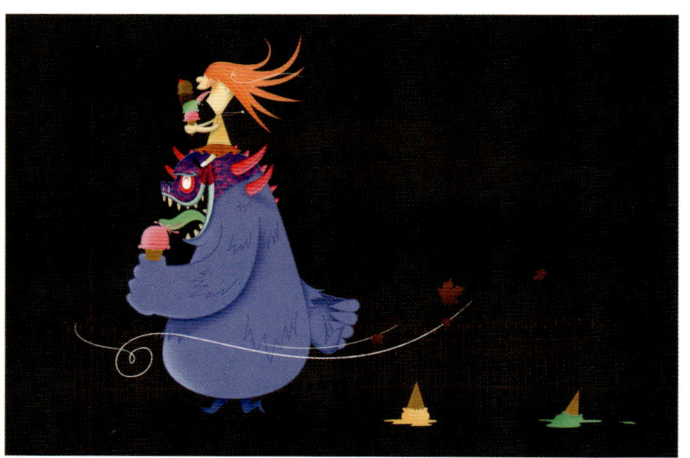

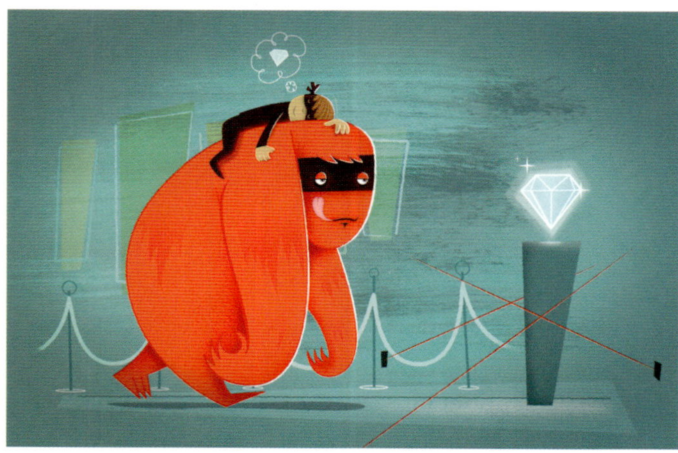

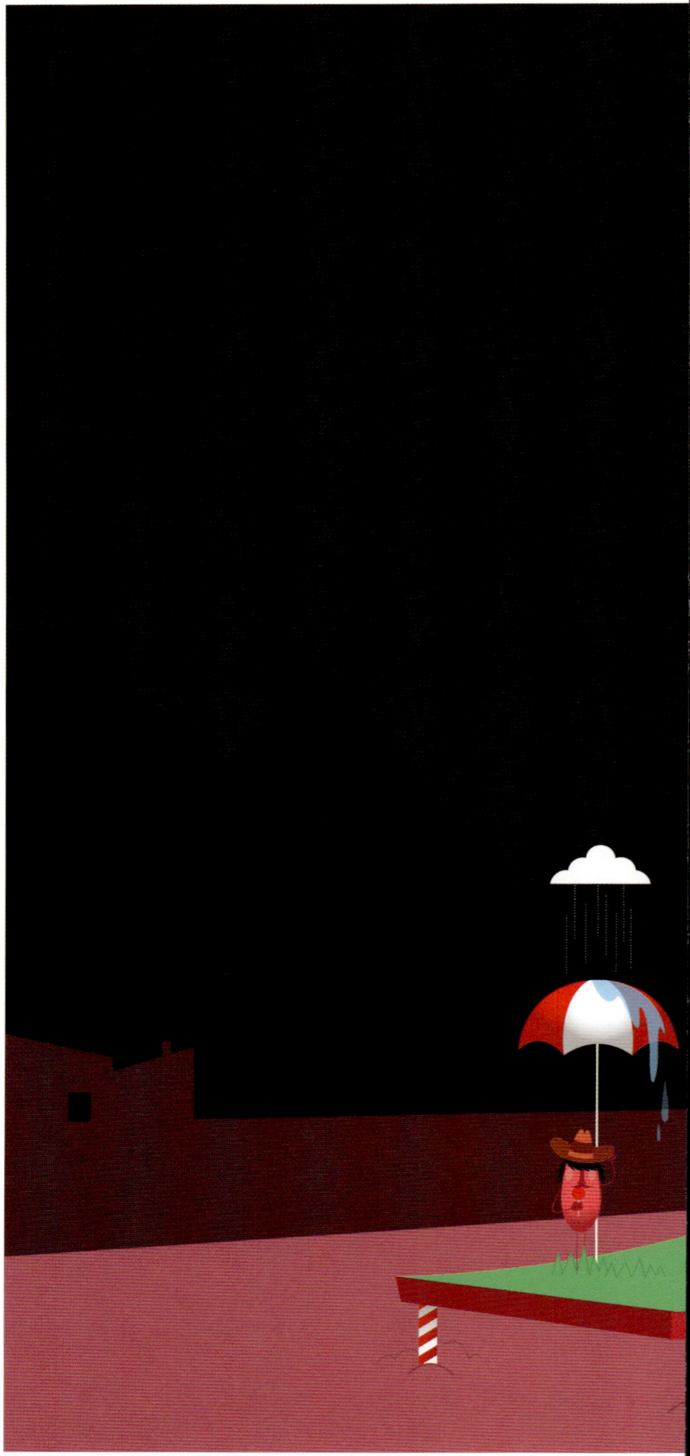

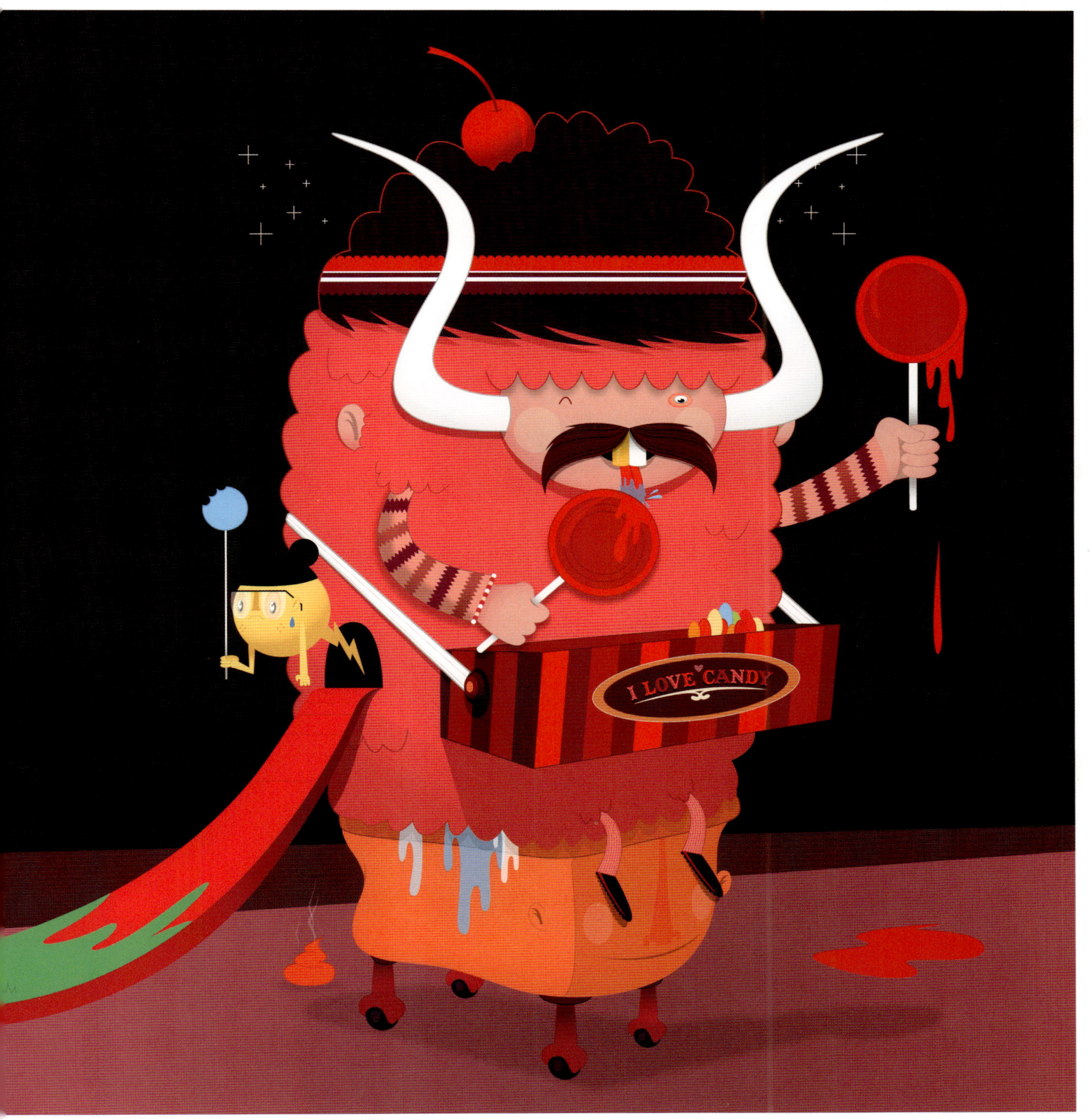

I LOVE CANDY

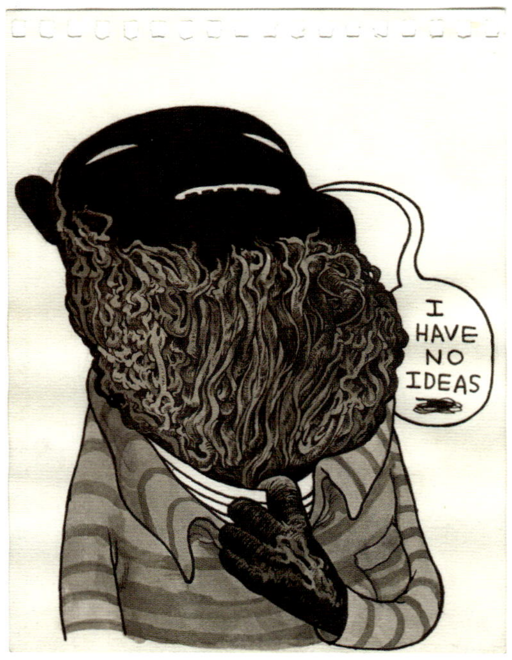

TRAVIS MILLARD

As a kid, Travis Millard's room was littered with magazines, comic books and piles of punk, heavy metal and rap tapes. "I was a sponge for the macabre," he says, "comedy with cuss words or anything offensive to my parents." Even so, Millard's dad tried to get him to take up golf. "He would explain why it meant so much to him. Something about competing with yourself, on a quiet course, with no one to impress, and trying to outdo what you did the last time around," he remembers. "I never got into golf, but I apply a similar mindset to making drawings or comics. Usually after I finish something, I get disenchanted with it, and try to do better the next time. More than anything else, it's a continual personal challenge to keep practicing, finding new twists and avoiding what I did last week." Before he became a full-blown illustrator, Millard worked a number of odd jobs. "Mostly it started as a refuge from my daily peon jobs around Lawrence and Kansas City—mail truck washer, dish dog, cook, retail guy, frame builder," he says. "I was always getting in trouble, or fired, at jobs for drawing at work." Now 10 years later—after leaving Kansas for Brooklyn, and then Brooklyn for Los Angeles—drawing is his fulltime gig. In 2007, Narrow Books published Millard's "Hey Fudge," a 240-page monograph of his personal comics and drawings.

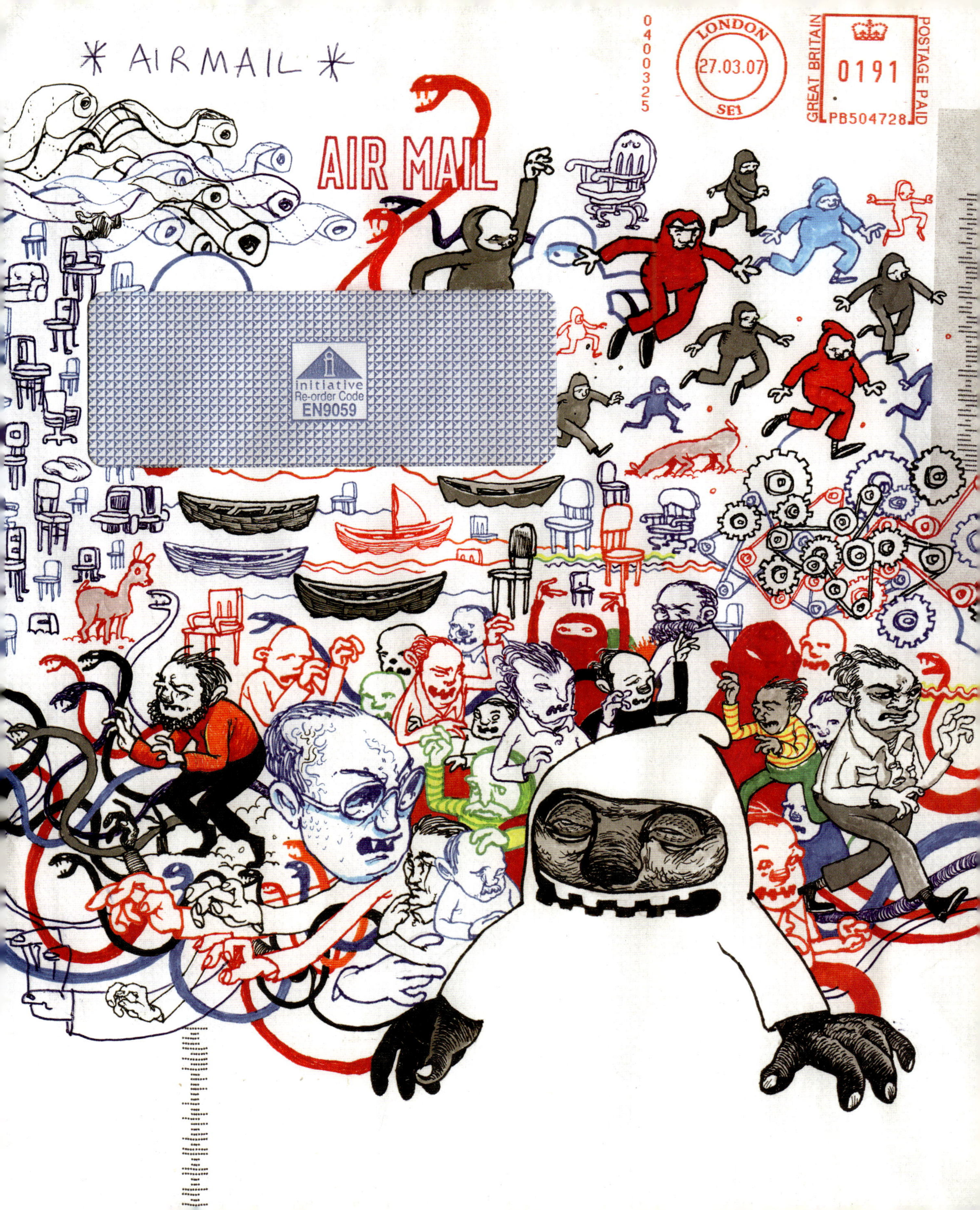

* AIRMAIL *
AIR MAIL
040 0325
LONDON
27.03.07
SE1
GREAT BRITAIN
POSTAGE PAID
0191
PB504728
initiative
Re-order Code
EN9059

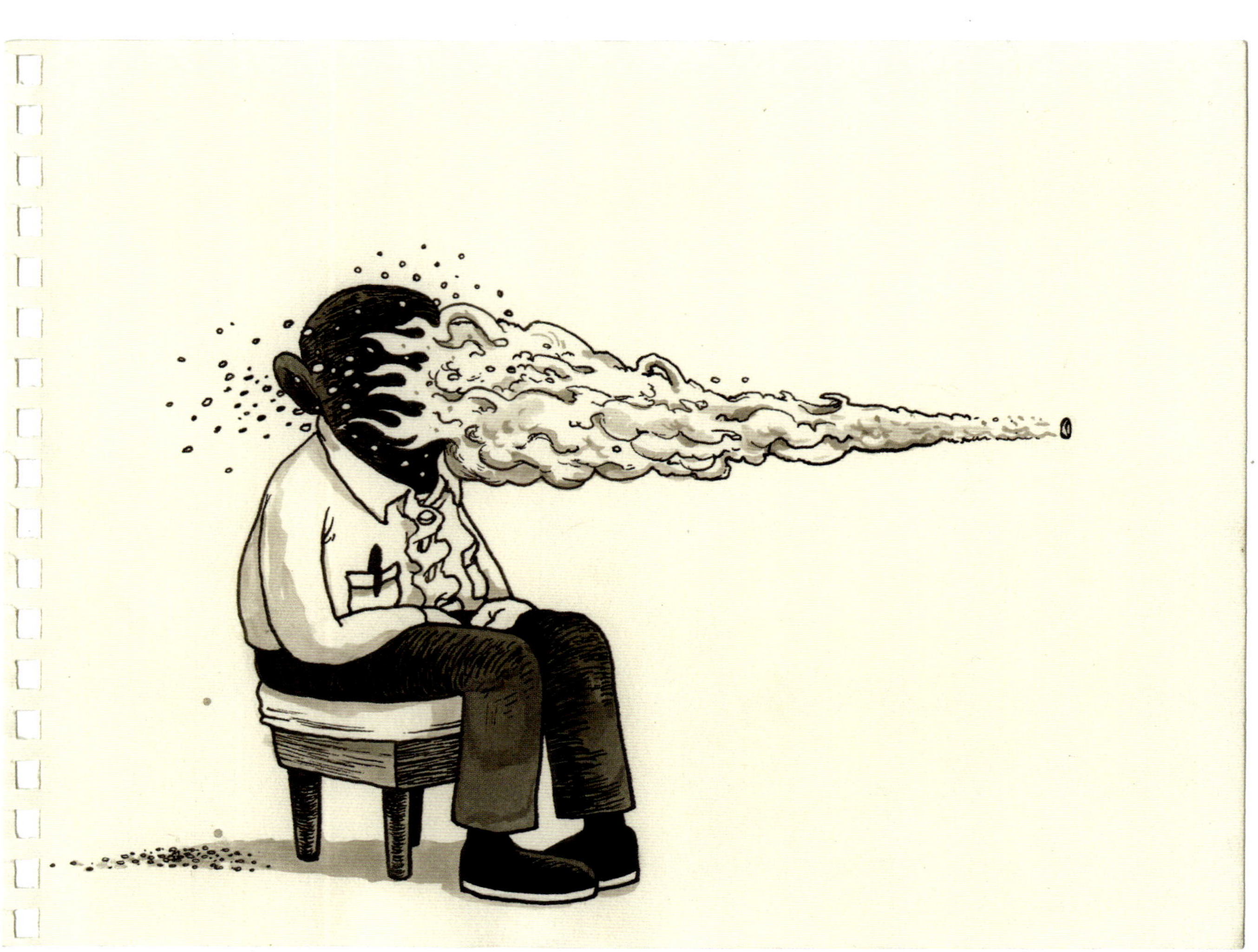

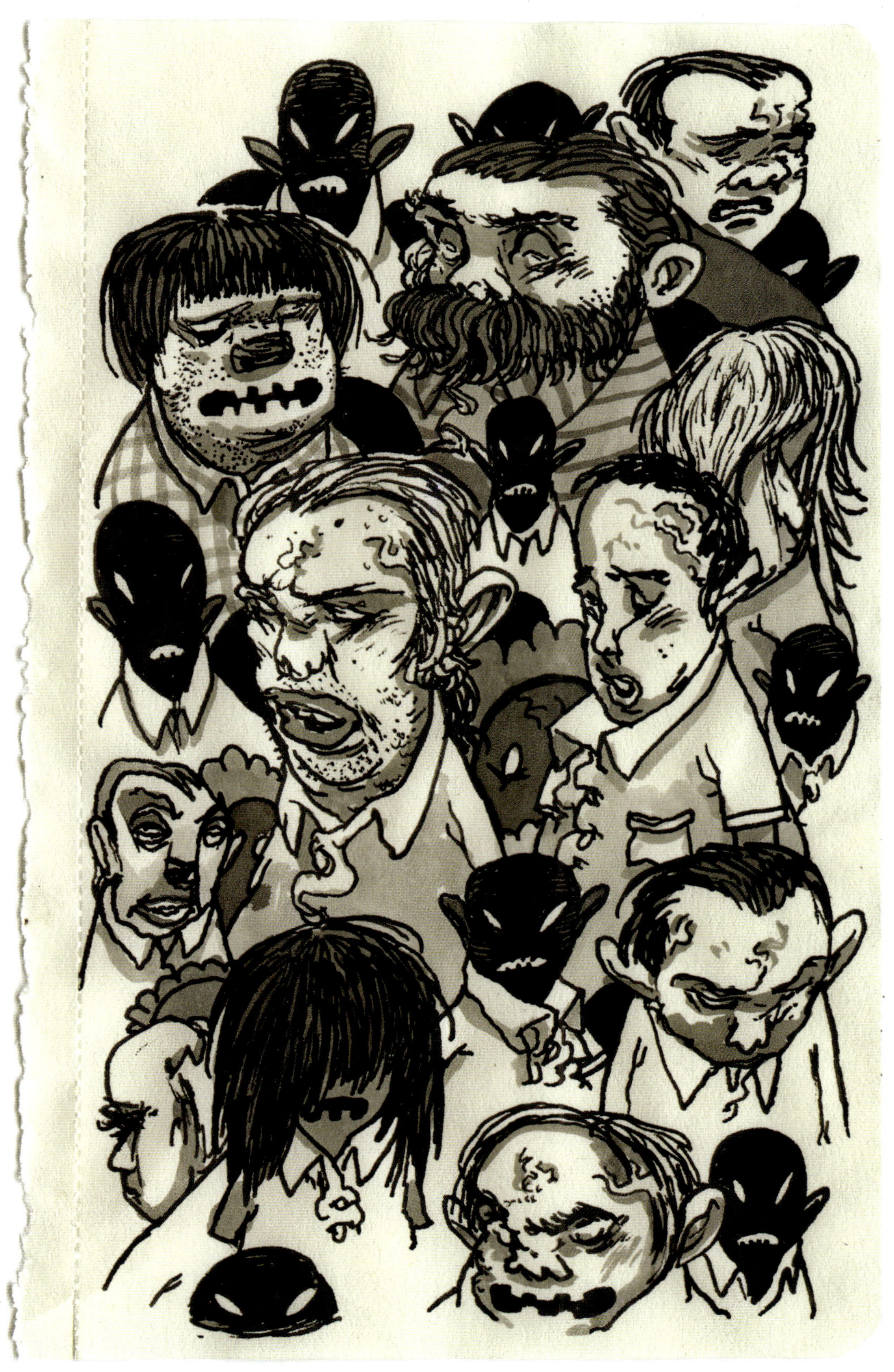

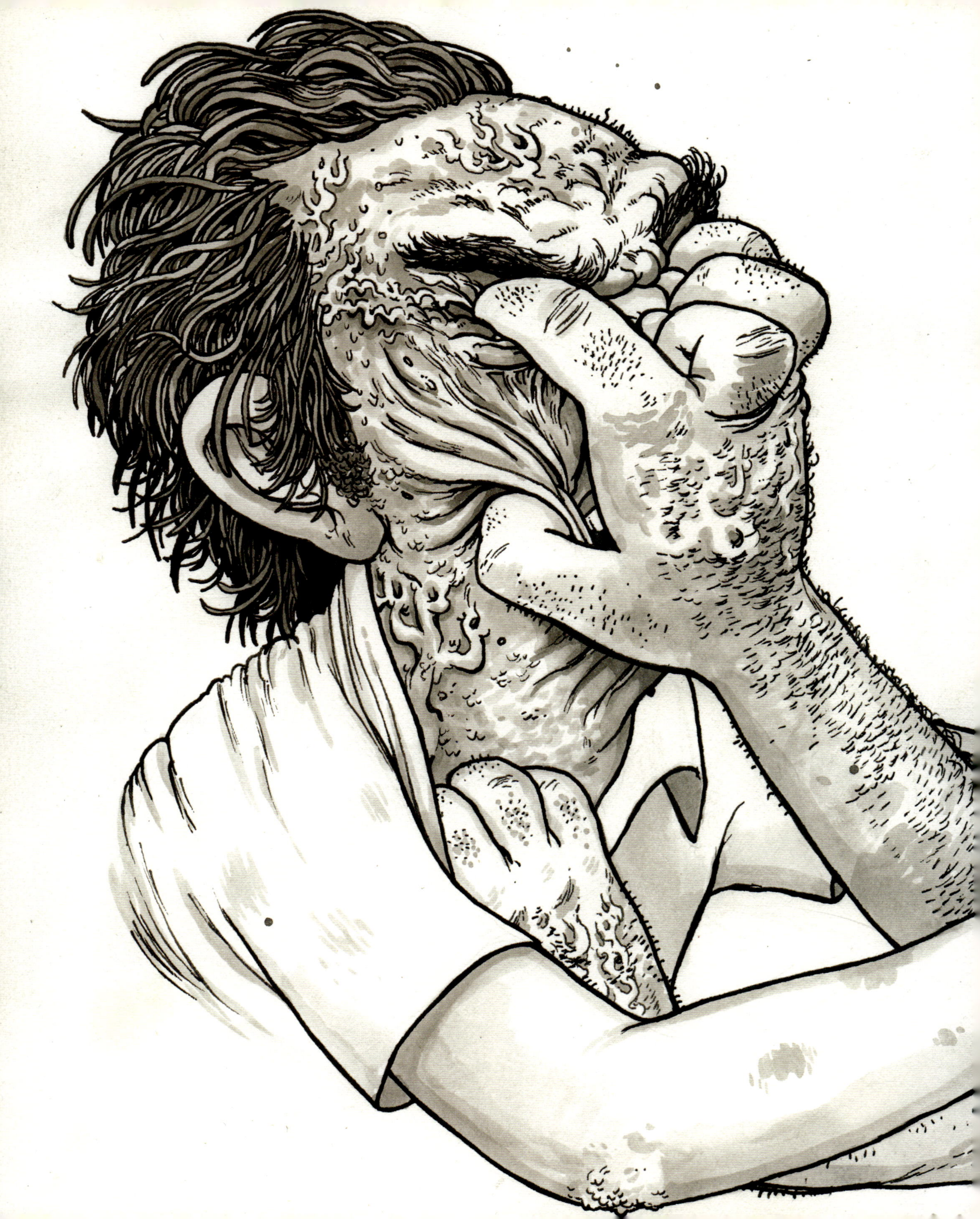

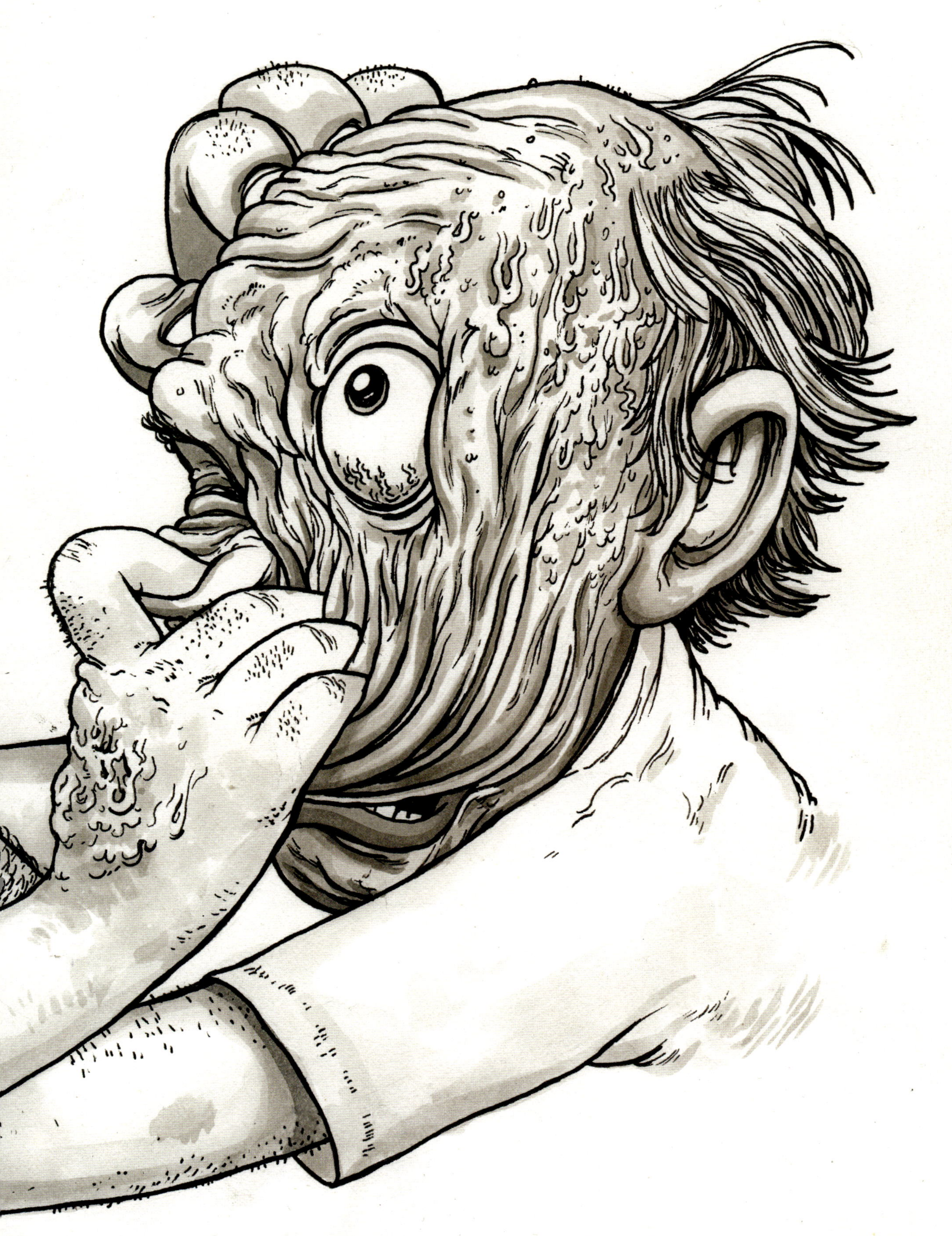

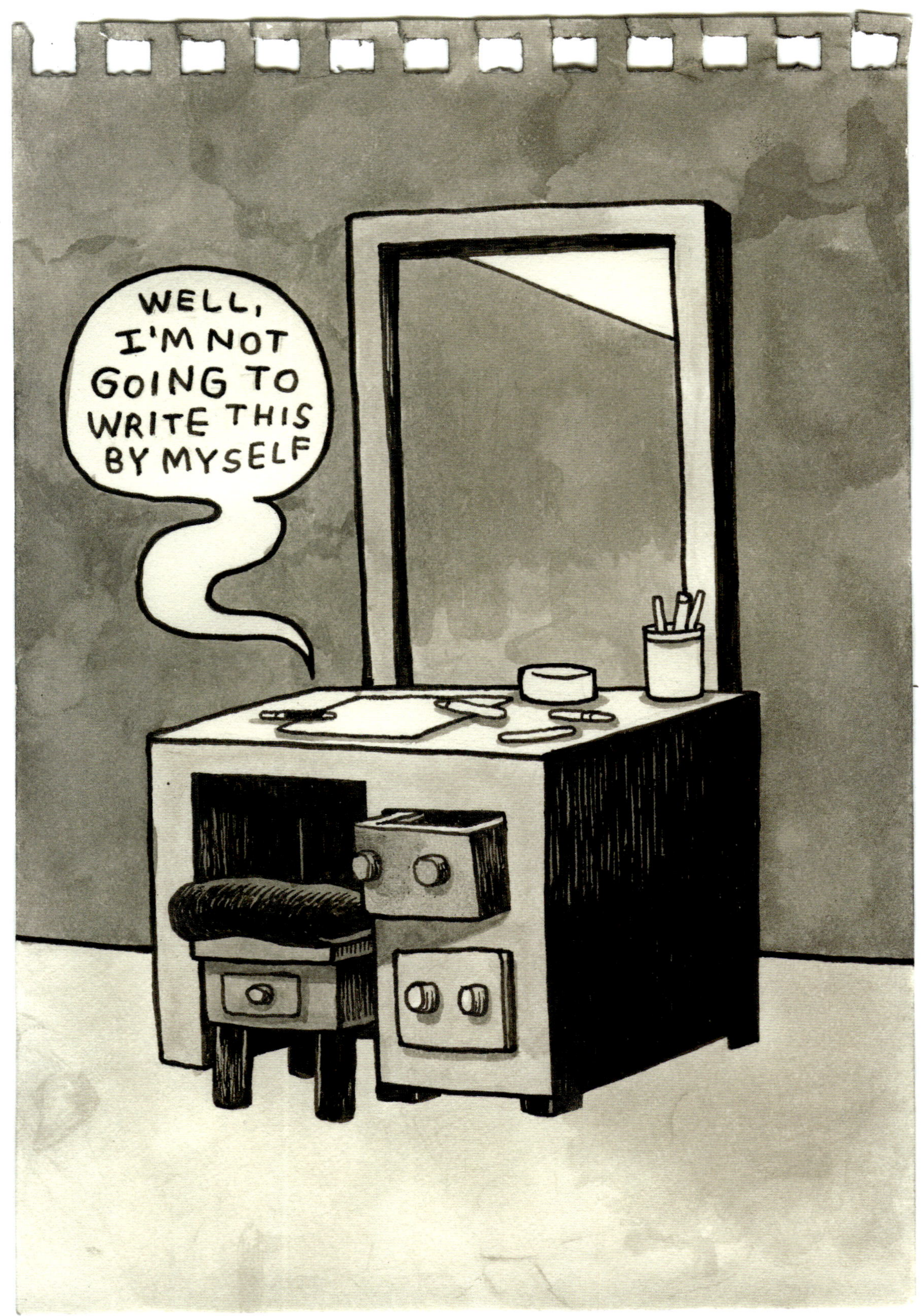

WELL,
I'M NOT
GOING TO
WRITE THIS
BY MYSELF

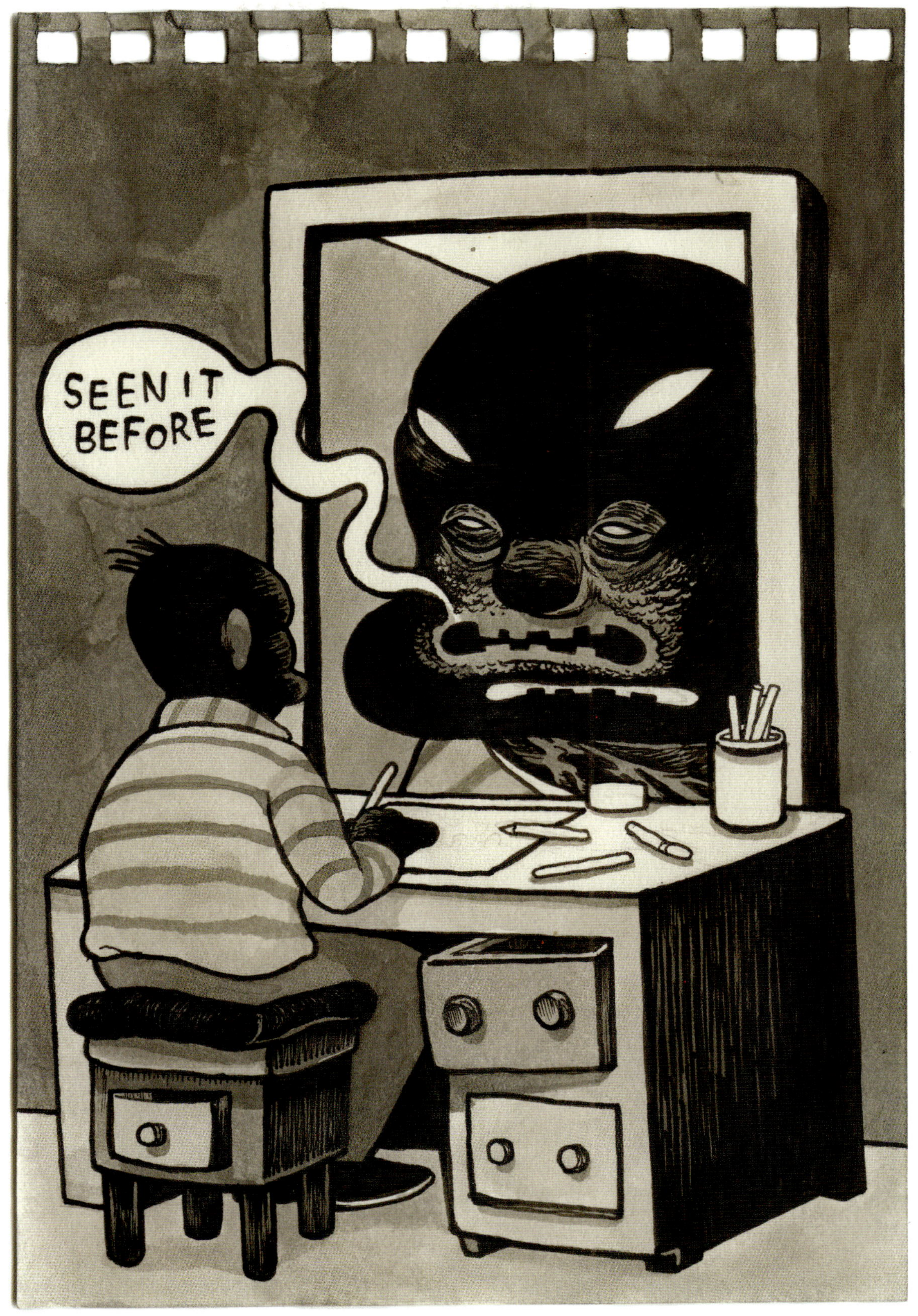

SEEN IT BEFORE

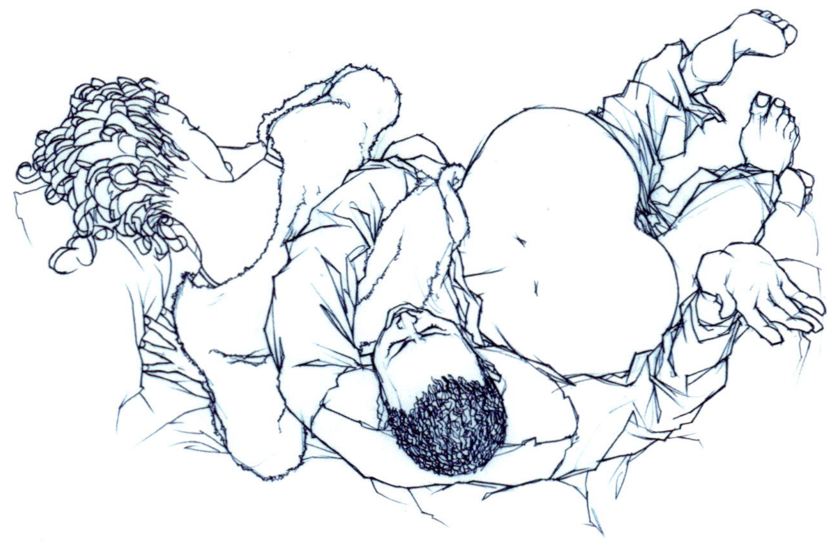

MODE 2

The world has been Mode 2's studio. Born on the island of Mauritius, he was raised in London. Some of his earliest influences included comics such as "2000 A.D." and "Heavy Metal," as well as the "Lord of the Rings" trilogy. In the early '80s he made a major discovery. "From the hip-hop years onwards, it was more about the music, dancing and rap lyrics from the likes of Kool Keith," he explains. Hip-hop of course led him into the world of graffiti. In '87 his work graced the cover of the influential graff book "Spraycan Art." Without any formal training, Mode 2 used knowledge of graffiti in his illustrations and developed a unique style. He defines his aesthetic as a "mix between hip-hop, '70s and '80s comics, paintings from the late 19th and early 20th centuries, and the whole thing remixed with an obsession for the female body." An admitted voyeur, he enjoys capturing the people and moments that most people overlook. Although he maintains his own style, Mode 2 is influenced by the works of Tanino Liberatore, Hans Bellmer and the Pre-Raphaelites. Of which, he says, "When it comes to drawing, I always feel that the ghosts of those who inspired are there looking over my shoulder."

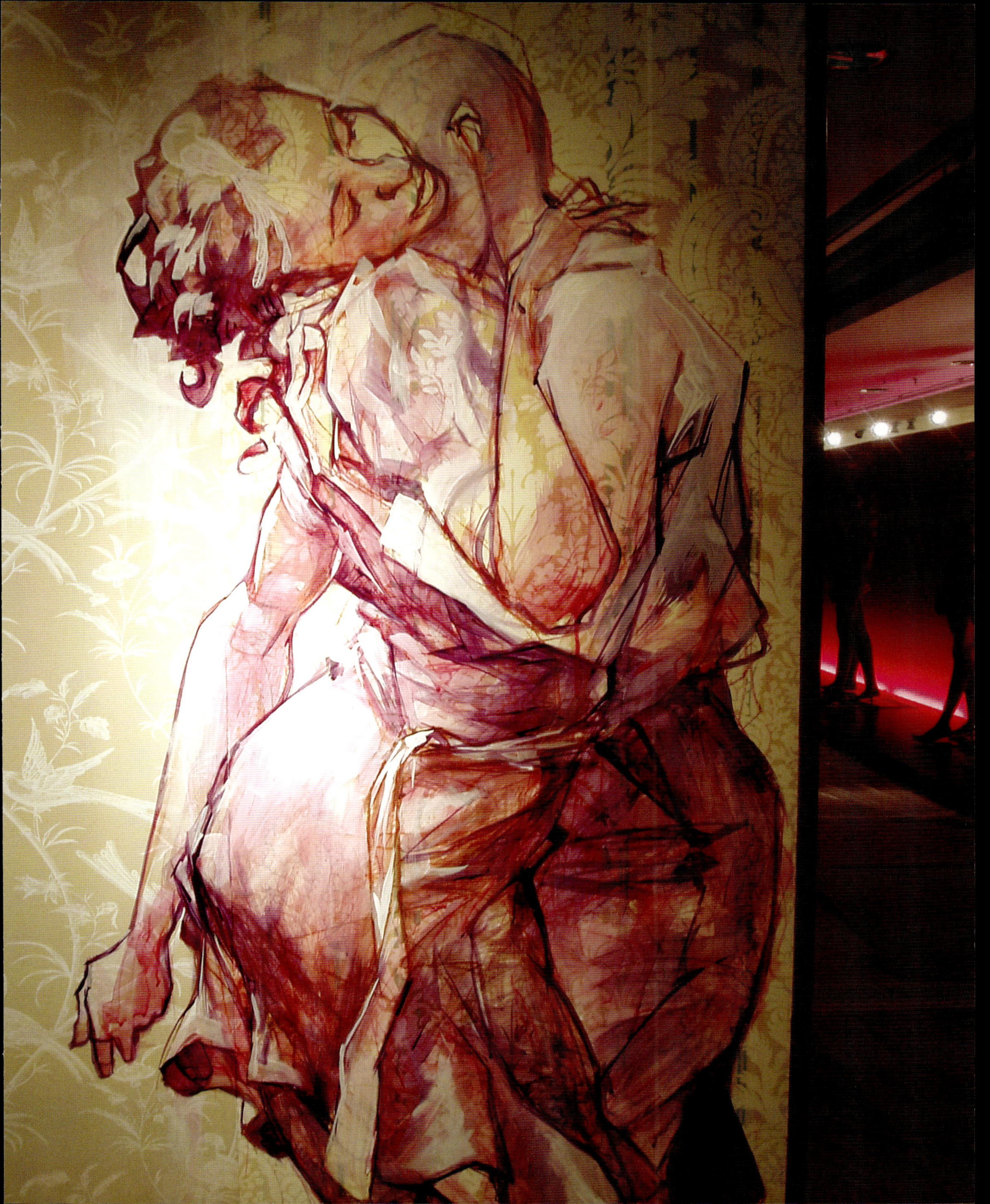

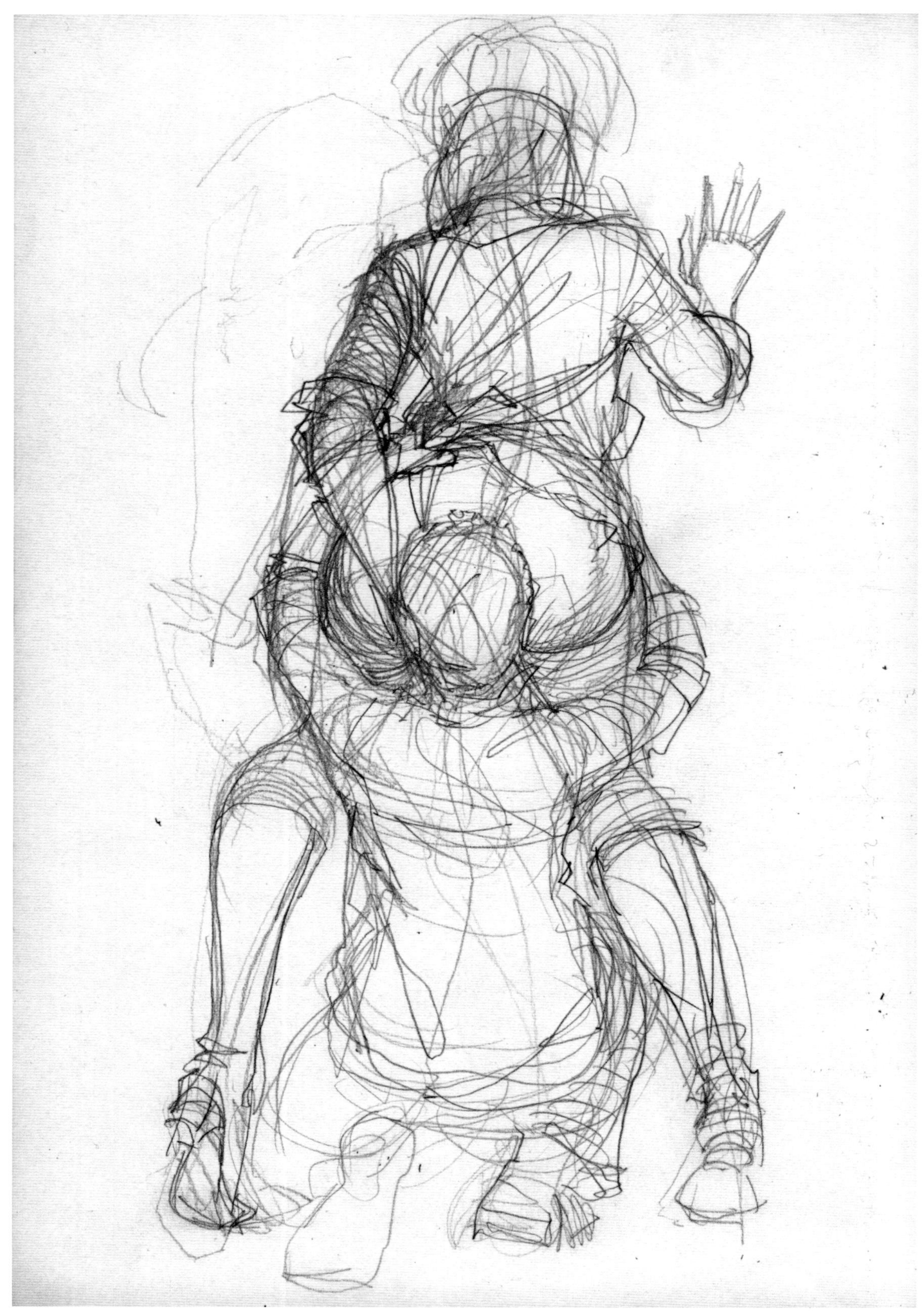

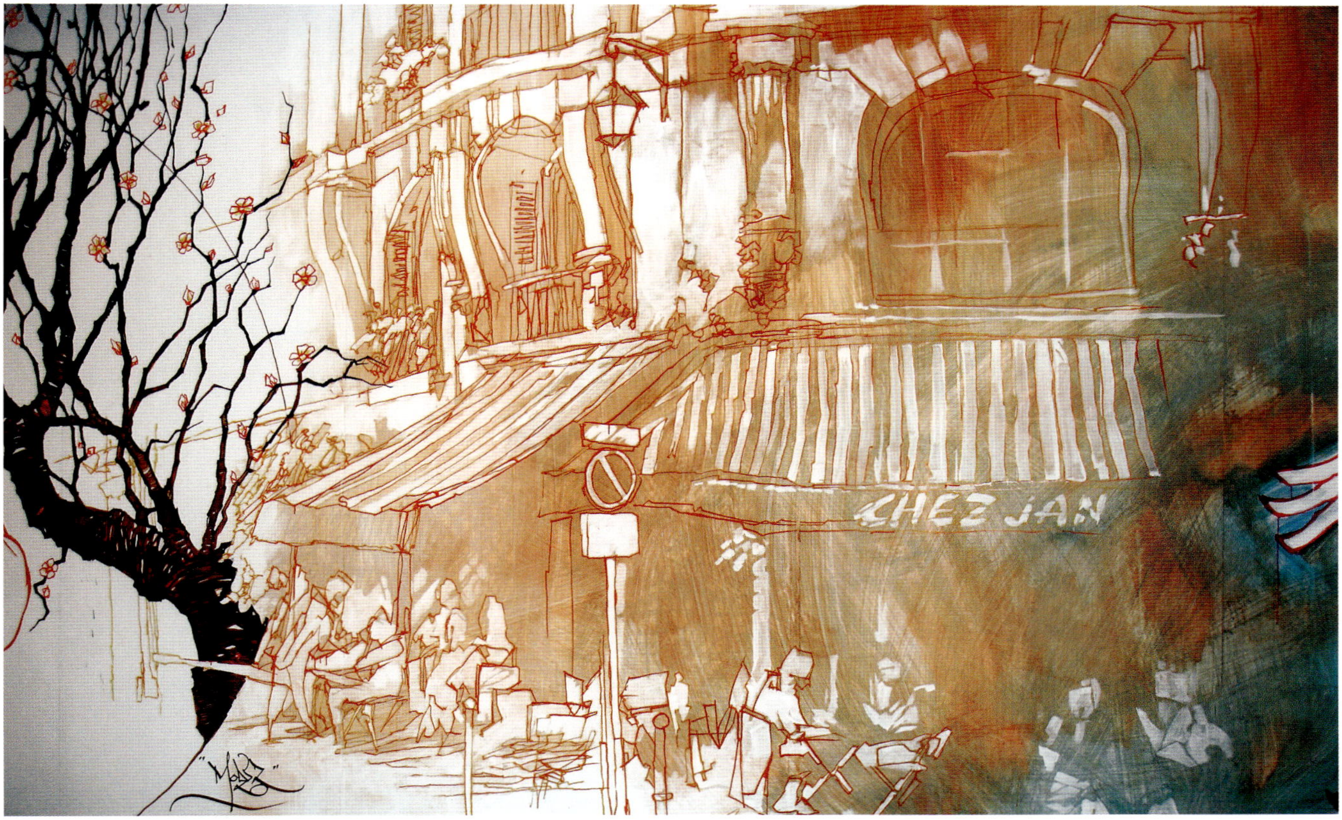

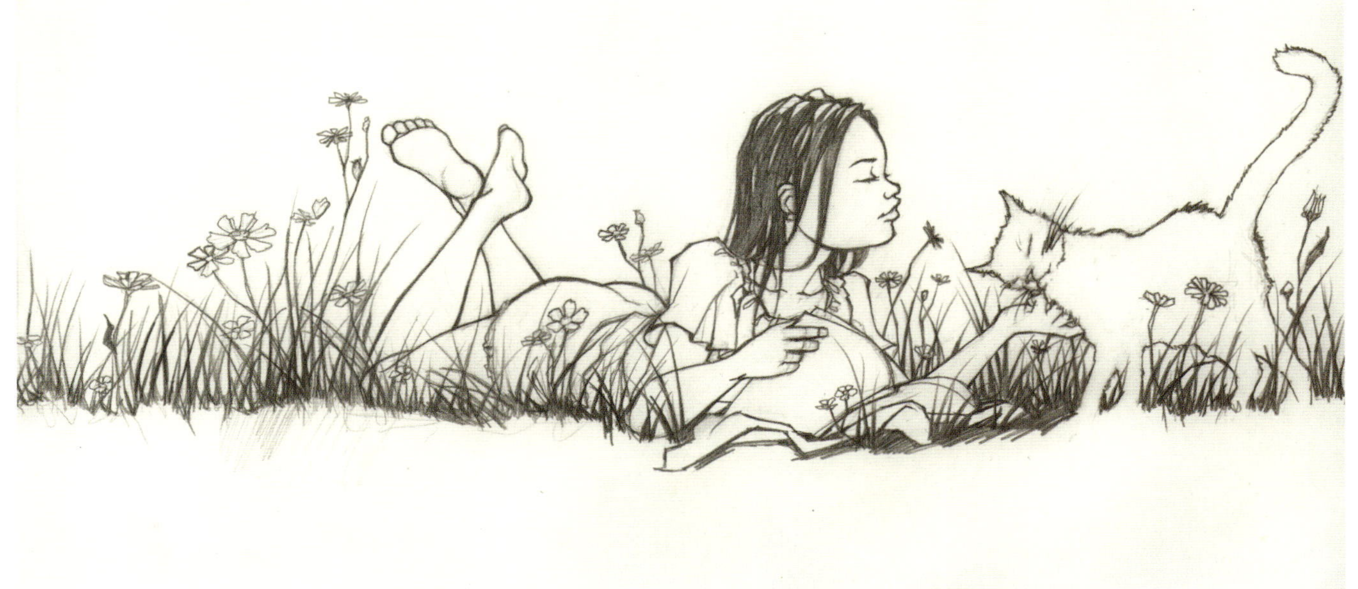

CHEZ JAN

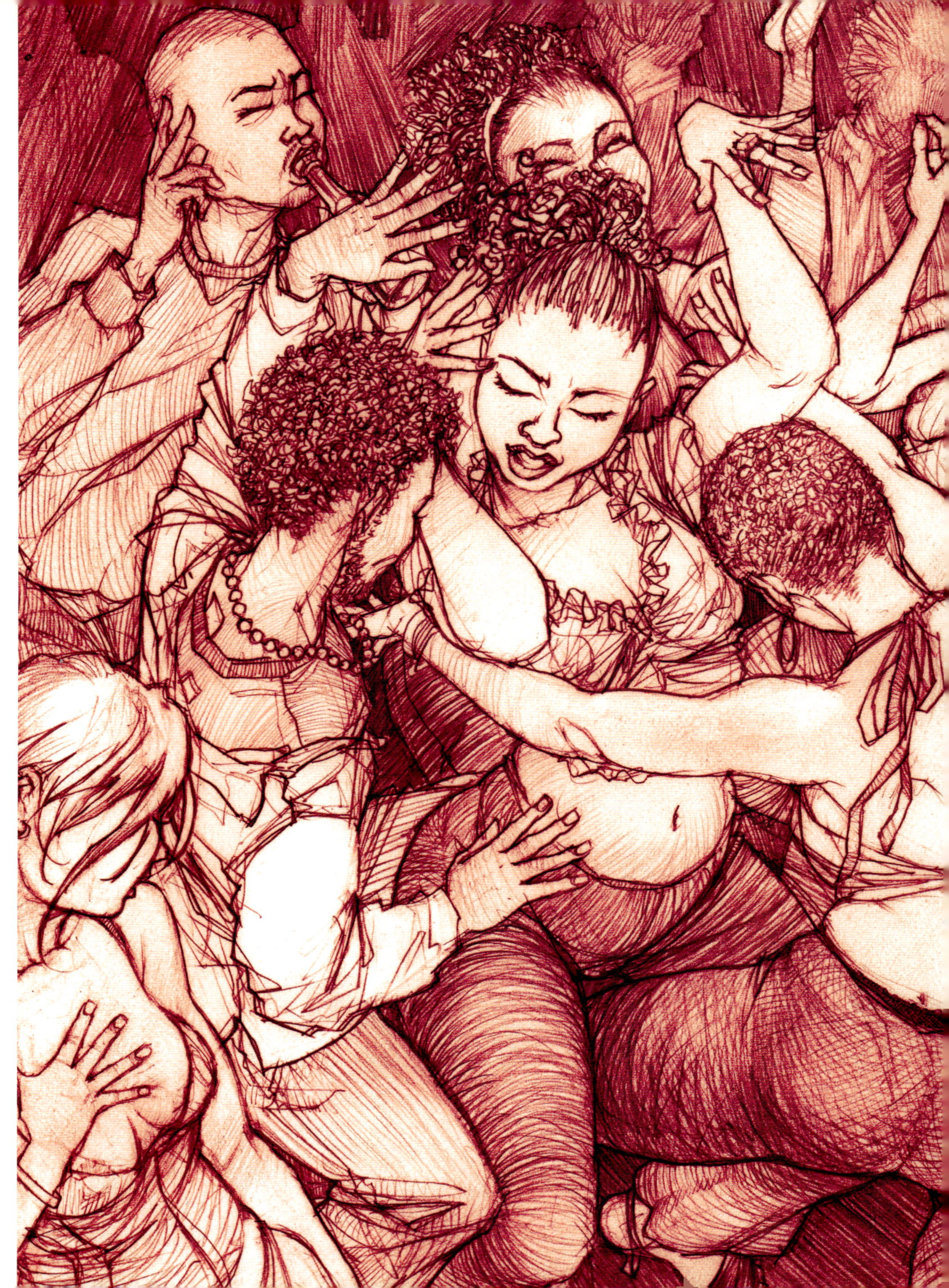

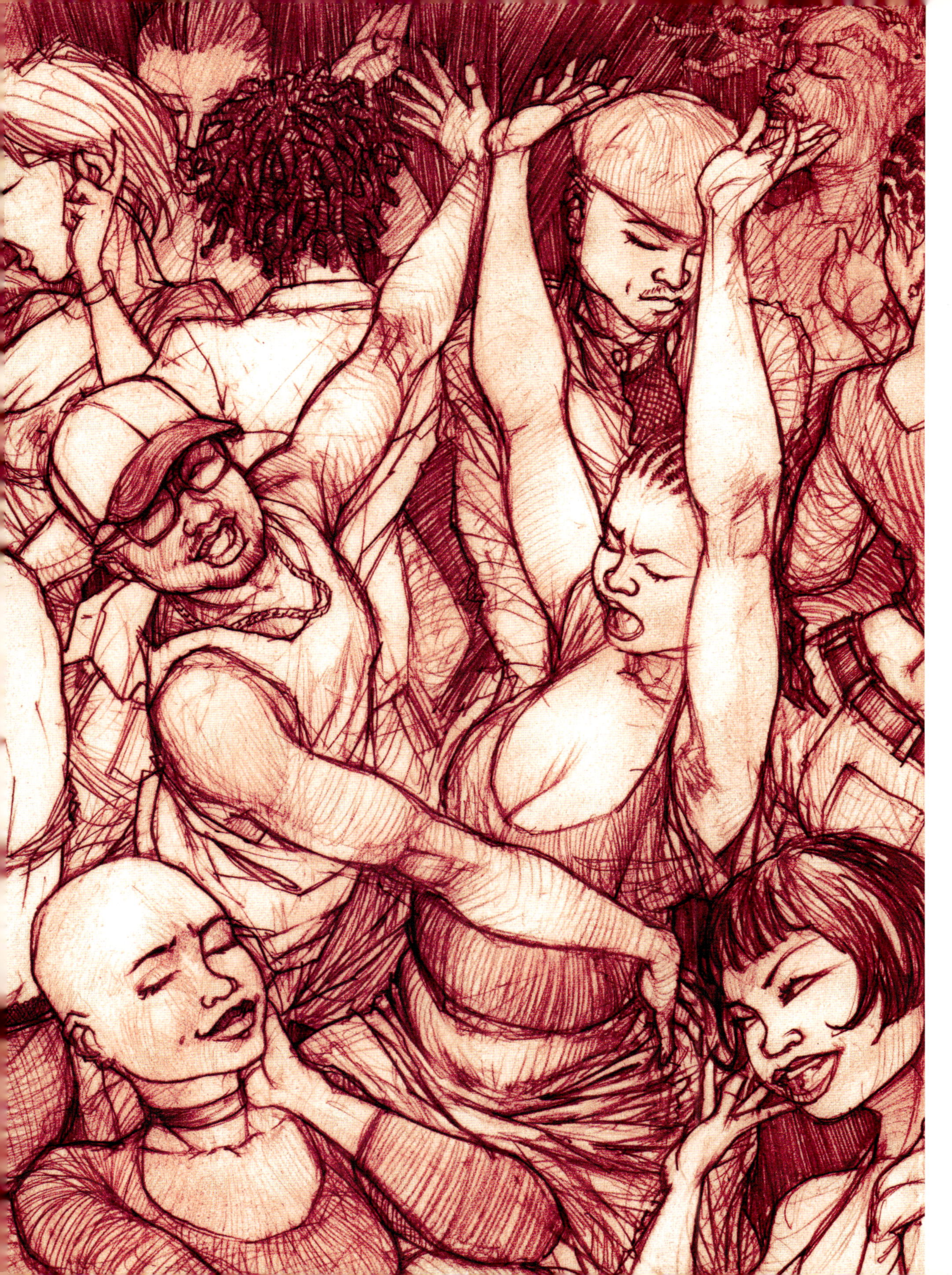

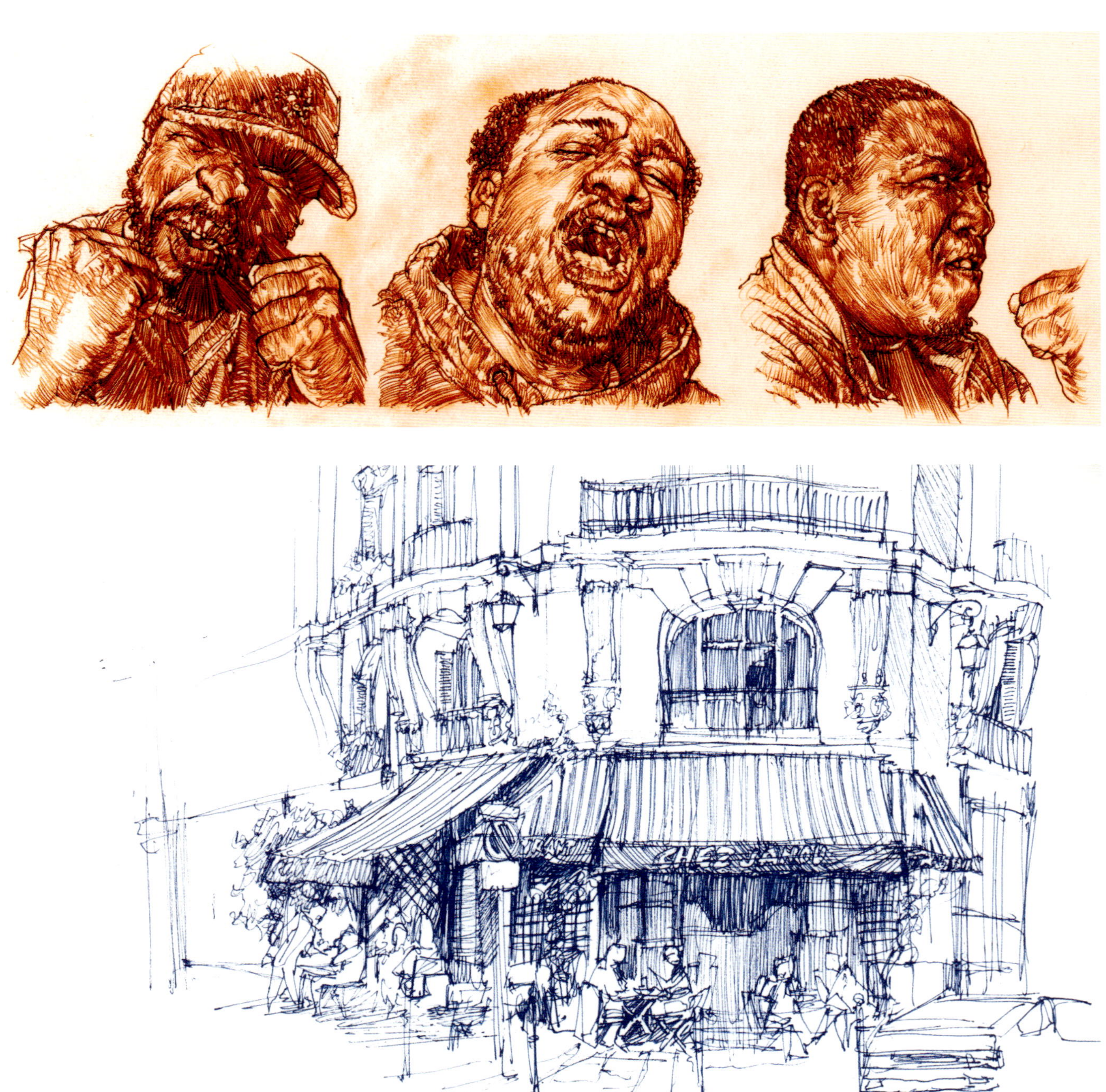

CHEZ JANOU

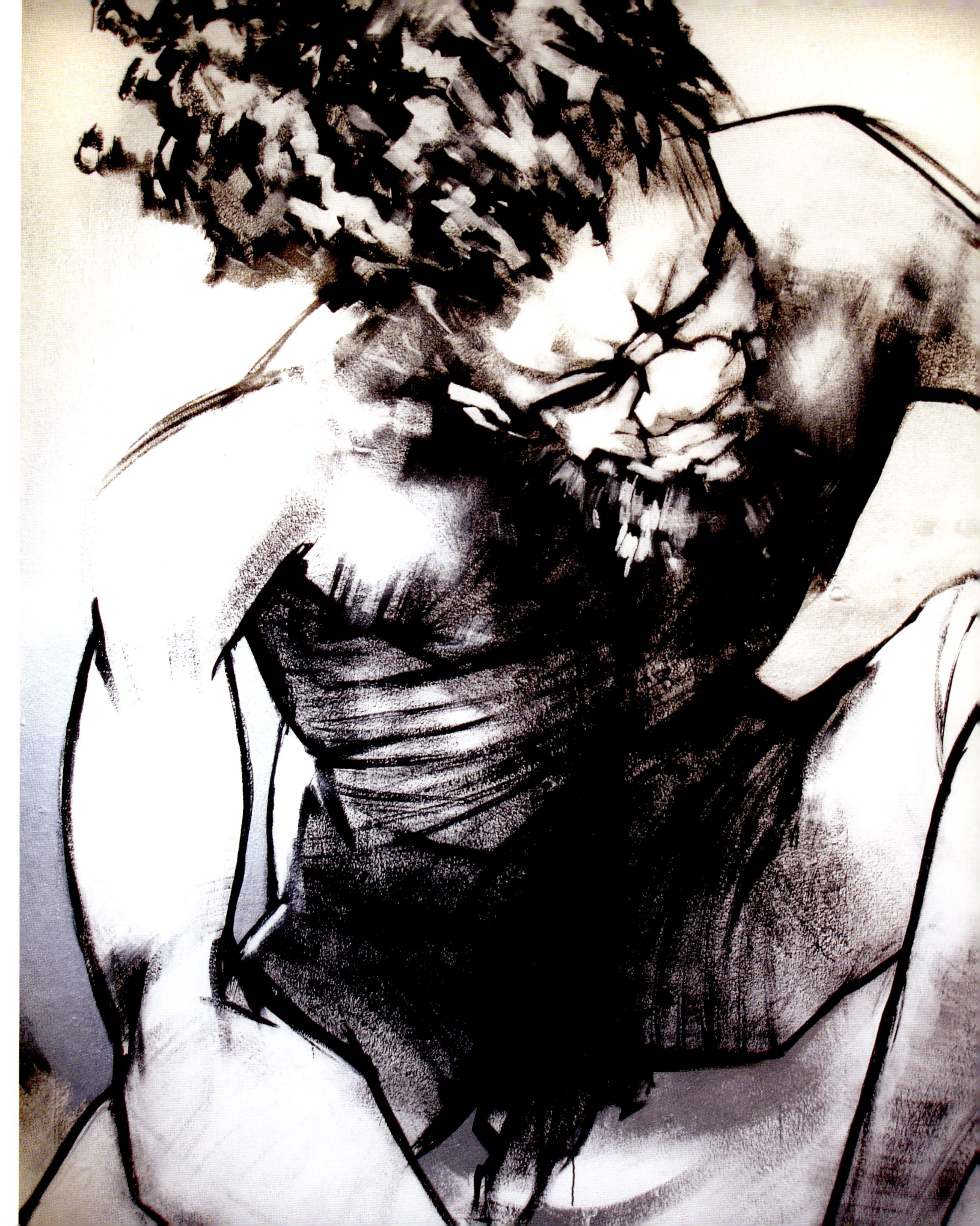

MORNING BREATH

While working in the art department at Think Skateboards, Doug Cunningham and Jason Noto bonded over their nostalgia for the '70s and '80s. "The world just looked different then," Cunningham muses. "Every business sign was unique, cars looked cooler, graffiti was relatively new, hip-hop and punk were just emerging, skateboarding was spreading…There's something exciting about a time when very few people knew what the fuck they were doing." Their shared interests led to a collaboration of illustration and design. In '02, the pair founded Morning Breath, an independent art studio based in New York. "It's about two individuals with similar tastes bringing two very different styles to the same canvas." Cunningham does the line drawing, while Noto adds the design elements—whether it's painting type or incorporating found objects. Morning Breath's work has achieved both commercial and personal success. They have created packages for a slew of musicians, and in '04 their work on AFI's Sing the Sorrow was nominated for a Grammy. Last year, Upper Playground released a book sampling some of their more personal work. "We feel that our biggest accomplishment has been making Morning Breath successful for us, both in terms of commercial and personal work," says Noto. "And keeping the integrity of both."

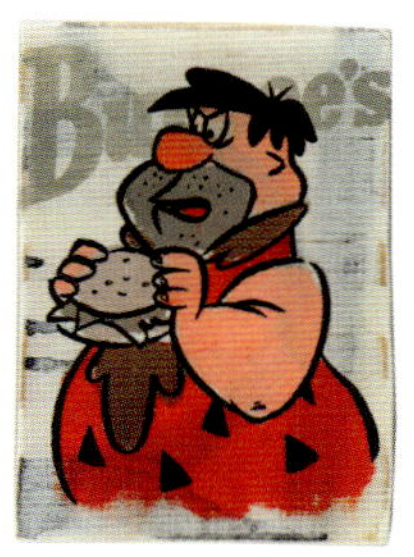
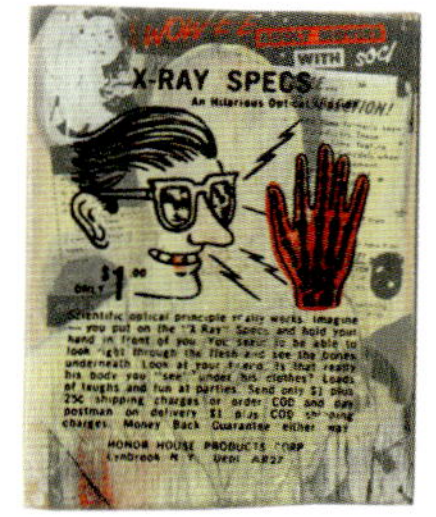

X-RAY SPECS
An Hilarious Optical Illusion!
ONLY $1 oo
HONOR HOUSE PRODUCTS CORP

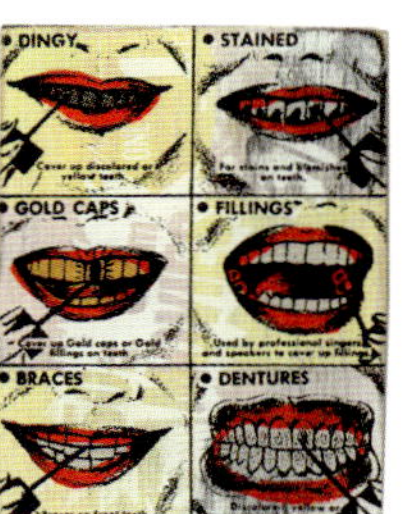

DINGY
STAINED
GOLD CAPS
FILLINGS
BRACES
DENTURES

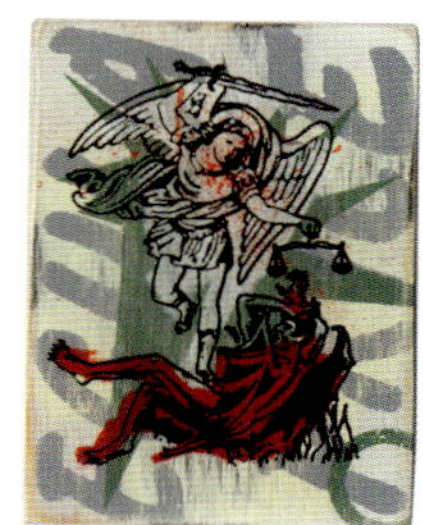

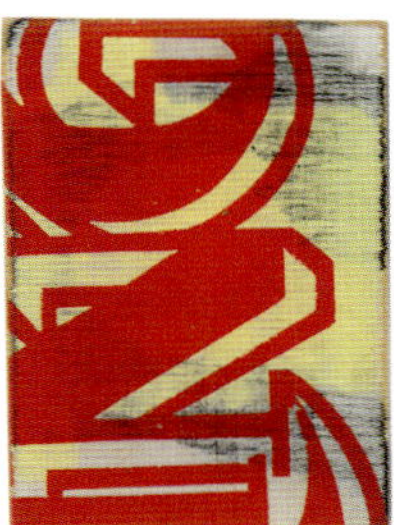
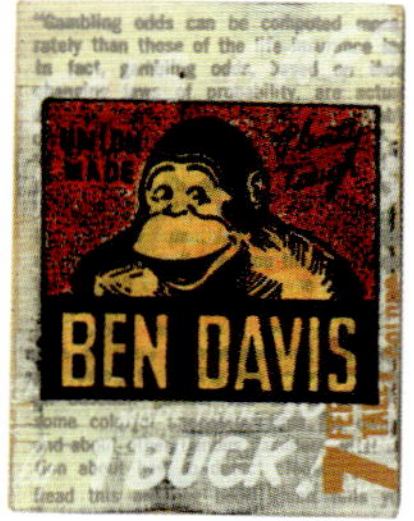

BEN DAVIS
BUCK!

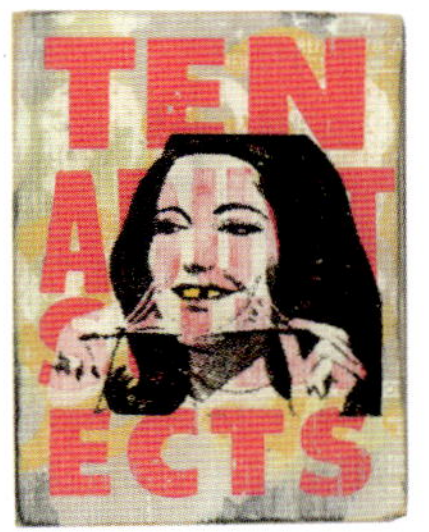

TEN
ECTS

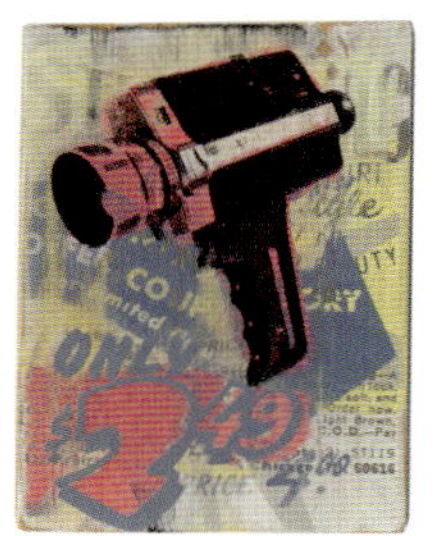

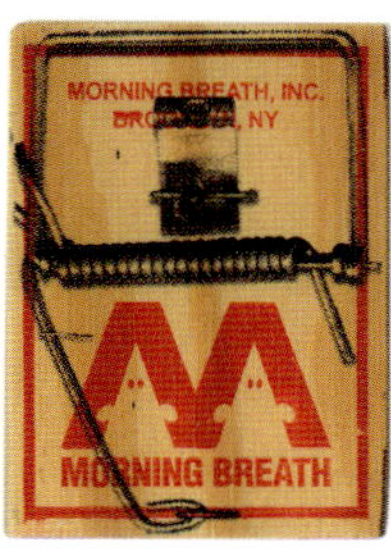

MORNING BREATH, INC.
BROOKLYN, NY
MORNING BREATH

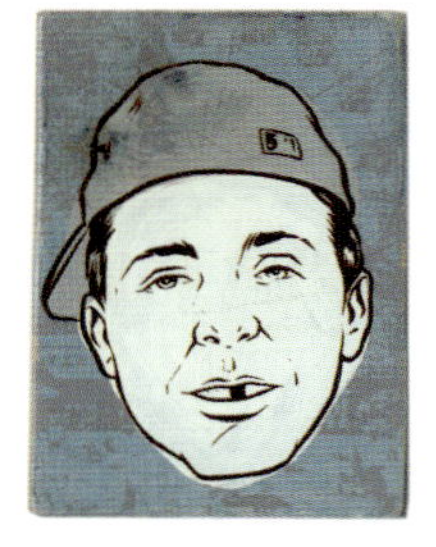
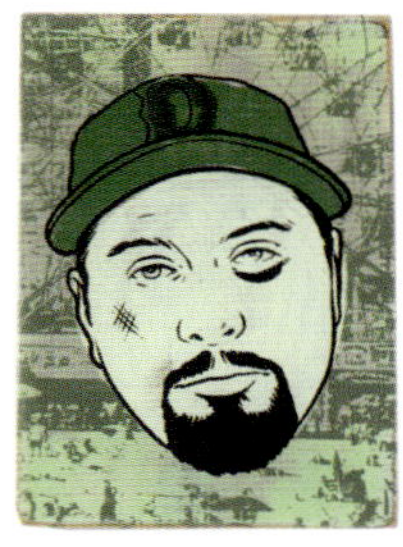
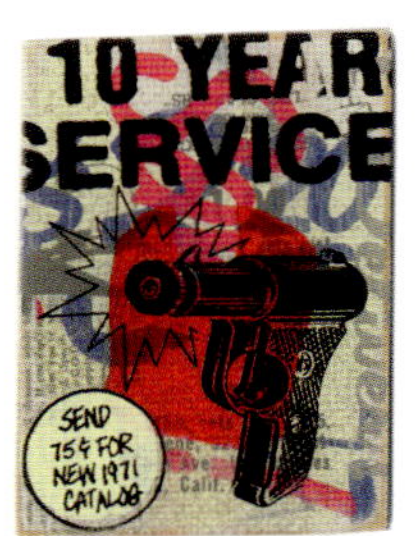

10 YEAR
SERVICE
SEND
75¢ FOR
NEW 1971
CATALOG

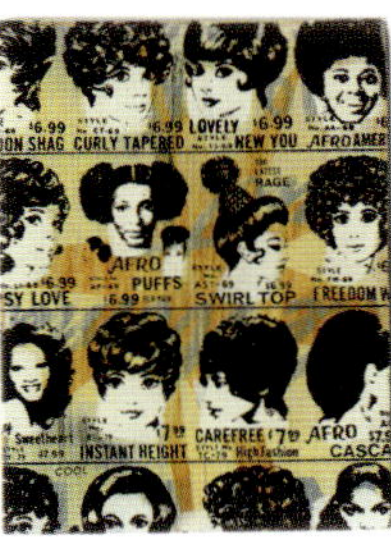

LOVELY
NEW YOU
CURLY TAPERED
AFRO
PUFFS
SWIRL TOP
FREEDOM
CAREFREE
AFRO
INSTANT HEIGHT

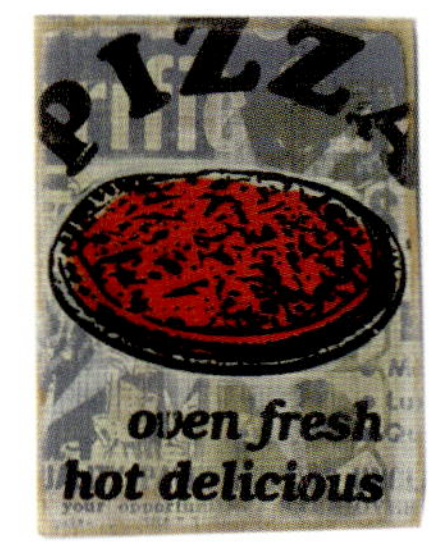

PIZZA
oven fresh
hot delicious

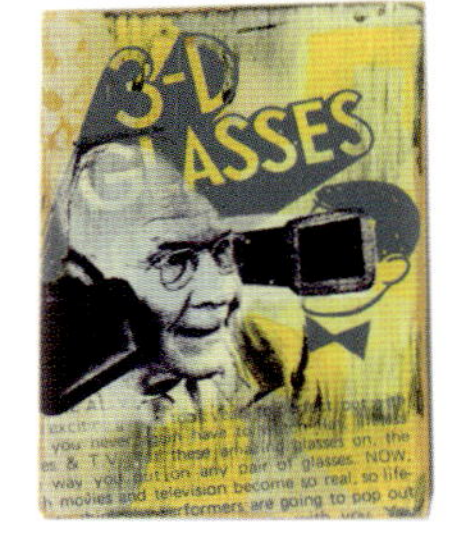

3-D
LASSES

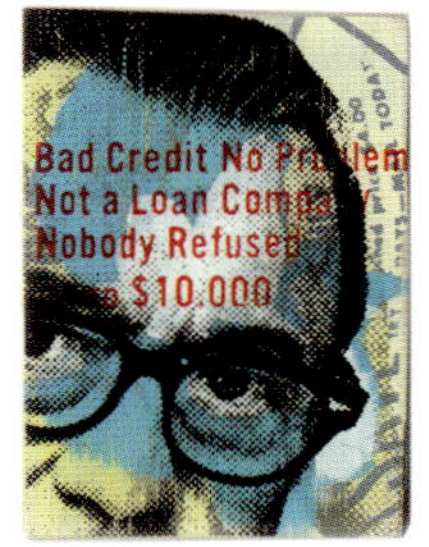

Bad Credit No Problem
Not a Loan Company
Nobody Refused
$10,000

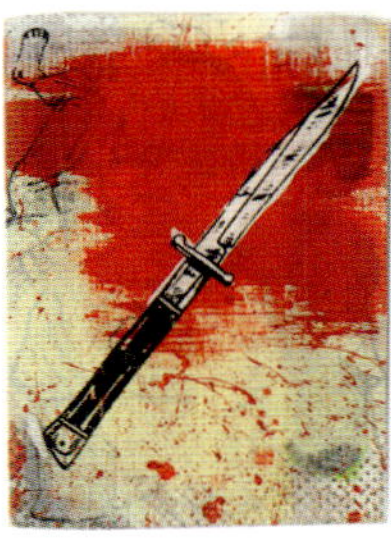
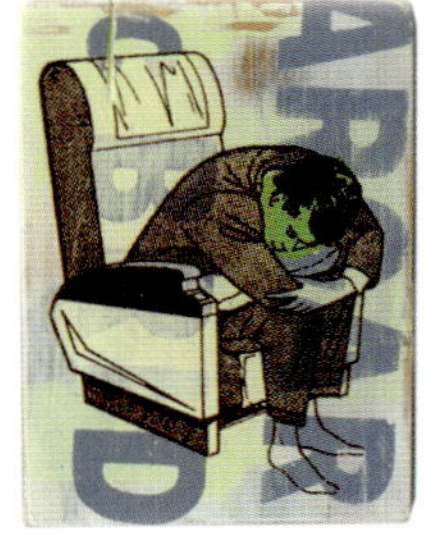
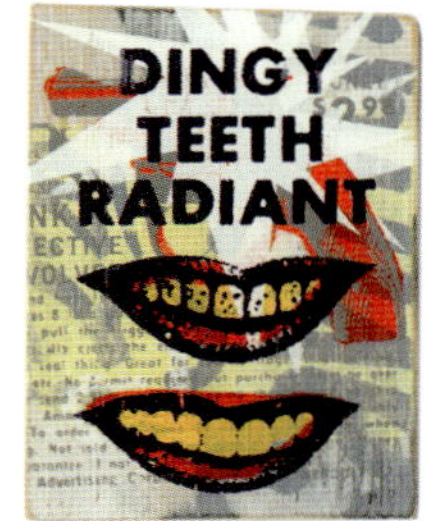

DINGY
TEETH
RADIANT

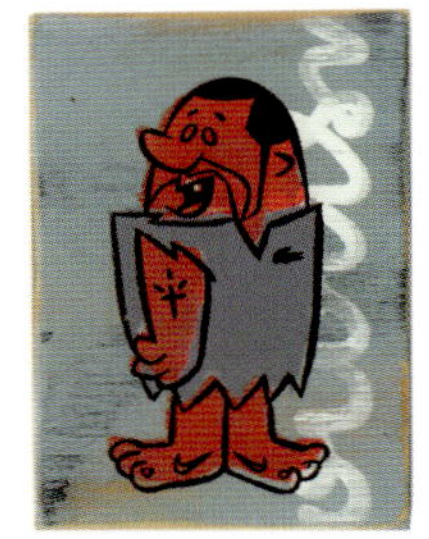

SSING?
YOU NOW!

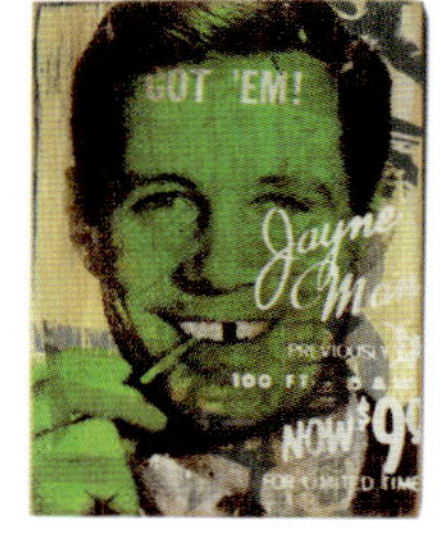

GOT 'EM!
Jayne Man
100 FT
NOW 9
FOR LIMITED TIME

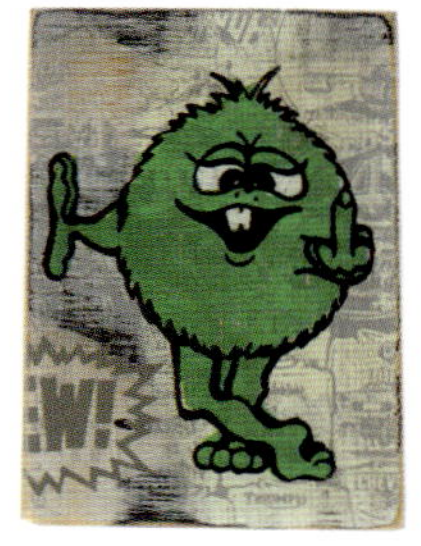
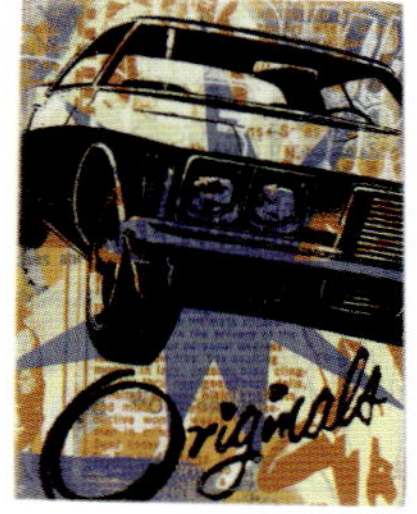

Originals

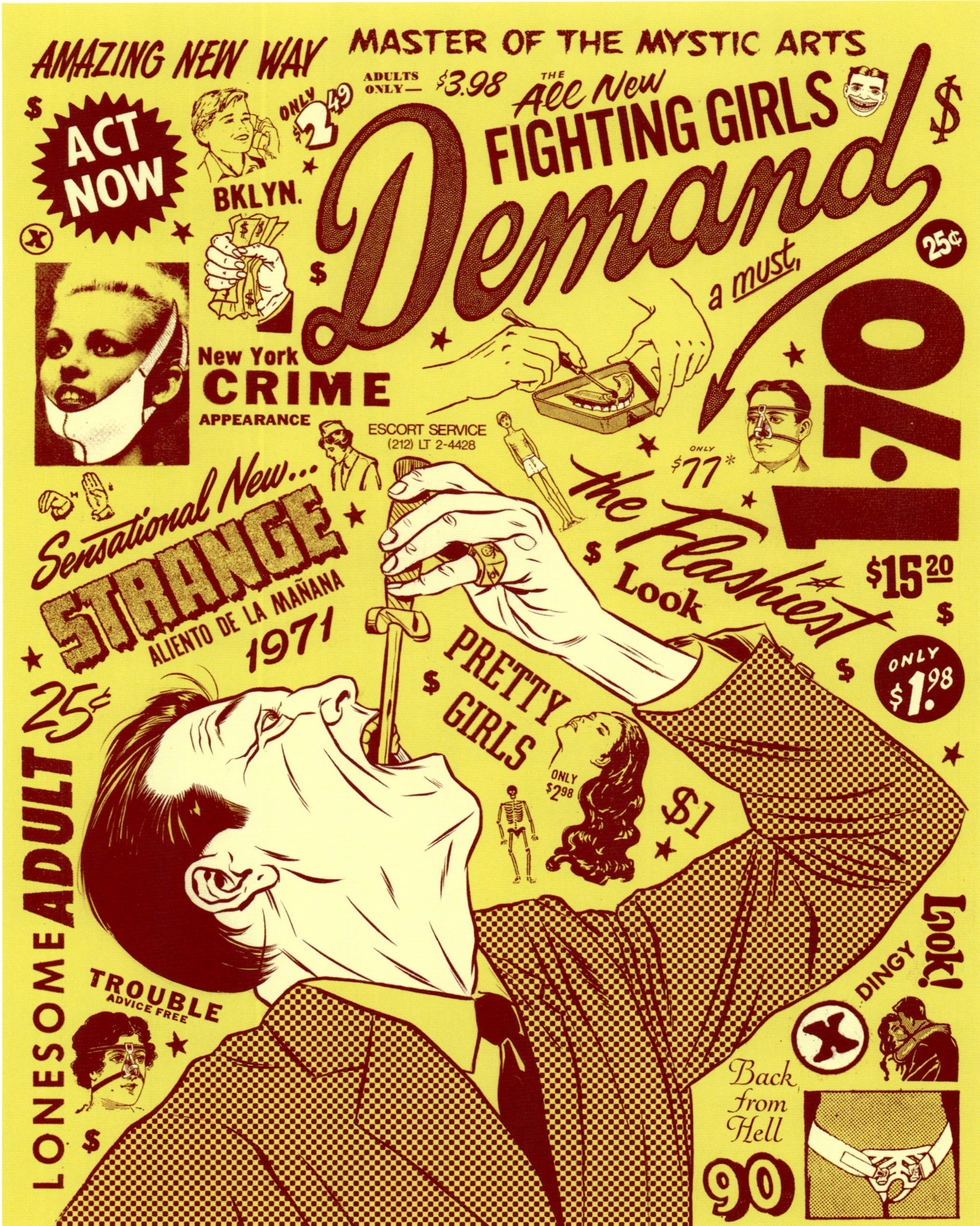

AMAZING NEW WAY
MASTER OF THE MYSTIC ARTS
ACT NOW
$
ONLY $2.49
ADULTS ONLY— $3.98
THE All New
FIGHTING GIRLS
$
BKLYN.
Demand
$
25¢
New York
CRIME
APPEARANCE
a must
ONLY $77*
1.70
Sensational New...
STRANGE
ALIENTO DE LA MAÑANA
1971
ESCORT SERVICE
(212) LT 2-4428
the Flashiest
$ Look
$15.20
$
25¢
$1.98
ONLY $1.98
LONESOME ADULT
25¢
PRETTY GIRLS
$
ONLY $2.98
$1
$
TROUBLE
ADVICE FREE
$
Back from Hell
90
DINGY
Look!

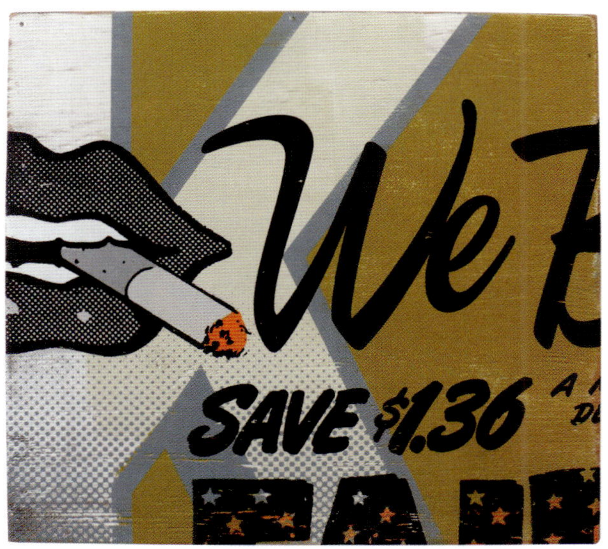

We
SAVE $1.36

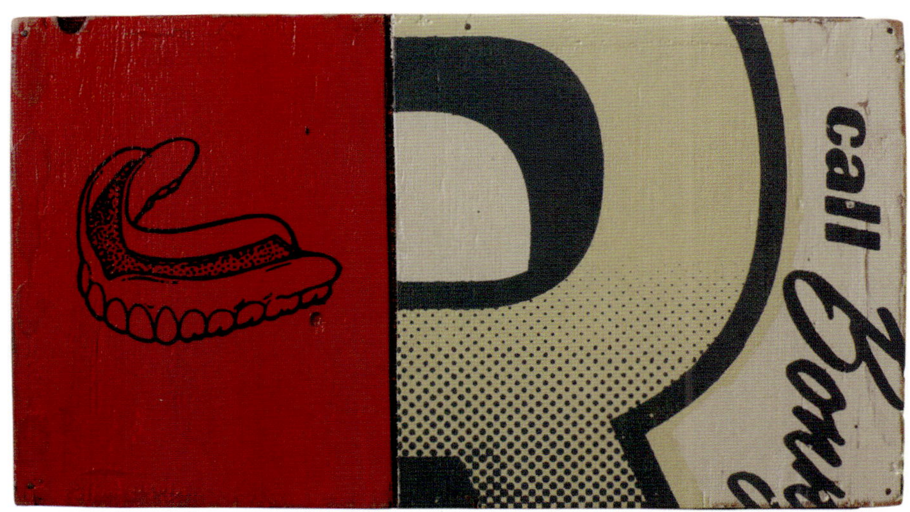

call

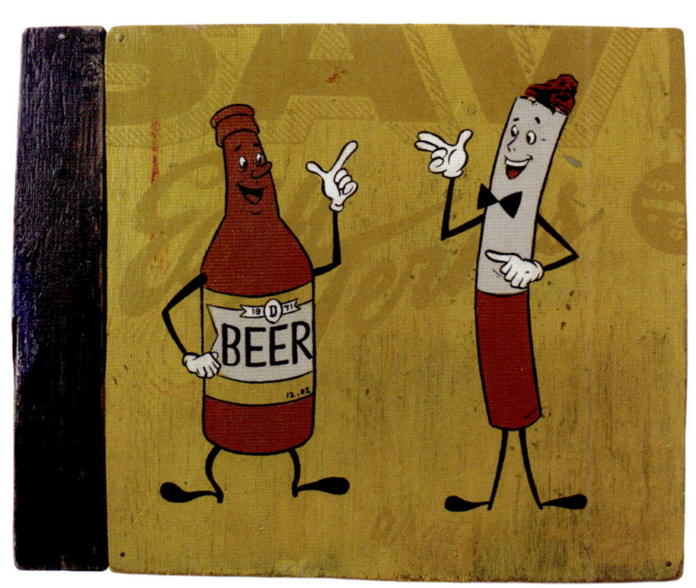

BEER

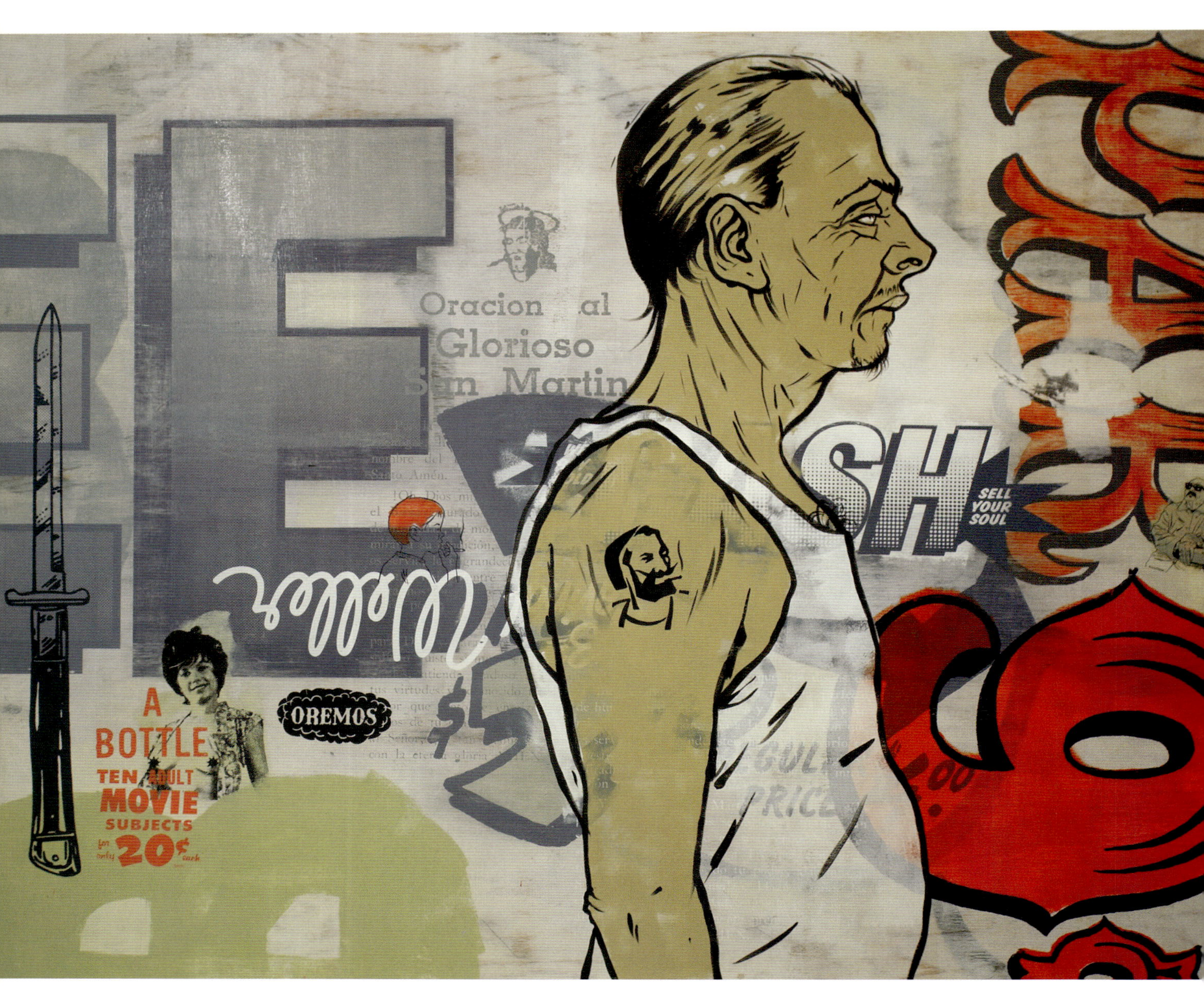

Oracion al
Glorioso
San Martin
A
BOTTLE
TEN ADULT
MOVIE
SUBJECTS
20¢
OREMOS
SELL
YOUR
SOUL

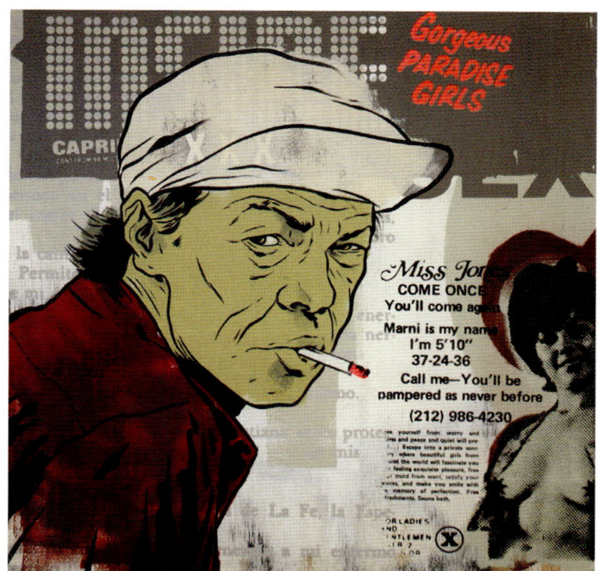
Gorgeous
PARADISE
GIRLS
CAPRI
Miss Jones
COME ONCE
You'll come again
Marni is my name
I'm 5'10"
37-24-36
Call me—You'll be
pampered as never before
(212) 986-4230

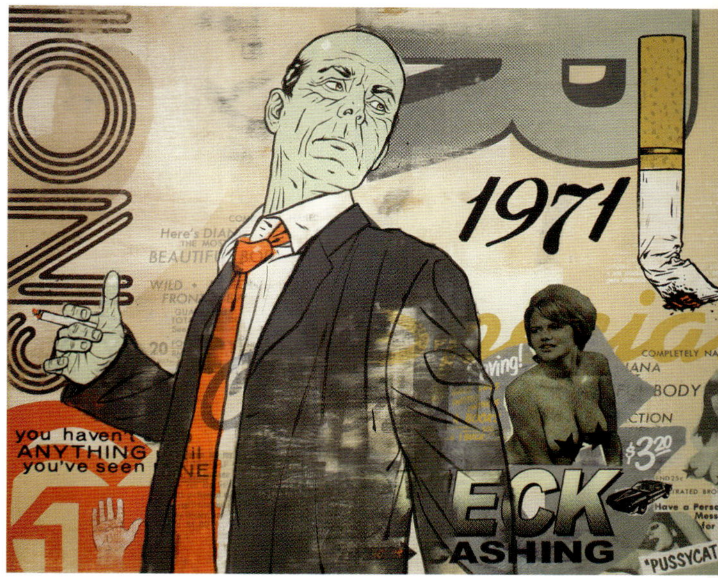
1971
Here's DIA
THE MO
BEAUTIF
WILD
FRON
you haven't
ANYTHING
you've seen
ECK
ASHING
COMPLETELY NA
BODY
CTION
$3.20
*PUSSYCAT

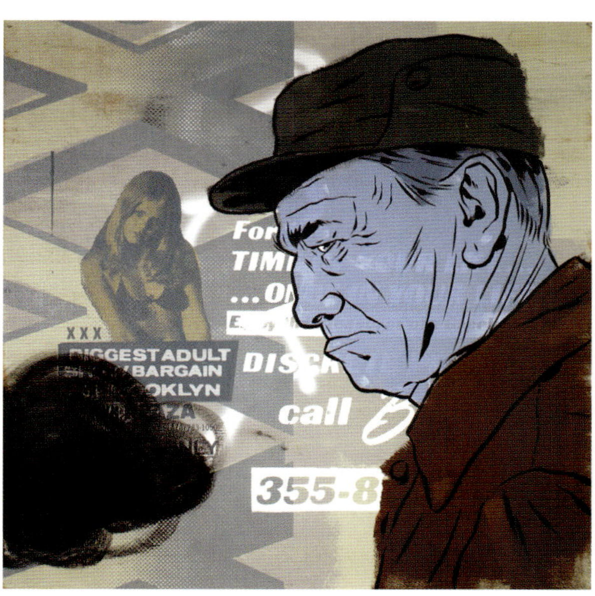
For
TIMI
...ON
DISC
call
355-8
XXX
BIGGESTADULT
BARGAIN
OKLYN

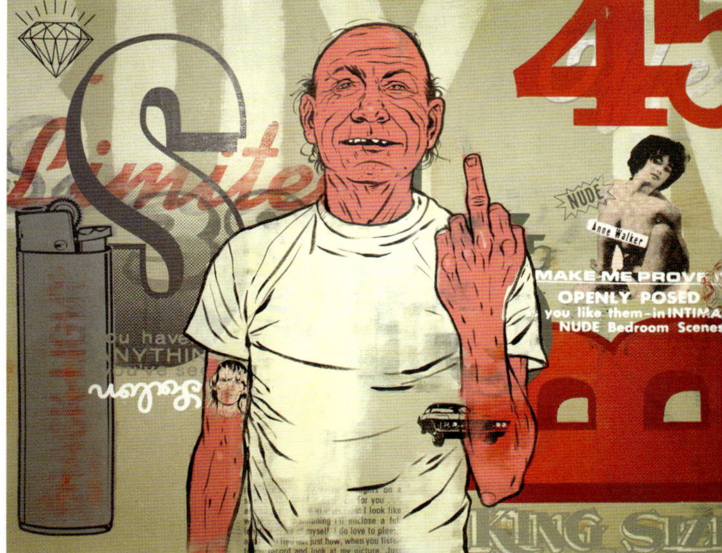
4
Limite
NUDE
Anne Waller
MAKE ME PROVE
OPENLY POSED
you like them—in INTIMA
NUDE Bedroom Scenes
ou have
ANYTHIN
KING SIZ

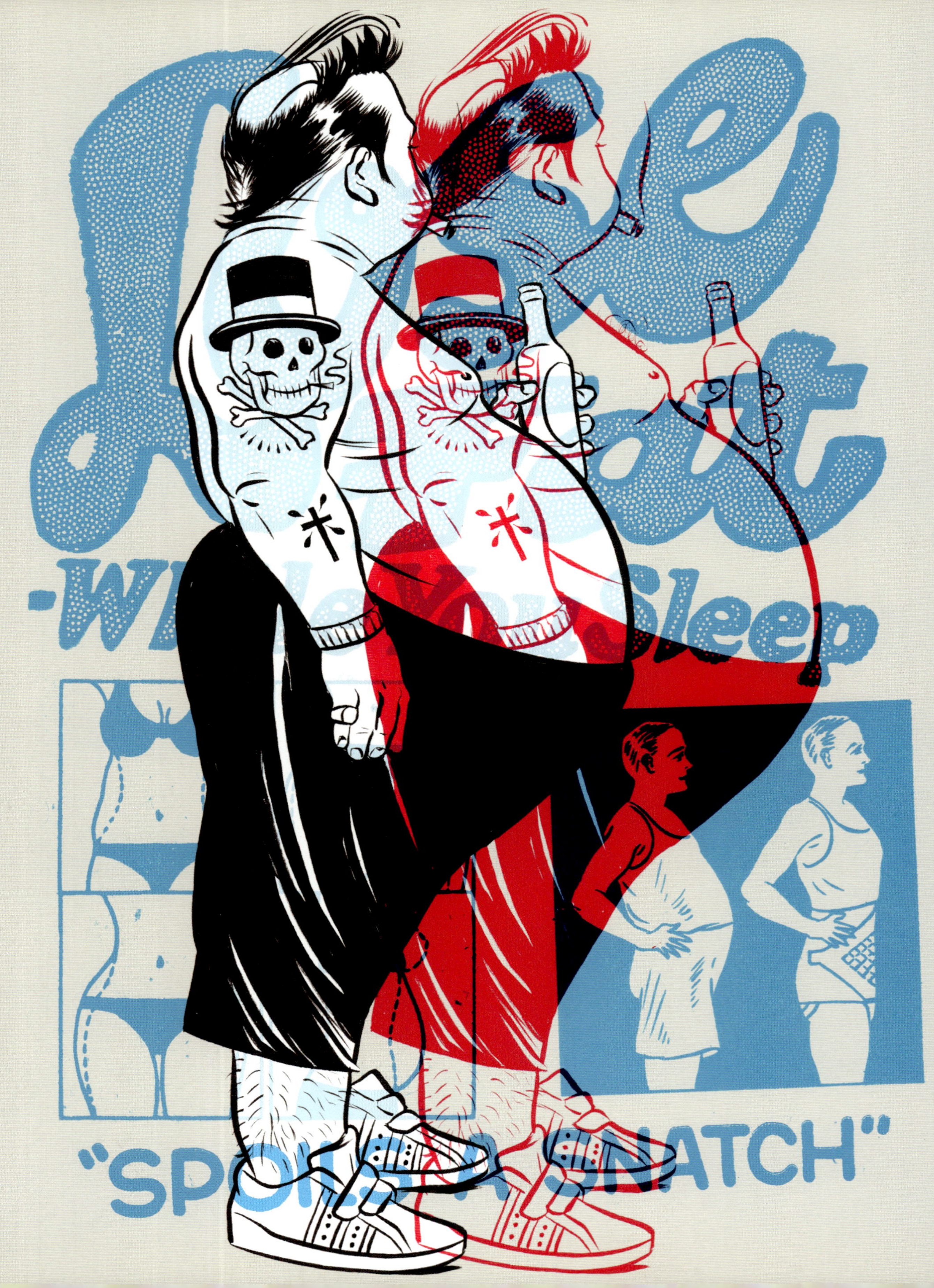
Life
-While you sleep
"SPORTS A SNATCH"

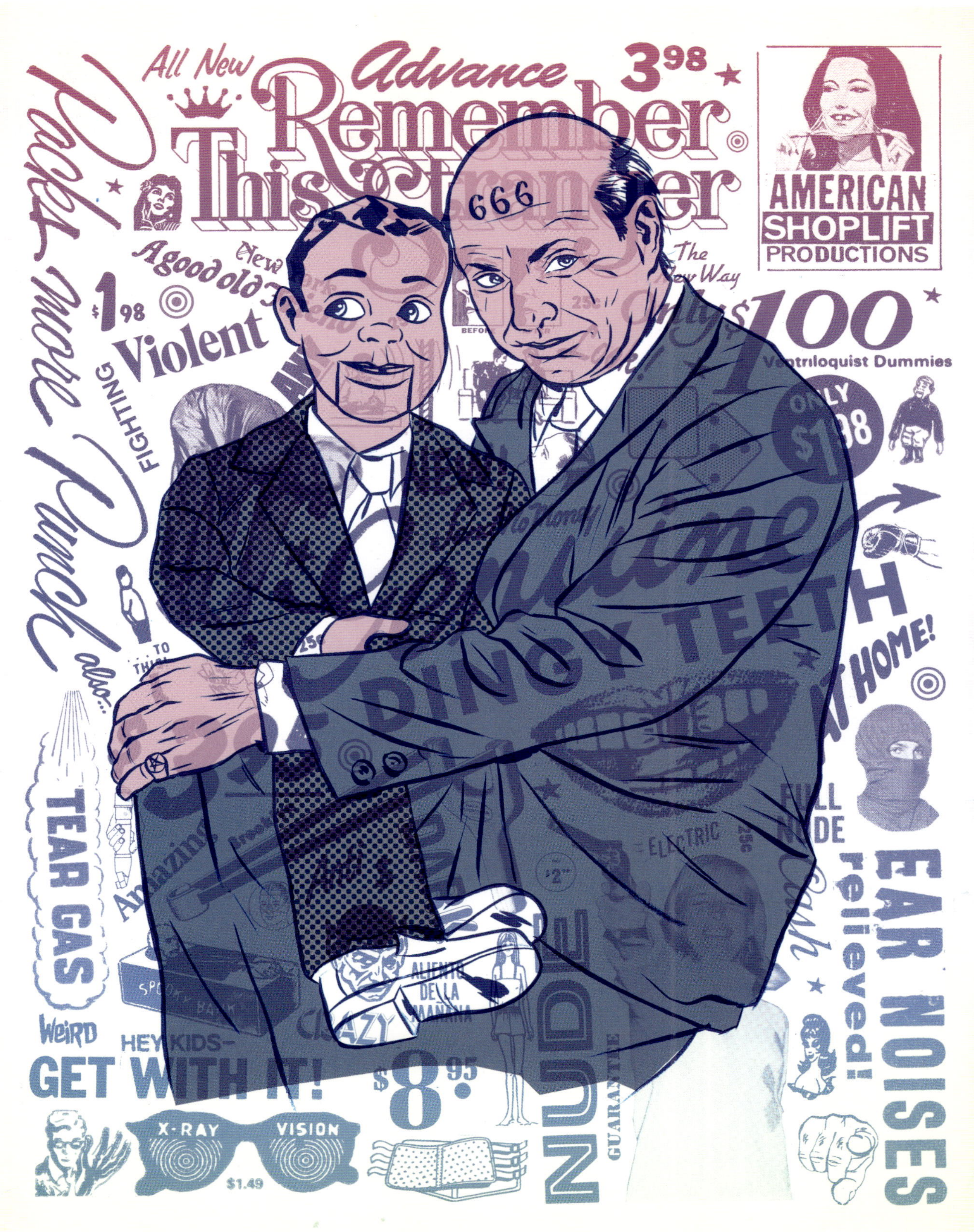
All New
Advance
3 98
Remember
This Stranger
Pack
$1 98
New
A good old
Violent
FIGHTING
AMERICAN SHOPLIFT PRODUCTIONS
666
The
New Way
$100
Ventriloquist Dummies
ONLY $1 98
Punch also...
PINKY TEETH
AT HOME!
TEAR GAS
Weird
HEY KIDS—
GET WITH IT!
ALIENTO DELLA MATTINA
NUDE
GUARANTE
$8 95
X-RAY VISION
$1.49
FULL NUDE
EAR NOISES relieved!
ELECTRIC

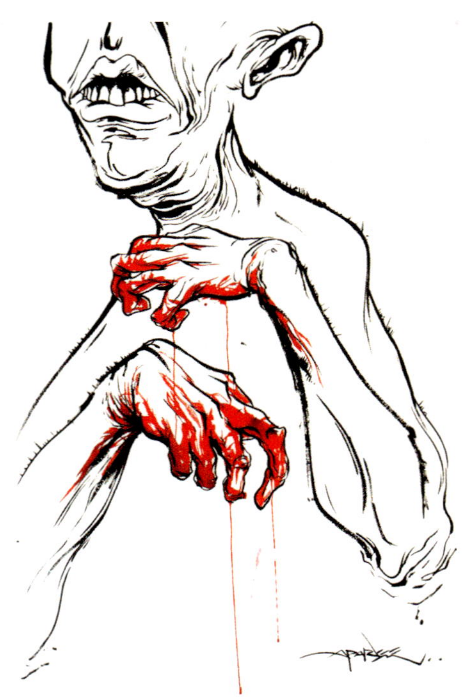

ALEX PARDEE

San Francisco Bay Area bred Alex Pardee applies graffiti's DIY ethic to his work. "I bypassed a publisher and spent my own money and effort hand printing books and secretly shoving them in people's faces by putting stacks of them on the shelves of record stores, bathrooms—anywhere." His persistence has paid off. His first major project culminated in a comic with illustrator Sam Kieth. Not only an art director and package designer for a number of bands, his book "Bunnywith" has sold more than 8,000 copies; and he recently held his first solo exhibition in San Francisco. Of his self-reliant approach, Pardee says, "It's probably the slowest, most gradual way to excel at anything, but I think it's the most rewarding." However, the road was not without bumps. At 14, Pardee was diagnosed with an anxiety disorder and depression and placed in a mental hospital. It was there that he began using art as a therapeutic outlet—a practice he still employs today. But his work—described as a "vibrant undead circus sideshow," reflects the tangled thoughts that still linger in his mind. "And with the things I think about," he says, "who knows what would happen if I didn't draw."

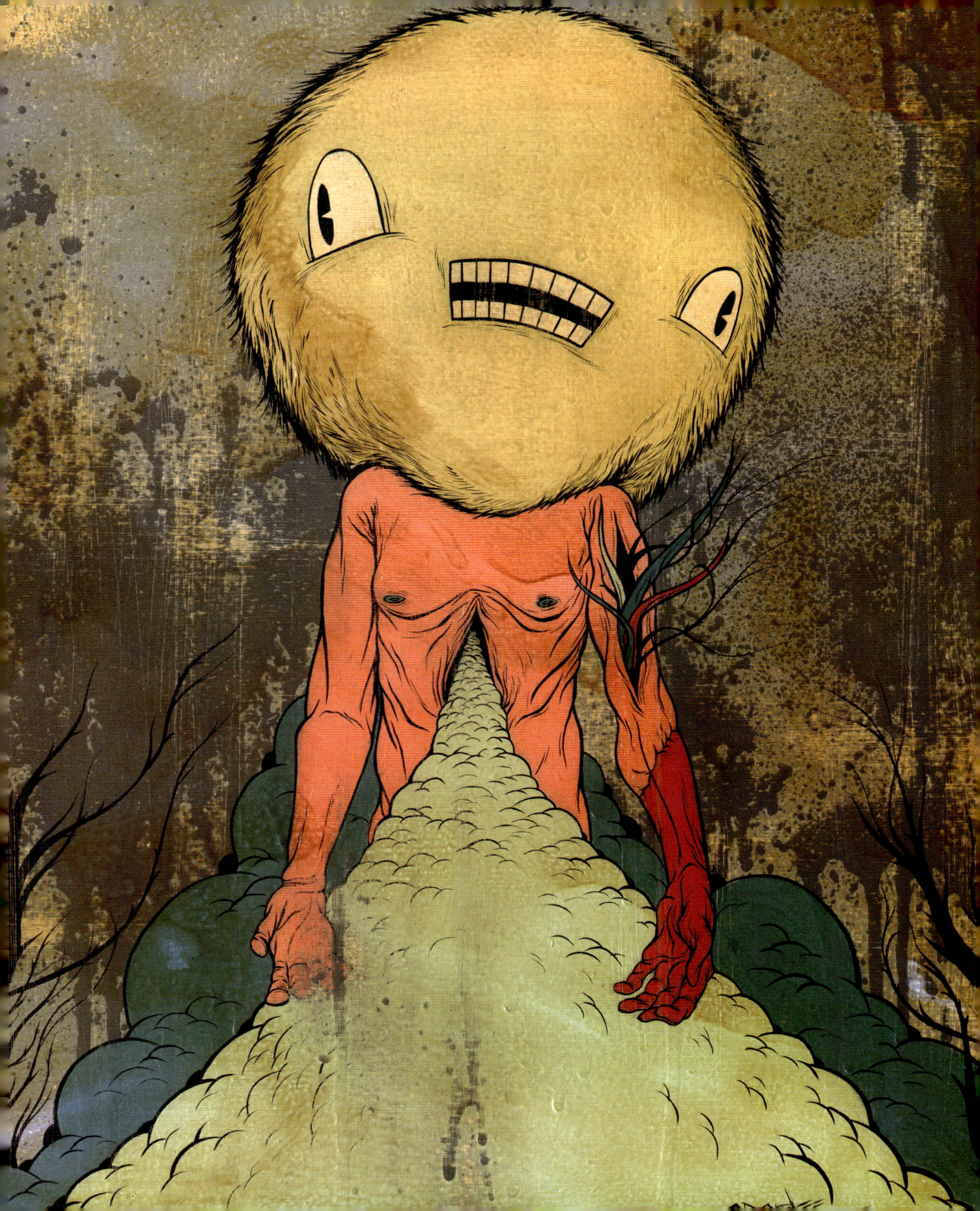

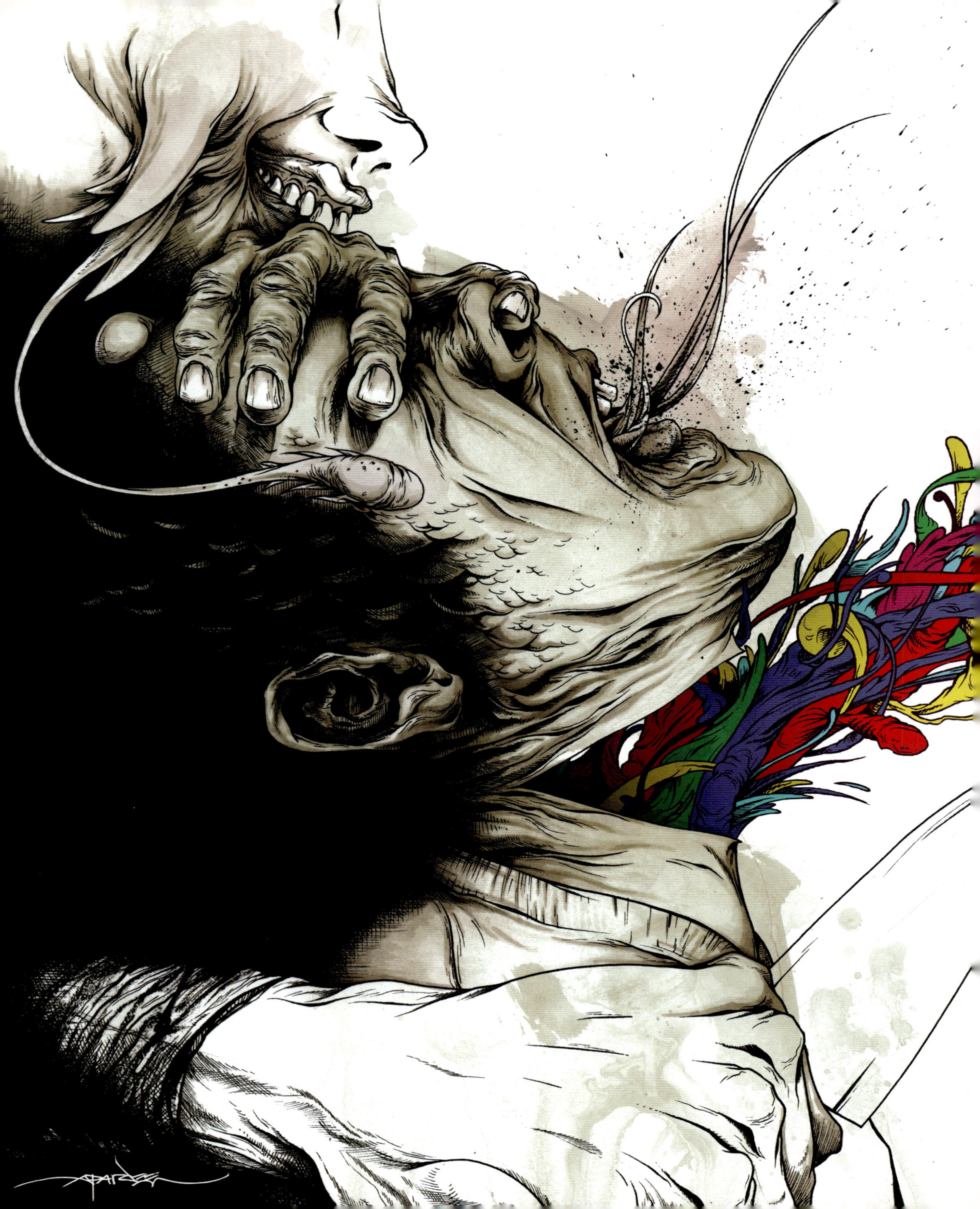

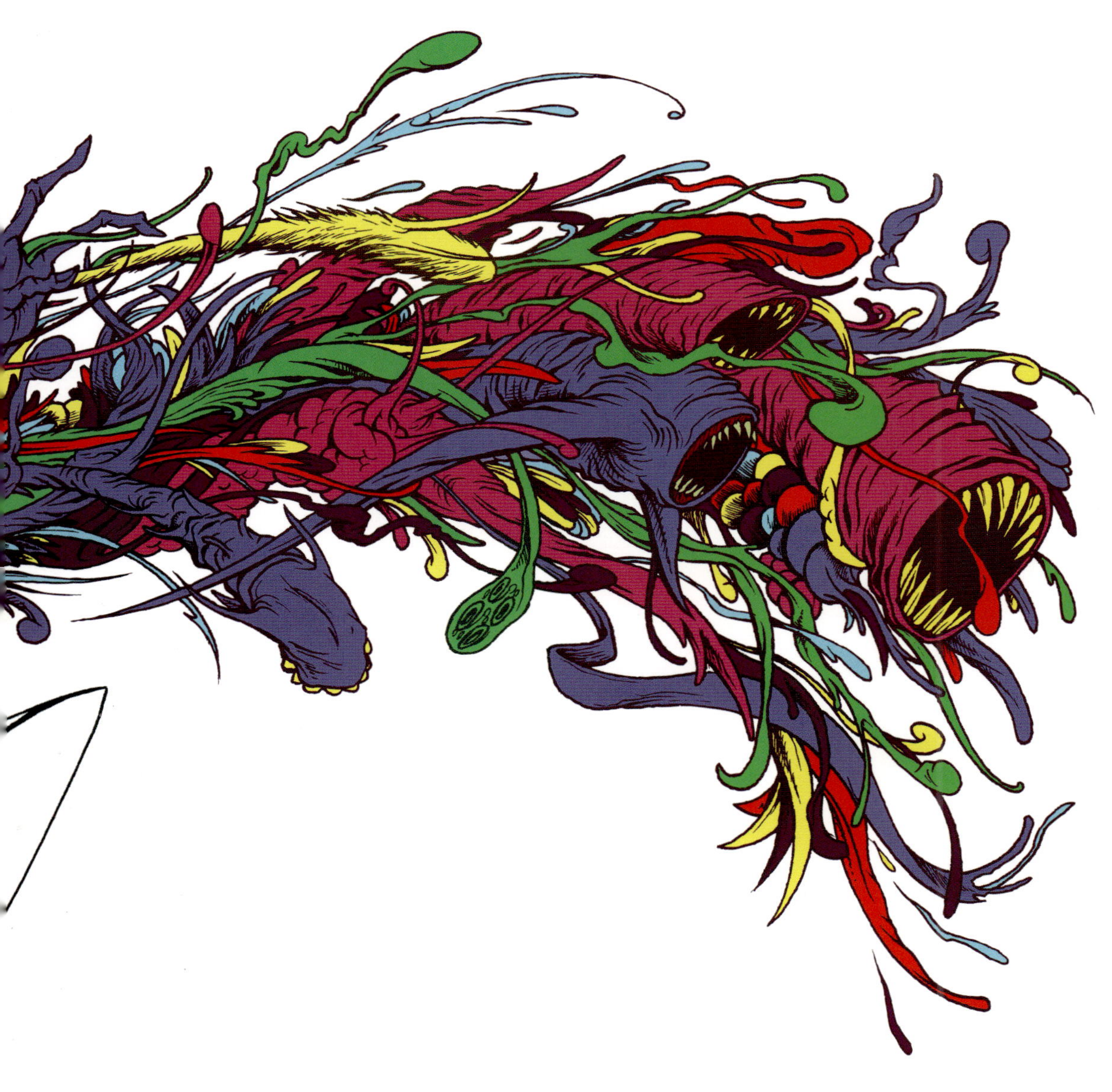

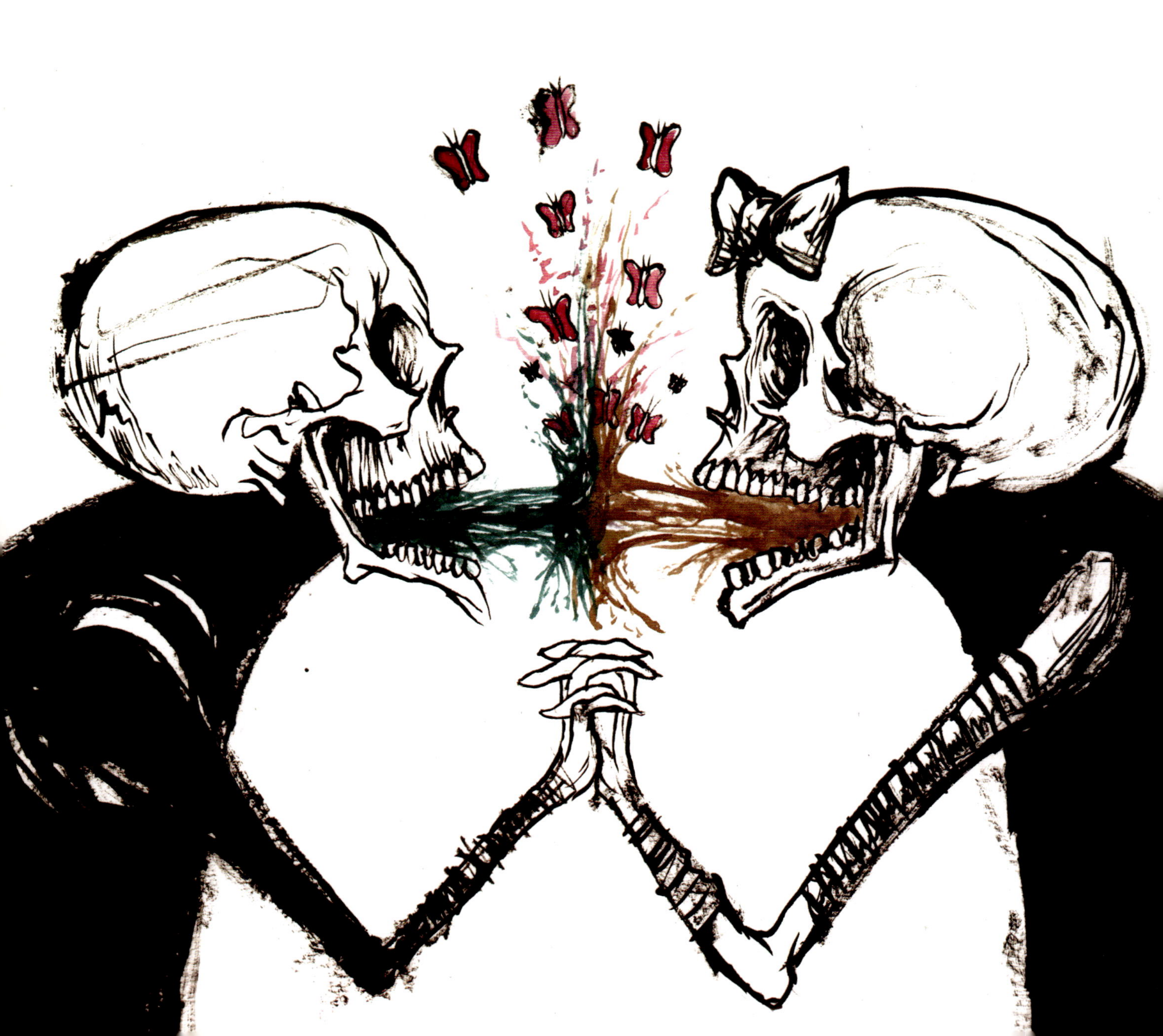

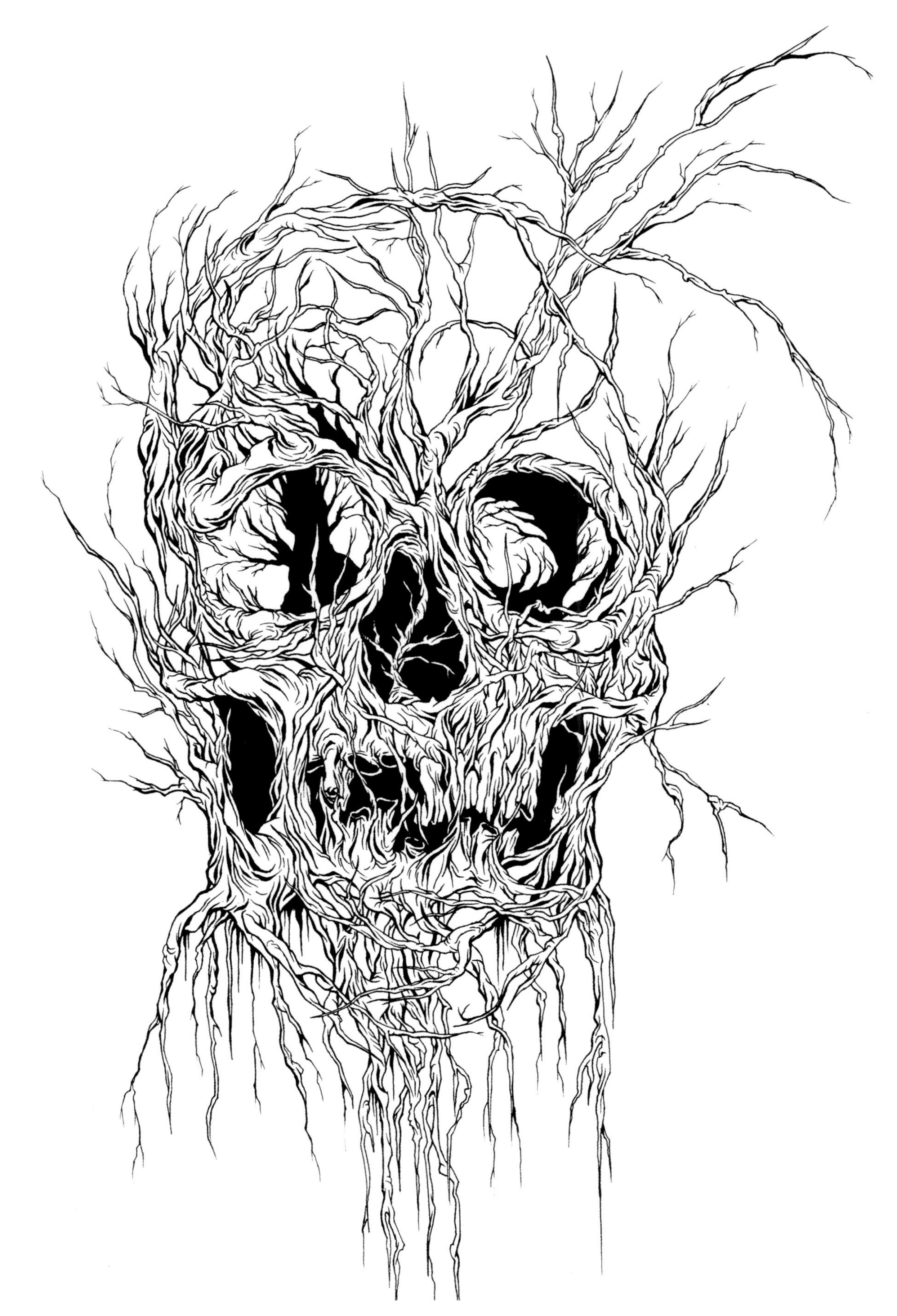

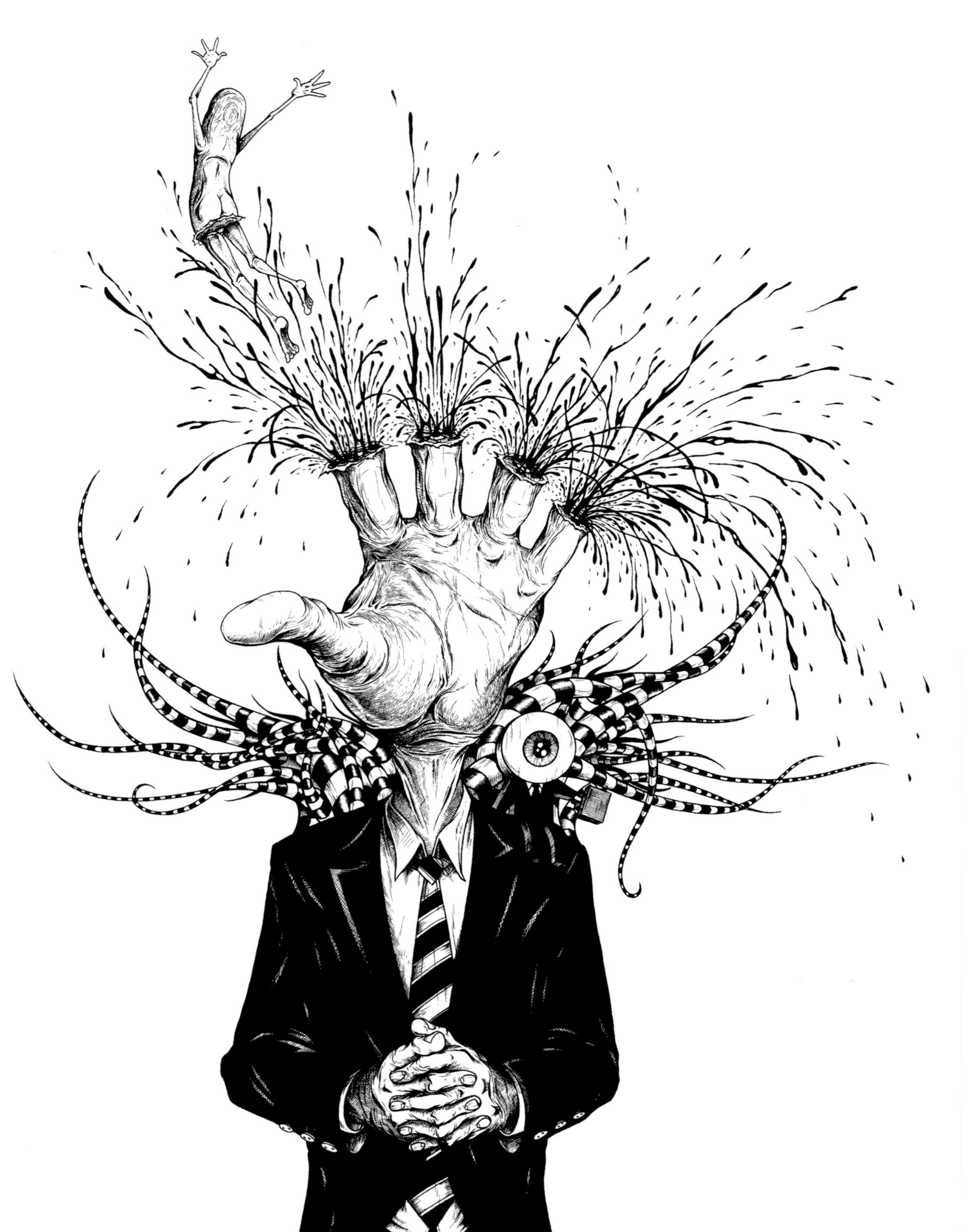

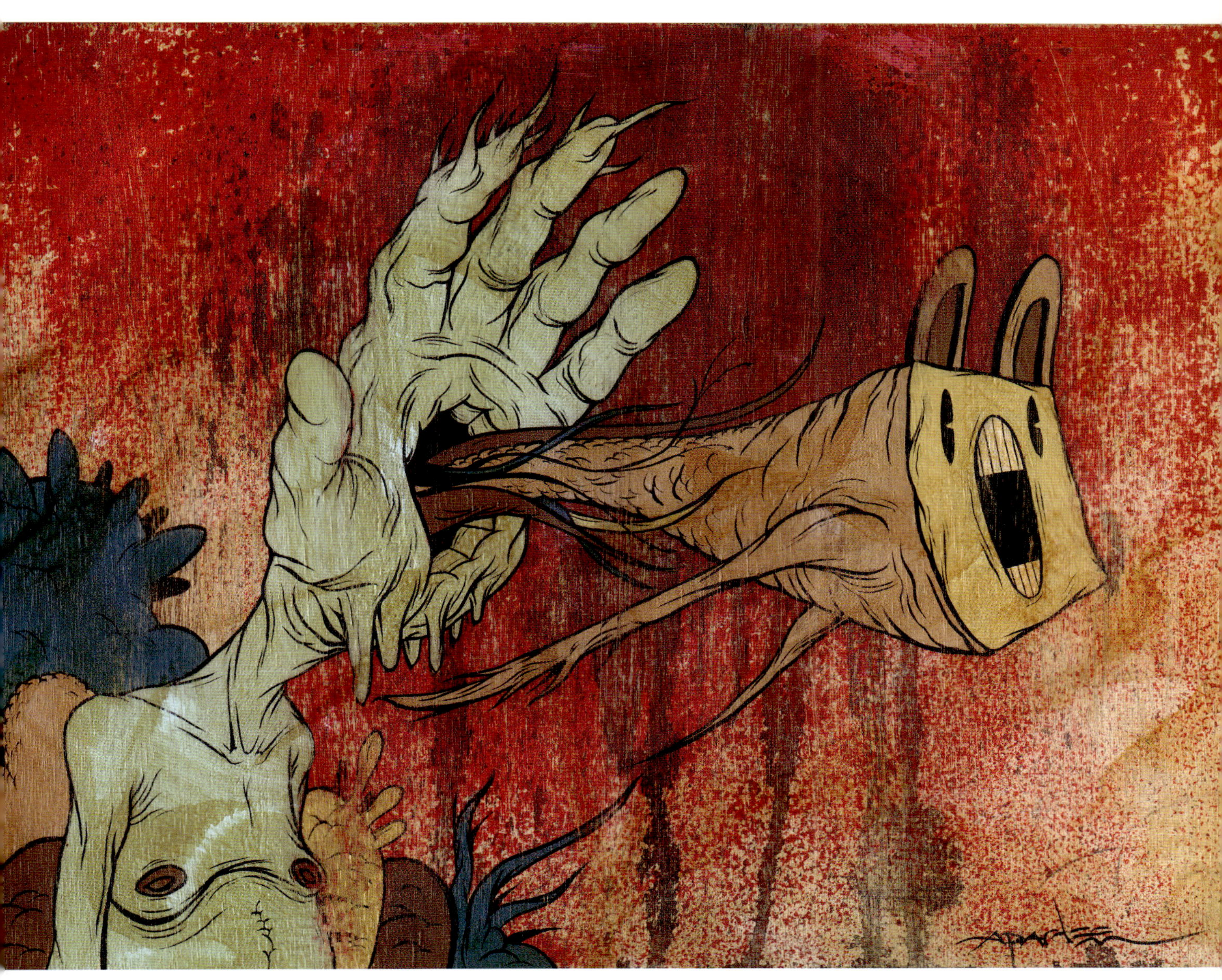

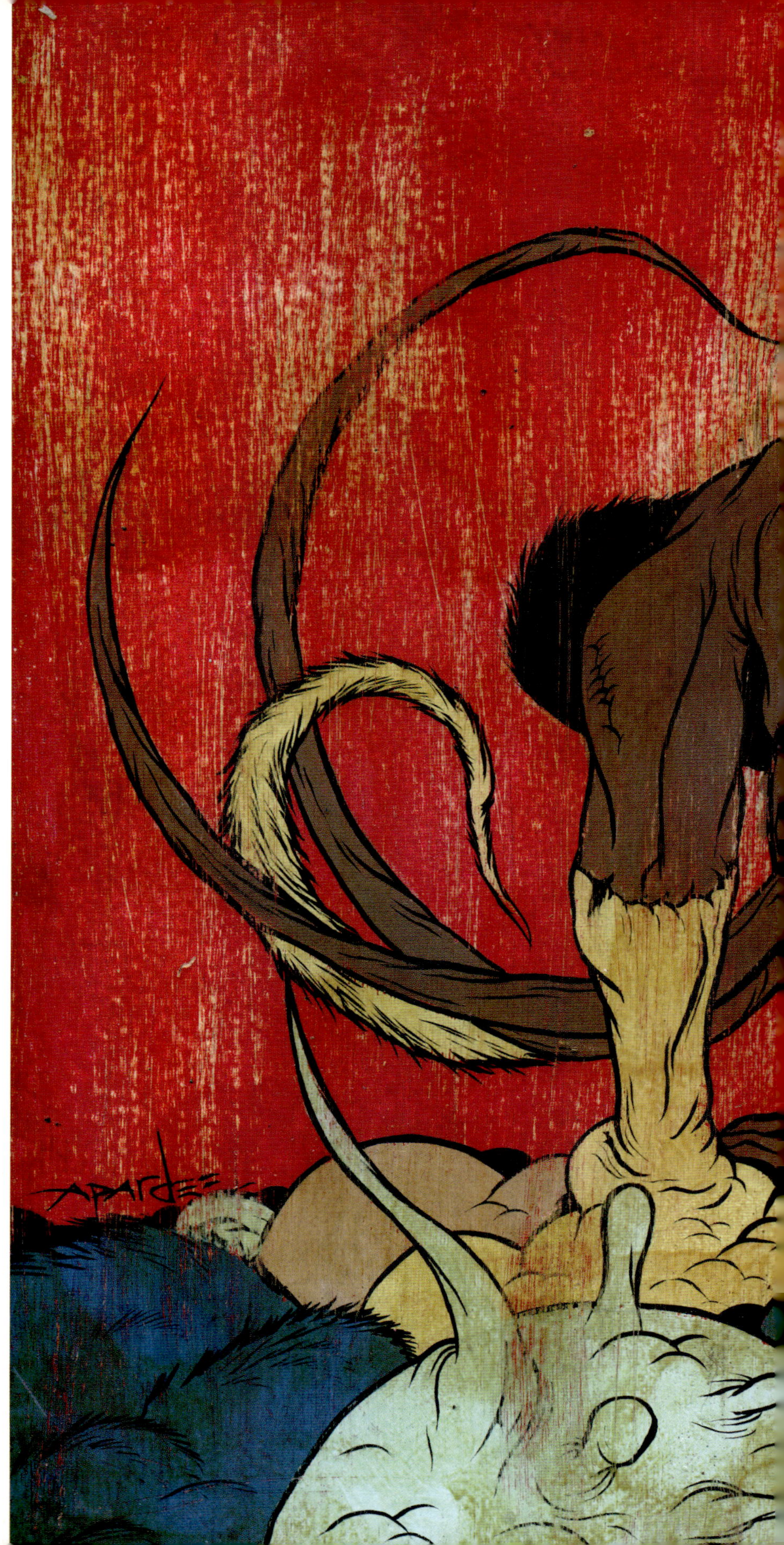

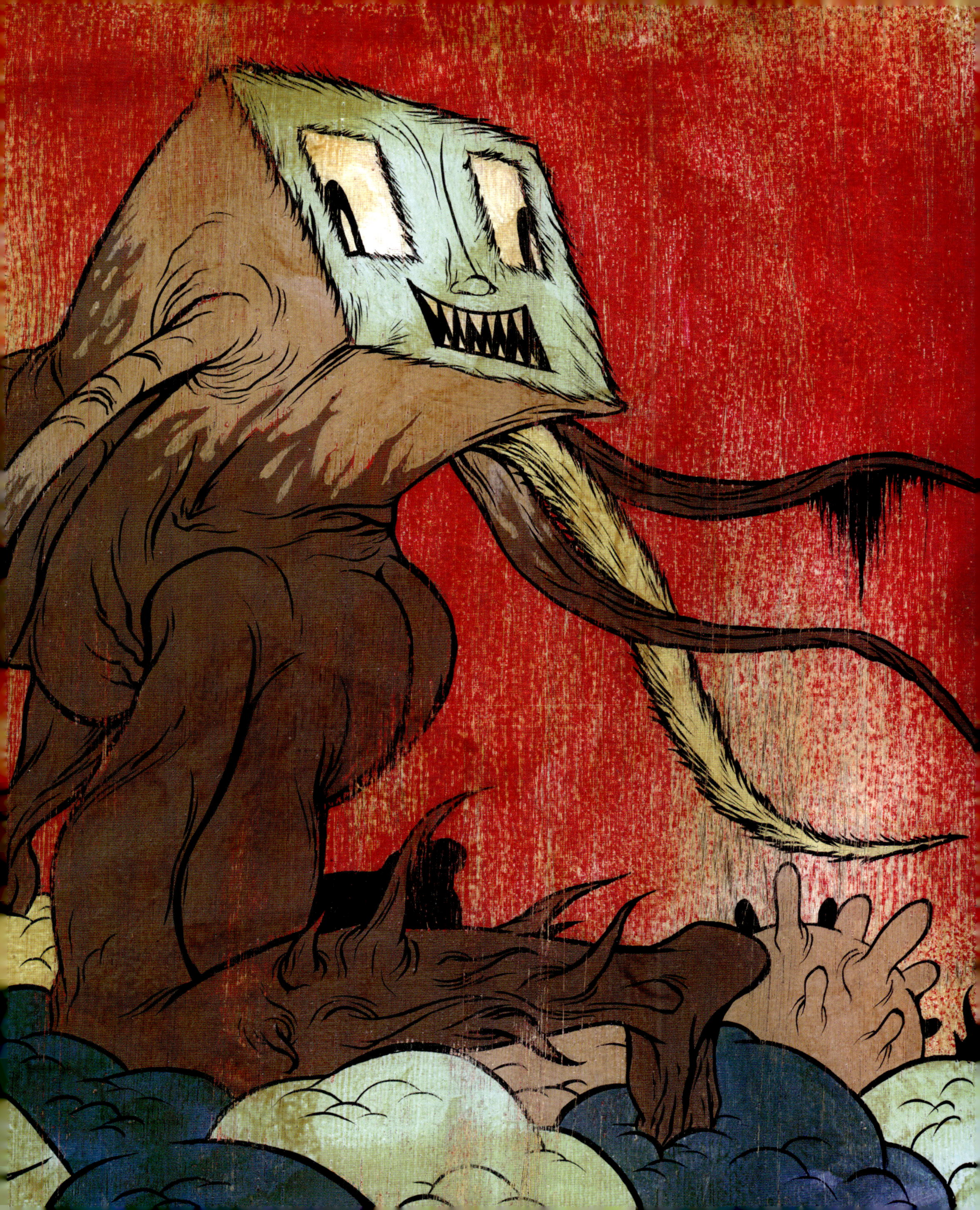

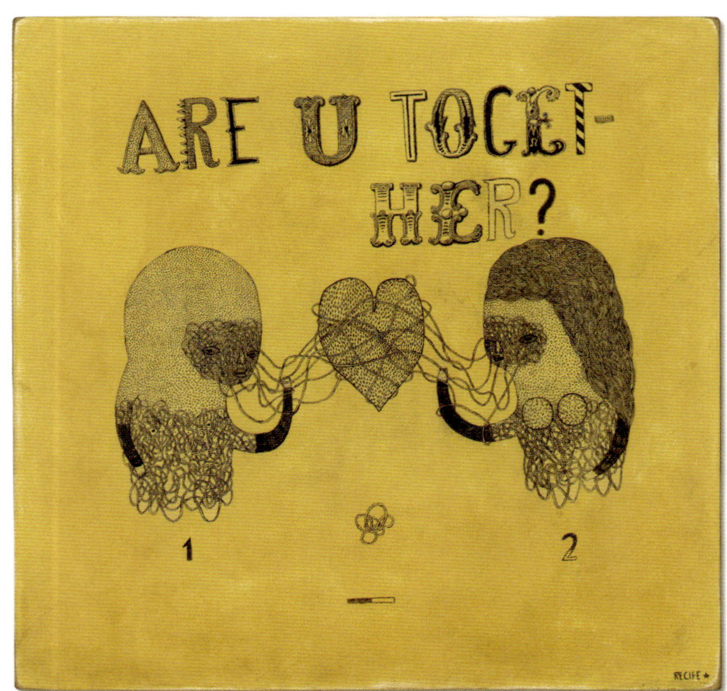

EDUARDO RECIFE

Eduardo Recife's resolute approach is rooted in his native country of Brazil. "I think that for us Brazilians we have to do the best we can with the resources we have," he explains. "Creativity plays a very important role in our lives." As a child, Recife filled his school notebooks with drawings and later dabbled in graffiti. "Then I found the whole 'grunge type design,'" he says. "It was love at first sight when I found the decayed, distressed types from the street in the digital world." When he discovered other artists' illustrations online, he wanted his work to be as good. "I experimented and practiced most of the day and night," he says. "I had an obsessive desire to improve myself in that field. Sometimes I wouldn't go out on weekends in order to work all day. There wasn't a teacher or tutorial or anything. It was pretty much trial and error and lots of dedication." Through hard work, Recife developed a unique aesthetic which pulls from various artistic styles and adds a personal touch. "I think we are very dependent on machines and computers these days," he laments. "Somehow we are losing our spontaneity and becoming cold like the machines we use. As far as images are concerned, I always try to employ some hand-made material in my work, or to make it feel worn and live. It gives a certain authenticity that it was made by the hands of someone."

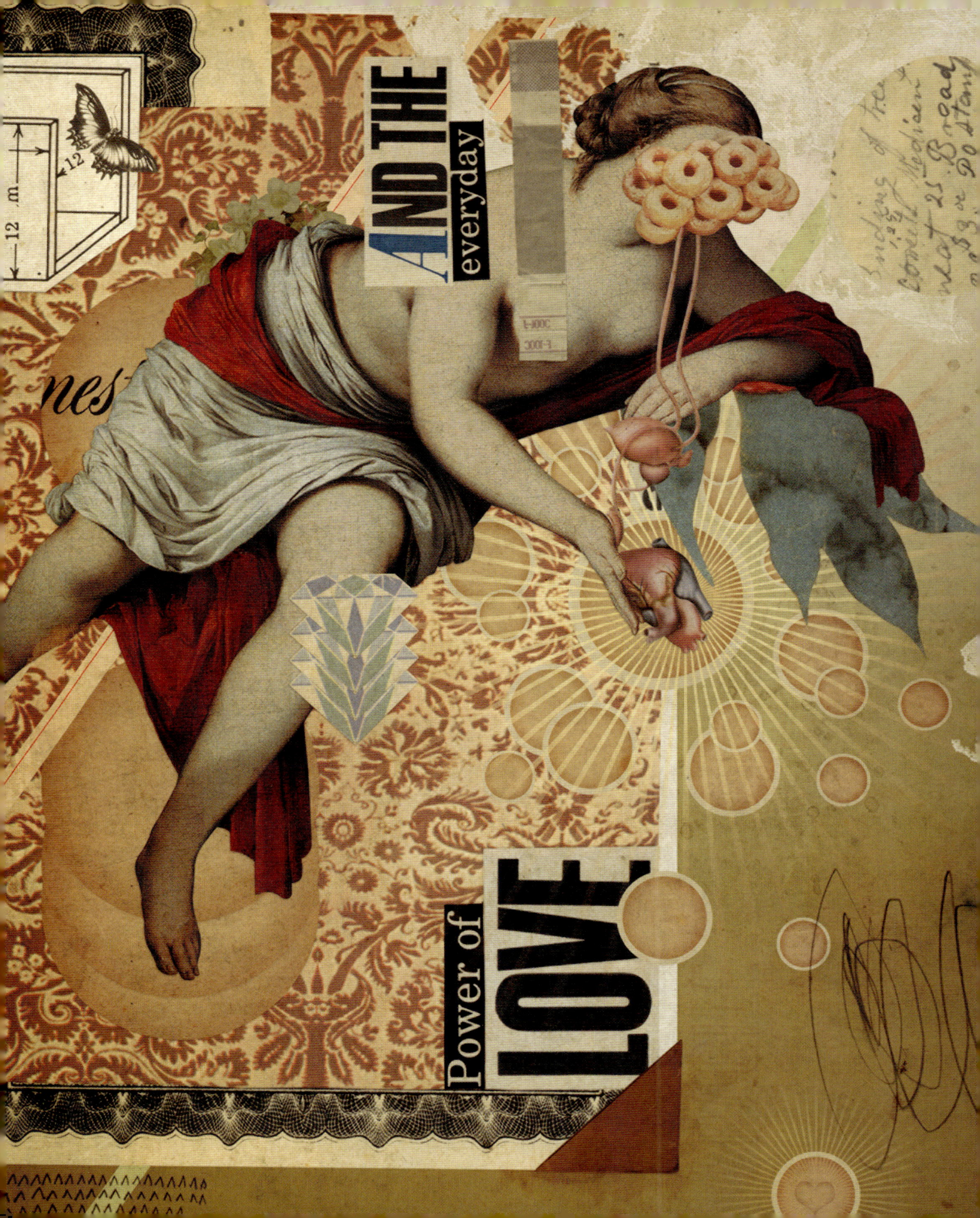
AND THE everyday
Power of LOVE
nes

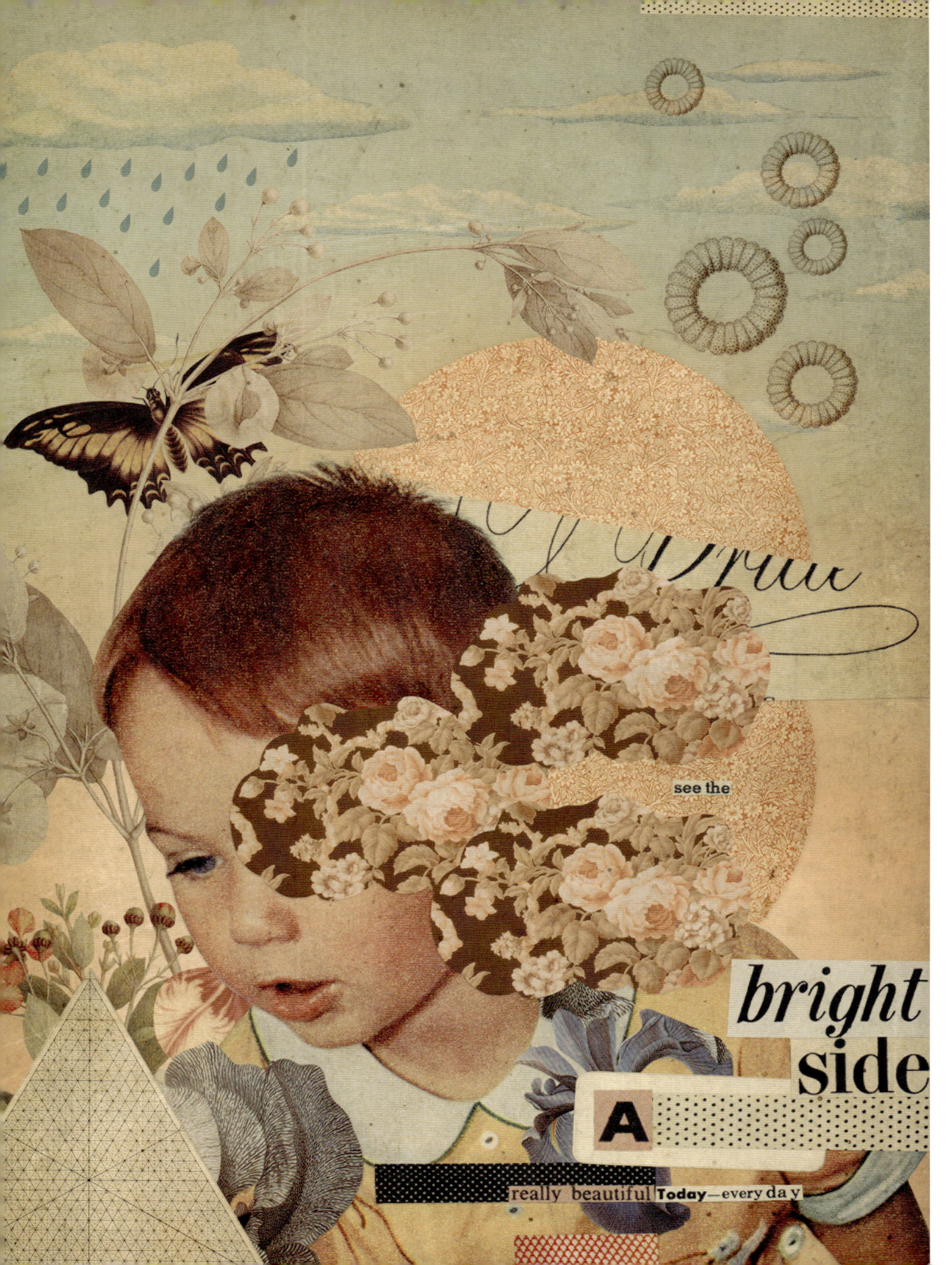

see the
bright
side
A
really beautiful Today—every day

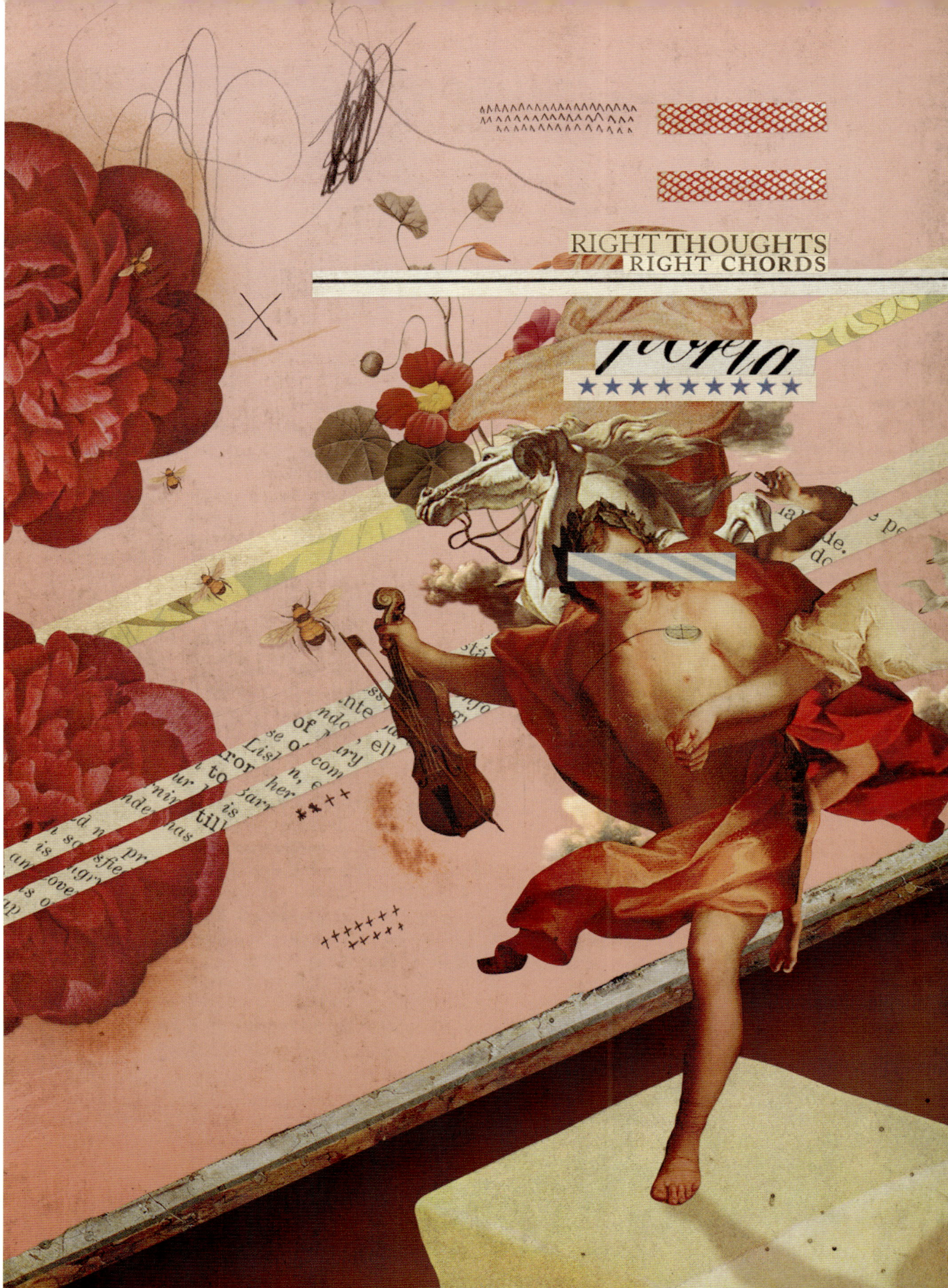

RIGHT THOUGHTS
RIGHT CHORDS

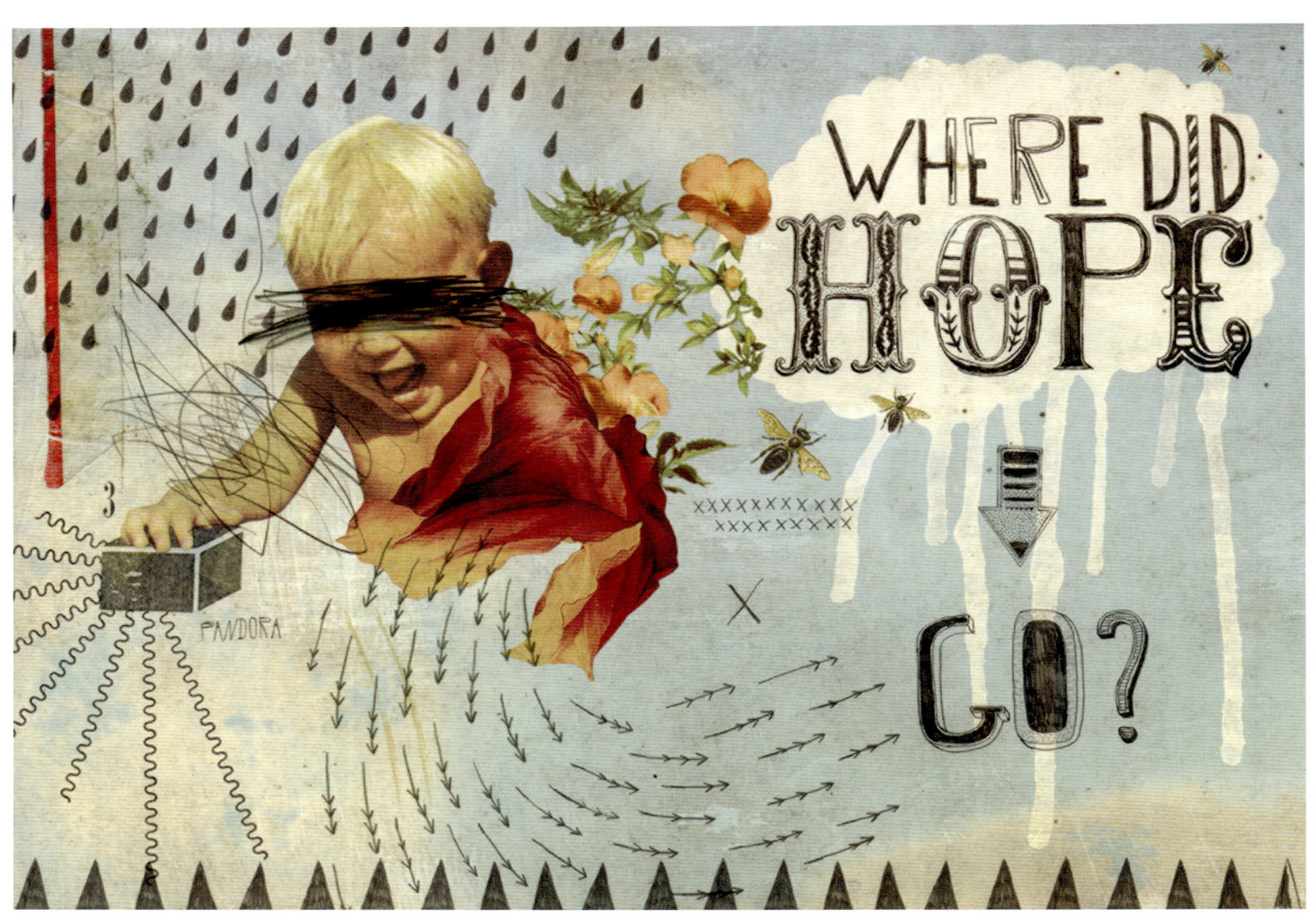
3
PANDORA
WHERE DID
HOPE
GO?

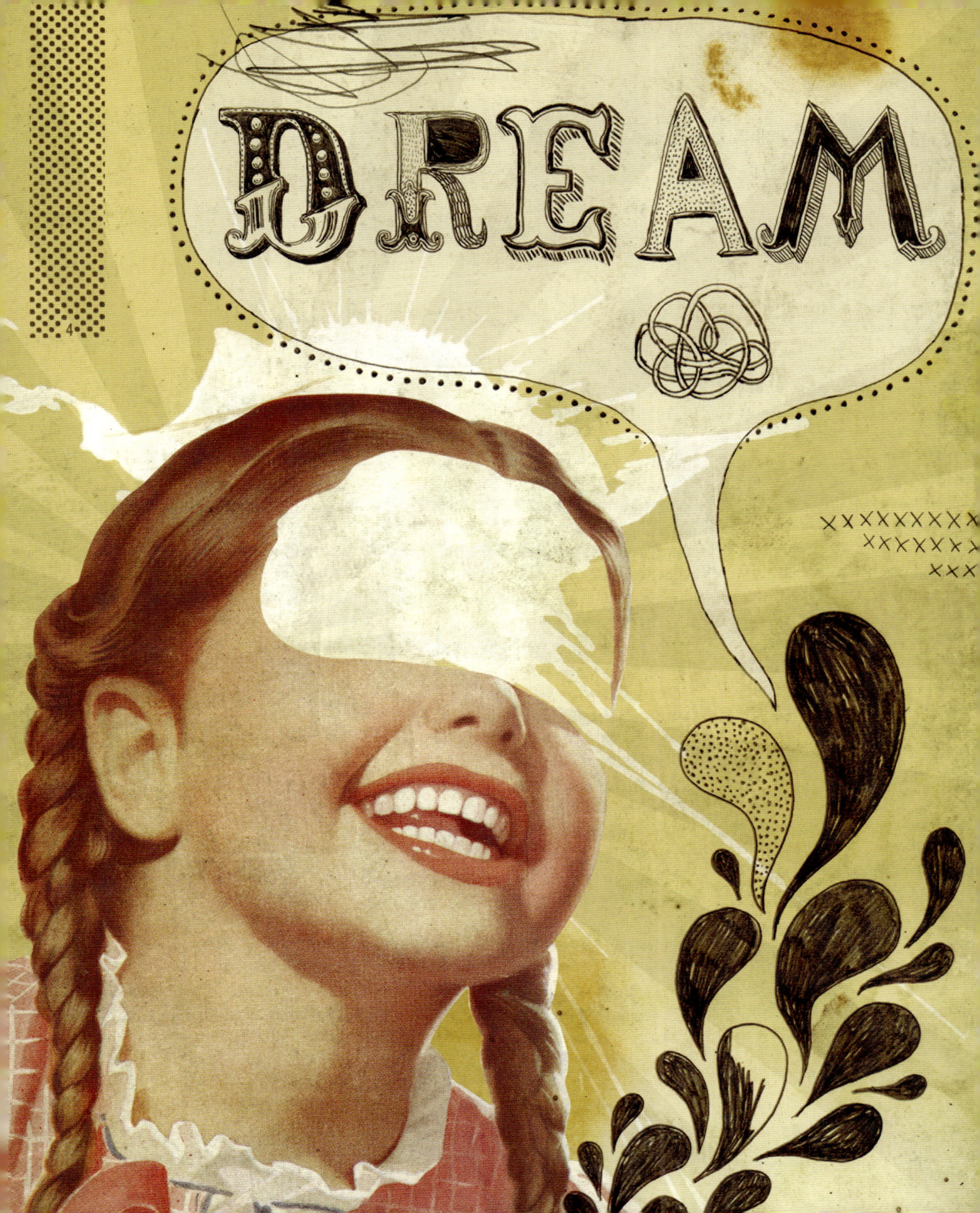
DREAM

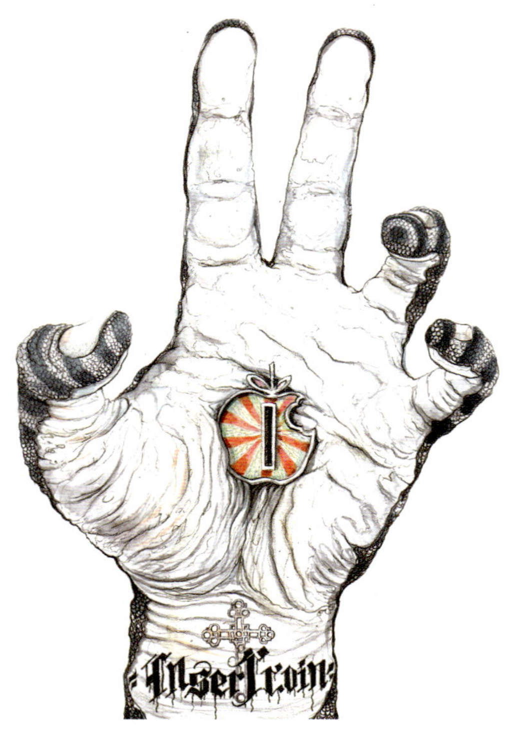

SAN

San, born Daniel Munoz in Moraleja, Spain, now lives and works in colorful Madrid. He started as a graffiti writer and later painted street art. The murals featured on his website, eseaene.com, are psychedelic and appear almost 3-Dimensional, pushing themselves off the wall. Before painting a mural, he outlines sketches on the street, but soon his passion for the drawing outweighed his interest in murals. "This activity has become my main dedication now," he writes. "I love to think about an idea and use drawing to express it because drawing is the most basic artistic instinct." In contrast to his murals, San's illustrations are simple, often composed in muted color or just black and gray. "I get inspiration from the things that express the development of time," he says. "Usually, I use symbols I find in the street, in nature or in human gestures." San used to do commercial projects, but, he thinks, "this kind of work kills your own creativity. Now, I prefer to use my time and my artistic potential to express myself and look inside myself." He concludes, "I try to make unique artwork using my brain, my soul and my hands. The outcome is just a consequence."

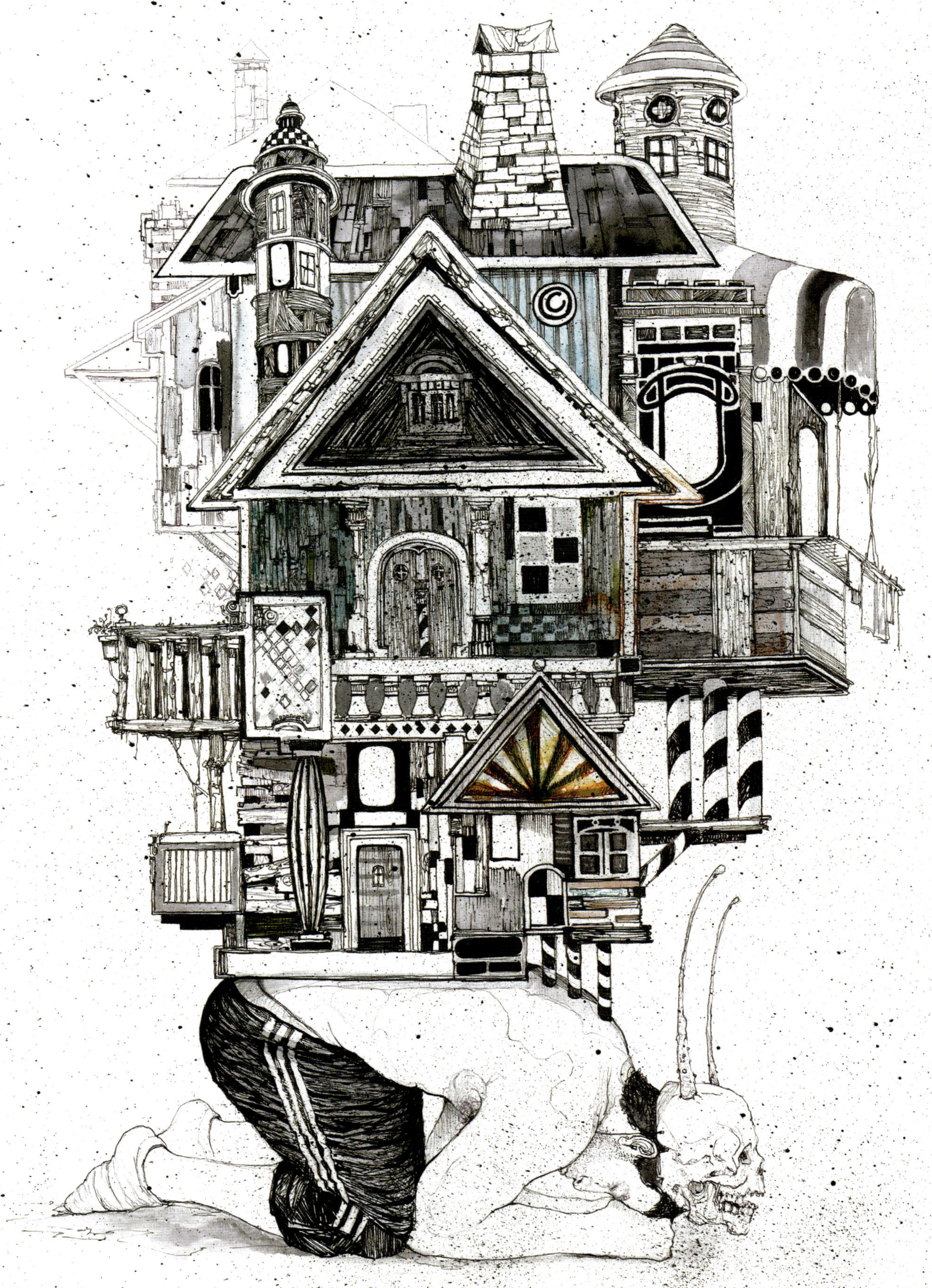

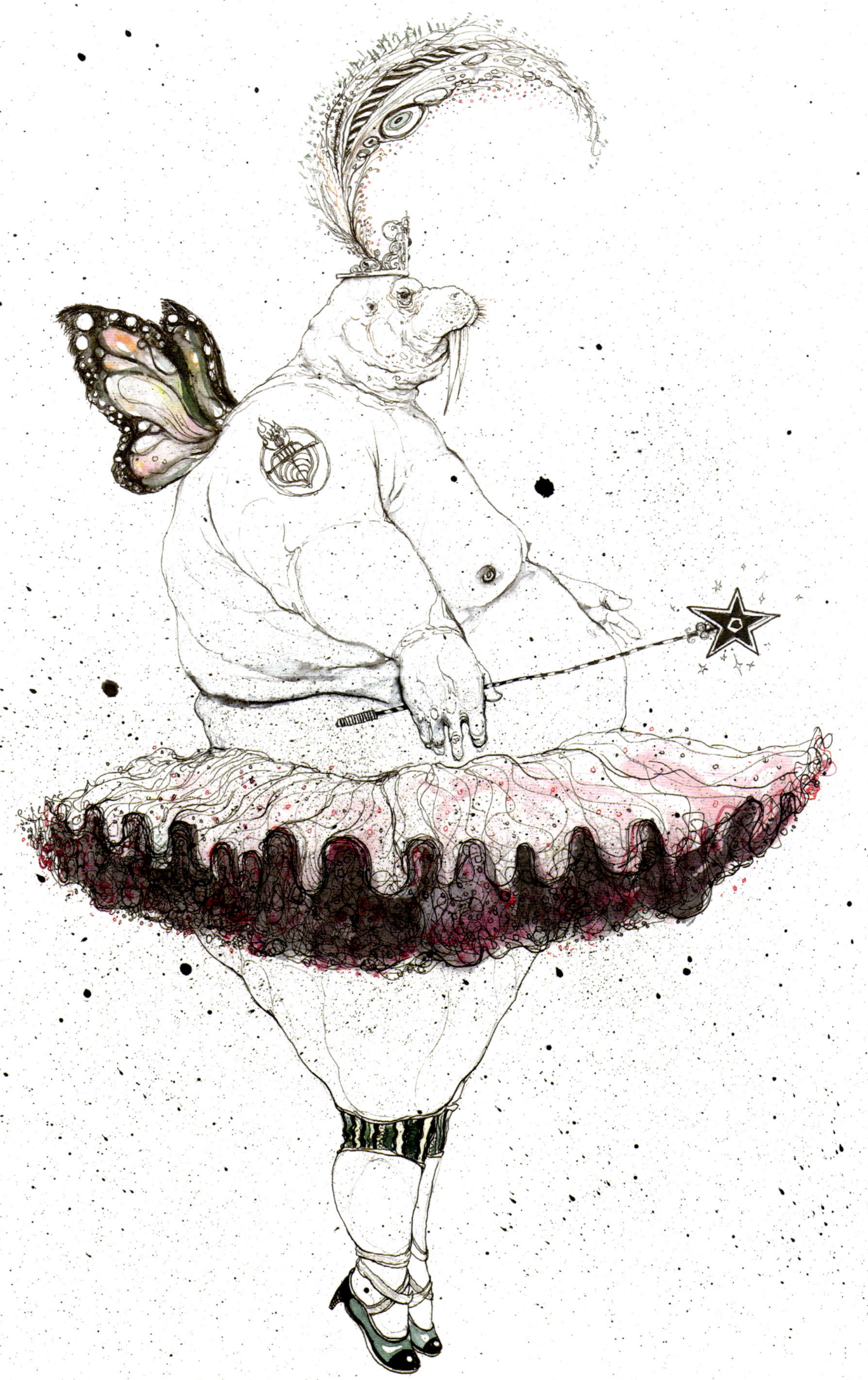

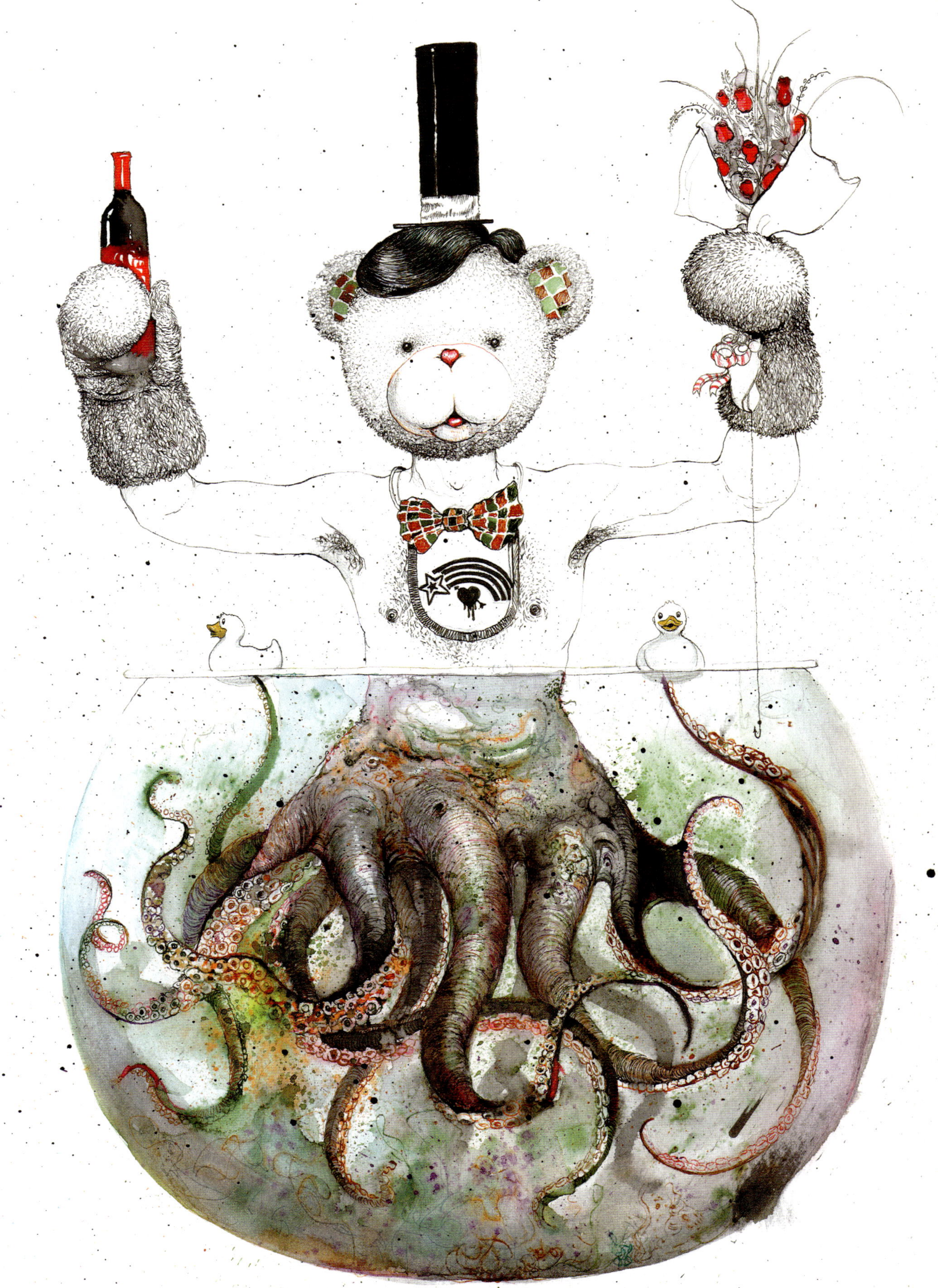

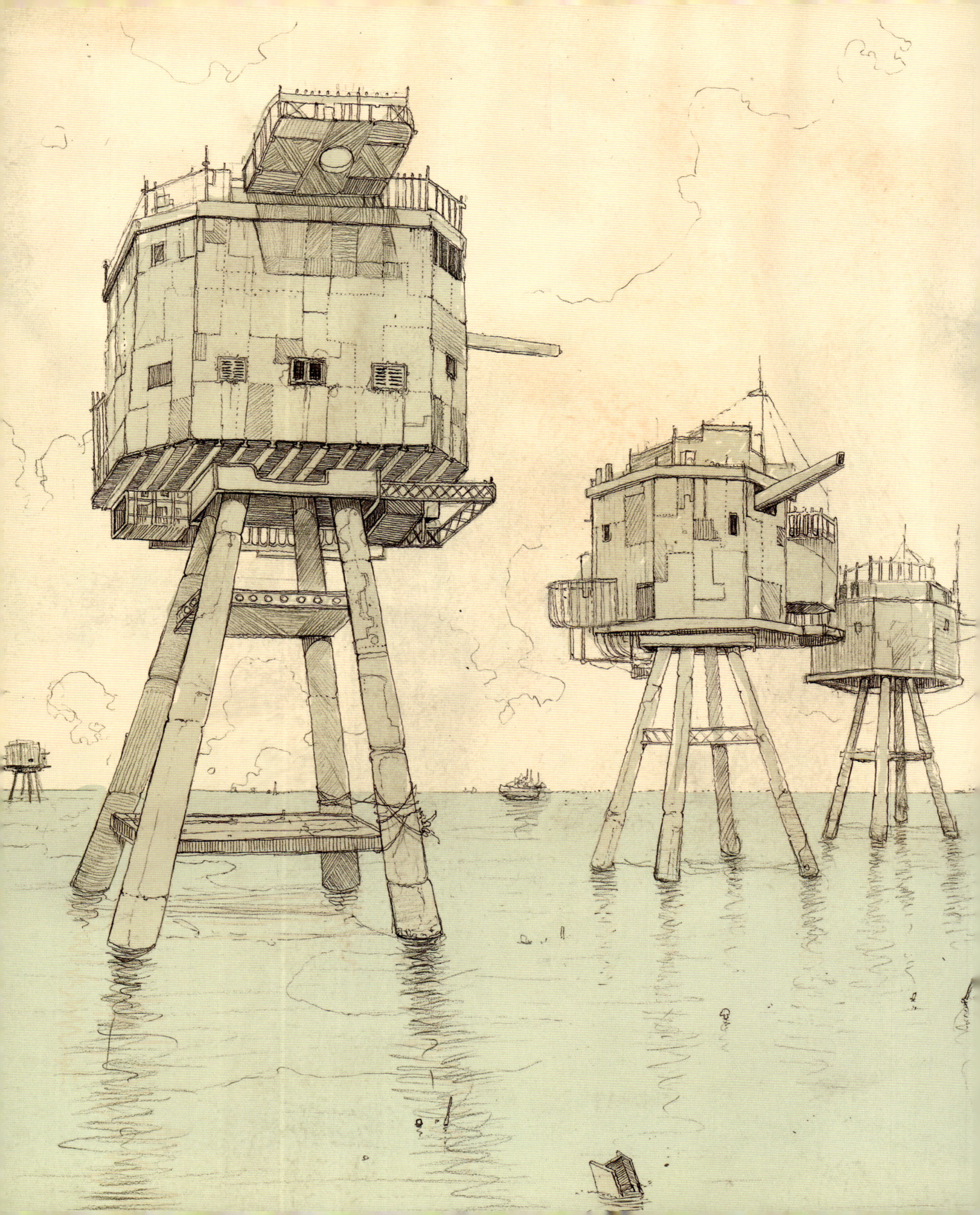

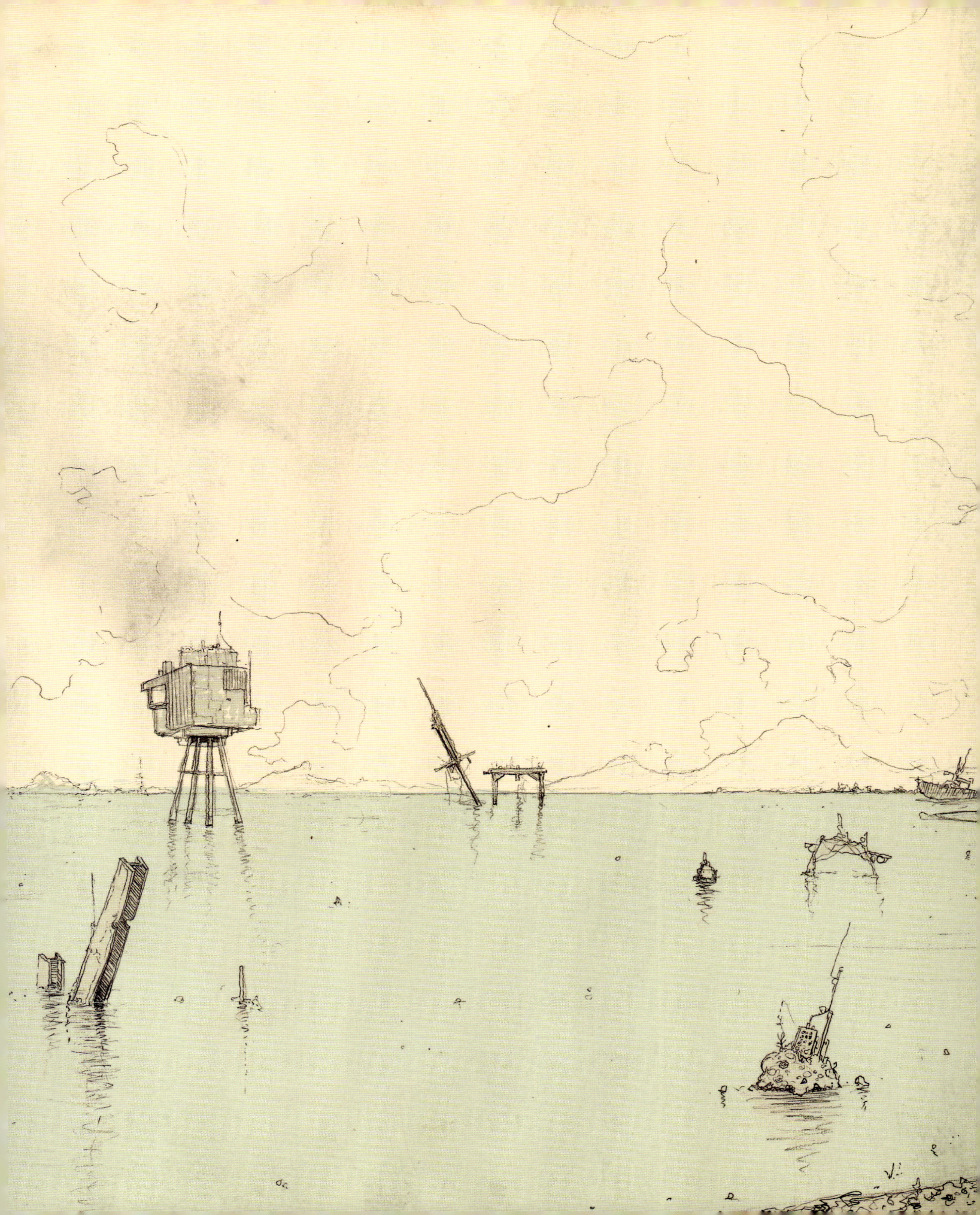

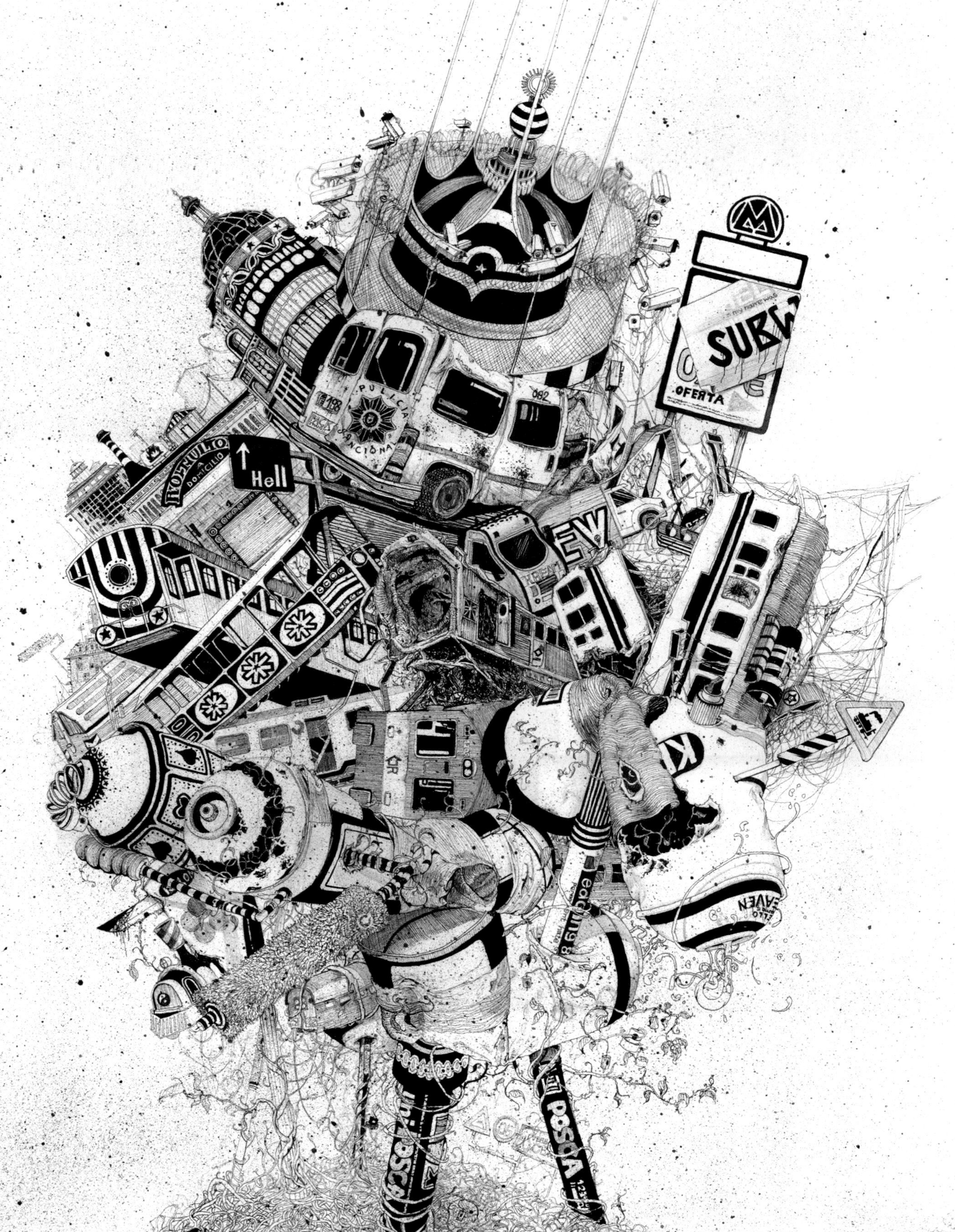

SUBW
OFERTA
POLICIA
FUNCIONA
082
DOMICILIO
Hell
EW
POSCA

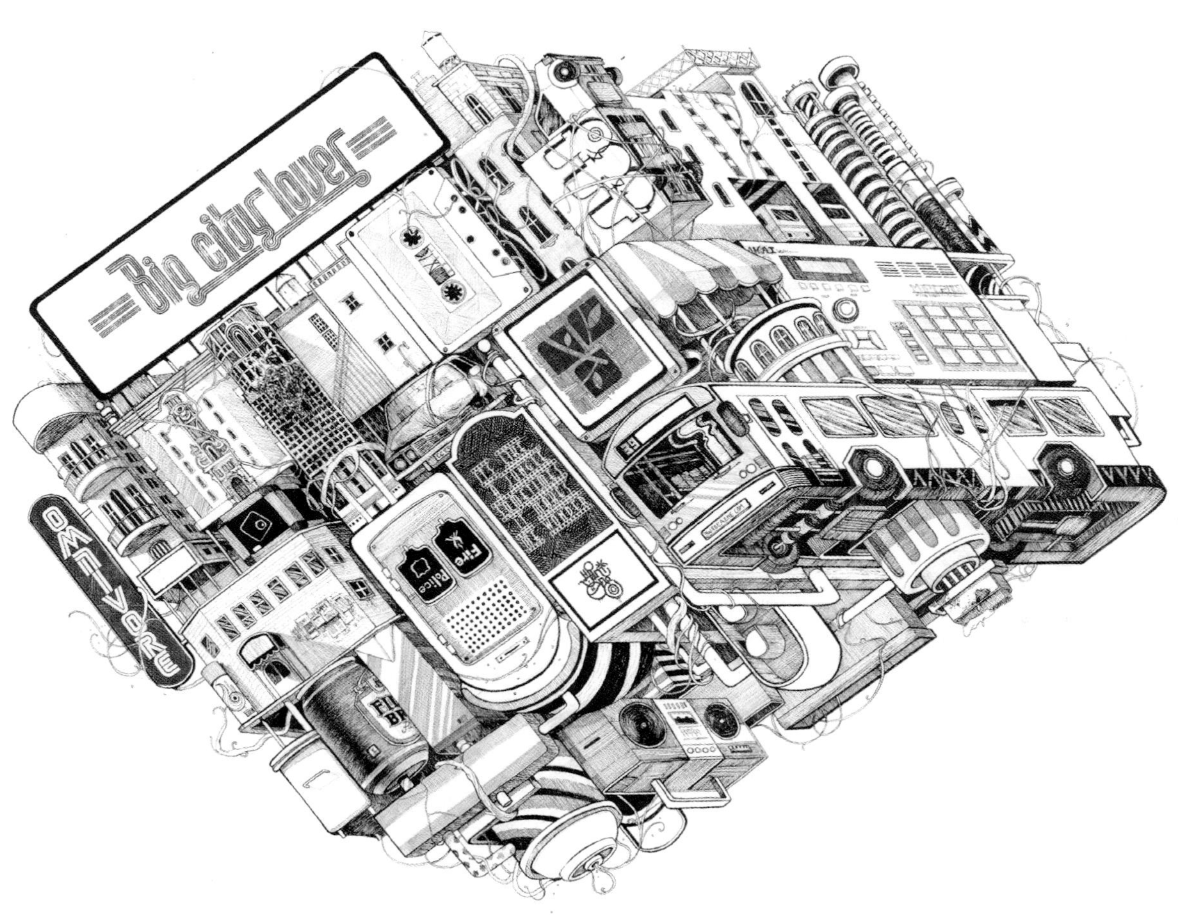
Big city lover

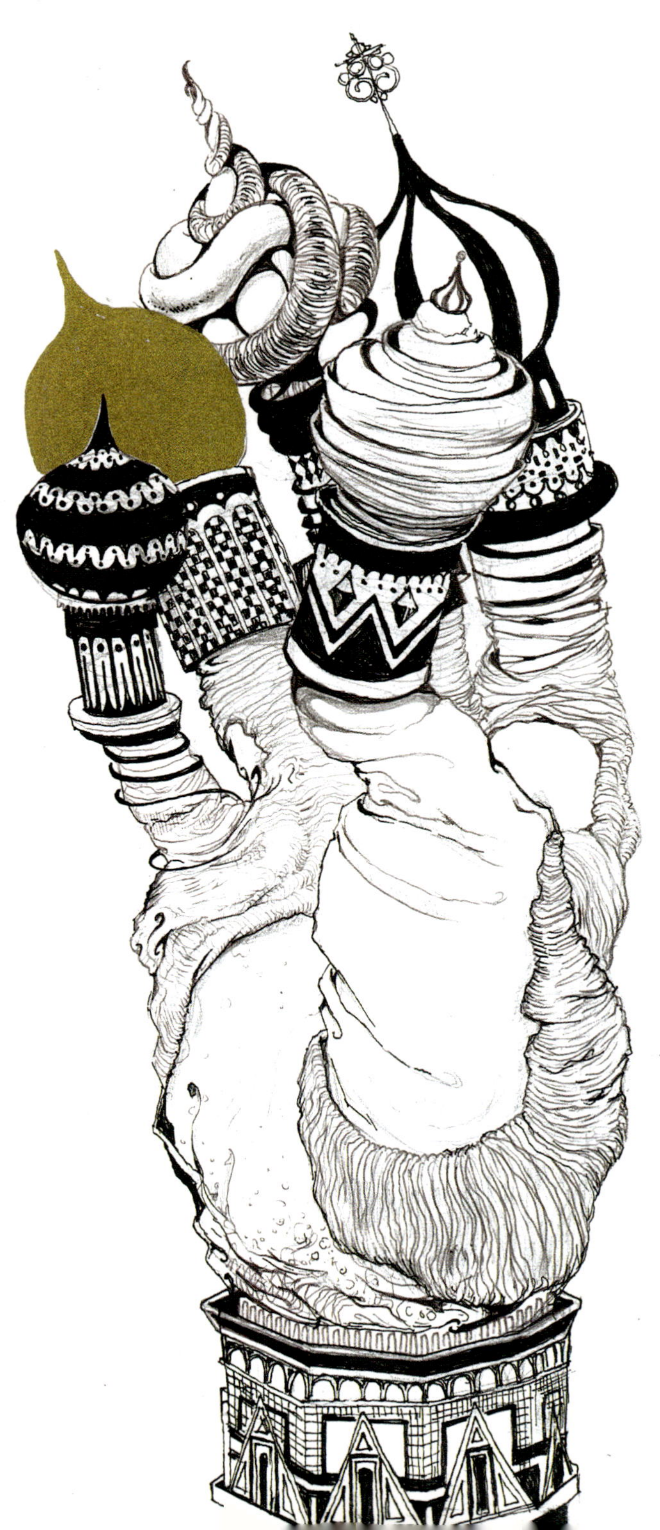

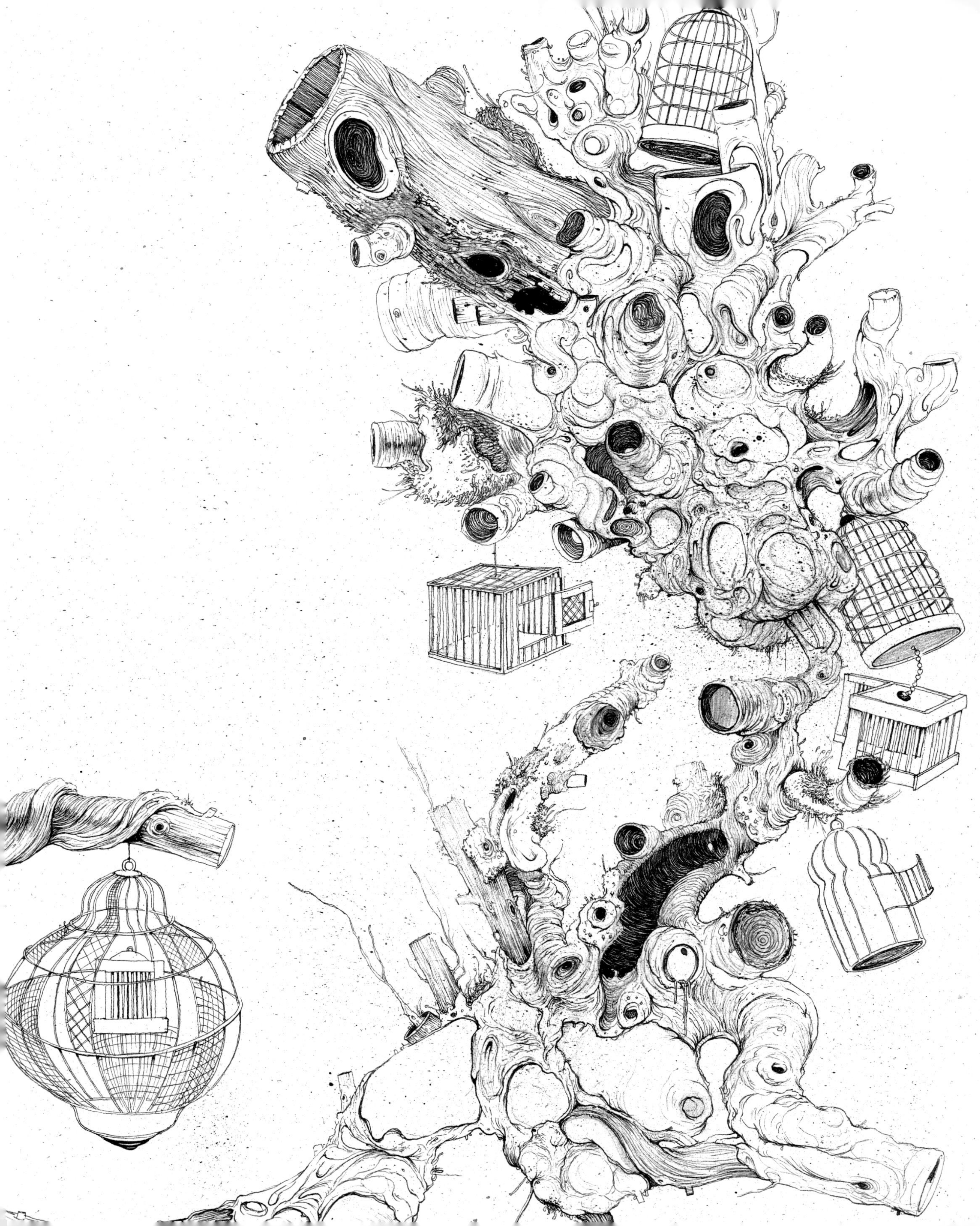

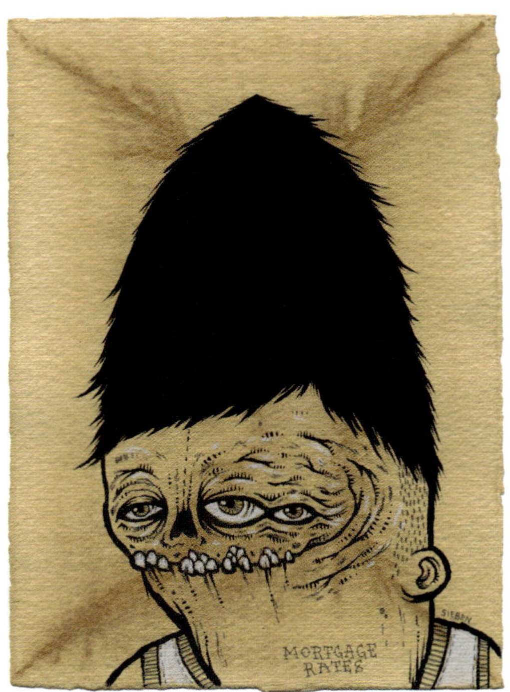

MICHAEL SIEBEN

Native Texan Michael Sieben was influenced by children's books like Maurice Sendak "Where the Wild Things Are" and skateboard designers such as Pushead. Sieben learned to use both styles in his artwork. "When I was younger I wanted to be a children's book illustrator, so I drew pictures that I thought would work well in a children's book," he explains. "When I got older, I started skateboarding and immediately shifted gears and decided that I wanted to design skateboard graphics. So I started drawing skulls and knives and imagery that I thought would look good on a skateboard. At some point I merged the two illustration styles that I had taught myself and ended up with something sort of cute and sort of gross." Sieben's work—often drawn with a subdued palette and framed by solid dark lines—keeps him rooted to his youth. "I feel like my work helps me hold onto some of the magic of childhood and adolescence," he says. Sieben frequently works on projects with the Volcom Art Loft, illustrates for skater mag Thrasher and co-owns the gallery Okay Mountain. "I love to draw," he says, "and the idea of being paid to do what you love has always seemed pretty awesome to me."

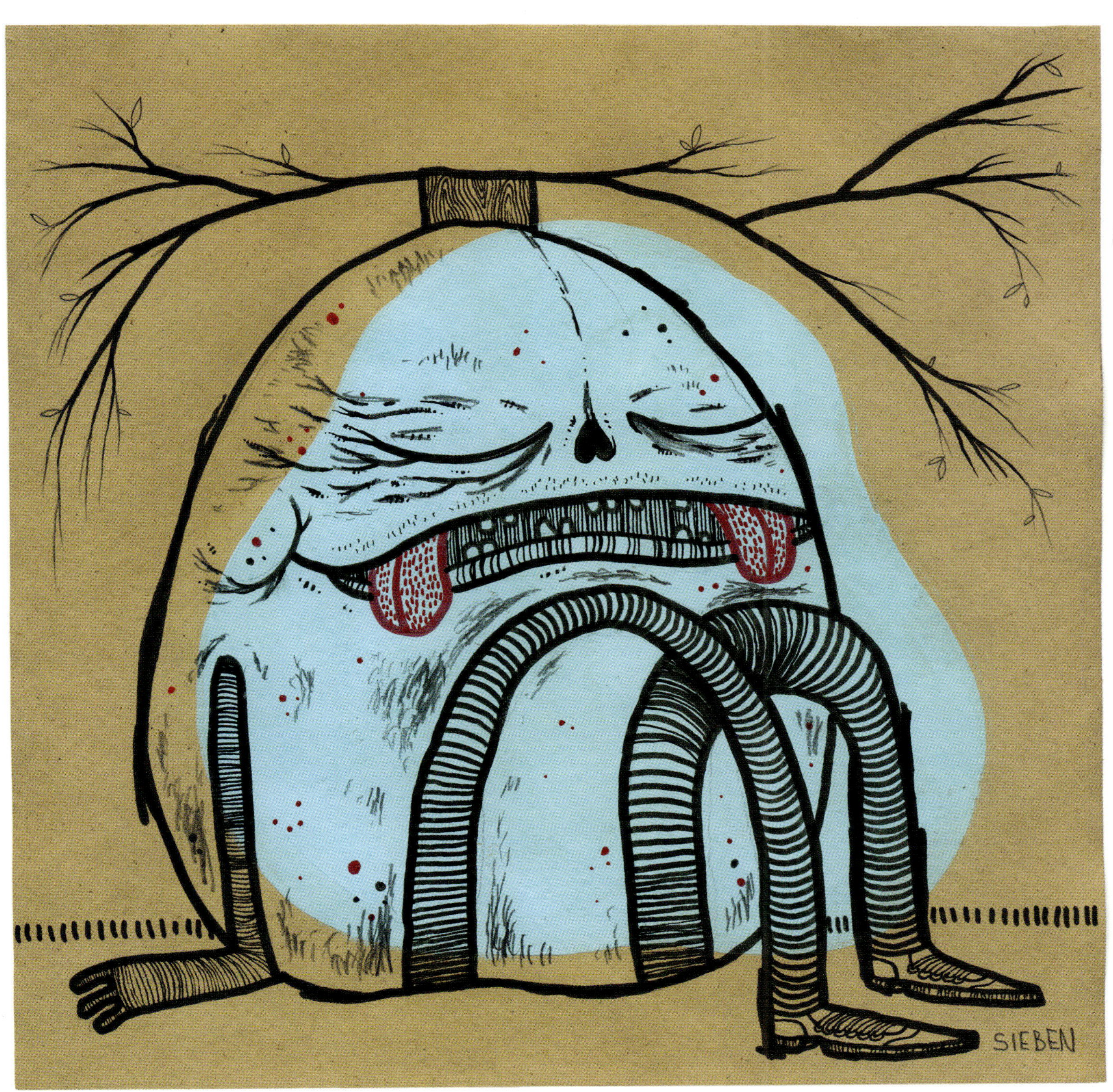
SIEBEN

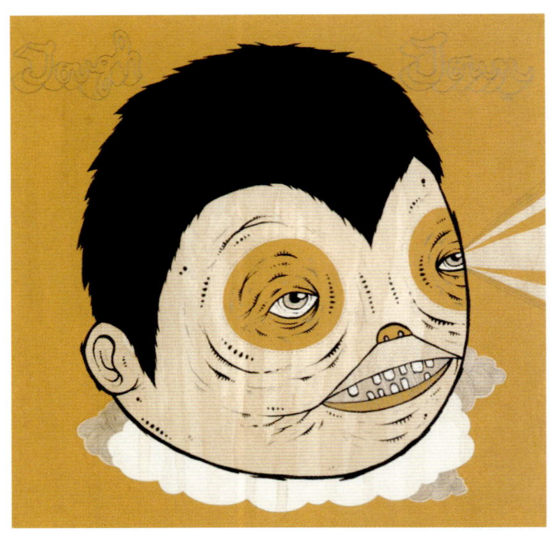
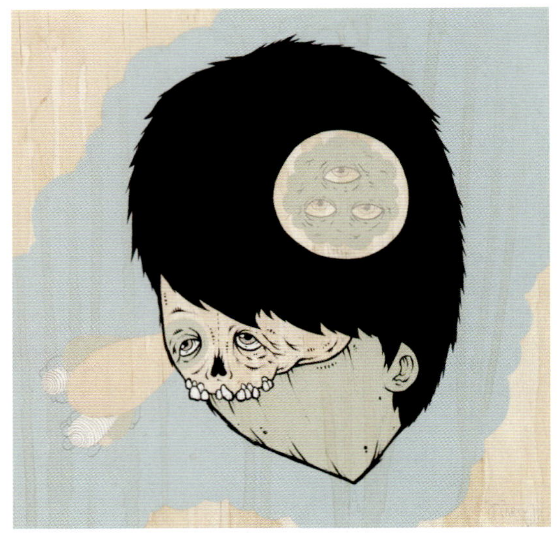
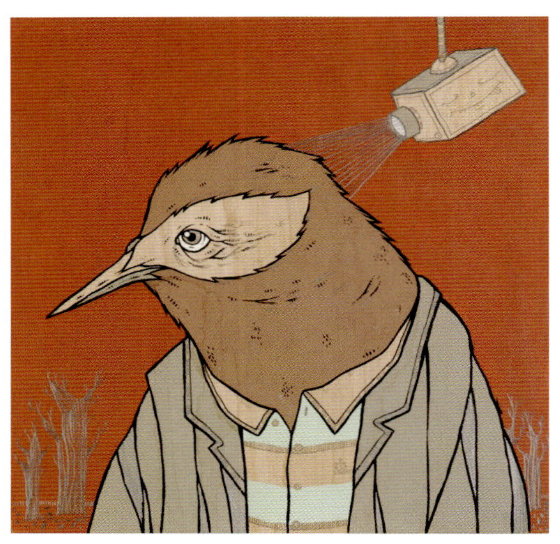
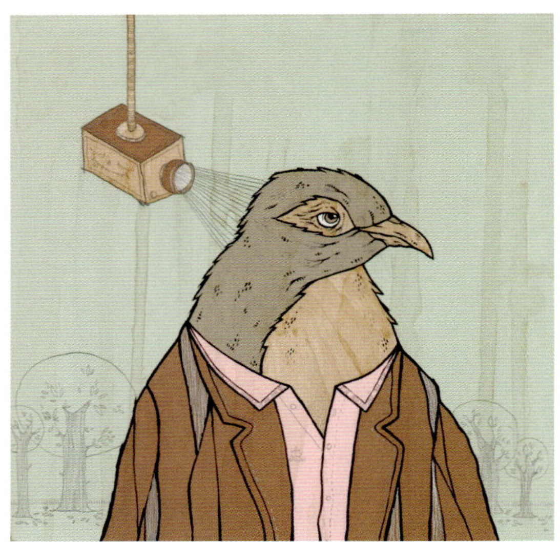
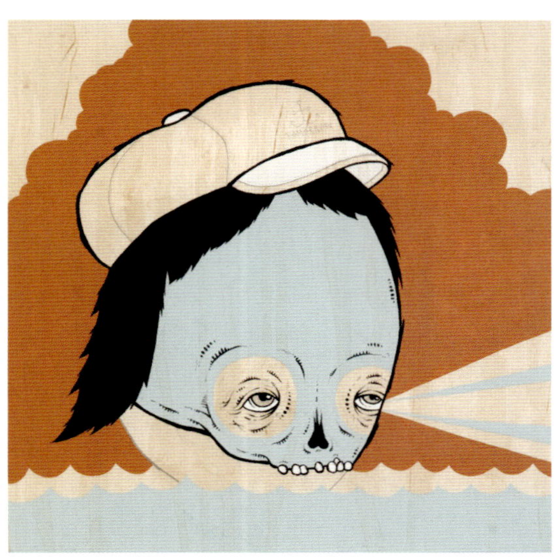
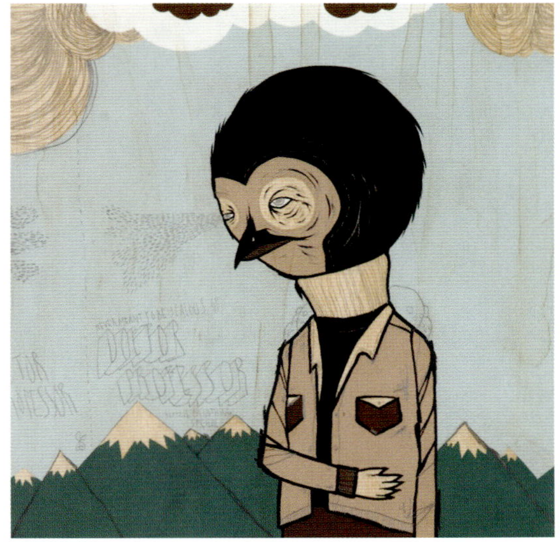

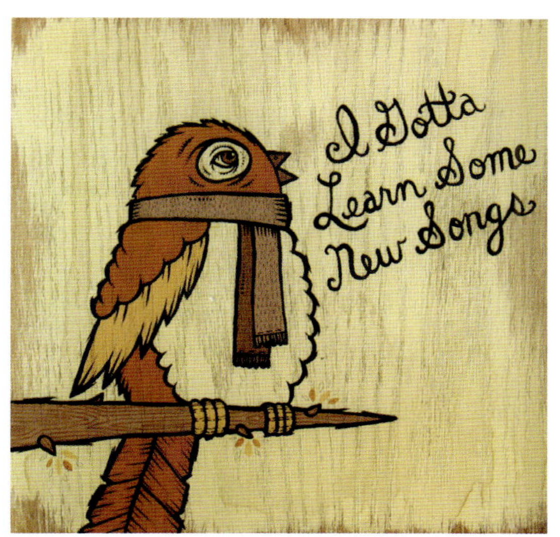
I Gotta Learn Some New Songs

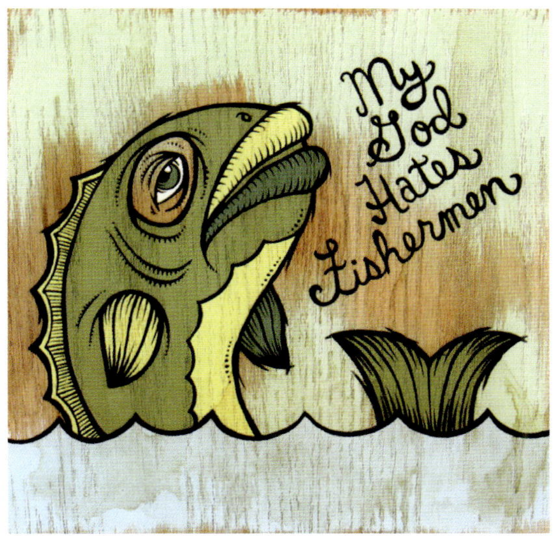
My God Hates Fishermen

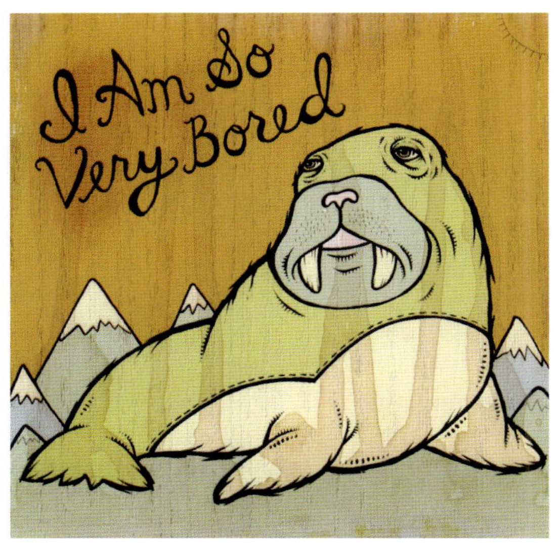
I Am So Very Bored

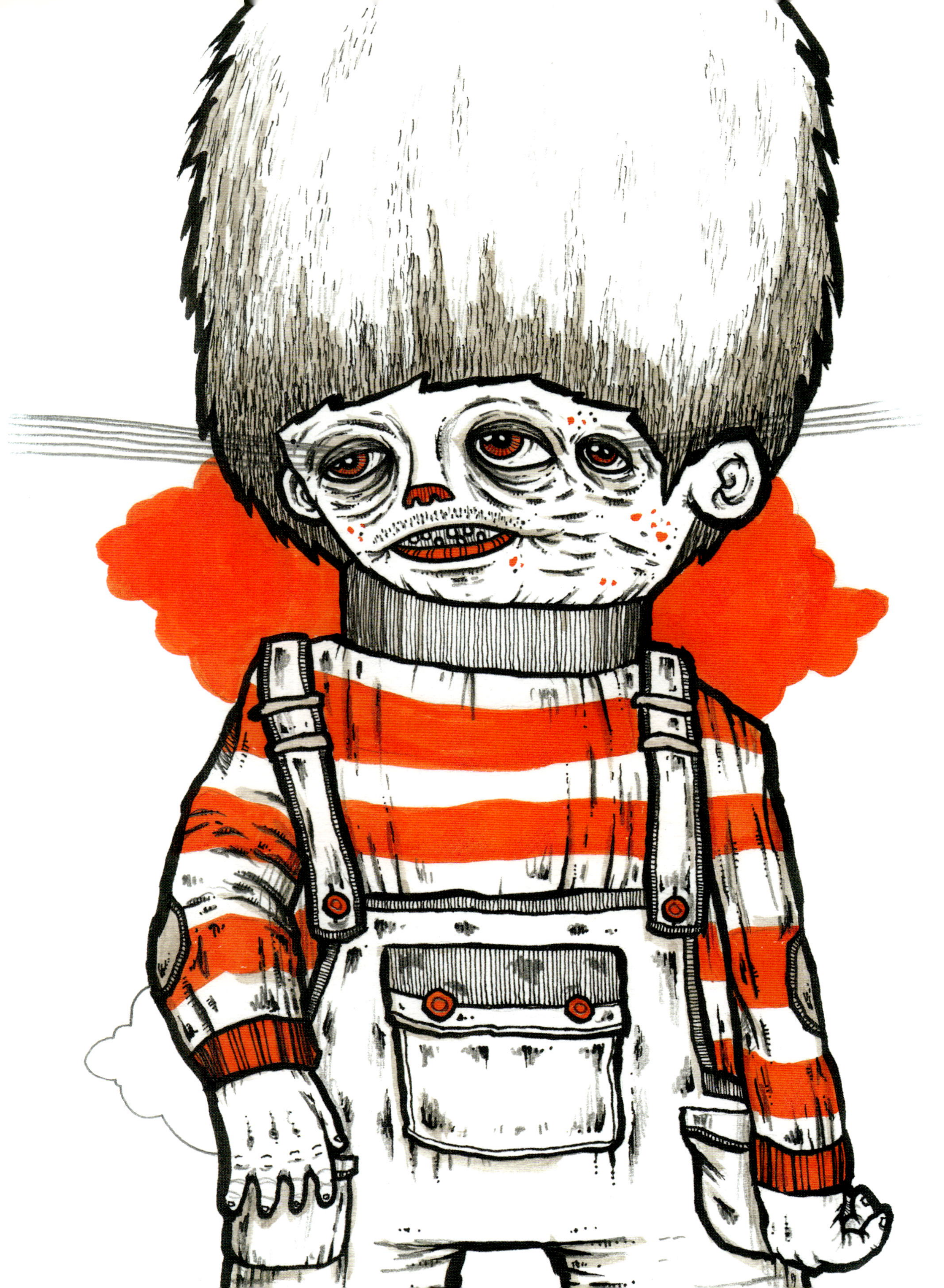

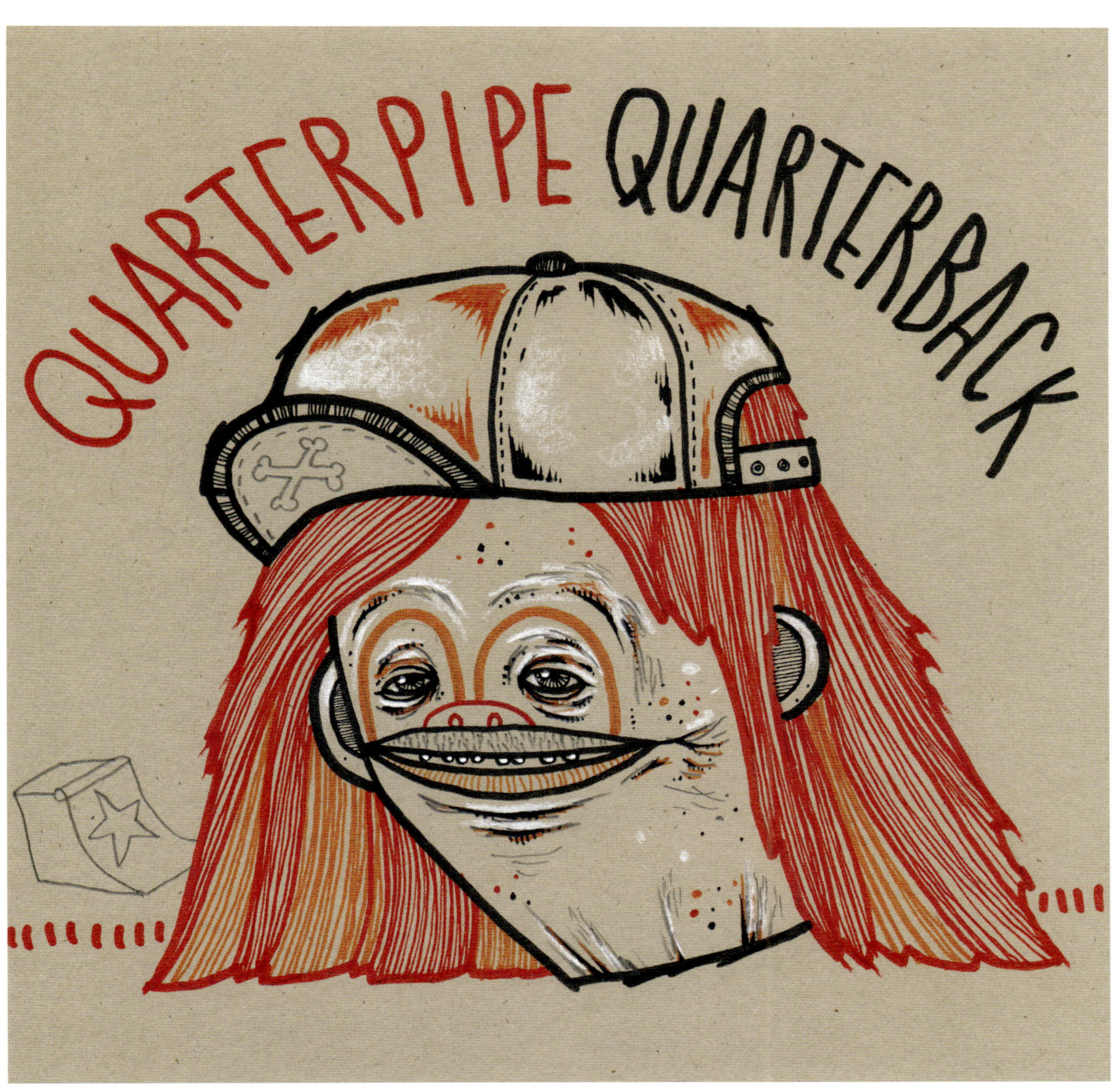

QUARTERPIPE QUARTERBACK

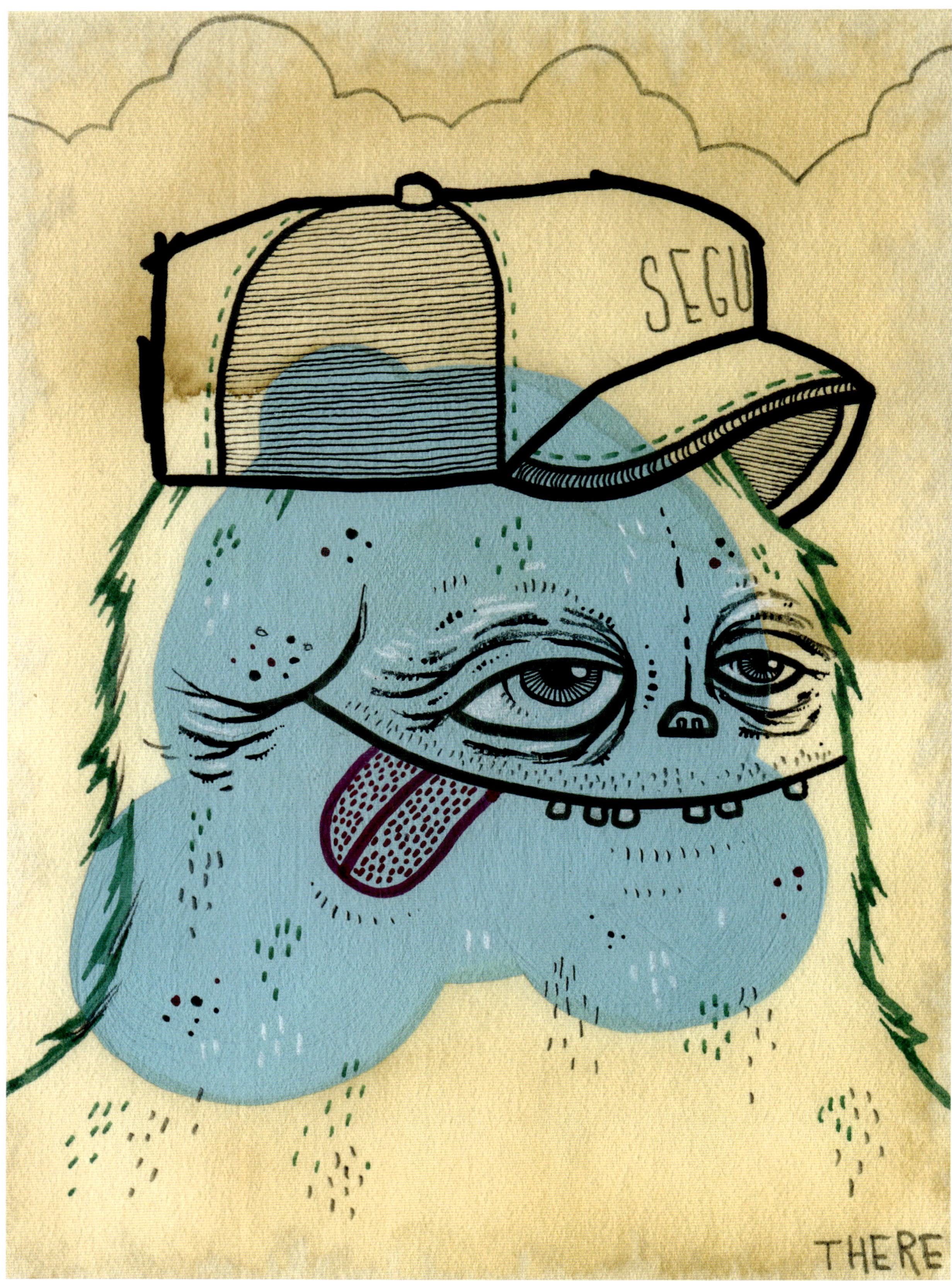
SEGU
THERE

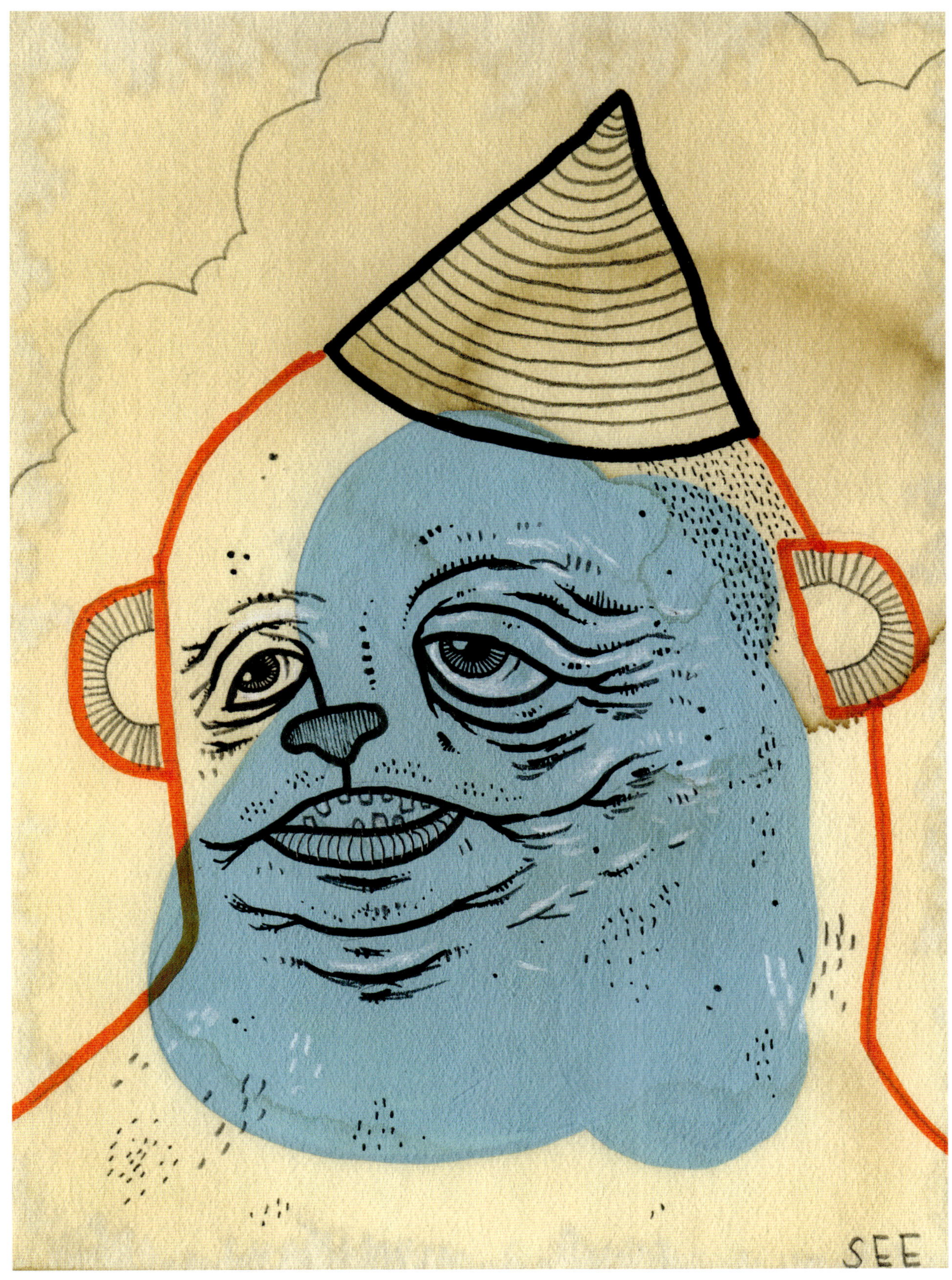
SEE

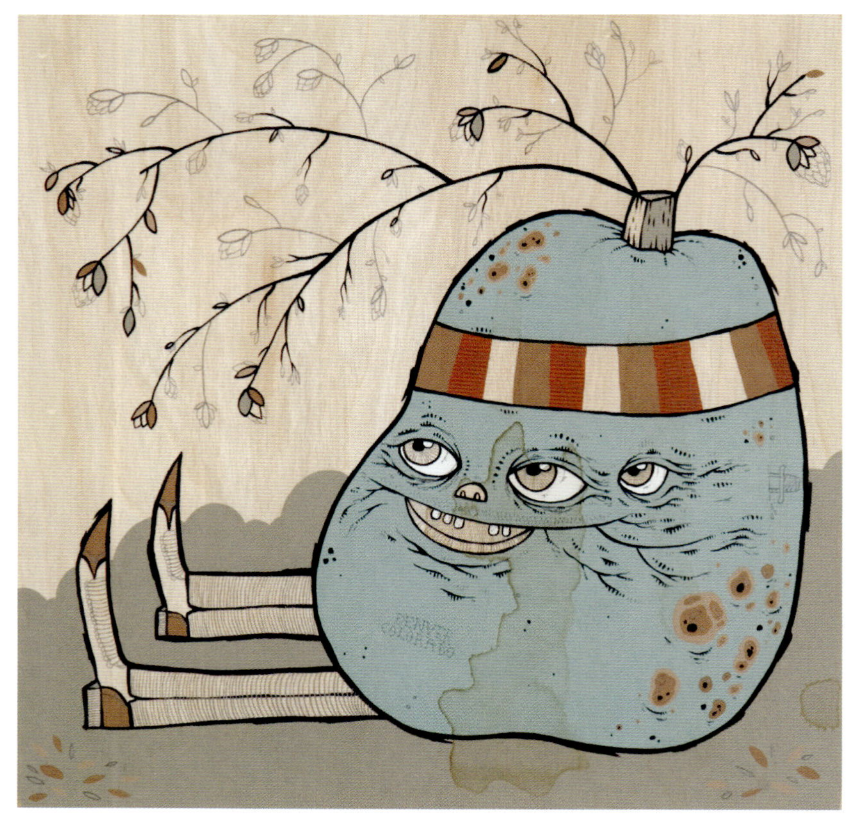

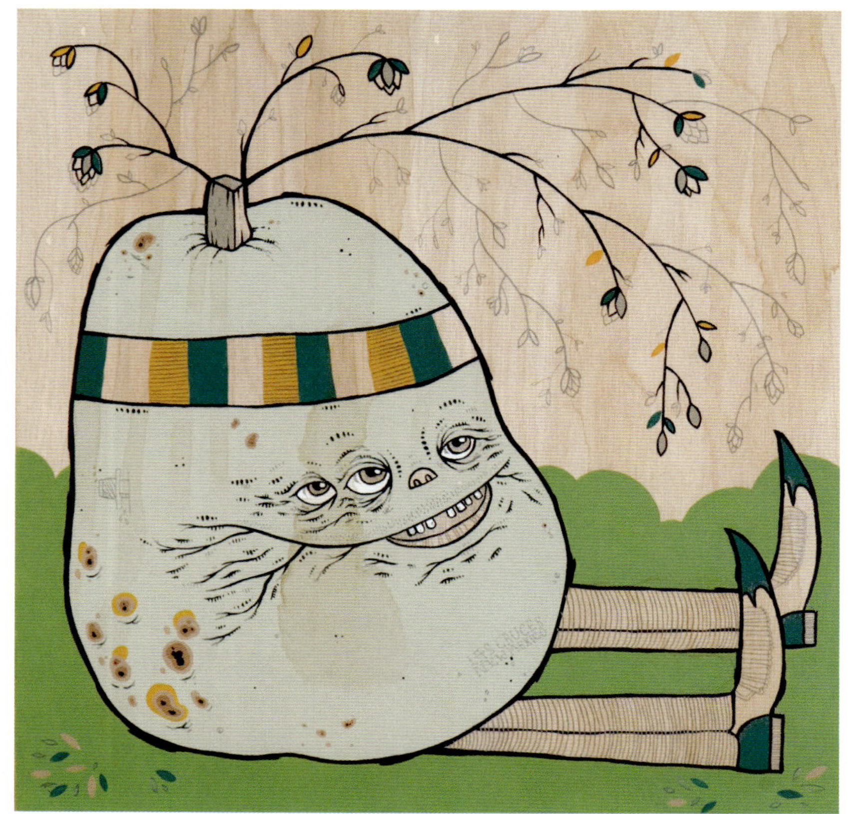

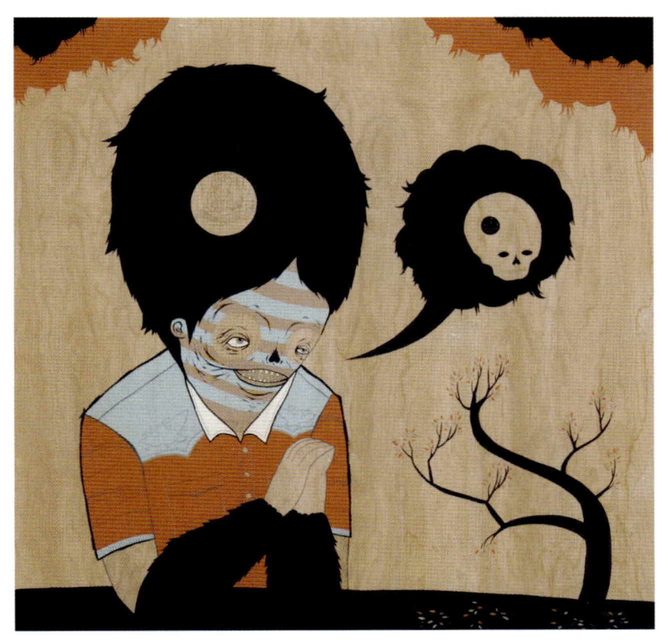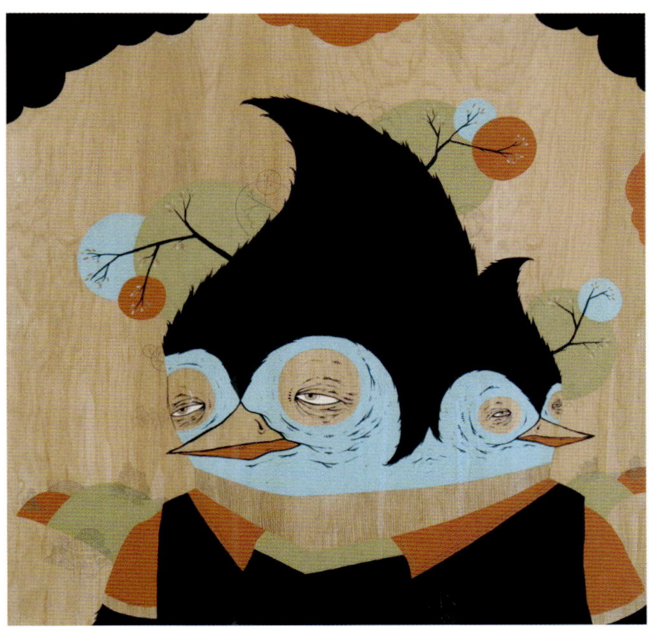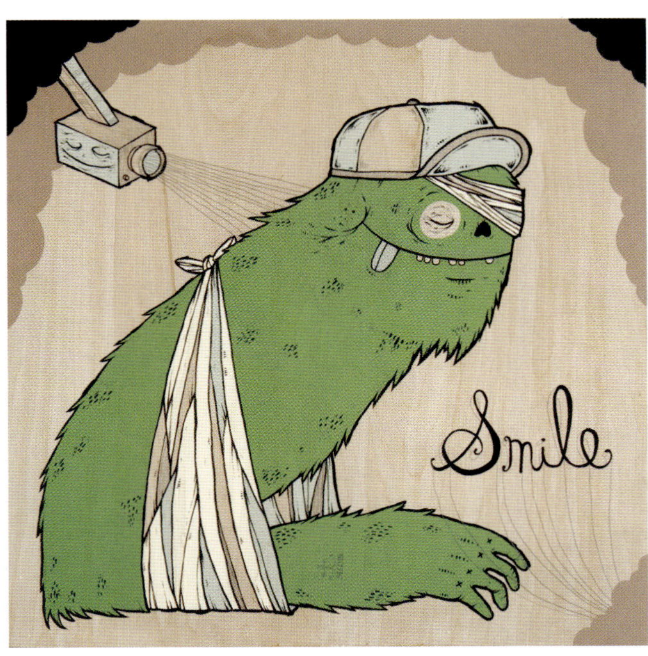Smile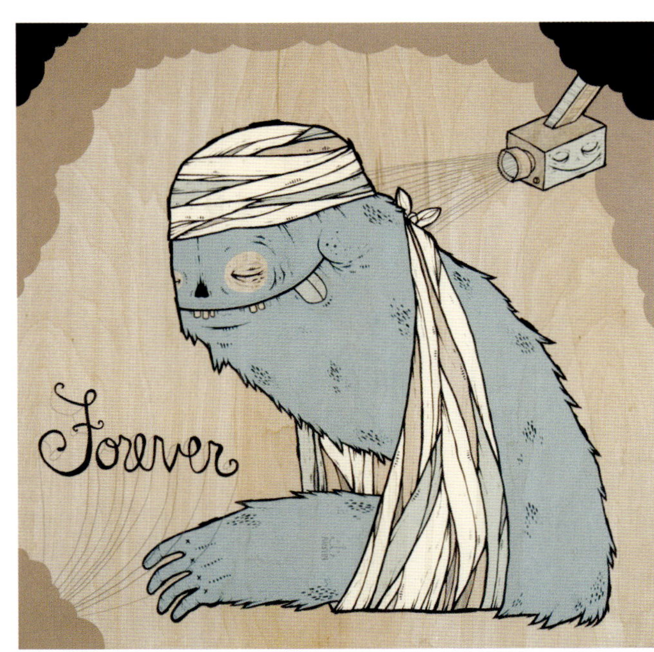Forever

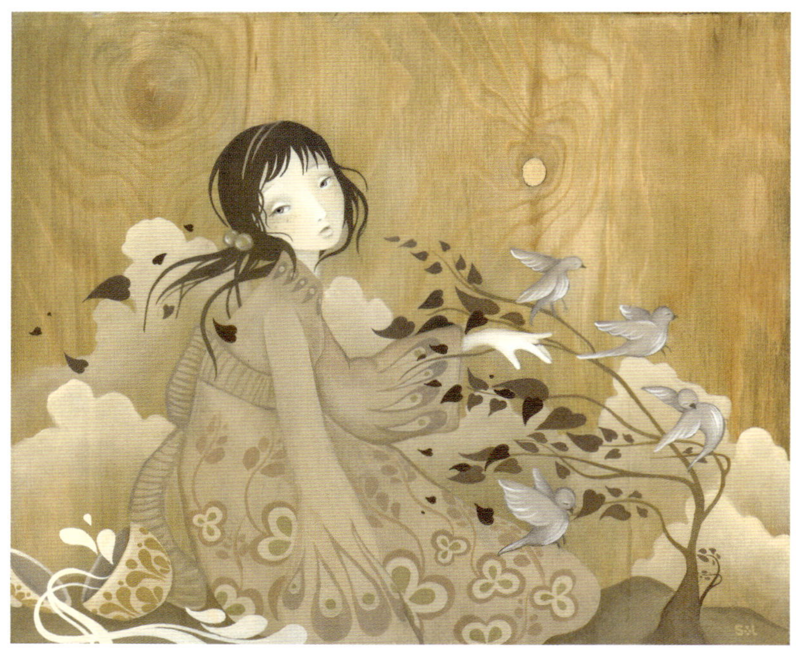

AMY SOL

Amy Sol has always had an active imagination. "I started drawing as early as I can remember," she reminisces. "I used to draw page after page of scenes and characters for hours everyday." Eventually, she grew into her skill and began experimenting with ways in which she could express her ideas. "I've just kept creating and my work seems to have developed and evolved along with my life and my understanding." Sol's work is beautifully rendered in overcast tones that seem to be pulled from an elaborate daydream. "There are times when I need to be somewhere, experience something or actually encounter a person who is part of my imagination," she says. Her work features varying elements, but seems to comprise one conceptual plane. "I dedicated much time to developing techniques that suit my particular ideas and tendencies. Conceptually, I feel that each piece is unique yet originates from the same place." Sol is inspired by science and nature, but finds that, "Inspiration comes unexpectedly and I always welcome it." Although she enjoys sewing, glue guns and "girly stuff," she is usually busy with exhibitions, an experience she describes as "wonderful." Early on, Sol lived in Korea, and now resides in Las Vegas, Nevada, but declares, "The studio is my favorite place to be."

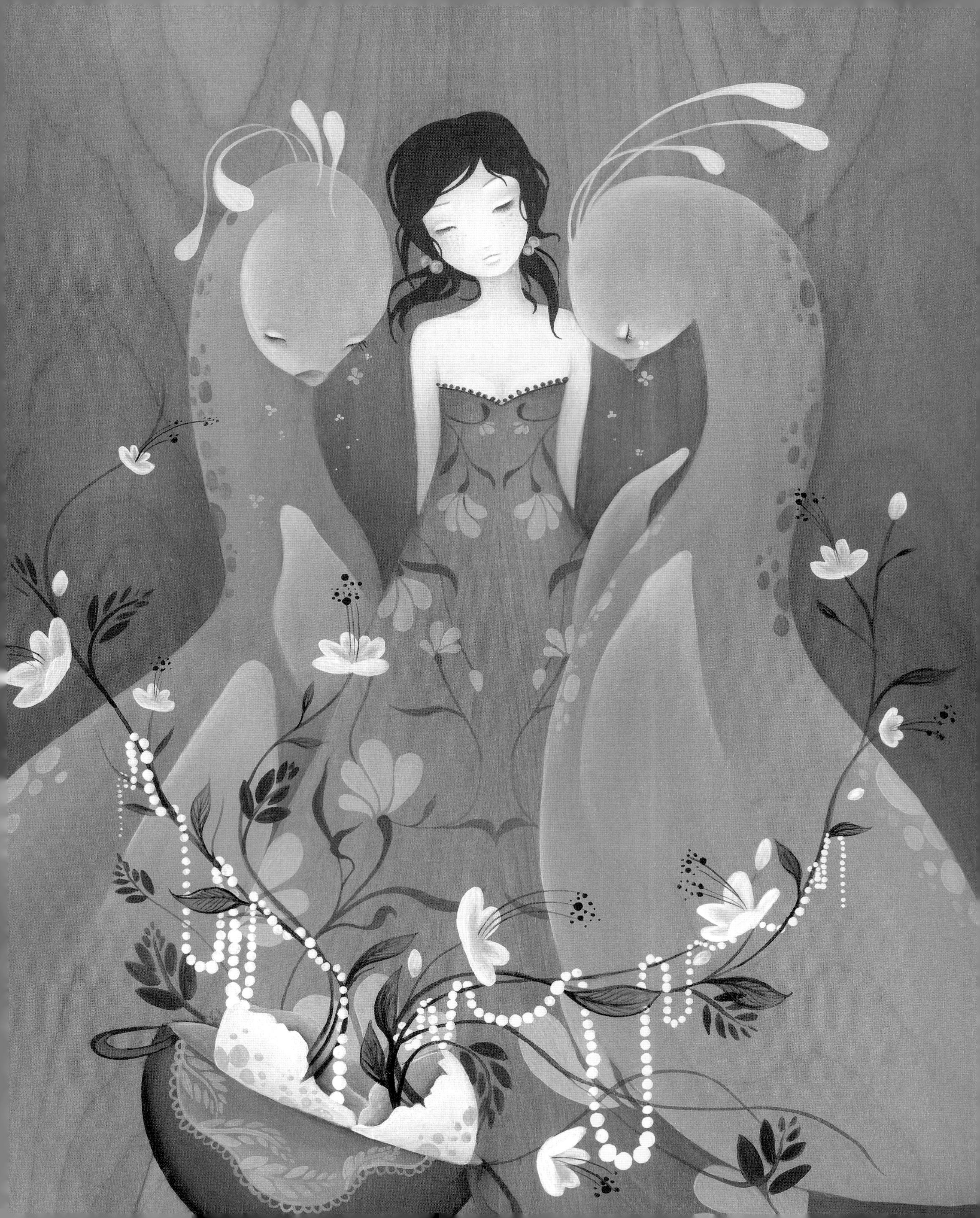

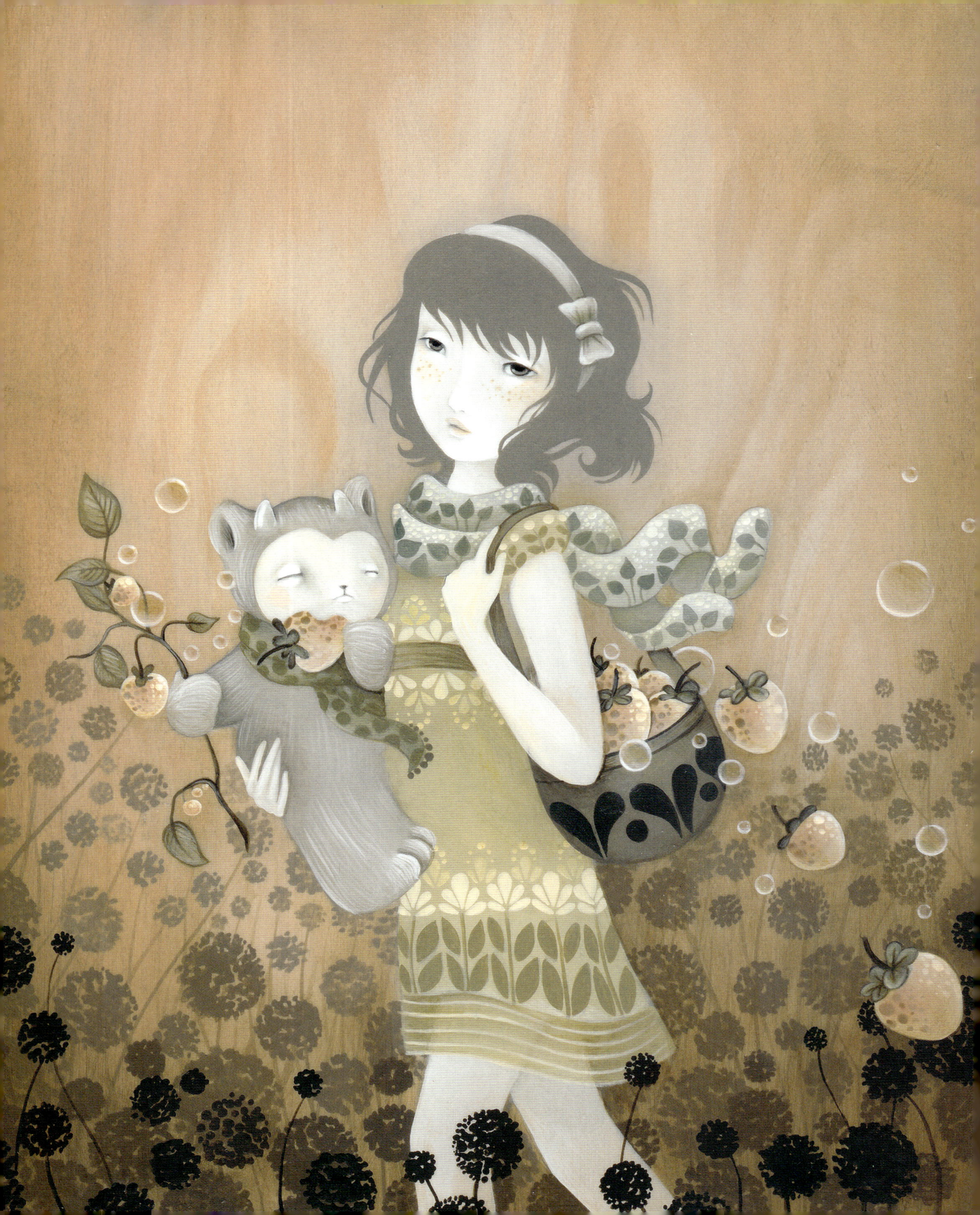

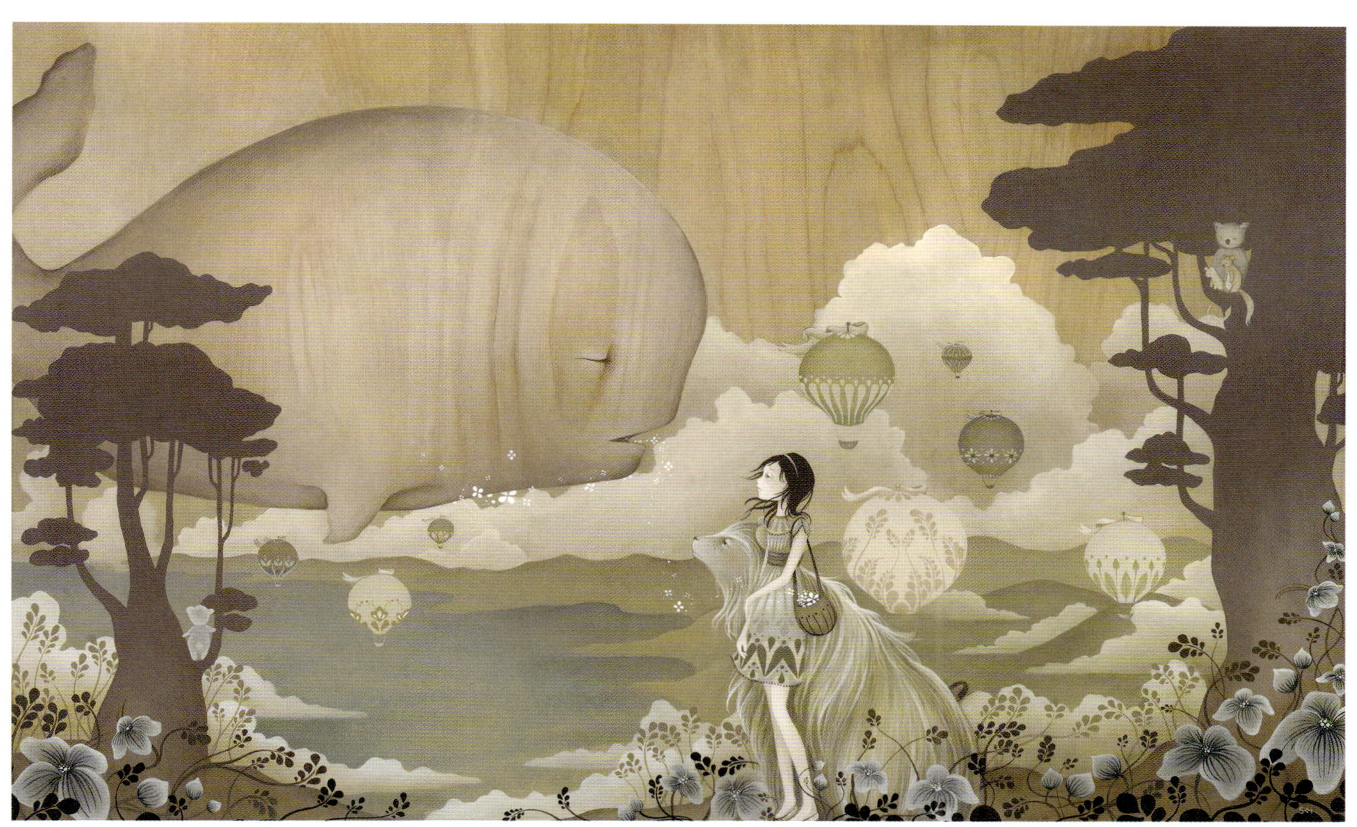

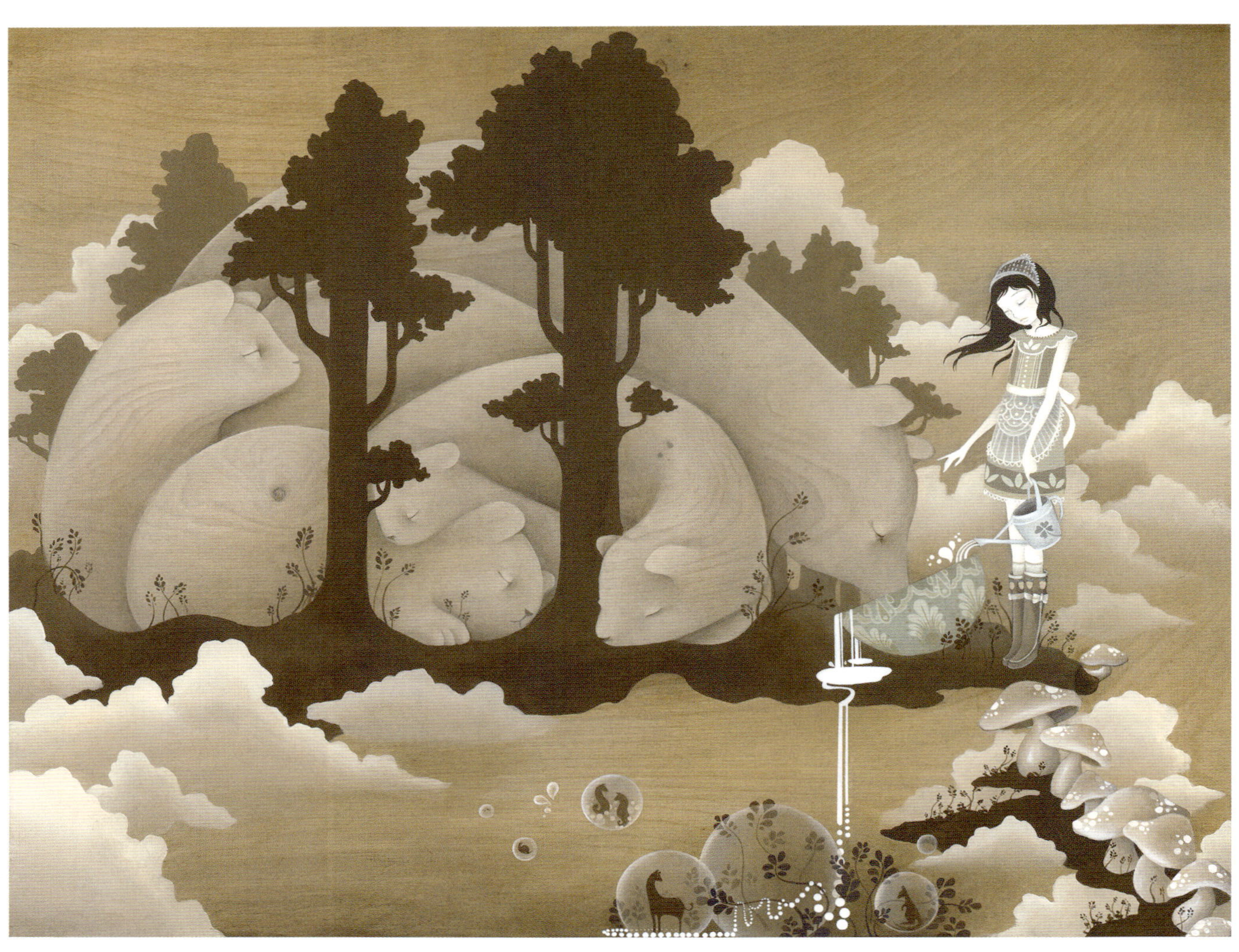

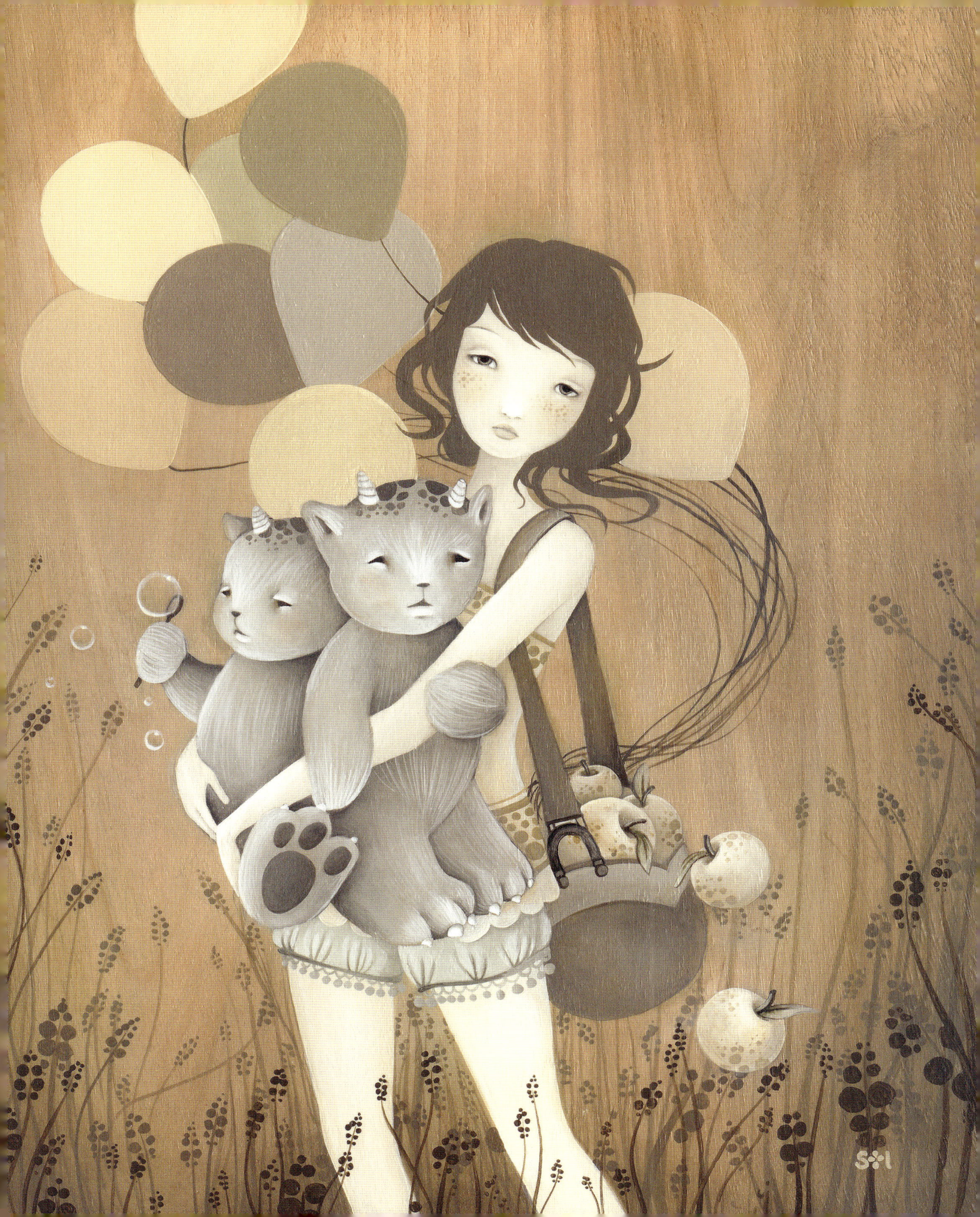

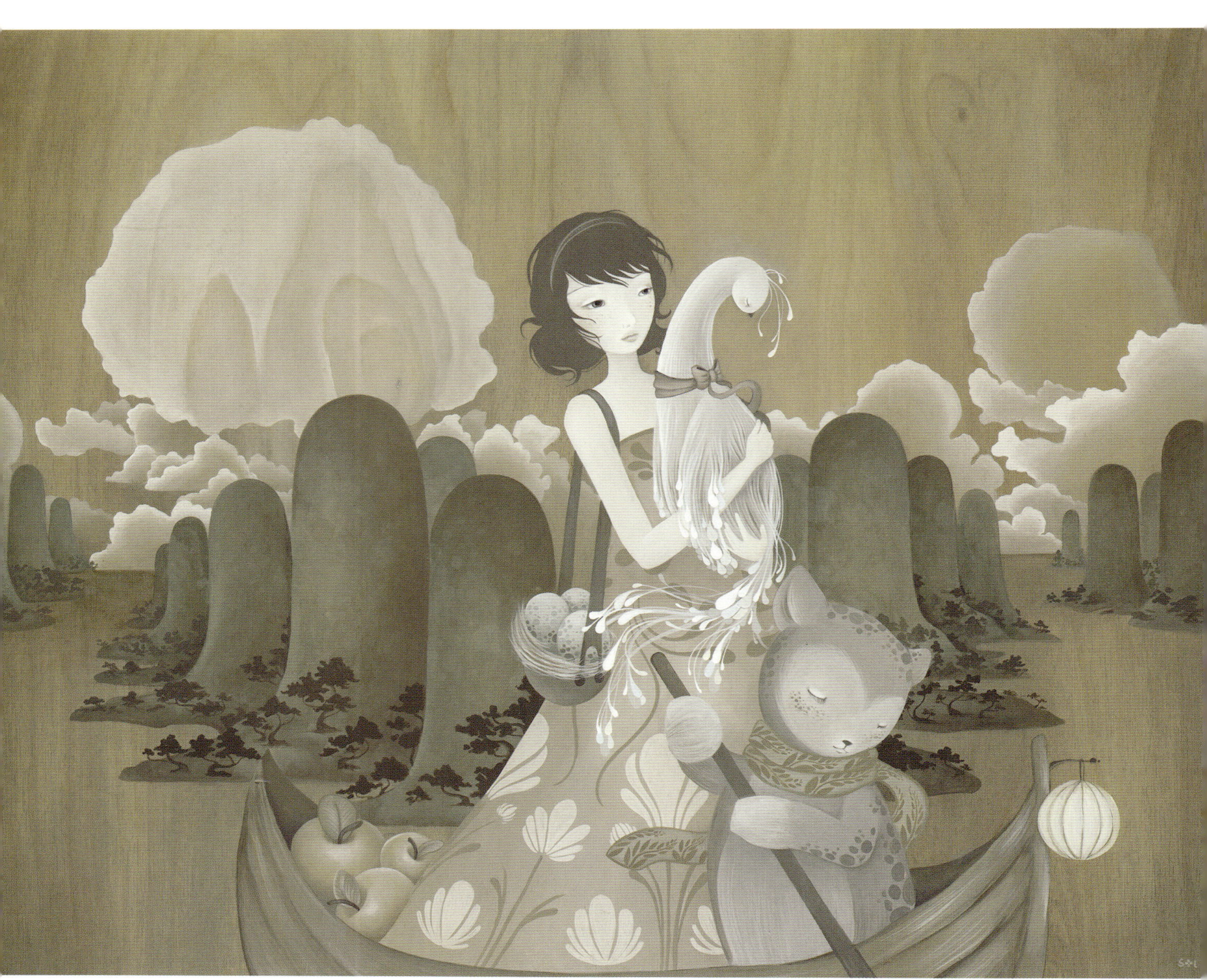

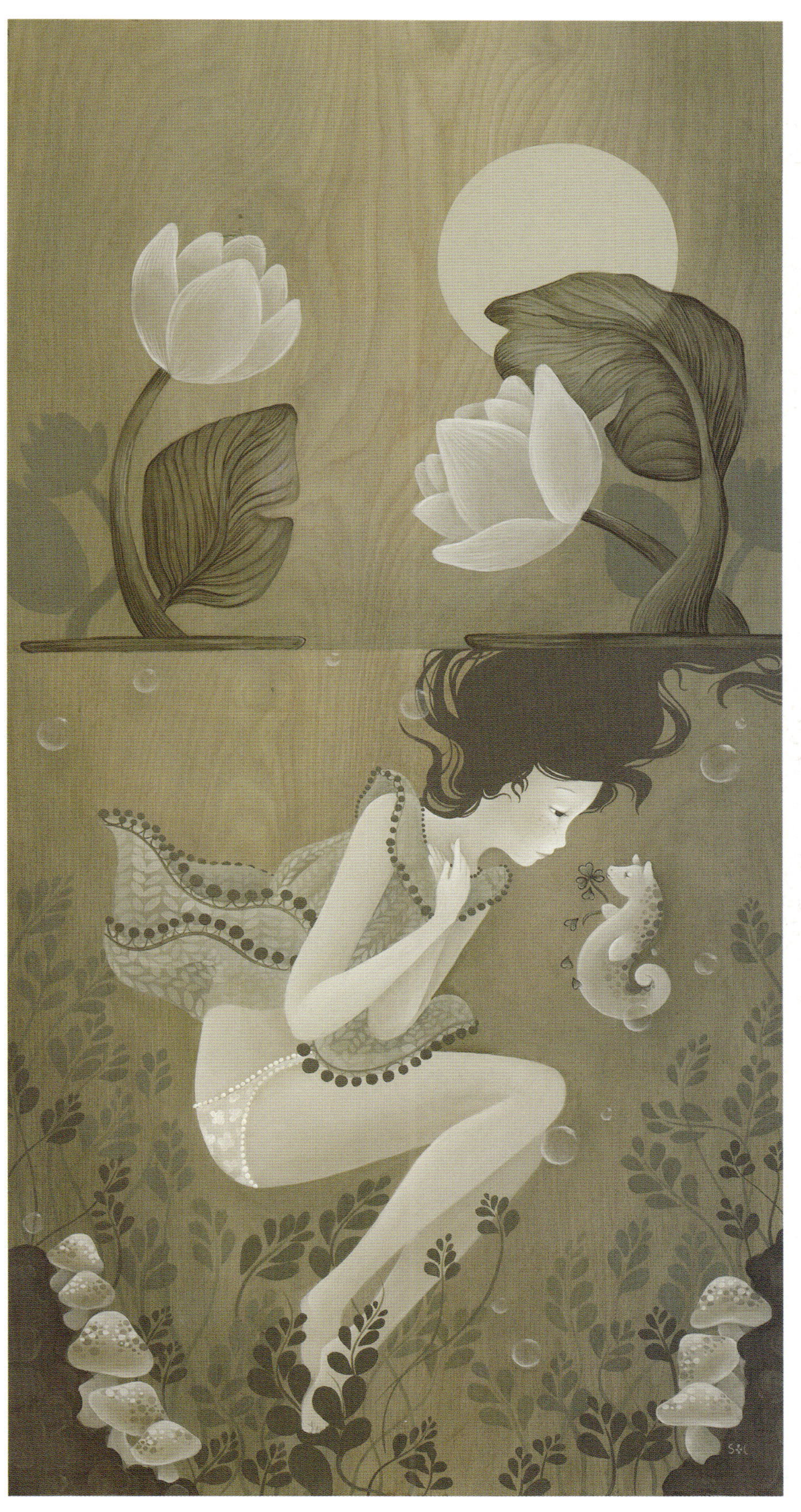

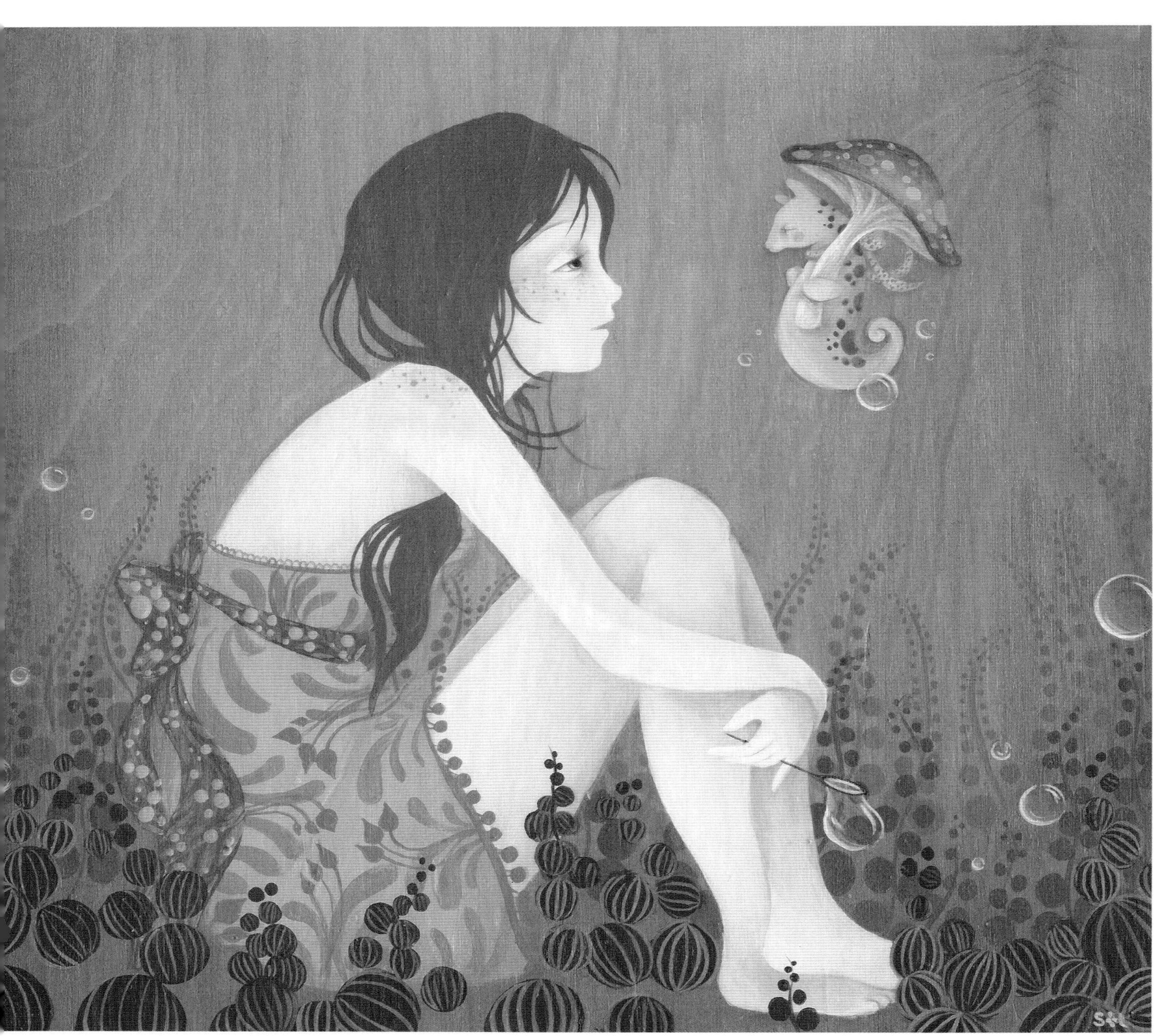

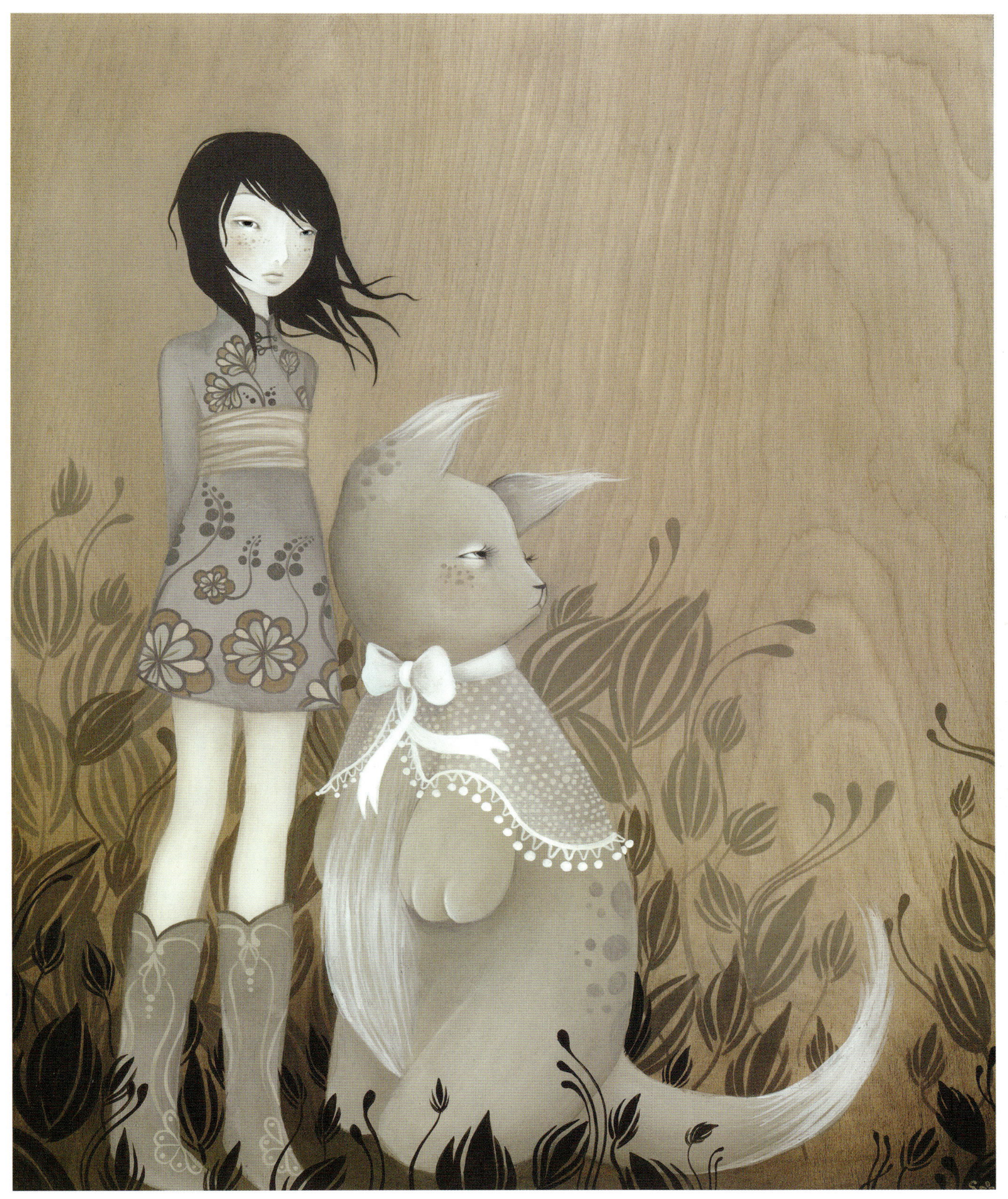

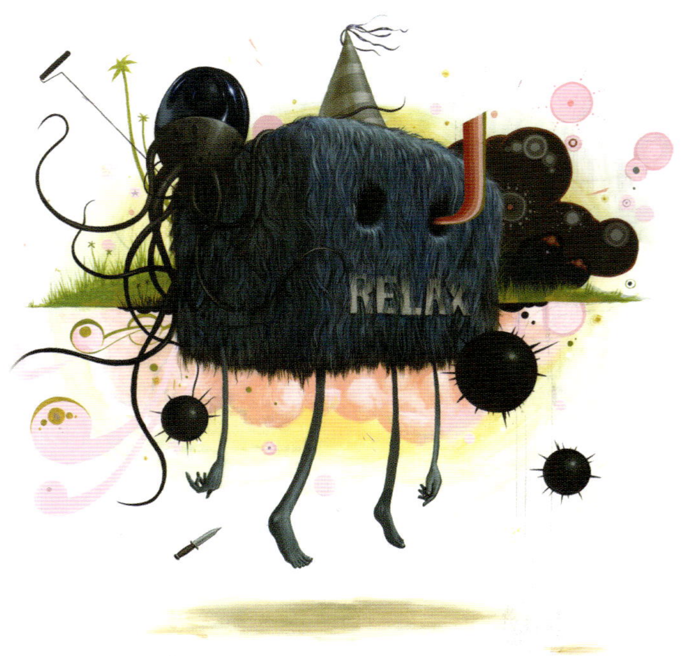

JEFF SOTO

At Art Center College of Design in Pasadena, Jeff Soto planned to major in fine art, but instead, opted for illustration with a fine art minor. "My goal was to make illustrations with backbone and to somehow weave it into my fine art," he explains. After graduating in '02, Soto began his professional career and has worked for clients such as Sony Music, The Village Voice and Esquire, among others. "It can be fun and sometimes it sucks beyond belief," he admits. "During tough jobs I have to keep reminding myself: Jeff, you could still be flipping burgers." But there's an upside, too: "I'd say my major accomplishment is that I've been able to do my thing and not compromise my vision." His work often displays images of both fear and hope. Recently, the latter has taken precedent, as swirling rainbows emerge from dark storm clouds. Nature is a main focus for Soto, who cites Sequoia trees and cacti as influences. "I try to show nature and manmade things either co-existing or fighting each other," he explains. "We can work with nature or we can destroy it slowly and suffer the consequences. We need to find better ways to live in harmony with our natural resources."

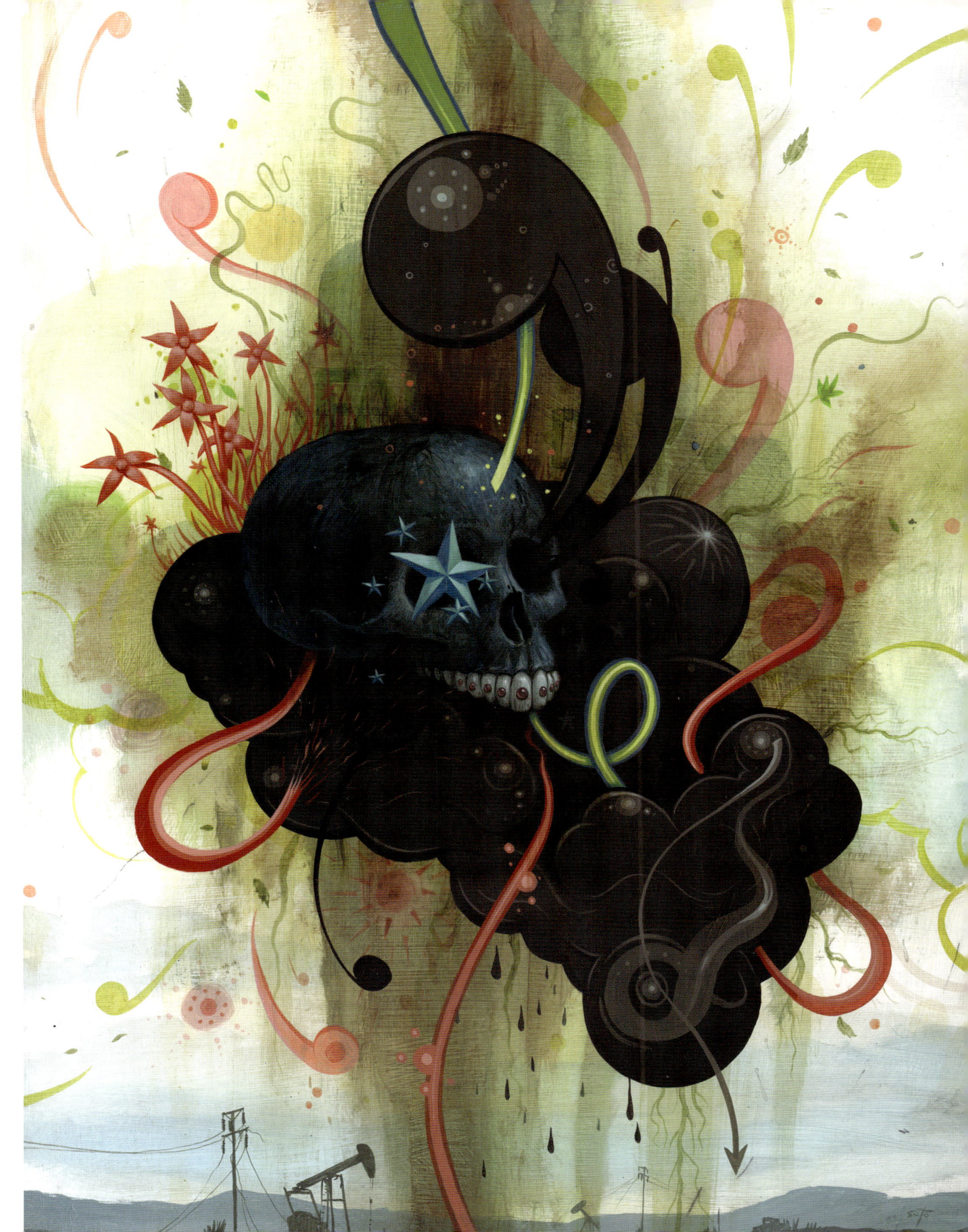

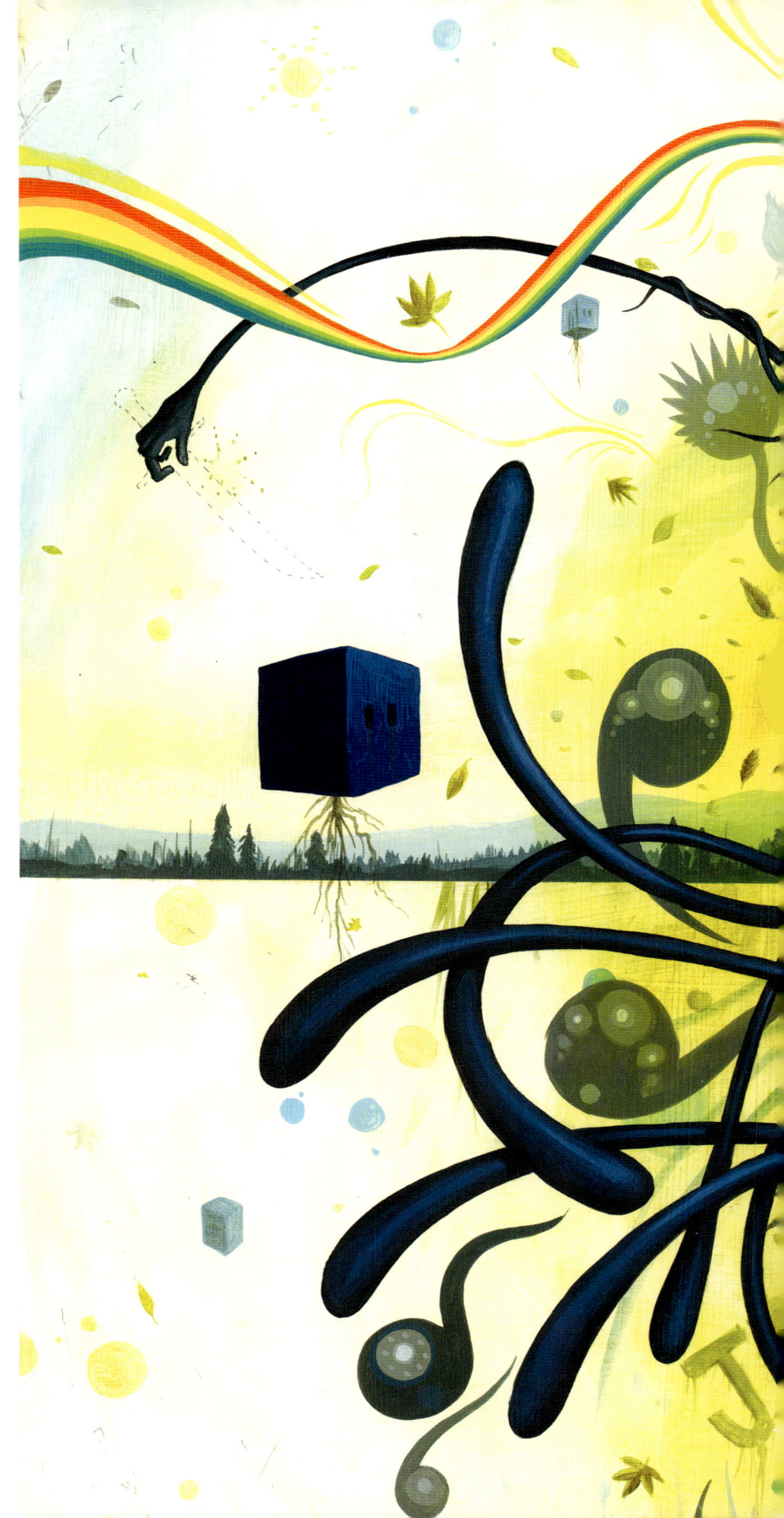

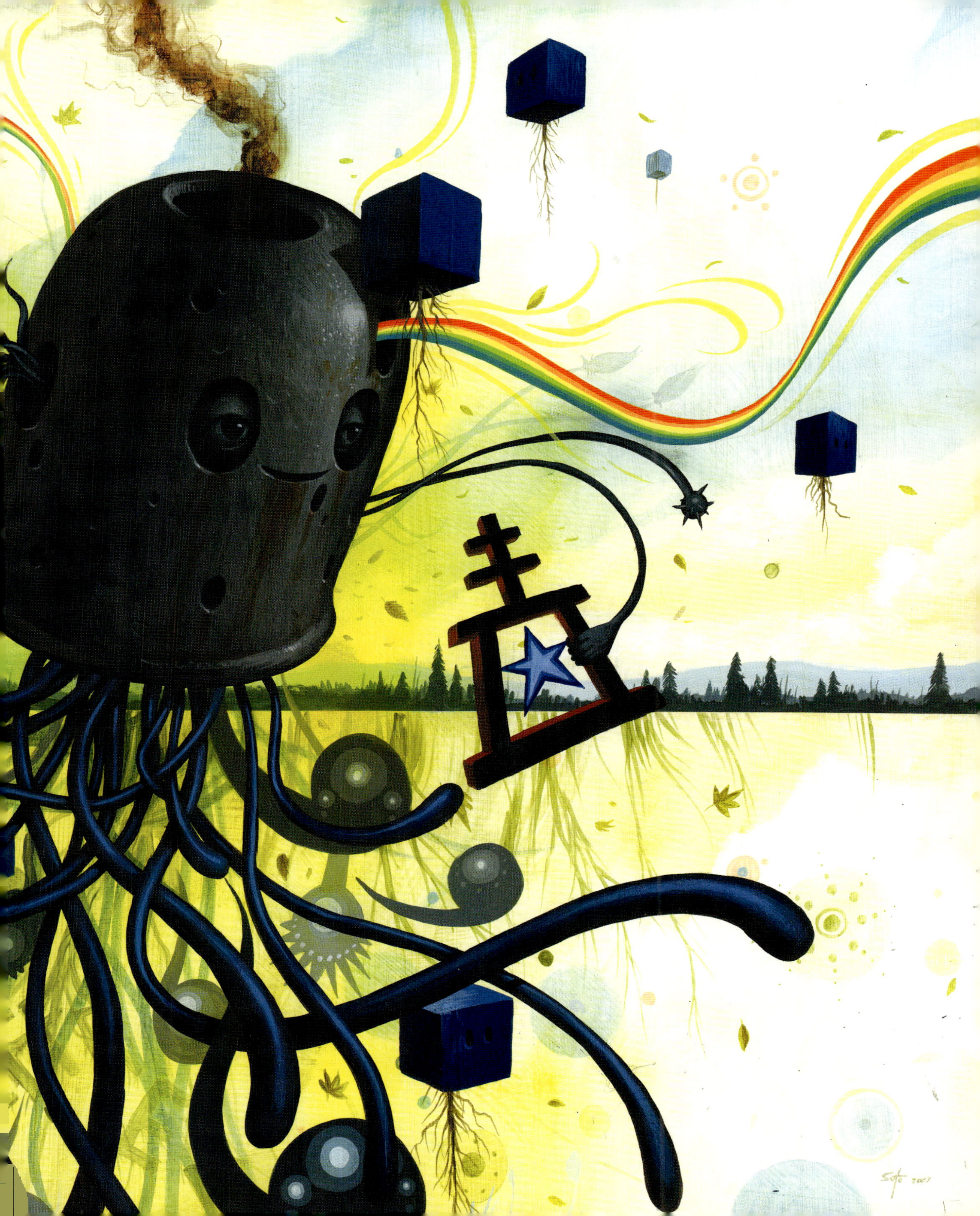

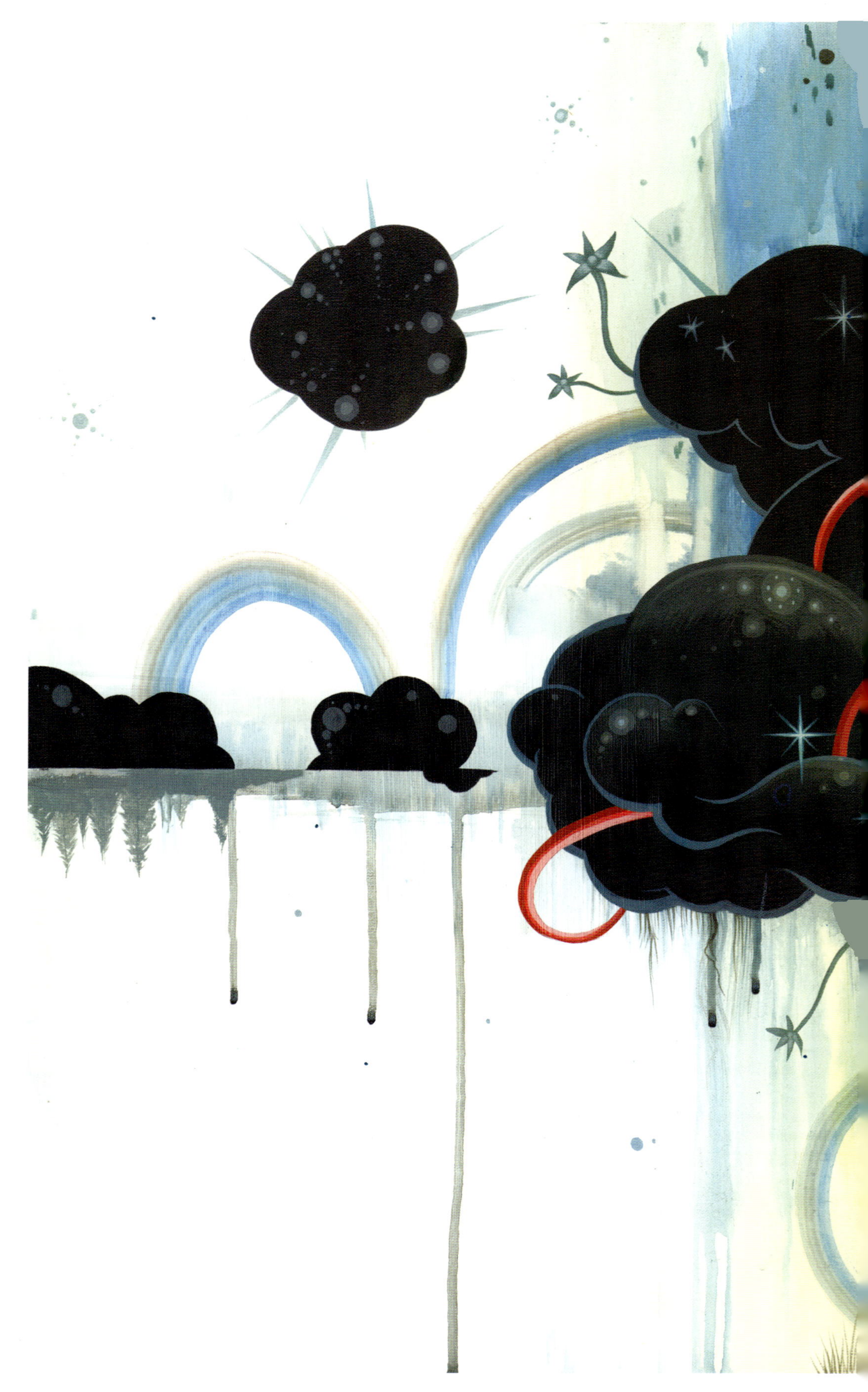

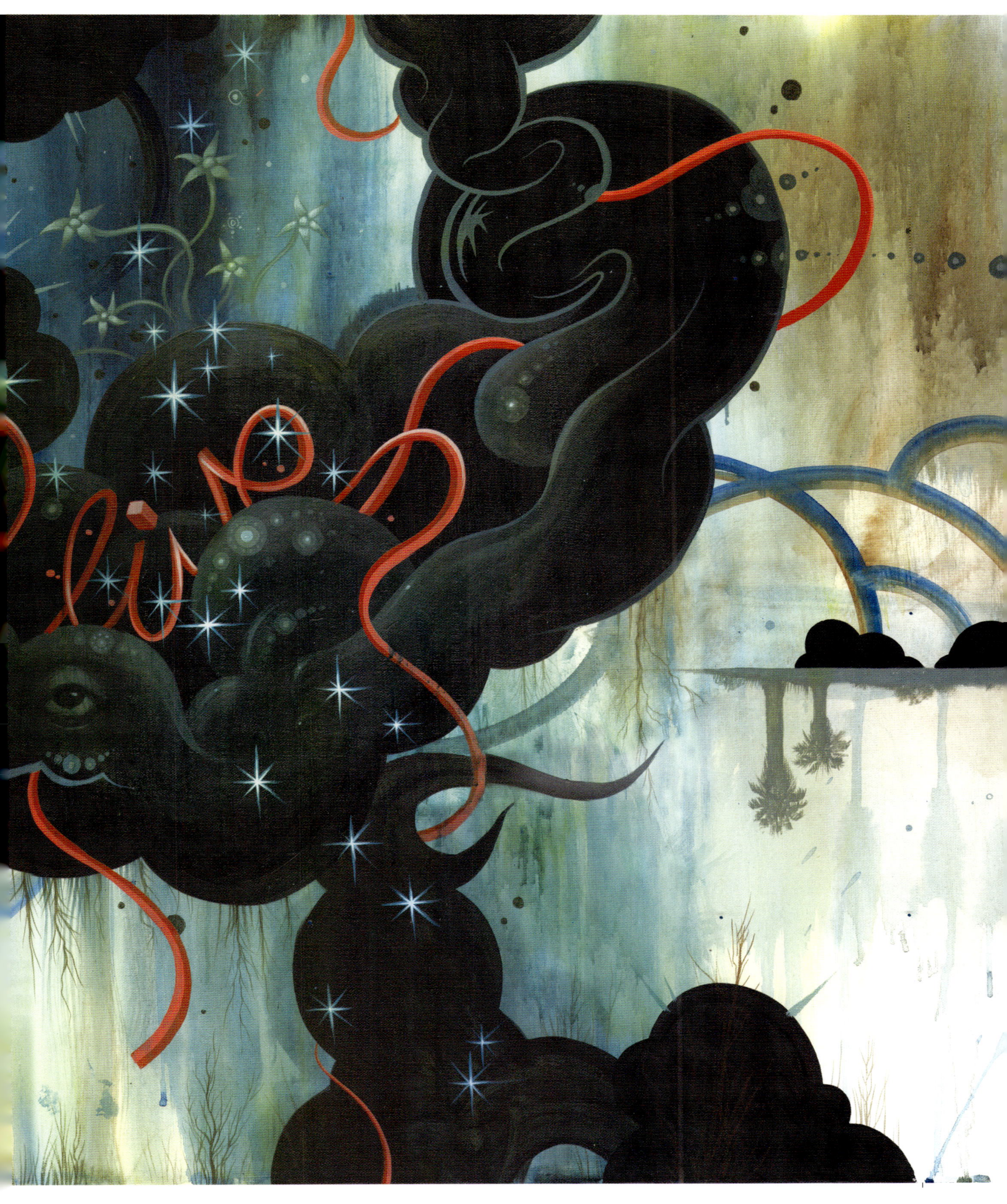

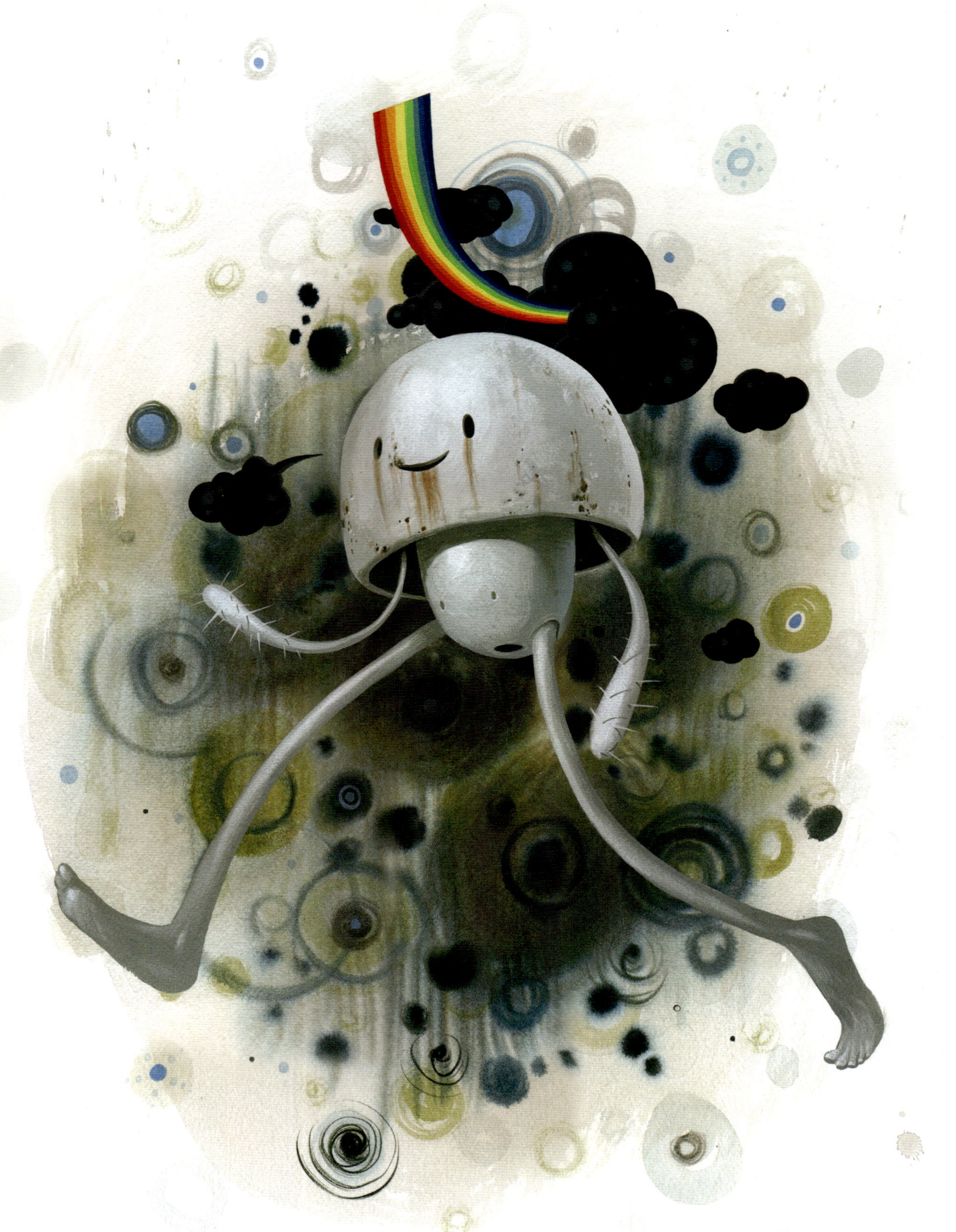

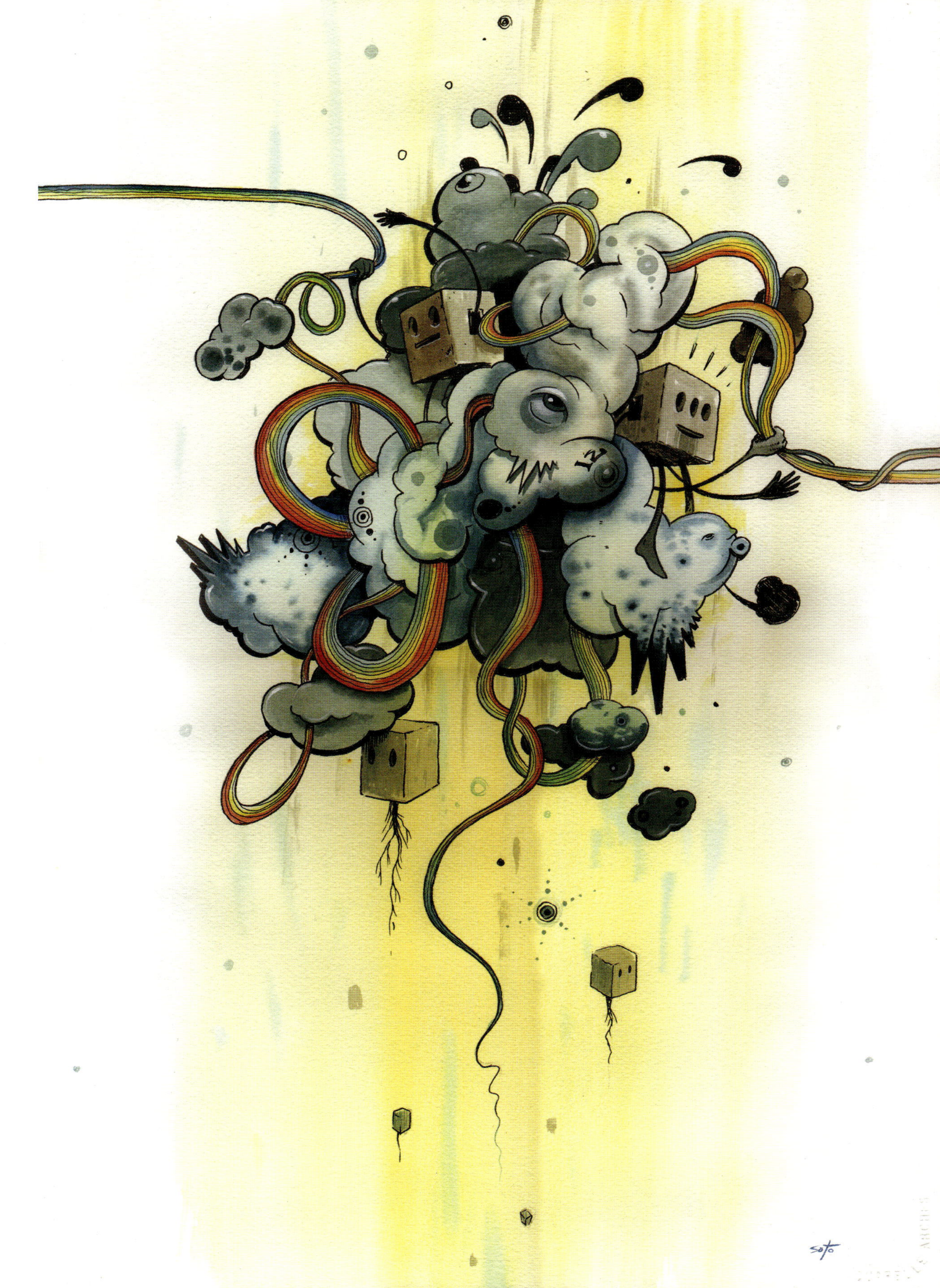

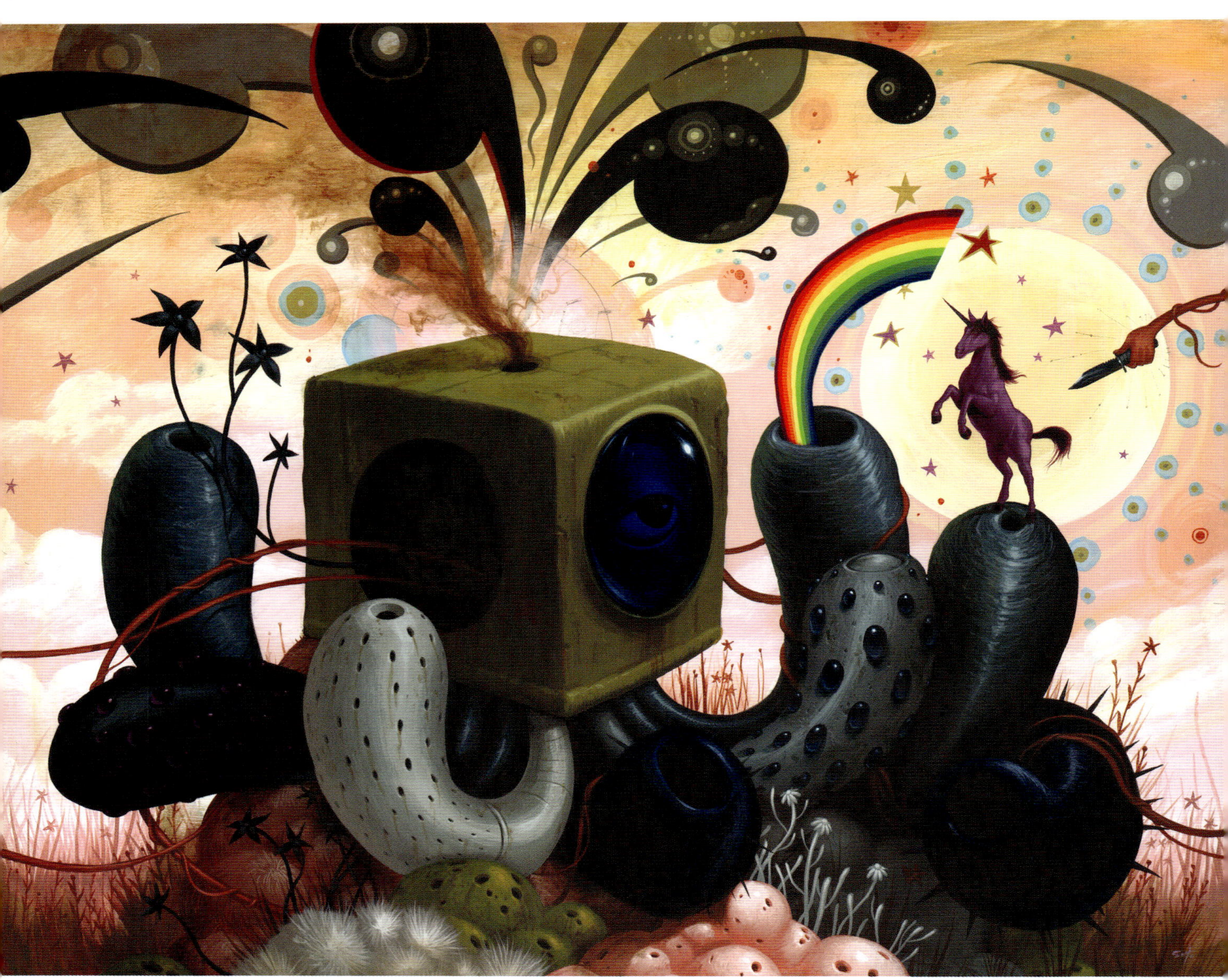

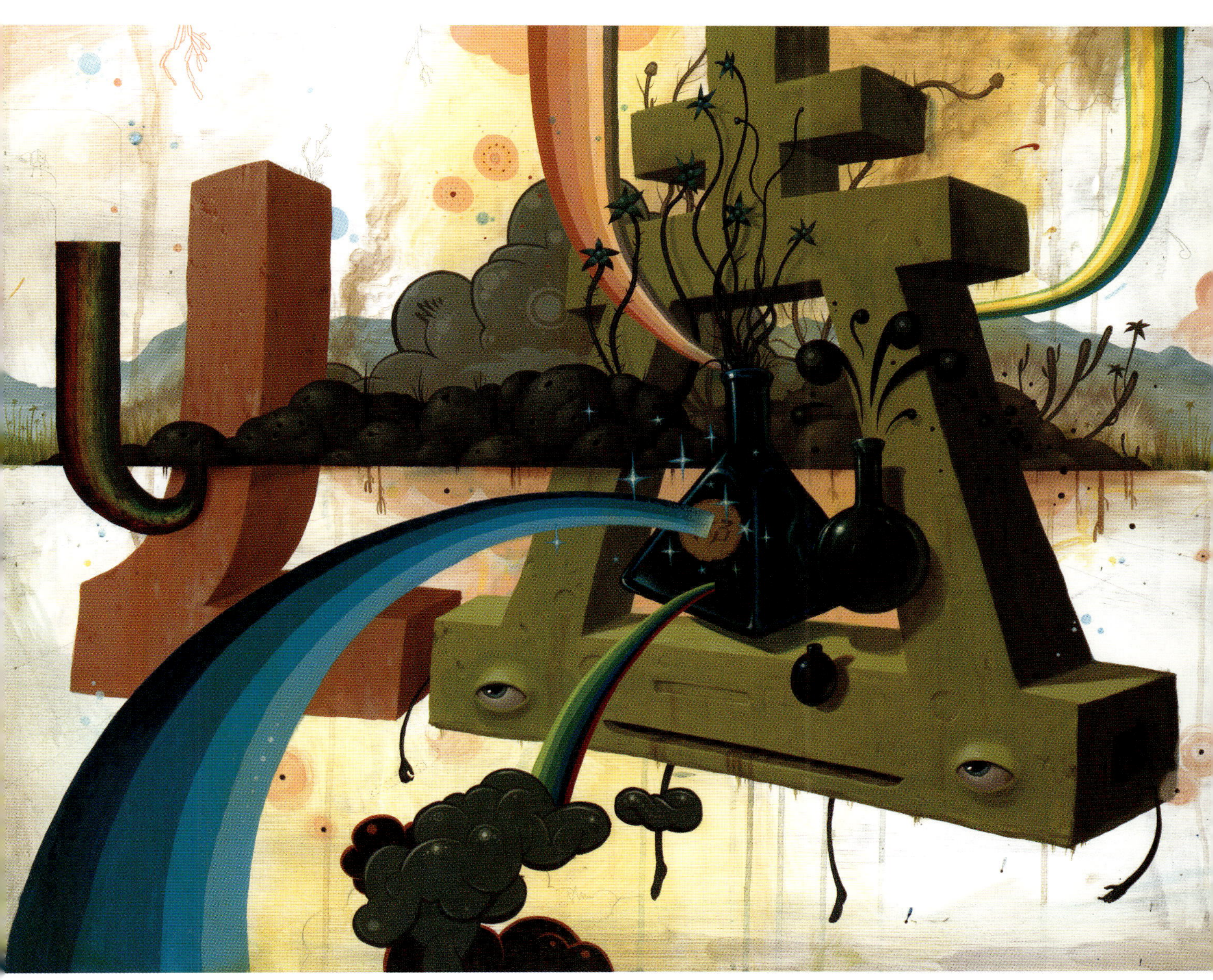

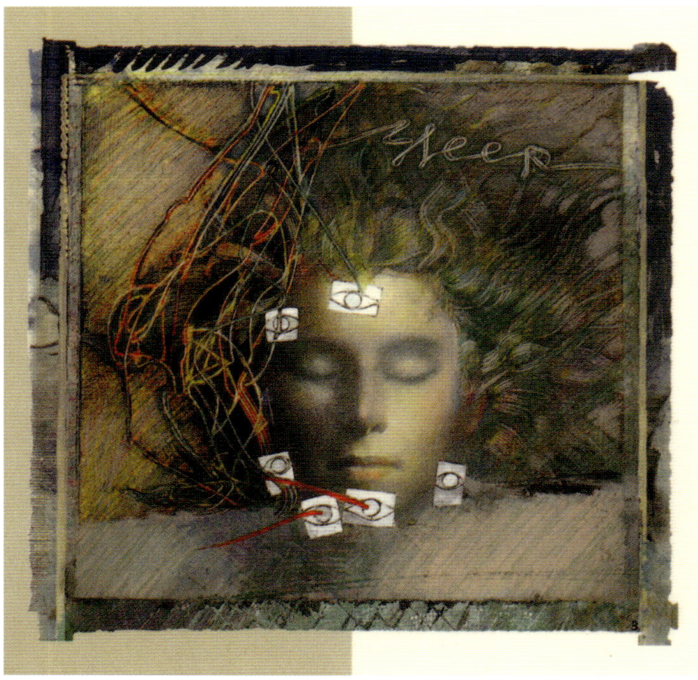

BARRON STOREY

Barron Storey plied his craft at the School of Visual Arts, where he "soaked up the cultural milieu of New York, came to grips with my artistic attributes—and limitations—and with the guidance of great illustrator Robert Weaver, embraced illustration as my lifework." From the gate, he wanted to illustrate man's inhumanity. But Storey had to start with what he knew, motorcycles. After being published in Cycle World, his subject matter began to expand, as did his clientele. He has since illustrated nearly a dozen covers for Time Magazine. "As I learned more, I could illustrate more," he explains. "Now, inhumanity is a major focus of my work." Led by Weaver's example, Storey decided to become a teacher. "Being close to the passion of young artists is a constant source of inspiration," he says. "I'm inspired by idealism and intelligence wherever I find it." In 2001 he received the Educator of the Year Award from the Society of Illustrators. In '07 he published "Life After Black," the follow up to his Harvey Award nominated "Marat/Sade Journals." Overall, Storey is most proud to be doing something that he loves. "Making art is a joy," he says. "Making art that assists in the understanding and affirmation of life is a contribution to all who live."

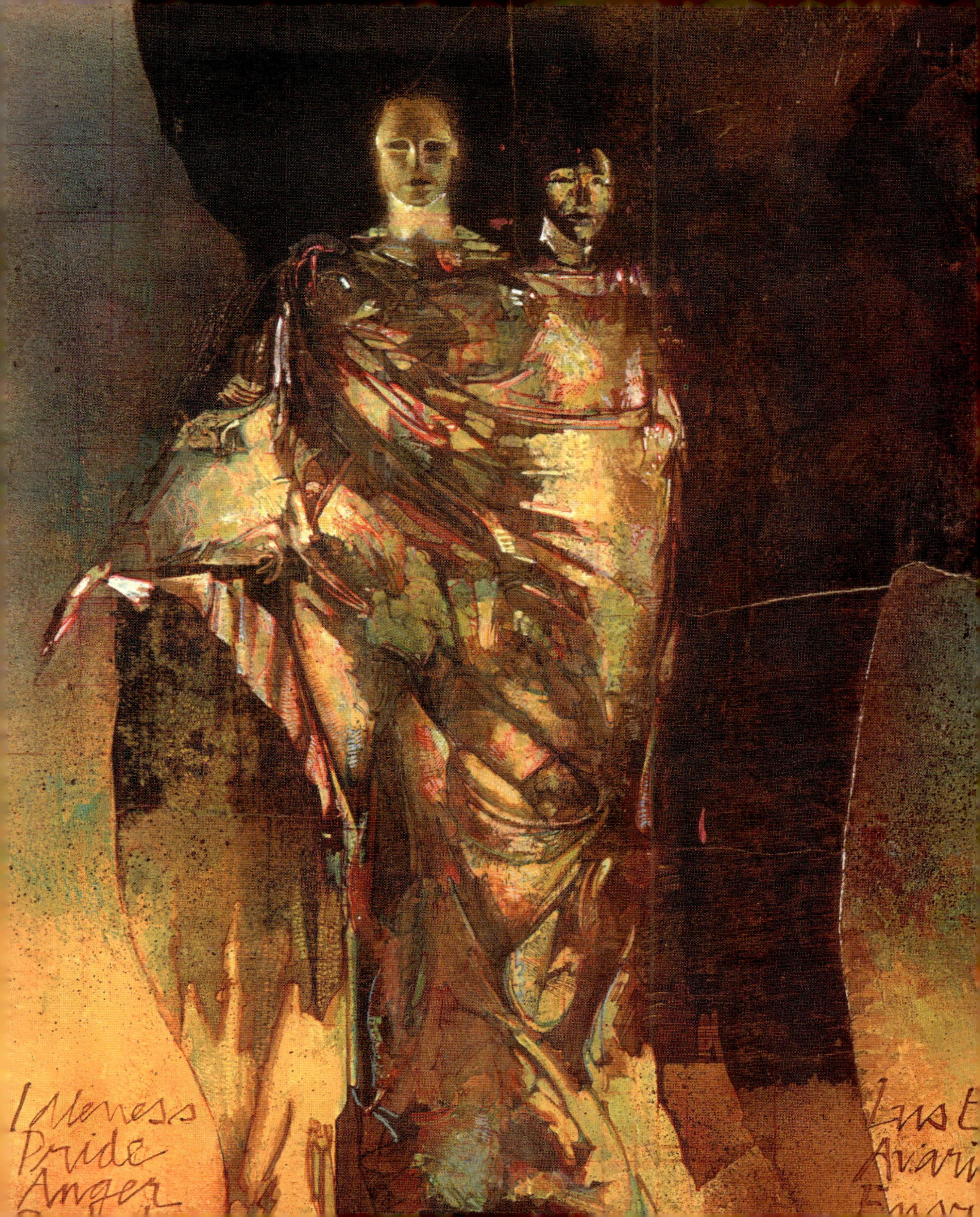
Idleness
Pride
Anger
Lust
Avarice

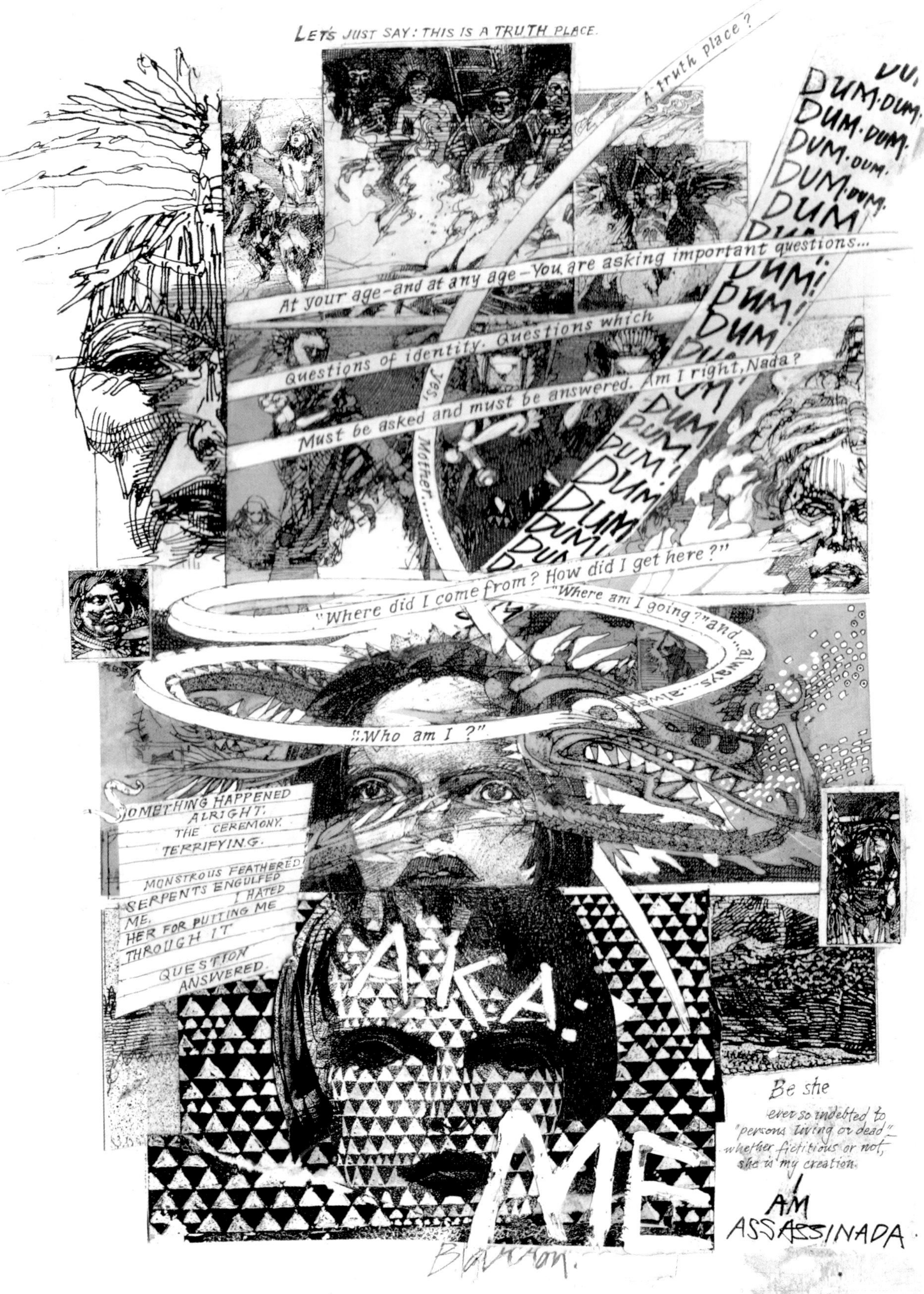

LET'S JUST SAY: THIS IS A TRUTH PLACE.
A truth place?
DUM. DUM.
DUM. DUM.
DUM. DUM.
DUM. DUM.
DUM
DUM
DUM!
DUM!
DUM
DUM!
DUM!
DUM!
DUM!
DUM!
DUM
At your age—and at any age—You are asking important questions...
Questions of identity. Questions which
Must be asked and must be answered. Am I right, Nada?
Yes, Mother.....
"Where did I come from? How did I get here?"
"Where am I going?" and...always...always
"Who am I?"
SOMETHING HAPPENED ALRIGHT. THE CEREMONY. TERRIFYING.
MONSTROUS FEATHERED SERPENTS ENGULFED ME. I HATED HER FOR PUTTING ME THROUGH IT
QUESTION ANSWERED.
A.K.A.
ME
Be she ever so indebted to "persons living or dead" whether fictitious or not, she is my creation.
I AM ASSASSINADA

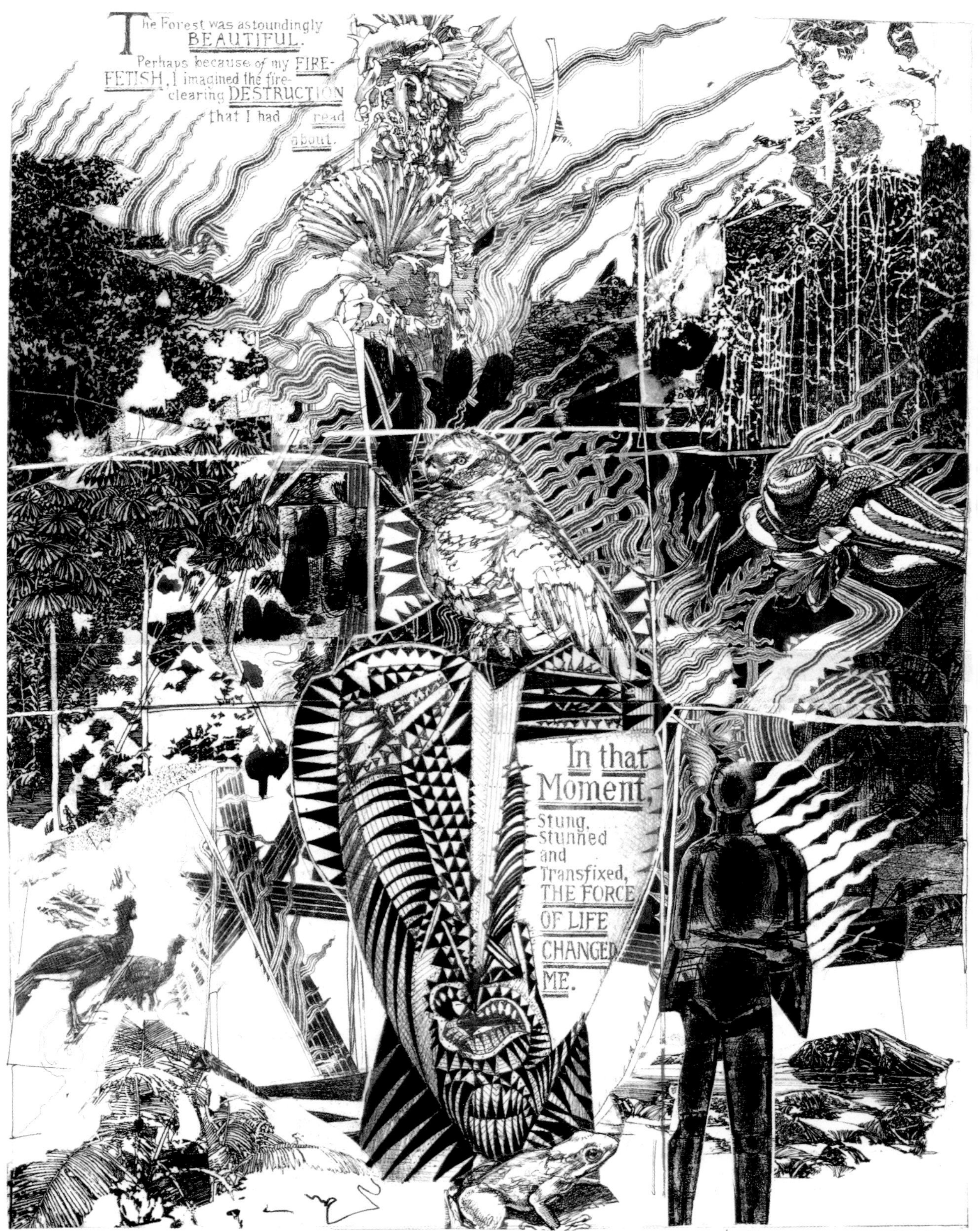
The Forest was astoundingly BEAUTIFUL.
Perhaps because of my FIRE-FETISH, I imagined the fire-clearing DESTRUCTION that I had read about.
In that Moment, stung, stunned and Transfixed, THE FORCE OF LIFE CHANGED ME.
Burn, Parrot! Burn, Bromeliad and Emerald Tree Snake! Burn Life and Culture, Burn, Mankind! Oh, Dear God: NO!

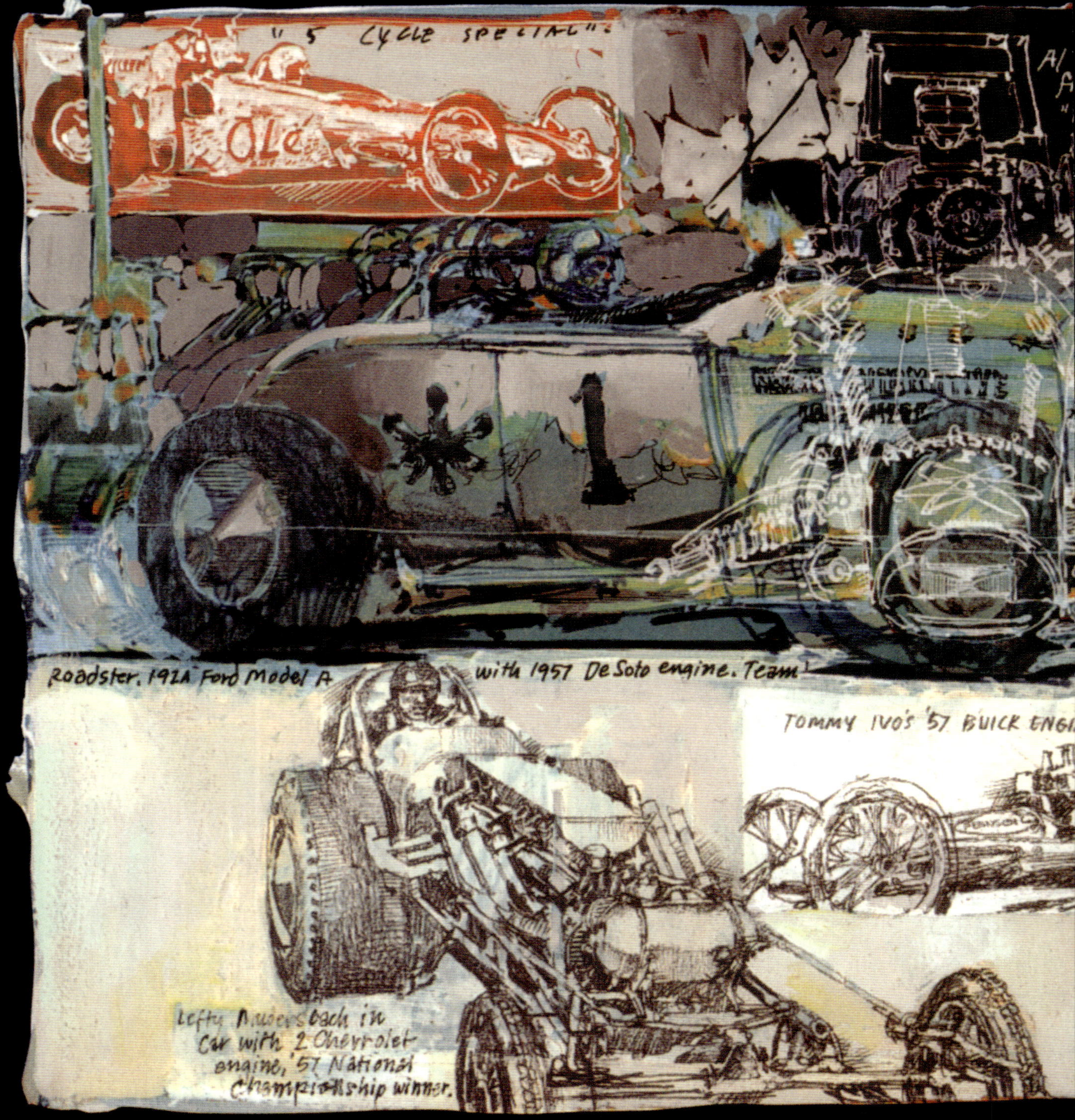

"5 CYCLE SPECIAL"
OLé
1
Roadster. 1924 Ford Model A with 1957 De Soto engine. Team
TOMMY IVO'S '57 BUICK ENGI
Lefty Nadersbach in car with 2 Chevrolet engine, '57 National Championship winner.

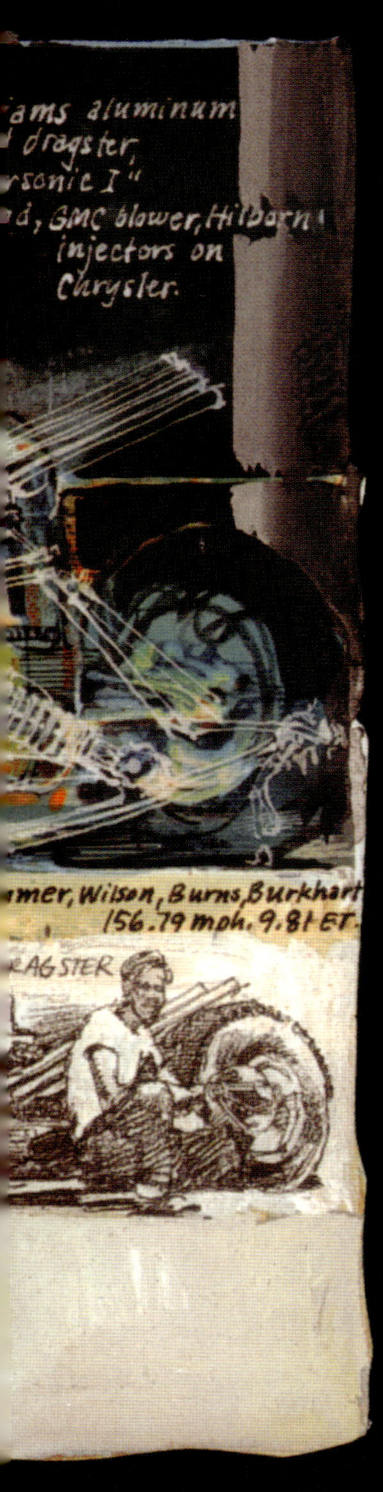
ams aluminum
dragster,
sonic I"
d, GMC blower, Hilborn
injectors on
Chrysler.
mer, Wilson, Burns, Burkhart
156.79 mph. 9.81 ET.
RAGSTER

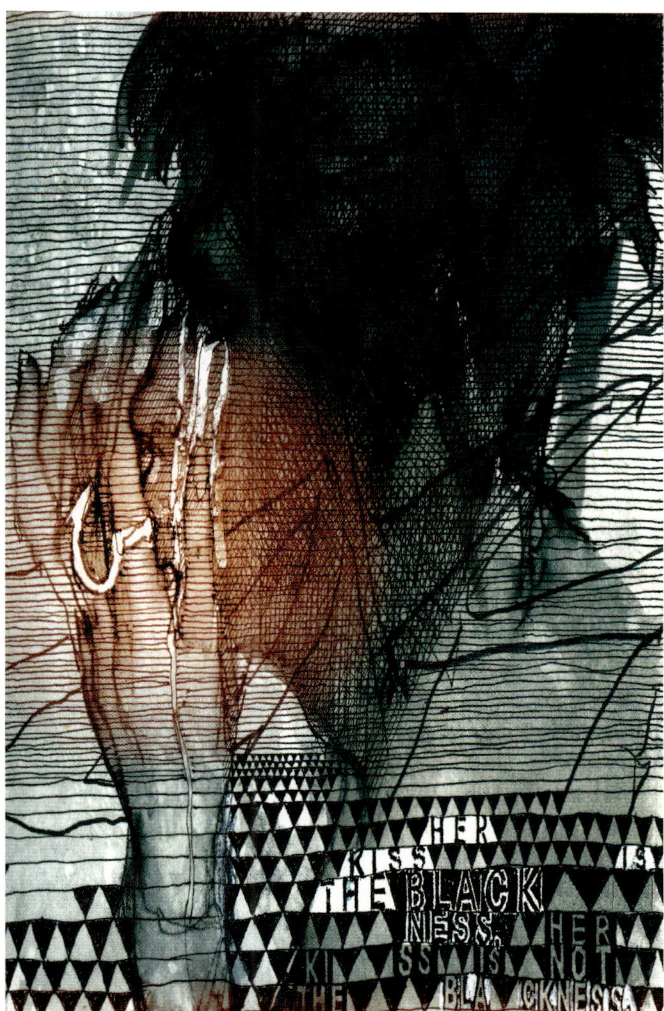
HER
KISS IS
THE BLACK
NESS HER
KISS IS NOT
THE BLACKNESS

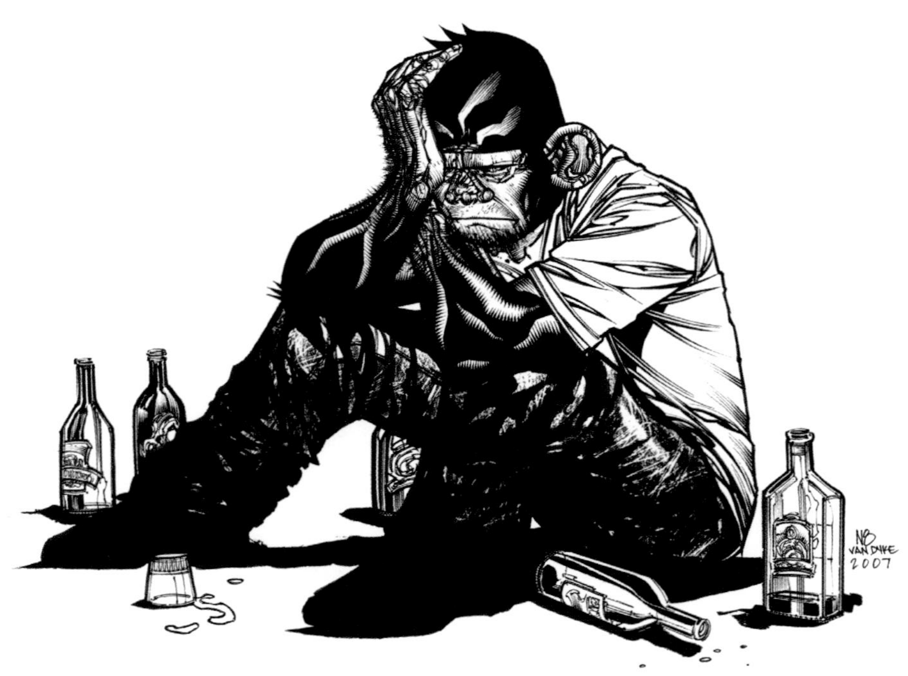

NATE VAN DYKE

Despite offers from prestigious art schools, Nate Van Dyke chose to forgo a formal education. "I believe that one of the reasons that I've gotten to where I am today is by having not gone to art school and come out a droid as so many kids seem to do," he explains. "It forced me to continue down the self-taught road and learn through trial and error." Contrary to this philosophy, Van Dyke has taught classes at California College of the Arts. "I find myself telling the students that not going to school may have been one of the best decisions I've made." His decision helped him develop a unique voice, and he is known for his mixed media illustrations. His work often features the "crazy chimp" he created for Heavy Metal Magazine (who recently released the book, Plan A: The Art of Nate Van Dyke). He has also designed custom Chuck Taylor shoes for Converse. "I want to give people a hint of what goes on in my mind," he says. "I want people to view my work and have it pull an emotion out of them. If I get them to feel disgust, to laugh, to feel sorry for the character or whatever else it may be, I've achieved my goal. I can turn the page and do it all over again."

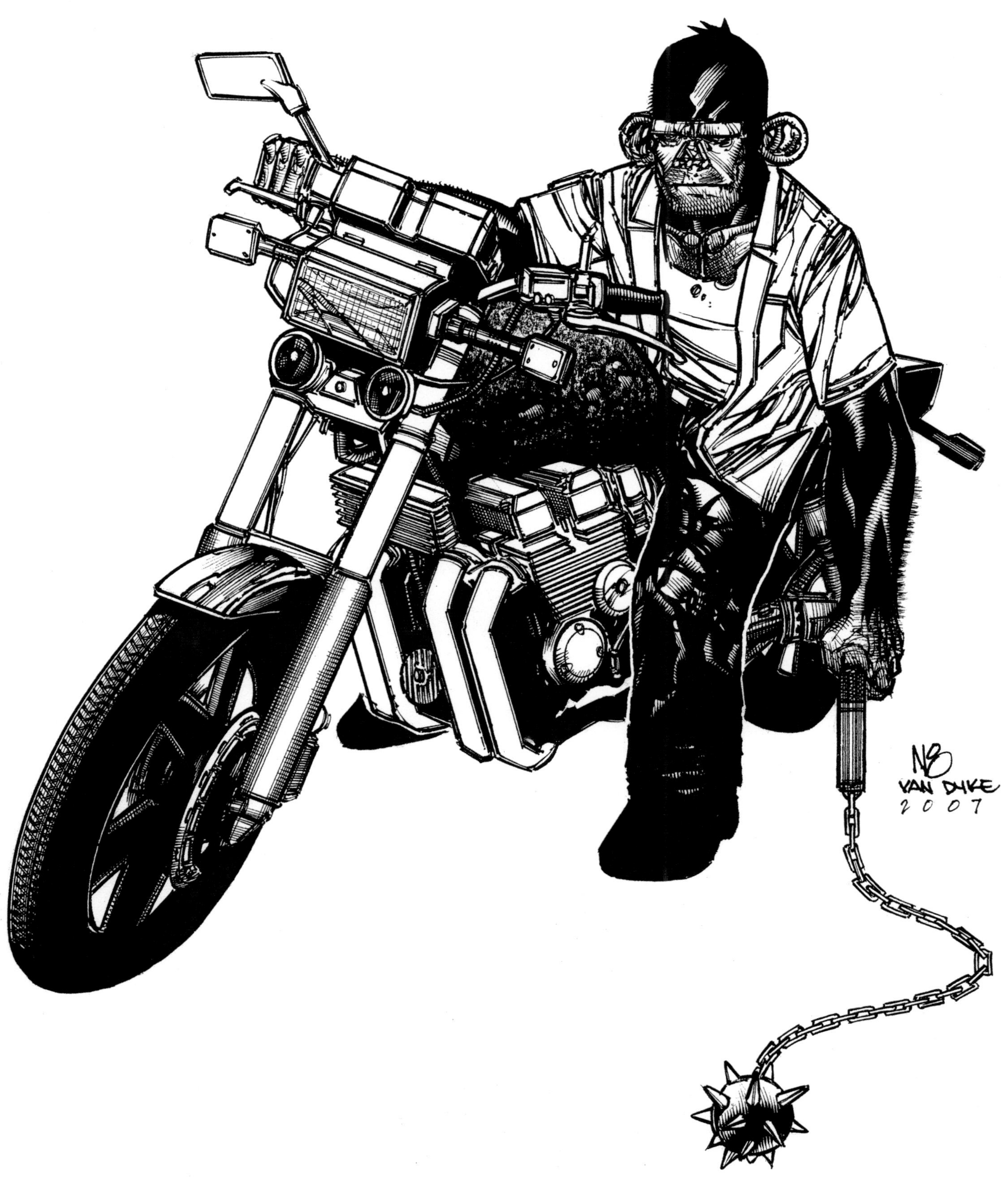

NB
VAN DYKE
2 0 0 7

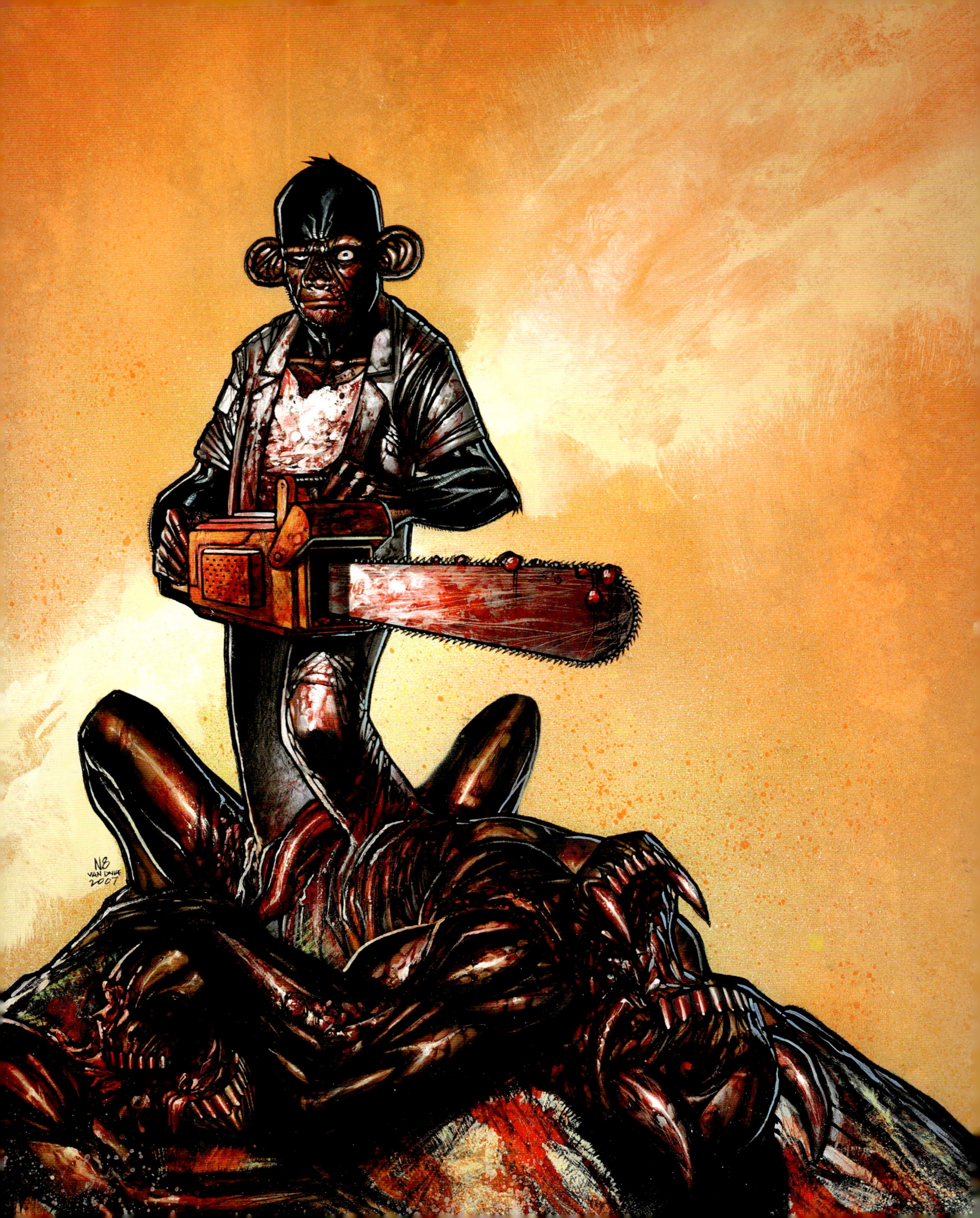

N8
VAN DYKE
2007

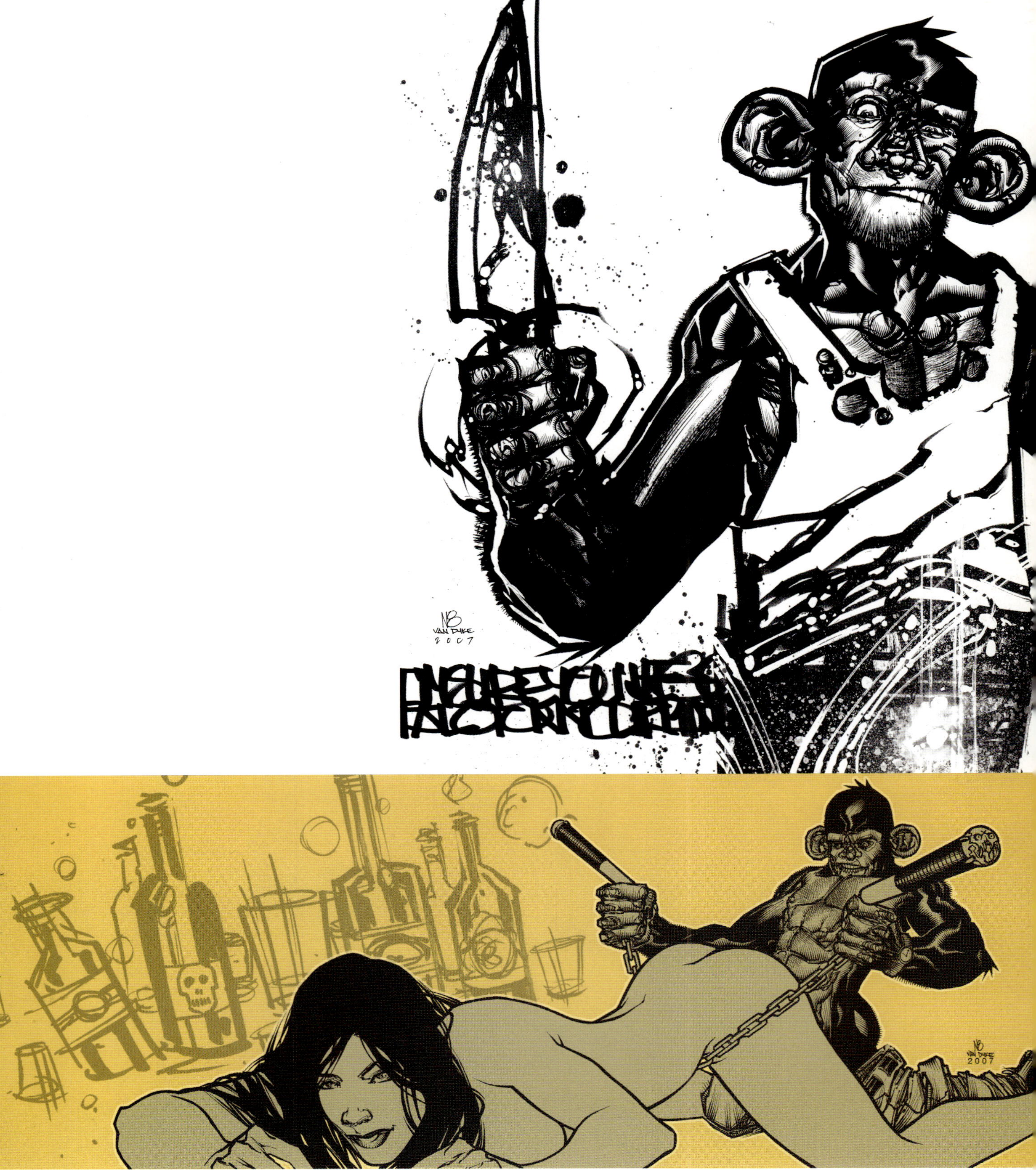

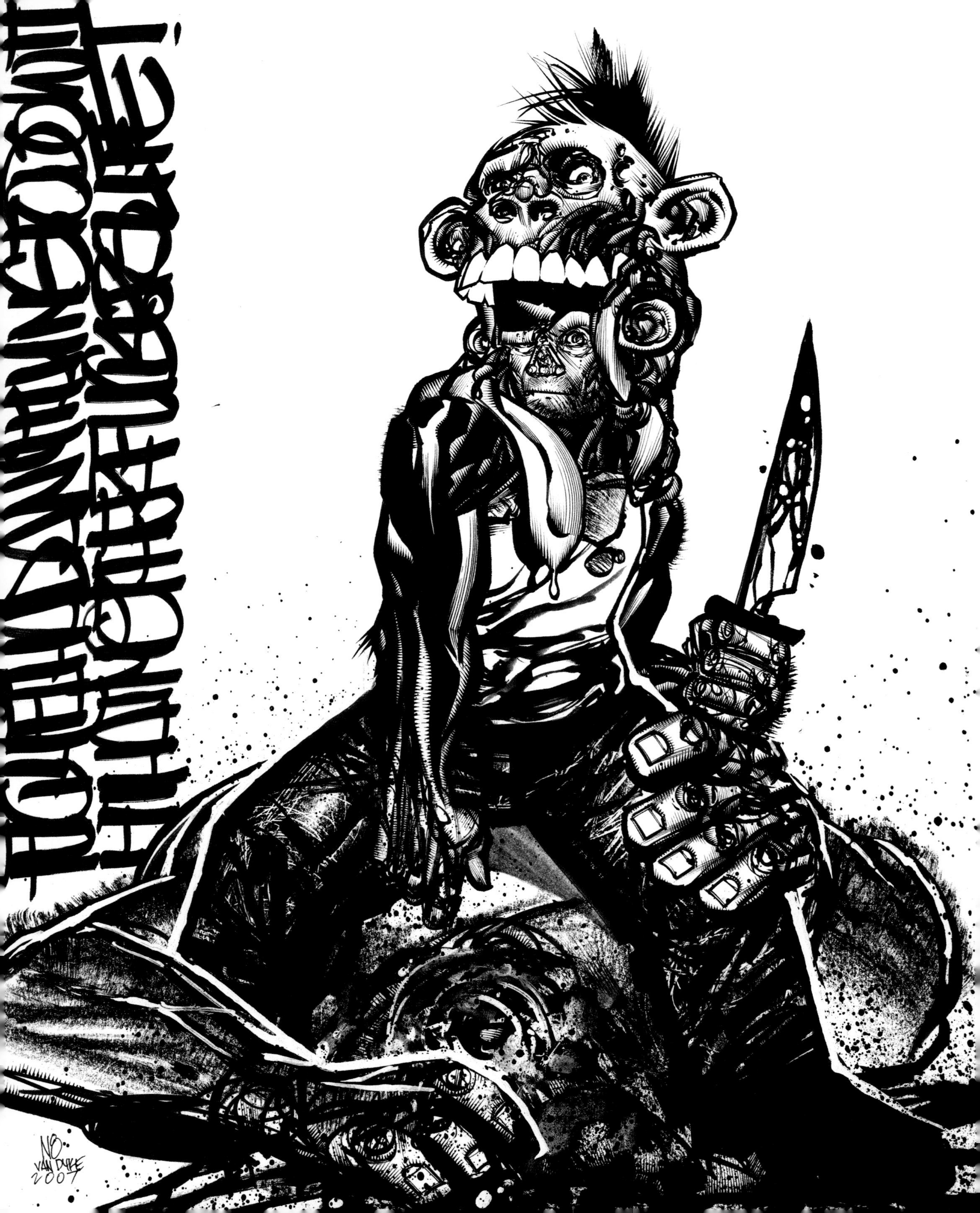

NB
VAN DYKE
2007

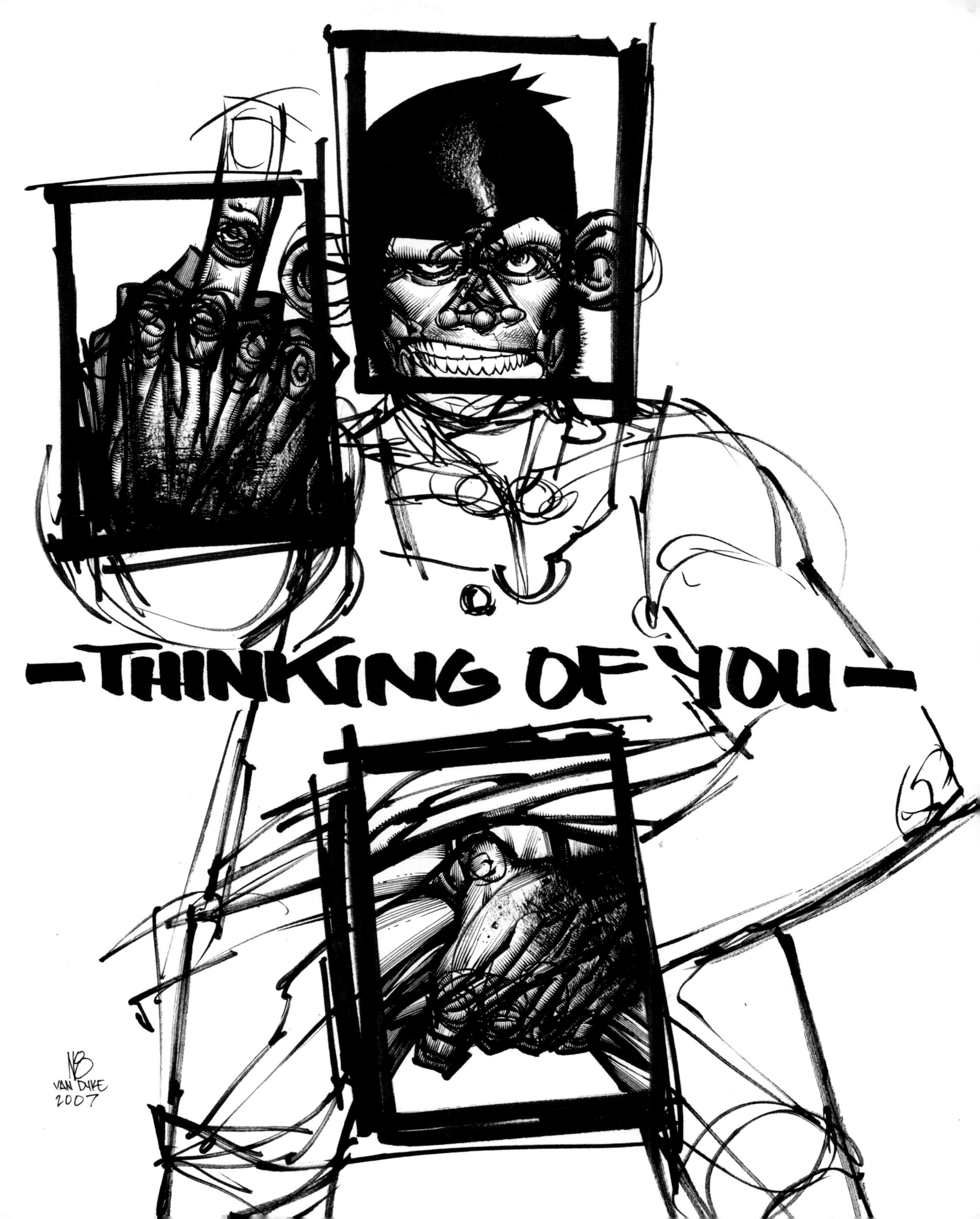

-THINKING OF YOU-
VAN DYKE
2007

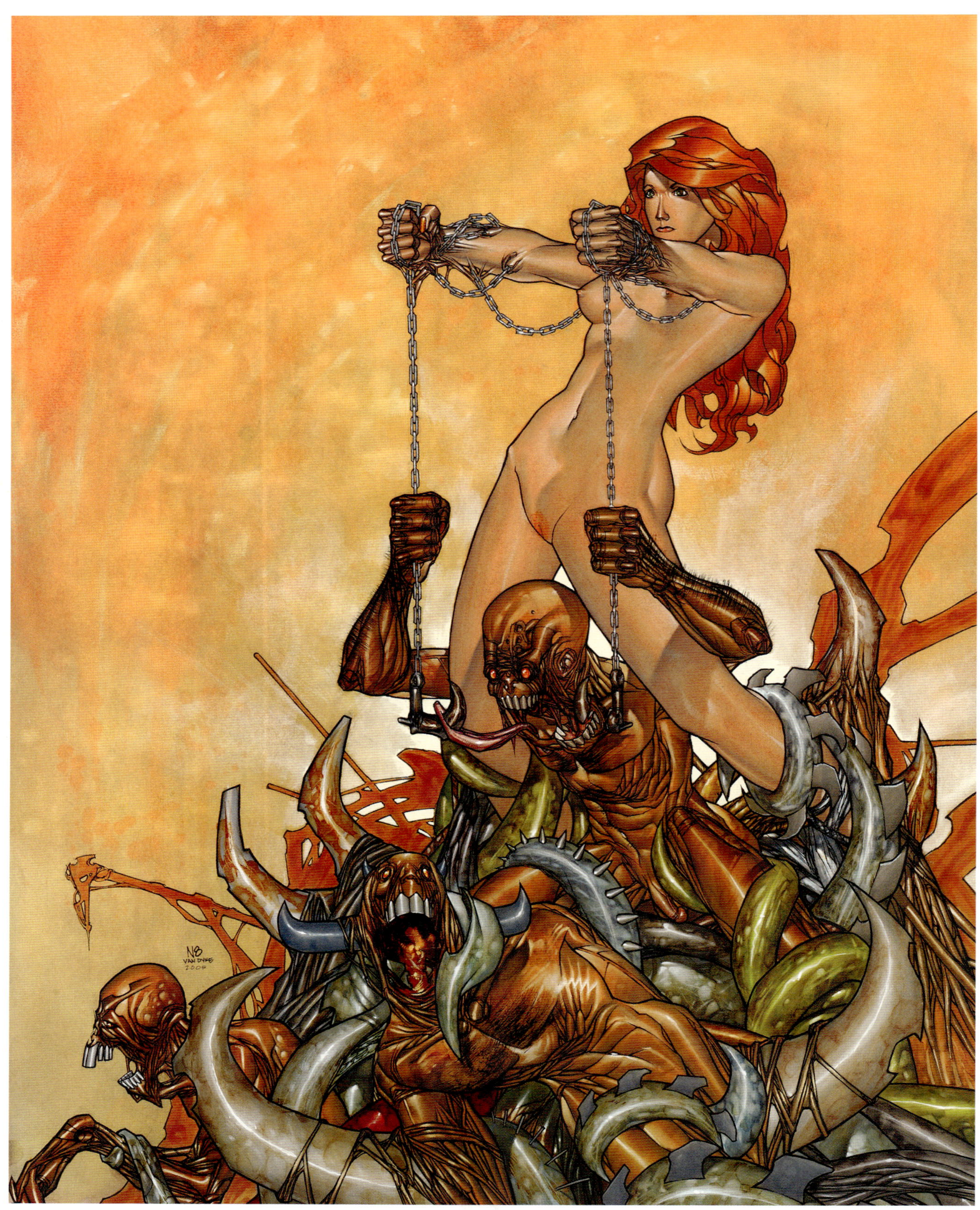

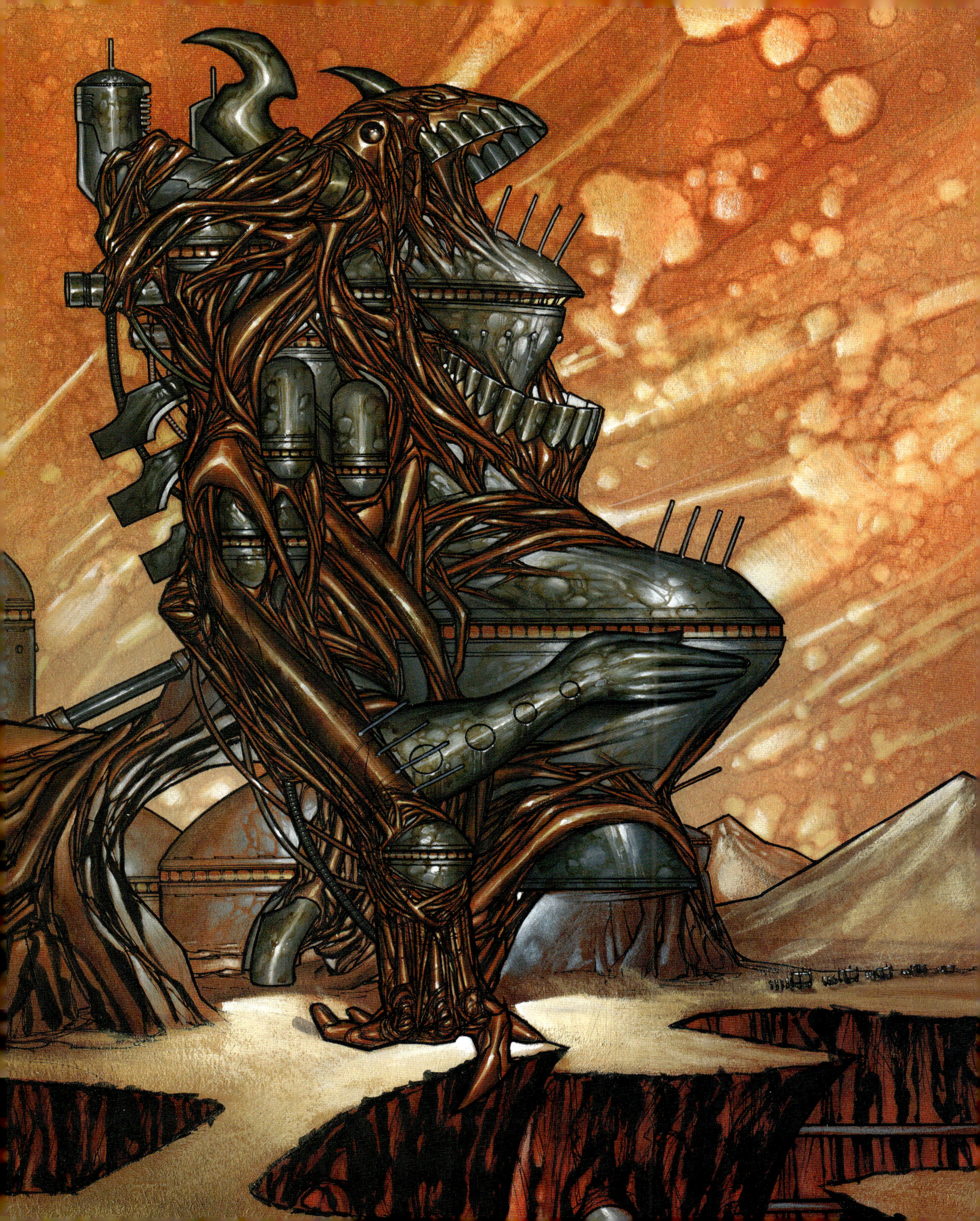

KELSEY BROOKES
www.kelseybrookes.com

DAVID CHOE
www.davidchoe.com

MICKEY DUZYJ
www.mduzyj.com

JEREMY FISH
www.sillypinkbunnies.com

MIKE GIANT
www.mikegiant.com

GROTESK
www.grotesk.to

TOMER HANUKA
www.thanuka.com

EVAN HECOX
www.evanhecox.com

JAMES JEAN
www.jamesjean.com

KOZY N DAN
www.kozyndan.com

TRAVIS MILLARD
www.fudgefactorycomics.com

MODE 2
www.mode2.org

MORNING BREATH
www.morningbreathinc.com

ALEX PARDEE
www.eyesuckink.com

EDUARDO RECIFE
www.eduardorecife.com

SAN
www.eseaene.com

MICHAEL SIEBEN
www.msieben.com

AMY SOL
www.amysol.com

JEFF SOTO
www.jeffsoto.com

BARRON STOREY
www.barronstorey.com

NATE VAN DYKE
www.n8vandyke.com

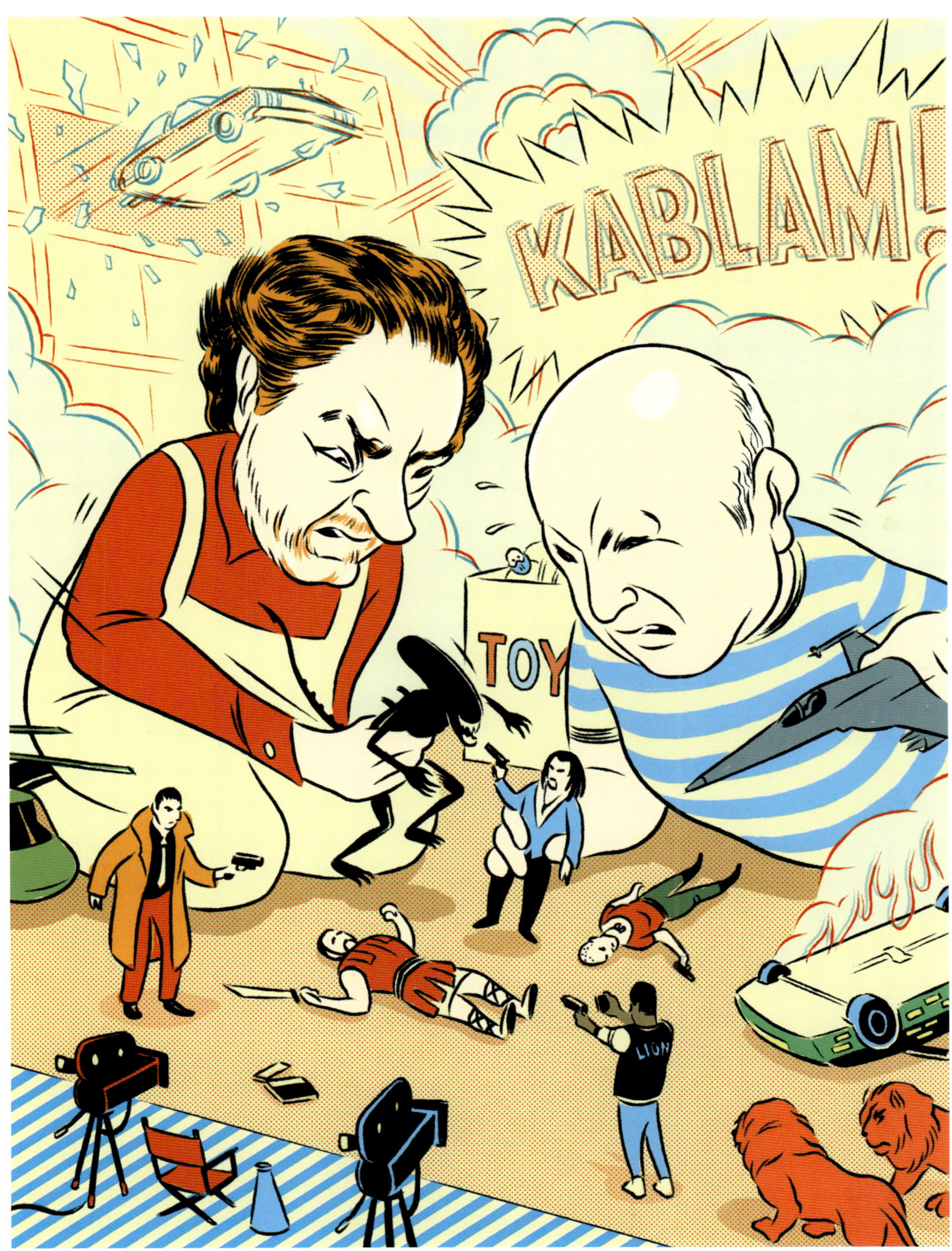

KABLAM!
TOY
LION

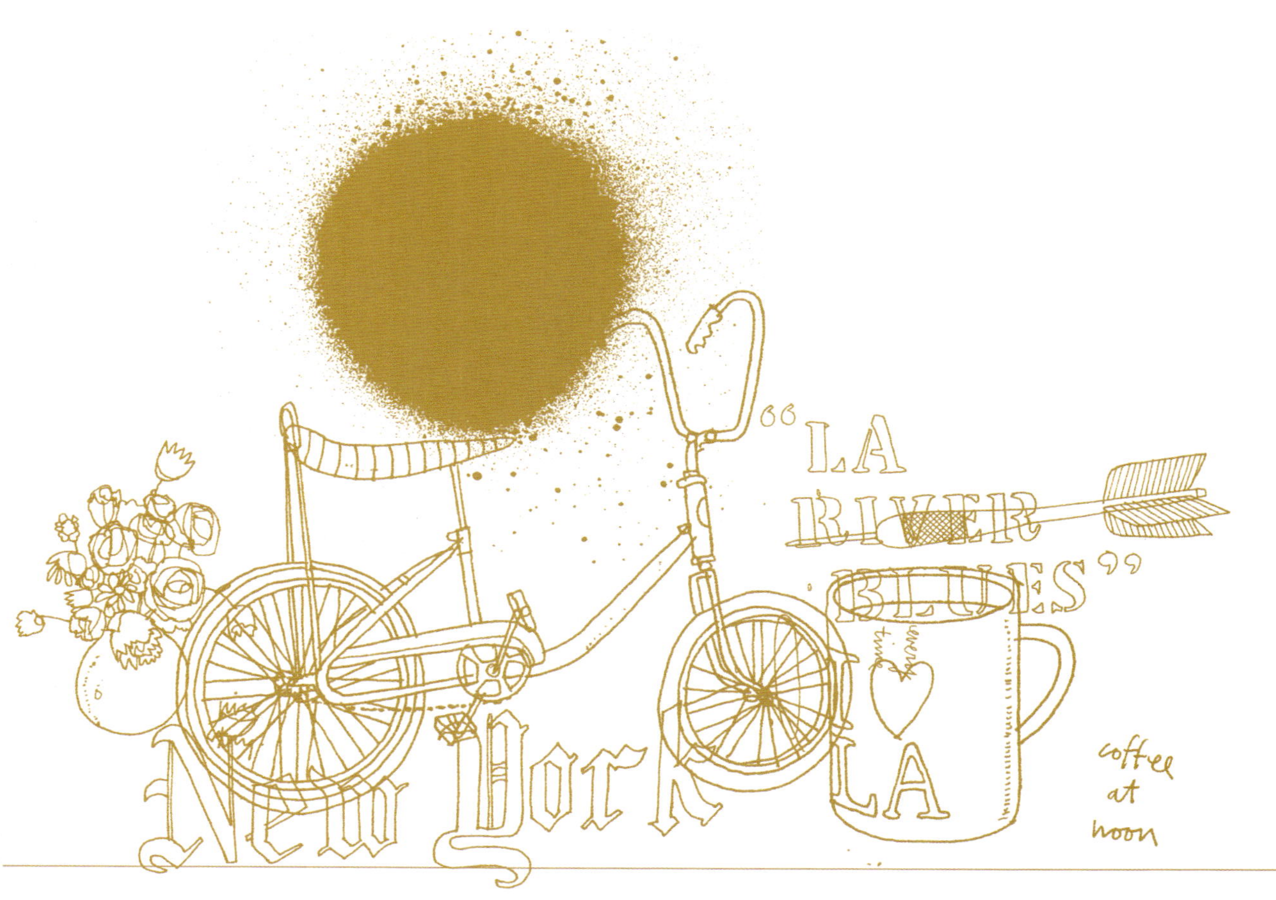

Image by Evan Hecox